With the appeal of *Zelda,* the fascination of *Act One* and the excitement of America's most loved Broadway productions, *The Life That Late He Led* is the magnificent story of COLE PORTER and the stars who surrounded him, including:

Fred Astaire
Tallulah Bankhead
Irving Berlin
Charlie Chaplin
Noel Coward
Bing Crosby
Judy Garland
Moss Hart
Rita Hayworth
Hedda Hopper
George S. Kaufman
Gene Kelly
Bert Lahr
Elsa Maxwell
Ethel Merman
Mike Todd

"A great portrait of the whole man. It will probably be the standard work on Porter." —*Publishers' Weekly*

"Put together with a sure eye for the values of the dream world in which Porter moved most of his life."
—*Los Angeles Times*

THE LIFE THAT LATE HE LED

A BIOGRAPHY OF

COLE PORTER

GEORGE EELLS

A BERKLEY MEDALLION BOOK
PUBLISHED BY G. P. PUTNAM'S SONS
DISTRIBUTED BY BERKLEY PUBLISHING CORPORATION

All photographs not otherwise credited are from the Cole Porter Collection.

Published by arrangement with G.P. Putnam's Sons

SBN 425-02191-7

G.P. Putnam's Sons
200 Madison Avenue
New York, N.Y. 10016

Berkley Publishing Corporation
200 Madison Avenue
New York, N.Y. 10016

BERKLEY MEDALLION BOOKS ® TM 757,375

Printed in the United States of America

G.P. PUTNAM'S SONS-BERKLEY MEDALLION
EDITION, JULY, 1972

ACKNOWLEDGEMENTS

Grateful acknowledgment is made of the generous help given by many persons, including classmates, teachers, friends, business associates and employees of Cole Porter. Special thanks must be given to Jules Omar Cole and James O. Cole—and their lawyer, John Wharton—for generously making available Cole's records and photographs. My thanks, too, to Sam and Harriet Stark, who never threw anything away. In addition, the following individuals not credited in the text were extremely helpful: Fred Koch; Robert Barlow of Yale; Clyde E. Small of Worcester Academy; L. G. Meldrun of the Indiana State Library; Elizabeth Faries of the Connecticut State Library; and all the members of the staff of the Theater Collection of the New York Public Library. I am also grateful to Leonore Silvian, Mike Valenti, Aurand Harris, Richard Segel and Jack Hamilton for research and criticism. In addition, thanks is given to John Ciofalo for designing the picture layout; to Henry Sell for permission to quote from a *Town and Country* profile; to M. J. Arlen for the right to use a portion of an article by the late Michael Arlen; to Schuyler Parsons for permission to quote from his amusing autobiography, *Untold Friendships;* to Stanley Green, author of *The World of Musical Comedy;* to Harms, Inc., for permission to use portions of the lyrics of "Weren't We Fools?" "Anything Goes," and "I Get a Kick Out of You"; to Chappell & Co. Ltd. for "The Blue Boy Blues"; to Buxton Hill Music Corporation for "Wouldn't It Be Fun!"; and to G. Schirmer for "A Shooting Box in Scotland."

TO

Madeline P. Smith

CHAPTER I

When the new baby arrived at 102 Third Street in Peru, Indiana, on June 9, 1891,* Kate and Samuel Fenwick Porter christened him Cole. Six years later, Katie, like many rich, pampered women, distracted herself by taking up with a gypsy numerologist. The gypsy had a theory that was just preposterous enough to intrigue her. He convinced her that any person whose initials spelled a simple word was assured of achieving success in life. Katie, who had a habit of making decisions without consulting Sammy, hurried down to the courthouse and extended their son's name officially from Cole Porter to Cole Albert (for his maternal great-grandfather) Porter. CAP.

That reaction of Katie's indicates the extreme limits to which she would go in attempting to ensure all manner of social and material advantages for Cole. Even before he was six, she had already instituted what was to be a lifelong campaign to secure a niche among the elite for her offspring. When Cole was three and a half and she was still clothing him in sack dresses, he was enrolled in a kindergarten for the well-to-do children in Peru. His mother's first instructions to the teacher were, "Never let Cole be selfish!"

* Sometimes given as 1892, 1893 or 1894.

What this meant was that Katie intended to keep complete control of her son. She dreamed of his becoming a musician. By the time he reached six years of age, she had engaged piano and violin instructors for him; and, because in her opinion "the best people" were socially accomplished, she placed him in dancing class. Not much later, she engaged Mme. Cattin, the local dressmaker, who was originally from Dijon, France, to tutor him in French.

Cole proved an apt pupil, chiefly, Mme. Cattin believed, because he possessed perfect musical pitch, which made it simple for him to mimic her excellent accent. Mme. Cattin's discovery only reinforced Katie's determination that Cole should pursue a career as a musician.

Thus, the course was set that was to establish Cole Porter as a unique figure in the world of light music, and the foundation was laid for acquiring the social graces that were to help shape a personality that for forty years fascinated a world not much given to curiosity about popular songwriters. Yet Cole was so unusual that one afternoon when critic Alexander Woollcott, actress Jane Cowl, editor Herbert Bayard Swope, cover artist Neysa McMein and other celebrated figures decided to while away time by selecting the person with the most original personality, they unanimously chose Cole.

Paradoxically, in his early years Cole's individuality was all but smothered by the machinations of two forceful personalities and one that was seemingly diffident and poetic. Yet each of these was to make an enormous contribution to the adult who became renowned as the working playboy of the Western world.

The strongest of the trio, who did as much good as harm, was Cole's maternal grandfather, the strong-willed J. O. Cole. J. O. was endowed with what was then known as "pioneer spirit." In 1834, as a lad of six, he had been brought to the roistering frontier town of Peru, Indiana, by his father, Albert. Albert had migrated from Kensington, Connecticut, to Zanesville, Ohio, to Goshen, Indiana, before settling in Peru, and throughout his life Albert retained sentimental ties with the East. But even as a boy,

J. O., always self-reliant and individualistic, resolutely rejected everything Eastern and stoutly insisted upon being educated at Peru Collegiate College rather than in Connecticut. In 1850, at twenty-two, like a true pioneer, he set out for the gold fields on the Pacific Slope, determined to make his fortune. Once he arrived in California, he worked briefly as a miner, then decided that there was more gold to be taken from miners' pockets than from the ground. To attract it, he built a sluice and sold water, and in addition operated a general store. He soon succeeded in amassing profits, which he saved. Eventually, he married Indiana-born Rachel Henton (whom he customarily and sentimentally referred to as "The Rose of Indiana") and fathered two children, Kate and Louis A. By 1867, having accumulated $30,000, he returned to Peru to open a brewery, and he operated it for forty years. As it prospered, J. O. proceeded to become something of a promoter.

He bought large tracts of land in Indiana and Illinois; and as a part of a syndicate, which he formed with other local businessmen, he acquired vast acreage in West Virginia—land which, luckily for all concerned, proved to be covered with hardwood forests and to hold copious deposits of soft coal beneath the surface.

J. O. was a shrewd businessman, canny, crusty, tough. Although he was an autocrat who demanded that the world do his bidding, he treated his adored wife, Rachel, with a romanticism that would have astonished the outside world, often sitting on the side of her bed for hours, gazing at the flawlessness of her face in repose. To her and their daughter, Kate, he granted an indulgence and a degree of tenderness that no one else ever evoked.

Katie was small, dark, round of face and, by her own description, "large" of mouth. She was considered reasonably attractive, but to J. O. she was perfection. Their relationship was both close and complicated. He pampered her, and she, in turn, adored him. Still, she inherited many of his qualities and even as a small girl showed unusual spirit. By the time she reached her teens, she was willful and more than somewhat spoiled. (His son Louis was more or less shunted aside.)

Although J. O. customarily fulminated against anything Eastern, Katie was pro-Eastern and announced that she intended to take her education at Vassar. For reasons now unclear (although, according to Cole Porter, not because of her father's opposition), the college plan fell through. Katie first studied at Colby Academy in New London, Connecticut, and later at Brooks Seminary in Poughkeepsie, New York. The latter placed far more emphasis upon "finishing" than educating young ladies. In Katie, it awakened cultural interests—interests that were eventually to have a profound effect upon her son.

After graduation, Katie returned to Peru. She appeared then to be a tightly reined, self-controlled young lady, but beneath the surface her true nature was wildly romantic. In addition, she was accustomed to being indulged and humored and allowed to have whatever she wanted. What she then decided she wanted was a struggling young druggist named Samuel Fenwick Porter.

The townspeople were puzzled. True, Sammy Porter was handsome, whereas Katie was somewhat plain. Still, she was the only daughter, the favored child of a powerful civic leader who was on his way to becoming one of Indiana's richest citizens. They could hardly believe that she would "throw herself away" on Sammy Porter.

When Sammy first arrived in Peru from Vevay, Indiana, he appeared to be a dreamy youth who knew how to spin a good tale and be an excellent companion, but he also seemed totally unsuited to the hurly-burly of business. To the townspeople's surprise, he bought and began to operate the drugstore at 12 North Broadway. Almost at once this hitherto self-effacing young man aggressively threw down a challenge to his competitors, whom he castigated as members of "The Peru Druggists' Monopoly."

Calling himself "Porter, the Druggist," Sammy ran weekly advertisements in the local newspapers. Indeed, his promotional material drew excited comment in the little country town, and it is easy to see why since most of it was as truculent as this example, which ran in the July 18, 1884, edition of the Peru *Republican:*

FOR SHAME!
The Druggists of Peru
Combine and Compel the People of Miami County to Pay Their
MONOPOLY PRICES.
BUT HOLD!
PORTER "The Druggist" to the Rescue!
And Exposes Their Monopoly and Sells Goods Not Low, But
DIRT CHEAP!
He Does Not Sell Any Goods
For Less Than Cost and Charge You Monopoly Prices on Drugs to Make It Up
HE DOES NOT STEAL FROM YOU!

Under ordinary circumstances a less likely suitor for Miss Kate Cole could hardly be imagined. Katie, of course, was well aware of the speculation centering upon Sammy and her; but from the beginning of the courtship through the nuptials on April 9, 1884, and for a long time thereafter, she was too happy to care.

For Sammy life with the Coles was difficult, since he was always in the shadow of J. O.'s overpowering personality. Sammy was ambitious, but no matter what he accomplished, it was doomed to insignificance by comparison to J. O.'s undertakings. As an admirer of Luther Burbank, Sammy performed numerous agricultural experiments. J. O. ridiculed them. When Sammy bought land and put in a peach orchard, the blossoms were of such uncommon beauty that a woman's magazine sent someone to photograph them. But J. O. was derisive, since nobody ever bothered to pick the peaches when they were ripe.

Nevertheless, because of Katie's efforts, relations between the men remained friendly enough so that when in later years J. O. built a big house on Westleigh Farms for the Porters, Sammy accepted it, just as he accepted an Isotta limousine. For everyday use, however, he continued to drive a little runabout for the simple reason that much of the time he didn't have enough pocket money to supply gas for the big car.

As time passed, the relationship between Sammy and Katie understandably underwent a series of subtle readjustments. The reversal of the roles of protector and protected had contributed to this, as had the loss of their first two children. Thus, when Cole was born, Katie, even more than most mothers, was quite prepared to make him the center of her life.

She soon noticed how quick-witted and ever-amusing this tiny son was, and almost at once an uncanny rapport sprang up between her and this boy, who in many ways seemed a miniature reproduction of herself. Perhaps their physical resemblance, at least in part, accounted for her determination that his life must come to something. It was an era when Ward McAllister had only recently originated "the 400" to describe everyone who mattered in the social sense, and Katie dedicated her considerable energies to preparing her attractive son to change the number to 401.

Her efforts took many forms. At the slightest opportunity, she decked him out in starched shirt-blouses, trimmed with elaborate hand-tatted lace cuffs. There still exists a photo taken at a friend's birthday party held on June 30, 1898. This was a time when "Remember the Maine" was a contemporary slogan, and most of the boys, including the host, sported Admiral Dewey white caps and sailor suits. Not seven-year-old Cole. He sat erect and lonely in his too-correct little white jacket, waistcoat, white shirt, wing collar and black tie.

Nor was he ever allowed to indulge in ball playing or roughhousing. Riding, a gentleman's pursuit, was encouraged, and by the time he was six, Katie saw to it that he owned a pony.

She held for herself the same goals as for her son. Her origins may have been solidly middle class, but her secret self identified with the most elegant ladies of society. In fact, custom and fashion ruled her life. Of her devotion to the latter there can be no doubt. Custom also had its appeal. For instance, Cole attributed her churchgoing to custom. He believed that she felt no real religious convictions, although she attended some church every Sunday. Her grandfather Albert had founded the Episcopal Church in Peru, but Katie at one time or another dropped in on every fashionable congregation in town. "I never felt religion was serious to her," Cole recalled years later. "It was of no importance. She went to show off her new hats."

Not unnaturally, Cole developed no deeply felt religious beliefs. On most occasions throughout his life, he spoke of "pleasing the gods" or lamented, "The gods are punishing me," but he seldom referred to God, except to deny belief in Him. Even at seventy, he told his social secretary, Mrs. Everett W. Smith, that he found no comfort in trying to believe in a Supreme Being.

If Katie failed to endow him with religious inspiration, she neglected little else, especially his musical education. For the piano, which required two hours' practice daily, Peru provided teachers who met Katie's standards. But for the violin, an instrument which Cole detested as "screechy," she put him aboard a train and sent him to the Marion, Indiana, Conservatory of Music, thirty miles away.

During the first year, Cole enjoyed the novelty of the trip, but even as a child he was easily bored and the monotony soon made itself felt. The situation was made worse because he finished his lesson by noon and there was no train leaving Marion for Peru until evening.

Finally Cole rebelled, but Katie took him firmly in hand and saw to it that he continued making the trip. Then, abruptly, he stopped complaining. Katie either assumed that he was acting as an obedient son or she simply wasn't curious enough to ask why he no longer protested, which was fortunate, since the reason was to color his future work.

During these trips, Cole discovered that the candy butchers sold much more interesting, though less well-publicized, products than sweets: spicy books. These risqué tales stimulated his imagination, and he became an insatiable consumer, buying penny dreadfuls on each trip and secreting them in his music satchel on the way to Marion. Once he arrived, he would hurry to the conservatory, take his lesson and then dash off to spend the day vicariously experiencing the exploits of the adventurers who were the leading characters. "I suppose some of my lyrics owe a debt to those naughty books," Cole noted late in life. (And who, recalling "But in the Morning, No!," "Love for Sale," "Nobody's Chasing Me" or "Always True to You in My Fashion," can doubt that statement?)

Meanwhile, all Katie's energies were focused upon helping the boy prepare himself as an interpretive artist. She announced to friends that she knew exactly what she was about and that any suggestions on child-rearing were not in order. Still, little remarks were dropped that bothered her enough so that she began looking for an answer to the criticism. How long it took her to discover her method of refuting her critics no one knows, but discover it she did. Once each year, she imported the Marion Conservatory Orchestra to Peru, bought out the entire house and distributed the tickets to anyone who seemed remotely interested.

There was in this arrangement an unspoken agreement between Katie and the management of the orchestra that Cole would be invited to perform a violin solo. This, he later said, was to serve notice that he was not being ruined and was no dumbbell. "The way I played," he added wryly, "I couldn't help feeling my ma was losing points."

For his part, Cole quietly despised the appearance until he discovered that there was one compensating factor: whenever he performed, he sensed that Katie's motherly pride and affection shone upon him with unusual warmth.

How he happened to take up composing at the age of ten, Cole could never explain, but in 1901 he wrote a one-song operetta, *The Song of the Birds*. Later, he referred to it as "my noxious operetta," but at the time he proudly dedicated it to his mother.

The little selection delighted her even more than it infuriated Cole's grandfather, who snorted contemptuously at such instructions as "mother's cooing," "the young ones learn to sing" and "one birdling falls from the nest *(pianissimo, lento).*" Katie now envisioned the possibility that her son might develop into a creative artist. J. O. ordered that there be no further encouragement of the boy's musical activities, but this deterred neither Katie nor Bessie (J. O.'s second wife and Cole's step-grandmother), who twittered as excitedly as Cole's birdlings. In fact, only Sammy Porter seems to have failed to react. When asked what his father's response had been, Cole said in later years, "He seemed not to notice."

Several months or possibly a year after writing the operetta, eleven-year-old Cole sat perched on a piano stool in the midst of his customary morning practice session. Suddenly, the song of a bobolink that was sitting on the white fence outside the window caught his attention. "I looked at him. He looked at me. Something stirred. I began trying to reproduce his notes on my piano. Then I began to improvise. That was how 'The Bobolink Waltz' came about." It was a pseudo-Strauss waltz, derivative enough that it might actually have passed for the real thing. Naturally, Cole dedicated it to his mother.

Katie was ecstatic. Euphoric in mood, she hurried off to Chicago where she succeeded in publishing the song. In one version of the incident, Cole maintained that the music publisher accepted the manuscript on its own merit and was ignorant of the fact that it had been written by a child. Later, Cole amended the story, saying that his mother had paid a vanity publisher $100 to have 100 copies printed. These she distributed among friends, some of whom misguidedly sent him copies long after he had reached middle age. The latter version seems likelier in view of the fact that he also said that he had never heard the song played by anyone except himself and that it had never earned a sou in royalties.

More significantly though, through the song Cole gained an insight that, for better or for worse, was to exert a profound influence upon the course of his life. Detecting in Katie's reaction to his creative activities a kind of loving acceptance that he otherwise seldom encountered, he dimly perceived, although he did not consciously formulate his discovery, that music could be used to gain affection and acceptance. This insight was anything but transitory.

Peru in the early 1900's was a citadel of puritanism. It was generally believed that the more unpleasant the remedy, the quicker the cure; the stiffer the punishment, the sturdier the character it developed; and that to be too responsive to a child was in the end to be unkind. Although the Coles were better endowed with material possessions than their neighbors, they, with the exception of Katie, subscribed to that point of view. However, there seems little reason to doubt that the family, including Katie, united to set young Cole apart from his contemporaries.

From photographs taken in the late 1890's and early 1900's, Cole's small, serious face, dominated by large expressive brown eyes, peers out. His somber mien hints that for him childhood was far from the carefree succession of golden days celebrated by Hoosier poets. Even in his earlier years, he saw his ineffectual father walking in the shadow of the seemingly omnipotent J. O. Nor is it possible that he could have been unaware of or have failed to be confused because his mother, so devoted to J. O., found it necessary to step in and protect her husband from her father's ridicule. Because Cole was shy and sensitive himself, he undoubtedly identified with Sammy, and yet, this very act of identification broadened the gap between him and his father and his grandfather as well.

As Cole grew older, Katie often lamented the lack of contact between Sammy and their son, yet paradoxically she often stepped in—protecting Cole, challenging her husband, withholding information from one or the other—thus further lessening the possibility of a close relationship developing between them. She found no trouble in handling Cole. Utilizing her firm but sympathetic manner, she cleverly controlled him, getting him to do whatever she wanted without arousing the slightest resentment.

Sammy, on the other hand, approached Cole with rigid demands. He lost his temper easily—as he may have wished to do with J. O.—and he succeeded only in overpowering and estranging his son. Cole retaliated by detaching and screening out all the unpleasantness. Confronted by his father's anger, he retreated behind a blank, inexpressive mask. Late in life, he observed that he retained only two or three early impressions of his father. The most important of these, he said, had been recalled to him by his cousin Louise Bearss. It seemed that his father had greatly enjoyed poetry. And so on winter nights when Cole was small, he and his father would sit in the parlor and read aloud from Shelley, Keats, Robert Browning, and other poets Sammy admired. Then they would discuss and analyze the work.

Soon, Cole began writing verse which Sammy criticized and corrected, suggesting improvements and helping his son develop ideas. "I suppose that he started me writing lyrics," Cole said.

Yet there was good reason for Cole to have forgotten these important sessions. For in them, as in all their contacts, Sammy expected too much. He would give Cole a long, complicated, metaphysical poem by John Donne or Robert Browning and lose patience when the boy failed to understand it. Again and again these scenes were repeated until they stiffened Coles' conviction that his father did not appreciate him. By the time he was twelve years old, Cole's relationship with Sammy had been damaged beyond repair. Sammy's failure was too pronounced for his son to forgive for another fifty years.

Even before that, J. O. had gradually supplanted Sammy in directing the upbringing of the boy. J. O. paid many of the bills and had a dominant voice in making decisions in the Porter household. Yet he set for Cole standards so high that any child would have despaired of meeting them, especially a small, shy, sensitive, unathletic boy.

Occasionally, it was true, J. O. would grow nostalgic for

his youth on the rambunctious Indiana frontier or in the California gold fields. Then he would delight Cole by spinning stories of canal badmen, fractious Indians and gold-crazed miners. At these times a closeness would spring up between the two, but it was always of short duration. As if by design, a day or two later, J. O. would have the hired man hitch up his team, and then J. O. would take his grandson for a spin through the Indiana countryside. Customarily, he chose to rein in the horses at the top of a rise that afforded an excellent view of an austere building. Then, in all solemnity, he would assure Cole that that was where he was headed. The building was the county poorhouse.

Consequently, Cole might admire his grandfather's power, his position and his determination, but he knew that he could not live up to the old fellow's expectations. Perhaps, too, he feared that he might be dealt with as his father or anyone else who opposed J. O. had been.

Fun was not a major element of these preadolescent years. On one occasion, Cole told columnist Leonard Lyons that his mother's insistence that he practice his piano lessons for two hours every day had ruined his childhood, but when Lyons asked whether he was sorry about this, Cole replied, "Frankly, no." Privately, he was not so sure.

Naturally, there were some childhood pranks such as the time that he and Tom Hendricks, whose father owned Hendricks Blue Drugstore, removed the Perfecto bands and buried the denuded cigars in the chocolate ice-cream container. Once, too, he and golden-haired Desdemona (her mother was a great admirer of Shakespeare) Bearss dressed up like a farm couple and went from door to door, speaking in exaggerated country accents, peddling apples from an orchard owned by Sammy Porter. More typical of his activities was the direction of a children's home talent show at the age of seven.

Summers, Cole spent most of his time at Lake Maxinkuckee, where he would join the other boys in meeting the big lake steamer, *The Peerless*. The boys would board and go to the roof of the top deck to dive off as the boat departed—all except Cole. Admidst the clanging of the bells and the roar of the engines, he would tarry at the piano until that moment came when the signal to change from reverse to forward blanked out all sound except Cole's piano-playing. Then the captain, outraged at the idea of Cole's wet bathing suit ruining the varnish on his piano bench, would come rushing aft to rout him and chase him to the rail, where Cole would dive into the water. That moment, more nearly than any other, approaches the picture of the conventional young Indiana farm boy. But it is a rare one.

As Cole grew older, he became even more of an outsider. He struck his contemporaries as witty, amusing and a little aloof. Discussing him years later, one of the crowd who summered at the lake noted that even as a child Cole had been aristocratic in appearance, with his fine-boned, fine-featured countenance and somewhat superior attitude. He was never one of the crowd, and apparently at the time he harbored no wish to be.

Only with little Des Bearss was his relationship intimate. Each seemed instinctively to know what the other was going to do. And when Des was still a small girl, there was no doubt that she was in love with Cole. Cole liked her, even loved her, but later said that he had never been *in* love with her. "We had great times together," he explained. "She was the first person I ever knew who was fun."

With the exception of this friendship, Cole's existence was so unsatisfactory that he soon learned to reconstruct it imaginatively. When some unpleasant incident occurred, he blanked it out. In the Porter household, irritations, slights and anxieties were not discussed. Katie maintained that no one was interested in anyone else's unhappiness. Consequently, Cole devised his own ways of escaping a regimented, boring existence. His reading, or at least those books which he later recalled fondly, was strictly escapist. *Alice in Wonderland, Swiss Family Robinson, Treasure Island* and Kipling's *Jungle Book* were favorites that he read more than once. But in later years, when his personal life was more satisfactory, he seldom bothered to read fiction.

His favorite toys, too, allowed him to indulge his fantasy life. Two that were especially cherished were a clown suit and a toy theater. The clown suit neatly fitted his need since it freed him from the obligation to remember his family's position in the community. And the toy theater with its operable curtain and numerous sets provided a place where he could act out his daydreams and create an environment more pleasant than the everyday one.

Even more treasured than the toys were his visits to the real theater and the actual circus. Peru had become a circus winter quarters almost by accident a year or two before Cole's birth. At this time, a livery-stable owner named Ben Wallace had taken over some wild animals from a bankrupt mud show to satisfy a feed bill, and after exhibiting them in a nearby town Wallace decided to go into the circus business. By the time Cole was a small boy, the Great Wallace Shows had winter quarters close to J. O.'s farm.

Cole was dazzled by Ben Wallace, a tall-grass showman of the old school, whom he called "Uncle Ben" and who gave him free run of the Wallace quarters. He also liked the circus people, and when free from his musical obligations he would wander through the animal barns, chatting with the keepers and observing animal behavior, including the mating habits that he was to chronicle so exhaustively ("birds do it, bees do it," etc.) in numerous songs for Broadway shows.

The high point of the year, he often maintained, came with the raising of the brown canvas big top, which took place over a full week. During that time, the itinerant performers would descend upon winter quarters and begin intensive practice of their routines.

Cole's particular pet for several seasons was "the world's most beautiful fat lady." Since her act required no rehearsal, she was free to spend her time as she wished. So whenever Cole could escape, he would load the hefty beauty into his pony cart and set off on a drive, the little cart listing heavily to one side. Together, the elfin, serious-faced boy and the elephant-sized woman, who customarily protected her delicately pigmented skin by means of a dainty sunshade, would explore the country lanes. Cole's step-grandmother Bess (Rachel died before he was born) found this highly embarrassing. She protested to Katie, but Katie, who never fully accepted Bess, resolutely refused to interfere.

The theater was also a beloved outlet. When Cole was still a small child, Katie often took him to Chicago for a frenzied week in which they attended the theater or the opera every evening.

In Peru, the manager of the nickelodeon discovered that piano accompaniment increased attendance. He hired a regular pianist and when she was indisposed, Cole was sometimes asked to fill in. This arrangement continued until boredom and mischievousness overtook him and he amused himself by playing chase music for a love scene and hearts-and-flowers for a horse race, which spelled a quick end to that career.

Still, there was the Emeric Theater on West Fifth Street, and whether the attraction featured stars of the Sothern and Marlowe caliber or such barnstormers as the Hickman-Bessy Players, Cole was happy to lose himself there. For no acting company, however accomplished, could compete with the polychrome curtain that hung at the Emeric. This marvel depicted the Grand Canal in Venice in all its exciting detail, and by the time Cole was ten years old, he had resolved that one day he would occupy one of those Venetian palazzos (he actually lived in three). But meantime there was the present to contend with.

So Cole daydreamed, earned extensive admiration for his musical accomplishments and tried to blot out the disconcerting, sometimes angry currents that flowed among the adults at home. He succeeded very well, too, until Katie announced that the following fall, at the age of thirteen, he was to go East to school. Years before, she had vowed that her children would have the advantages of a classical education and Eastern social connections. Some writers have erroneously reported that it was J. O. who sent Cole to Worcester Academy to discourage the boy's interest in music. Actually, J. O. fought hard to keep him in Indiana where he could learn farming, hunting, business and other manly pursuits. Katie, however, gave no quarter and Cole departed amidst a family disagreement that caused his grandfather and his mother to stop speaking for the next two years. Thus, Cole, who was the means by which a number of disappointed people hoped to fulfill their own thwarted ambitions, found himself embroiled in a painful situation. After he left Peru for Worcester, he did not return home for three years, nor did his family visit him because of the bitterness of the quarrel which his departure caused. The outcome was that for all practical purposes he temporarily became a boy without a family.

CHAPTER II

Luckily, Worcester Academy provided Cole with a chance to escape the isolation that his family had imposed. Not without something of a handicap, however, since he was preceded by numerous trunks, pieces of statuary, paintings and an upright piano—a rather unusual assortment of possessions for a thirteen-year-old Midwestern farmboy to bring to school in 1905 or, for that matter, any other year.

Cole was at the time unexceptional-looking, aside from appearing two or three years younger than his classmates. He was short, slight and wiry. He parted his hair squarely in the middle and had button-bright brown eyes. His greatest asset was a smile that transformed his features so that he appeared almost handsome.

From the first, he used his considerable array of talents—wit, music, energy, intelligence, enthusiasm and precocious conversational powers—to ingratiate himself with everyone from the headmaster's wife to the athletic coach. It was typical of him that during his freshman year, having discovered picture postcards, he bombarded acquaintances with witty messages, even those classmates whom he saw every day.

That year, 1905, Worcester Academy's registration reached 240 and there were 21 faculty members, a growth that had been attained chiefly through the tenacity of Harvard-trained Daniel Webster Abercrombie, a dour Scotsman whose tenure was referred to by iconoclastic students as "the fifteenth (or sixteenth or seventeenth) year of the reign of the tyrant Abercrombie." Dr. Abercrombie's strictures were, in fact, so harsh and inclusive that a camaraderie sprang up between his victims—both teachers and students—creating an admirable school spirit.

Cole soon attracted the headmaster's favorable attention, since he was the likely kind of material (far preferable to roughneck athletes) with whom Dr. Abercrombie enjoyed working. For it was Dr. A.'s aim to convert middle-class American boys into young gentlemen. To accomplish this, he tried to imbue his charges with the ideals of the best Continental schools. Self-discipline was expected. Gentlemanly behavior was to be taken as a matter of course. "Democracy," Dr. A. was fond of saying, "is not a leveling down, but a leveling up."

Cole proved to be an apt subject. Certainly anyone who dined with him in later years could see that his style reflected the attitude of the headmaster, who announced, "A gentleman never eats. He breakfasts, he lunches, he dines, but he *never* eats." Good manners and good taste, Dr. A. proclaimed, were to be sedulously cultivated. "It was he," Cole once remarked, "who first taught me that there is always enough money in the world—never enough beauty."

One place that Cole discovered beauty was in Dr. Abercrombie's classroom. At that point in his life, the educator confined his teaching to Greek, and, as his students attested, he was a marvel at bringing ancient characters and societies to life and illuminating the rhythms and the poetry of the great classical writers. If Cole's father first aroused his interest in poetry, it was Dr. A. whom Cole later credited with causing him to realize that he (Cole) alone could match the rhythm of *his* words to the beat of *his* music.

As one classmate later noted, Cole always had a

remarkable capacity for winning favor with anyone, even the dour Dr. A. Nor was Cole above doing a bit of apple-polishing by jotting down every sentence that the headmaster uttered in the classroom. As a result, he eventually enjoyed an unusual degree of freedom from the academy's rules.

If Cole was a favorite of Dr. A.'s, Mrs. Abercrombie became his real patron after he had taken tea with them. In her drawing room, she plopped a cushion on the piano stool (so that Cole could reach the keyboard) and sat enthralled as he played selections from MacDowell. Mrs. Abercrombie thought him brilliant, and Cole soon realized that his musical accomplishments were to stand him in even better stead in Massachusetts than in Indiana. For after his success at the Abercrombies, he was often invited to faculty wives' parlors where his good manners, worldly chatter and easy amiability delighted adults.

He also used music to ingratiate himself with fellow students. Significantly, in recalling him years later, almost without exception classmates remembered him in one of two ways: either he was seated at the piano in his private quarters, playing and singing songs he had heard in touring musical comedies or he was in the Megaron (recreation hall) playing for groups of boys who gathered to harmonize during idle moments. About his own voice, Cole had no illusions. "It was unpleasant but adequate," he often said.

Cole, even in those days, was matter-of-fact about both his liabilities and his assets. To all outward appearances, he had made an easy adjustment to prep-school routine, yet he had not succeeded in leaving behind disturbing memories of the trouble caused by his mother's insistence that he come East. His guilt about the rift that this had caused was so overpowering that few of his classmates ever heard him mention his family. Several school friends later said that they were under the impression that he was an orphan who was being educated by a rich relative. Instinctively, Cole conducted himself by his later credo: neither to show weakness nor to beg indulgence. Whatever anxieties he suffered within, he suffered in silence, presenting a lighthearted serenity that fooled most companions.

One who was not fooled was bluff Donald Baxter MacMillan, who taught French and mathematics but whose main job in those days was to coach the Worcester Academy athletic teams. MacMillan, only temporarily a teacher, was a hearty outdoorsy type, who in 1908 left teaching to accompany Commander Robert E. Peary on his successful "dash" to the North Pole. For fifty years thereafter, MacMillan made trips almost annually to Arctic regions where he challenged nature and triumphed over it in the interests of science. It would seem that Cole could scarcely have chosen a less likely confidant (unless it were Dr. A.) than this rugged adventurer who was seventeen years his senior. Yet the fact remains that he cast MacMillan in that role.

"Cole was a lonesome kind of boy," Admiral MacMillan recalled in 1964. "Didn't seem to have a home. Never heard him speak of his father, grandfather or any brother or sister. Rarely of his mother. They never visited. And either they didn't want him to come home or he didn't want to go. He went around like he hadn't a care in the world, but I could see something was bothering him."

As Cole's first year at Worcester drew to an end, MacMillan suggested that he obtain permission to go to Camp Wychmere, possibly the first nautical boys' camp in the United States. MacMillan had founded it a few years earlier on Bustin's Island in Casco Bay off the coast of Portland, Maine. The older man thought that Cole, who was not proficient in athletics, would profit by being given a chance to study navigation and seamanship, which would "put some iron in his spine."

Cole obtained permission from Katie and went directly from Worcester Academy to Wychmere and back to Worcester for two summers. While at Wychmere, he spent considerable time both on the water and in the woods, but MacMillan was disappointed to discover that his charge cared nothing for outdoor life. "He slept out. Slept in a tent with some other boys, but during the day he'd come to my cottage. I had an old piano there. He'd have stayed at that all the time if we'd let him. Swimming and boating—that was just an interruption. The time there didn't toughen him up a whit. Everything was music with Cole. And everybody naturally liked him. Dutch Cottrell, Damon Howard—all the big athletes from the Worcester Academy—they all liked Cole. Even if he couldn't play ball, he could play the piano. Very entertaining, he was. He wrote a song about someone charming the birds from the trees. That's how he was," MacMillan recalled. "Truth is though—he was a little soft. I felt sorry for him. Never thought he'd amount to much."

In spite of MacMillan's estimate, Cole managed to make the honors list a majority of the semesters while he attended the Academy. This meant that he earned at least one A and no grade lower than B. From the beginning, since it was his intention to enter Yale upon graduation from prep school, he pursued a strictly classical course.

By the time Cole reached his junior year, his grandfather and his mother had made up their quarrel and J. O. once more undertook to direct his grandson's upbringing. But Cole was so busy he had little time to ponder his grandfather's advice.

He had been elected president of the Mandolin Club, chosen co-pianist for the Glee Club, elected an editor of the school paper, was front-runner in the Dexter Speaking Contest, had been tapped to serve as an usher at the Senior Promenade and stood by as an alternate in the Inter-Society Debate.

But for him, the high point of his junior year came on April 10, when he appeared in the leading role in the class play. This production had special meaning to Cole, since by log-rolling and agitation he had succeeded in bypassing the traditional Shakespearean offering and had persuaded his classmates to choose Richard Sheridan's *The Rivals*. Why? "Because I was crazy to play Bob Acres," Cole later explained. For some time he had been considering the possibility of becoming an actor.

The notice that appeared in the school paper, *The Vigornia,* gave Cole a good review: "Cole Porter, as Bob Acres, was excellent. He was the carefree young man at first, then the bold fighter, known to the country as 'Fighting Bob,' and last the terrified duelist, wishing to receive the fire on his side and shaking with fear. He was full of life and vim throughout."

What higher praise could Cole have wished? Much higher. Despite the kind words given his performance, those heaped upon the young man who played David, the servant boy, were more enthusiastic. Cole had no stomach, either then or later in life, for coming out second best, and his interest in acting swiftly declined.

Still, he retained an inborn sense of showmanship. From his freshman year on, as he progressed through the Dexter Speaking Contest, he had invariably chosen comic works to entertain his audiences. Now in his junior year, as the contest drew to a close, Cole selected William Wordsworth's "The Complaint of a Forsaken Indian Woman" as a change of pace. *The Vigornia* critic's reaction illustrates the shrewdness of this choice. After describing Cole's performance in detail, the reviewer noted: "Those who thought Cole Porter could only specialize in humorous selections were agreeably surprised by his serious work." No one, however, was at all surprised when the announcement was made that Cole had won the $25 first prize.

As a pragmatist, Cole continued to give recitations and to play the piano, endeavors that earned him adulation. On the other hand, he became more and more reluctant to do anything that made him seem unpopular, such as playing the violin. Yet, at Glee Club director John Leydon's urging, he did agree to play a solo for the musical club's final concert. He chose a selection from Flotow's *Martha,* and to Dr. Abercrombie's delight the boys whistled and stamped so enthusiastically that the headmaster complimented them on their appreciation of the finer things. This also met with cheers. In the expansive mood, Dr. A. invited Cole to treat them to an encore.

This time Cole took his place at the piano where he immediately launched into a series of satirical quatrains poking fun at well-known foibles of faculty members. Dr. A. had walked into Cole's trap. Prior to the concert he had composed the verses and arranged for the enthusiastic response to his violin solo. From that evening on, he made every effort to avoid further identification with the violin.

Sometime in June, 1908, Cole took preliminary entrance examinations for Yale. His showing in Greek was below par and it was apparent that he would need the assistance of George L. Fox of the Fox Tutoring School in New Haven. In fact, Cole suggested that he spend the summer there, but his grandfather was adamant that he return to Peru for the first time since going East to boarding school.

Cole reluctantly agreed and proceeded to spend as much time as possible at Lake Maxinkuckee, playing the piano on *The Peerless*, the lake excursion boat. Soon he was drawing large crowds whether he performed English drinking songs, Gilbert and Sullivan or a particular favorite, "The Spaniard Who Betrayed My Life." In later years, those Maxinkuckee friends have always smiled when critics have speculated upon the origin of Cole's beat. Night after night, they've said, he developed the heavily accented phrasing in order to make his music heard above *The Peerless'* engines. "If he could drive an automobile with the same heavy foot he plays the piano, what a race driver he'd be," Indianan racer Ralph DePalma once said at the finish of a number.

When Cole wasn't at the piano, he was generally with Des Bearss. Des was now a fun-loving, witty girl, and she shared Cole's interests not only in music but also in a rather critical view of people. That summer she had discovered a book ridiculing clichés, and after she read it to Cole and Tom Henricks, the three of them spent hours rating their families and friends for "bromidic content." Before returning East, Cole invited Des to the Worcester Academy's senior prom and naturally she accepted.

Still, Cole regarded her chiefly as a good companion.

That fall, he began to escort Worcester girls to the theater and, soon after school opened, he attended a reception for the academy boys at Piedmont Church. Among the girls, most of whom were clad in fluffy white frocks, was one who was wearing a little black-and-white checked dress. Her name was Beulah Mae Singer. "He always liked smartly dressed women," she said later. "How he happened to take a shine to me, I've never understood—although I had curls, blue eyes and a pretty little face. He singled me out almost at once and came up and started talking. Instead of writing my name on my identification card, I'd pricked out the letters with a pin. He noticed it and commented. Then he began to talk about himself. All evening. It wasn't a bit boring as it sometimes can be. It was fascinating. Gen Russell, the girl I'd come with, thought so too. He wasn't what you'd call attractive. He moved like a frisky monkey and looked like a solemn bullfrog. With slightly buggy eyes. Well, he captivated me by sheer force of personality. I took a fancy to him that lasted all my life—even though when I married I burned my Porter collection. Of course, I couldn't let him know. Girls couldn't in those days. They ran instead of encouraging boys."

At 9:30, most academy students departed in order to be on campus by the 10:00 P.M. curfew. Cole, a person of special privilege, remained behind. Finally, he asked to escort Beulah home. She refused, saying that she was with Gen Russell, and he left. At 10:00, Beulah and Gen departed, bade one another goodnight and Beulah stood awaiting her trolley. "Suddenly," she later said, "a figure stepped out of the shadows across the street. He came up, gave me an accusing look and said in a masterful way, 'I'm taking you home.' I was very worried about Mother. She was almost Spanish in her restrictions." On the trolley, Cole invited Beulah to the Worcester-Wilbraham game. She informed him that her mother wouldn't allow her to go without a chaperone and insisted that he leave her at the corner of the block in which she lived.

Nevertheless, at the game, Beulah (who was with a

chaperone) was on the lookout for Cole. When she spotted him, he merely tipped his hat and strolled on. She was so chagrined that afterward whenever she saw him in town, she crossed the street to avoid meeting him. Yet at Easton's, she continued to linger over college ices (as sundaes were called in those days), hoping to catch a glimpse of him.

That spring, on Easter Sunday, Cole and Martin Van Buren III appeared at the Piedmont services and chose to sit in the pew which Beulah was occupying. "Cole talked all through the service. He was one of the most irreverent persons I've ever encountered—but *so* charming," she said. "While he talked, he cracked his ankle bones in a kind of castanetlike accompaniment. I'm certain he did it to draw attention to his new brown silk socks and snappy new footwear. He was quite a Beau Brummel—even then."

A week or so later, Cole once more asked Beulah to a dance, but her mother insisted she refuse. "I was hoping he'd ask me again, but by that time he had turned his attention to a Worcester girl named Grace Allen—and that was that."

At the academy, meanwhile, Cole was increasing his popularity by entertaining the student body with original compositions. Years later, he characterized them as the kind of special material numbers heard in second-rate dives. But in 1908 these songs garnered enormous popularity for him as he performed them privately for his classmates and the more liberal-minded faculty members. The only three numbers that he could recall in later years were "The Tattooed Gentleman," "Fi Fi Fifi" and "The Bearded Lady."

One way or another, Dr. A. discovered their existence and summoned Cole to his office to inquire about these "so-called original compositions." Cole was evasive, but Dr. A. insisted upon a demonstration. A few lines from the lyric of "The Bearded Lady" were enough. Dr. A. threatened Cole with expulsion and prohibited further creative activity of that kind. Thereafter, Cole was more selective about his audiences, but he was not about to give up any display which earned him such warm acceptance.

At the end of the year, Cole made his final chapel address, taking inspiration from Des Bearss and inquiring "Are You a Bromide?" On May 28, he also participated in Class Day exercises as historian and was named valedictorian. By strange custom, Worcester confers the valedictory upon the student who takes second honors. But Cole's natural distaste for coming in second-best was short-lived in this case since J. O., who believed excellence was by no means its own reward, announced that the boy was free to choose any graduation present he desired. Cole, who had had four years of exposure to Dr. Abercrombie's paeans to the glory of Continental culture, knew exactly what he wanted—a trip abroad. So after writing his second set of entrance examinations to Yale on June 30, he set off for Paris at the beginning of July, already a confirmed Francophile. There he lived with an ordinary French family, the Delarues, at 23 Rue Boissonade and became at ease in conversational French. Leaving the Delarues, he made a quick tour of the countryside, went into Switzerland and then to Germany. By this time the summer had ended and he was ready to return to the United States and Yale, Yale, Yale. The two months in Europe had wrought many changes, and when Cole arrived at 242 York Street in New Haven, he was no longer the ingenuous country boy who four years earlier had set out to charm everyone in sight the moment he arrived at Worcester Academy.

CHAPTER III

Judging by his behavior, when Cole arrived in New Haven in 1909 he was a young man destined to play many parts. Unlike at Worcester, where he had set out to make everyone like him, he now appeared to be undergoing a rebellious period.

Certainly he attracted attention at once. If this seems an exaggerated claim, it must be remembered that college life in those days followed proscribed rituals. Each class moved as a unit, and Cole was a maverick who had no apparent intention of conforming. Consequently, he alienated conservative upperclassmen.

Howard Cullman, a classmate who was to know him well later, has said that Cole refused to take notice of the dictates handed down by the older boys. Despite rules demanding conventional attire, he wore pink or yellow shirts and salmon ties. "He was a very colorful young man and the hierarchy resented it," Cullman once said. "They used to ask whether he was wearing the uniform for Main Street in Peru, Indiana. But Cole rode it out very well."

To do so required enormous self-control. A naturally shy person, Cole was made more timid by early exposure to his despotic grandfather. The easier course would have been to conform, yet a stubbornness and determination to please himself prevented him from capitulating. Instead, he developed a habit of "lowering the curtain" (as Fanny Brice was to say years later) or, as some said, "putting up a wall."

By the middle of his freshman year, definite pro- and anti-Porter groups had formed. Heading the latter was a young man named Thornton Thayer. Thayer, who possessed a beautiful bass voice and admired Cole's musical accomplishments, disliked him personally. His reservations sprang up initially, he recalled, when the father of a classmate offered to send his sailboat for an outing between New Haven and New London. Invitations, limited to four, were highly coveted. And Cole, who had never evidenced the slightest interest in boating, entered into the competitive spirit and managed to earn a bid. "We were tremendously excited about going," Thayer said, "Cole as much as any of us. But I guess the trip wasn't as eventful as he had hoped. When we got to New London, he met up with some Yale cronies and jumped the boat without so much as an apology. That was the nature of the animal—always selfish and a little snobbish, I thought."

More students might have shared Thayer's viewpoint had a fortuitous situation not arisen. Yale in 1909 needed fresh rally songs. Actually, Cole had been on campus only a couple of months when the *Yale News* deplored finding "genius for original compositon" lacking in the student body. Thus, Cole's familiar social passport had been handed to him. Alert as always to the opportunities at hand, he began turning out songs.

He also began to utilize his talents as an entertainer to establish a more likable public personality. In December, he was invited to New York by Vanderbilt Webb, whose family lived in one of the complex of interconnected Vanderbilt mansions on Fifth Avenue in the low Fifties. There, Cole for the first time encountered "the rich rich," as he always called them. For a brief time, he felt something of an interloper, but their milieu was the most compatible he had encountered and he applied the same intensity in learning to move among them that he brought to his other passion, music. Their formality, their vanity, their style and their material extravagances all appealed to him. They lived, as he had always felt people should, in veritable palaces; and they were waited on by personal maids, valets, butlers, housemaids, laundresses, cooks, and footmen in knee breeches, silk stockings, pumps and painted hair. Cole found the surroundings and the ritual enchanting and promised himself to emulate it one day.

In Indiana, he had hated "the too long dinners, with too much heavy food—not well served." Here, he reveled in the twelve-course dinners served on fragile china, accompanied by five or six wines poured into the finest crystal. The style with which each delicacy was presented struck him as being as important as what was proffered. He was, as always, acutely aware of every nuance in both material and social senses. He liked, too, the custom of addressing all but one's closest friends as "Miss So and So," and "Mr. So and So." It appealed to his natural fastidiousness.

Van Webb, despite his background, did not become one of Cole's close friends. Cole found him too serious, too hard-working, too eager to get on with life. (Webb completed a four-year course at Yale in three years.) Instead, Cole's circle was more likely to include such musically inclined freshmen as Johnfritz Achelis, Arnold Whitridge, Robert Lehman and Leonard Hanna, Jr., son of the Cleveland industrialist, who had the largest allowance of any boy in the freshman class. "Perhaps of any at Yale," Cole said. "And he was hurt a great deal by it. I received less than Len, but more than most of my classmates."

While Len's extravagances may have "hurt him" with some Yalies, naturally Cole sought his friendship. Like Len he preferred—and could afford—custom-made suits, mink-lined stadium coats, jeweled cuff links and gold cigarette cases. He envied Len his automobile, a real luxury in those days, but ownership was beyond him. As it was, he was often overextended and his bills brought increasingly severe reprimands from J. O. Once, finding himself pressed for funds and his grandfather unyielding,

Cole decided to pawn a watch which had a heavy, intricately carved case. He had treasured it since his mother had brought it to him as a gift from Switzerland when he was ten years old. He felt sure that if pawned it would relieve his difficulties. Reluctantly, he took it to the pawnbroker, who examined the timepiece and offered him a single dollar. The case was lead, not silver as Cole had always assumed. Upon receiving the news, Cole turned on his heel and left, taking neither the dollar bill nor the till-now admired watch. "All my life I've been accused of being a snob," Cole said in telling the story. "I'm not. I simply like the best."

When he discovered that Len shared his interest in the theater, the two became even better friends. Sometimes alone, sometimes accompanied by other students, they would finish classes, pick up bags already checked at the railroad station and dash to catch the 6:00 train, changing clothes on the back platform and arriving in New York in full dress. Then they would attend the theater, spend an evening on the town and take the milk train home. The train, which left New York at 4:00 A.M., arrived in New Haven just in time for chapel. Cole often slipped his choir robe over his evening clothes, with not an extra moment to spare.

During the Christmas holidays, he spent most of his time in New York. At this season, students from various Ivy League schools congregated to attend balls held in private residences. One of these was held at the home of Harriet Post, a vivacious young lady, the first girl he knew who had a private ballroom.* By the end of his freshman year, Cole had learned his way about New York almost as fully as about Yale.

That summer, J. O., sensing his grandson's frivolous

* Schuyler Parsons disputes this. He says that the Posts had a large room which was sometimes used as a ballroom, but also was used for the Thursday Club and other social activities. It did not, according to him, compare with those Cole had seen at the Vanderbilt, Beekman and Livingston homes.

bent, made still another attempt to have him familiarize himself with farming, as Cole's cousin James Omar Cole was doing. Katie opposed the idea. So did Cole, who viewed the prospect of working one's way to the top of a family-owned enterprise with cool distaste. His views grew even chillier when the experiment was inaugurated by a trip to Illinois where J. O., in partnership with four other Peru businessmen, had bought several thousand acres of undeveloped land. Cole, who had no intention of roughing it all summer, was totally uncooperative, and the trip was cut short.

But J. O. was tenacious. Since the haying season was in full swing, he insisted that his grandson help. On the appointed day, Cole sullenly set out for the field. Unaccustomed to manual labor, he feared ridicule by a field comedian. So, after working for half an hour, he keeled over and was carried home. Nor did he recover until Katie put her small foot down and announced the experiment was at an end. When he told the story many years later, Cole always maintained that he had suffered a "heatstroke." Whether real or counterfeit, as his grandfather suspected, no one can say. The odds are that he had already adopted what was to become a lifelong habit, offering an acceptable explanation for an unacceptable motive.

Still, in the end, J. O. triumphed—or thought he did. Although he accepted the fact that Cole would never take to farming, it was agreed that law was an appropriate career. This would endow the boy with an understanding of business and handling money. Without fully committing himself, Cole agreed—and bided his time.

Along with most of the sophomore class, Cole returned to Yale a few days before the start of the new term in September, and took up residence in a single room at 112 Welch Street. That fall was a busy one musically. "Bingo, Eli Yale," one of the football songs he had entered in the competition the previous year, became the campus hit of the season. In addition, he wrote a patter number, "Miss

Chapel Street," the first of almost 100 compositions that he was to turn out for college smokers. He also succeeded in publishing a Tin Pan Alley contender, "Bridget," through James H. Remick & Co. of Detroit and New York. In creating the song, Cole was already sophisticated enough to attempt to break with the traditional thirty-two-bar formula. The publisher, however, assumed that the use of an unconventional number of bars grew out of ignorance and doctored the song—which was the last that was heard of "Bridget."

Of more immediate consequence was Cole's participation in musical clubs. When the Glee Club and the Mandolin Club began their 1910 tour, Cole's specialty number, "Perfectly Terrible," was the eighth selection. By the time the final concert was held during prom weekend, "Perfectly Terrible" had been moved to the next-to-closing spot.

It was natural that Cole's initial efforts during his sophomore year at Yale should have attracted the attention of upperclassmen, such as Monty Woolley and Gerald Murphy. (Murphy was later to gain recogniation as a painter, as head of Mark Cross, Inc., as a friend of F. Scott and Zelda Fitzgerald and as an international host.) At the time, he was a senior and the big man around the Psi chapter of Delta Kappa Epsilon. (He was later voted "best dressed," "most thorough gentleman" and "greatest social light" of the class of 1911.) Murphy was eager to have Cole affiliate with DKE. Other members resisted the suggestion, until Murphy finally stilled their opposition by bluntly telling them that Cole was worth ten of them in talent, character, personality or any other qualification they cared to name. After that, it was agreed that a delegation was to visit him.

Cole, who had been aware of their reluctance to accept him, was absent from his quarters at the time the DKEs arrived, but the indefatigable Murphy investigated and discovered that he had been demonstrating his latest entry in the football song competition. It was "Bull Dog," a song still sung at Yale today.

Murphy persisted, and a second visit was arranged. This time Cole was "at home" and was tapped for the fraternity, being elected on April 12, 1911.

Earlier in the semester, Cole had met Monty Woolley at the *Yale News* banquet. Since this function (which saw the installation of the new staff) was a gala affair, all important college organizations and figures were invited. Significantly, the sole representative of the class of 1913 was Cole.

During the informal portion of the entertainment, he was asked to perform a few songs, including his own. He sat down at the piano and soon young voices were enthusiastically raised, drawing much admiring attention to him. But at least one guest was annoyed—Monty, or as he was known then, Edgar Montillion Woolley. Monty was a bitter, witty, unattractive young extrovert who was president of the Yale Dramatic Association, and he regarded the spotlight as *his* domain. Seizing his opportunity as Cole left the piano, Monty stopped him and suggested that his keyboard performance dazzled the player as much as the audience.

Cole denied the charge. "Look, Mr. Woolley," he later reported saying, "if I broke one little pinkie, no one would give me a second thought."

Thus unexpected show of humility so disarmed the anything but humble Monty that he thereupon decided to accept Cole as a protégé. Thus began a friendship which was to endure through the years and to spill over into the drawing rooms of the world, as well as the Broadway musical stage. Afterward, Cole claimed that he considered meeting the loquacious Monty one of his finest experiences at Yale. "He taught me to listen," he explained, flashing a wicked grin.

A survey of the junior class in 1911-1912 disclosed that fifty-two percent of the men had never taken part in any extracurricular activity. Cole, on the other hand, had majored in outside work and minored in the prescribed curriculum.

He acted the butler in a filmed screenplay shot at Yale, appeared in the Yale Dramat's annual production, danced the night away at the luxurious new Taft Hotel and generally outraged the conservatives. His social life was full.

A writer to the *Yale News* maintained that whenever two underclassmen discovered a common enthusiasm for licorice, they formed a club and gave it an esoteric name to mystify other students. Cole belonged to his share. In addition to the Dramat, Glee Club and DKE, he was a member of an enormous number of long-forgotten associations, including The Grill Room Grizzlies and the Mince Pie Club (he was the Spice). As a part of the Hogans he repaired to Morey's once each month to make out bills in return for dinner and drinks on the house.

Slightly more serious was The Pundits, a club organized by Professor William Lyon Phelps. Billy Phelps, who was a great character to generations of Yale students, was an inveterate lecturer. The Pundits, ostensibly founded to arouse interest in literature, actually, according to one member, existed "solely for the idolatrous worship of William Lyon Phelps." The students were invited to Professor Phelps' house for a good dinner and then one of the group was scheduled to read a paper. But Phelps soon found that he would rather lecture than listen, and the club degenerated into a weekly monologue delivered by its founder. Cole, who idolized Phelps, gave it his full attention.

In addition, he was a Whiffenpoof (the Whiffenpoofs is an autonomous group of singers within the Glee Club who serve as major attractions at athletic events and on Glee Club tours). Most important to Cole's ego, however, was his election on May 17, 1912, to Scroll and Key. For however much of a maverick he may have seemed, unlike some personalities Cole was not constituted so that rebuffs stimulated him to further effort. Rather, he thrived in an atmosphere of acceptance and adulation.

From the beginning, Cole's work with the Glee Club was attention-getting. During his junior year, he wrote and performed "The Motor Car," which caused critics to hail him as the big featured soloist. The man from the Washington (D.C.) *Star* went even further when he wrote: ". . . In addition to having a good singing voice and being a clever imitator, Mr. Porter is a comedian and his performance entirely out of the ordinary in college glee club concerts brought down the house."

Naturally, then, Cole was chosen as leader of the Glee Club for 1912-1913 and, being an ambitious youngster, he organized a tour, going as far west as Denver, and playing en route such cities as St. Louis, Chicago, Minneapolis and Detroit. The tour closed in New York City on January 1. That night the girls from Finch School gave a dance in honor of the Yale men. At this dance, Cole added a personal mischievous touch by dedicating "Heaven Will Protect the Working Girl" to Mrs. Finch. Years later, Edwina Stone, a Finch graduate wrote: "How we marveled at your courage and wondered what the outcome would be. For Mrs. Finch was at the time quite a suffragette, and labor sympathizer. Well, she took it in her stride for which we were truly thankful." It was the kind of situation Cole enjoyed creating.

On that note, the two weeks of "unadulterated pleasure" covering 4,700 miles, the longest trip undertaken by the club since 1901, ended. The group was lauded in every city for what the Denver *Times* described as their "snap and dash." Cole earned unstinted praise both for his work as the leader of the Glee Club and for his performance of still another original composition, "A Football King."

Certainly Cole's self-fulfillment reached a peak in the college smokers which he created for DKE and the Yale Dramatic Association. The first such show was inspired by a casual visit to the Grand Opera House to witness Leon Washburn's ten-twenty-thirty-fifty-cent presentation of Stetson's Big Spectacular *Uncle Tom's Cabin.* There, Little Eva's spotless purity and Simon Legree's dreadful villainy provided Cole and T. Gaillard Thomas II with the idea of spoofing a melodrama for the Yale Dramat's smoker. They set to work at once, interrupted their collaboration for the

Glee Club's Christmas tour and took up the project anew after Cole settled down from the excitement of the trip and his election as Glee Club leader for 1912-1913.

When that first smoker was presented on April 24, 1912, with Monty Woolley (who was doing postgraduate work) as "the Villain," they called it *And the Villain Still Pursued Her*. Highly praised in the press, it was transferred to New York for one performance. Still, there are few hints of Cole's later style in the lyrics. For the most part the songs were pedestrian and have little to set them apart from those found in run-of the-mill college shows. In one number, however, there was a bit of lyric which went:

> *Though we don't want to say it, we*
> *Are so chock full of gaiety*
> *Everybody knows*
> *Anything goes. . . .*

Once Cole seized upon a good idea, he never entirely discarded it. More than twenty years later, expanded and deepened, the same idea was utilized in his second-biggest Broadway hit, *Anything Goes.*

Before leaving Yale for the summer, Cole sought out a brilliant DKE pledge, Almet F. Jenks, Jr., who in his freshman year had won the $100 prize offered by the Yale Dramatic Association for the best play written by a university member. Cole suggested that it would be mutually advantageous for them to collaborate on the 1912-1913 DKE smoker. To give them sufficient time, he proposed that Jenks write the libretto during summer vacation and send it to him in Peru so that he could make a head start on the songs.

Jenks proved a facile worker and by the time Cole departed for Indiana, he already had an outline of the show. It took place in a "rundown hotel" owned by Oliver Delor whose only assets were, according to the author, a certain latent cleverness and a beautiful daughter. To the hotel comes Lawrence Thorne (eventually played by Cole) to meet a long-lost rich uncle. Thorne falls in love with

Delor's daughter, but in order to win her must change the fortunes of the hotel. He does so by creating a scandal involving his uncle, General Harrison, two Russian nihilists and several other assorted eccentrics.

Working from this outline, Cole turned out five songs which he sent along with the first letter to Jenks from "Westleigh on the Mis-sis-sin-e-wa." He entreated his collaborator to be "obvious and uninteresting. Otherwise we will suffer defeat for my music was never the result of inspired imagination." He closed by imploring Jenks to send along the completed scenario so that he could get at the opening choruses, and he also asked who Jenks thought should be cast in what parts so that he could write fitting songs more easily. "Be naif and I can join you," he ended.

Jenks' reply is lost, but Cole's next letter to him was in a euphoric mood, while at the same time he played the part of the practical man of the theater. "I am delighted," he announced. "I received a letter from you in which you showed a descent from the Etherial. [He was never a good speller.]

"As for the title *The Pot of Gold* being trite, I think it is truly wonderful. A title is good only when it means nothing until the fall of the final curtain and you must admit that in *this* case, the final curtain must fall.

"As for the caste [*sic*], it seems rather large but I suppose you consider it necessary. Of course with so many, rehearsals will be exceedingly difficult. Then too, a chorus girl is worth more than a useless part. I notice you have H. Sawyer down for a part. Please make it 'thinking.' I love your two Russian nihilists. I got the blank after one of the names. Of course, you will be Turnesky in your own inimitable way. I am trying to write a talking mysterioso song for you and your fellow conspirator. As soon as you finish the conversation between the nihilists in which the plot is formed write it to me and I will convert it into a *recitatif*. I have written your motif already. It combines the splendor of Wagner and the decadence of Strauss.

"You speak of three acts. I beg you—Don't. Three would be interminable or choppy.

"Remember what a change in costume and scene means. It is a terrible thought always and if possible try to condense your action to two acts.

"Another thing (Forgive me): Dink Stover was altogether too short. It gave one sensation but not perception. Please write this play a long one, for we can easily cut parts if we time it and find it soporific.

"I wish we could make this play a little masterpiece in its own foolish way. Take it horribly seriously and I will join you. It really is important for after all it can never happen again.

"The minute you finish it send it to me. I have a great deal to do when I return to college and I must have most of this play in black and white by October 1st.

"If you get done soon enough (and by that I don't expect you to tear it off) I can have the incidental music, an overture, an entr'acte, combined motifs, melodrama, etc.

"Perhaps I sound altogether too serious about it, but I feel that it is up to you to show New Haven a little of that brain. You have no idea how much is expected of you. You have a reputation.

"I have written a song for Anstruther [Arnold] called 'My Houseboat on the Thames.' "

Along with his practical suggestions, his starry-eyed idealism about the theater and a bit of condescension to a lowerclassman, Cole included two songs and the information that he would be in Peru until September 6, after which he could be reached in care of Vanderbilt Webb, who was getting married, at Shelburne, Vermont. Following Webb's wedding, he said he would be at Garrison, New York, with Humphrey Parsons. He planned to begin rehearsals by "the second week" and predicted that together they would "open a few eyes."

In his third letter on August 23, he informed Jenks he had written the overture and explained in detail what he was attempting. "It begins with the motif—Chlodoswinde's yearning for Larry; then follows the waltz representing her pangs on finding him false, ending in the motif of supreme happiness, which appears again at the end of the play.

Following this comes Larry's love song. Then a thing in 5/4 time introducing the foreign influence on the hotel, modulating into a death march representing the monotony and decadence of the place. This is connected with the opening chorus by a movement which grows more excited as it progresses. The opening chorus is the 'Rainbow Song' which would be sung by the guests who depart at the end of it."

As this letter makes clear, Cole was no simple college boy writing a handful of hit-or-miss tunes to dot an unpretentious little show. And in his final letter, he reiterated "Finish the second act. I can do nothing until you do. You see my only means of making the songs relevant is by writing verses which give the idea of belonging to the person who sings them."

When school convened on September 25, Cole immediately dined with Jenks and announced that he would leave the casting up to him but prudently added that of course those who can't sing can't have songs.

Cole, who was not living alone for the first time, shared quarters at 31 Vanderbilt with Humphrey Parsons, a moody pre-law student from New York, who had been chosen as manager of the Glee Club.

Scholastically, Cole was faced with the necessity of getting down to work. During his freshman year, he had failed the second semester of History A-1, Geology both semesters of his sophomore year (causing the dean to note in pencil on the back of his grade card "*Watch him!* No more irregularities, 1911.") and had earned no more than Bs, Cs and Ds in music.

Even so, Cole, who had never shown any inclination to participate in athletics, so envied top athletes their popularity that in the fall of his senior year he served as a cheerleader, experiencing a little of the thrill vicariously. That fall, too, he wrote a song for the DKE smoker, "A Football King," which reveals his private yearning to be a different type of human being than he was.

Despite his need to study, Cole spent a major part of his time at the DKE house preparing the ambitious production, *The Pot of Gold,* exerting pressure to allow non-DKE talent (Professor Haesche of the Yale Music School, orchestra leader Eddy Wittenstein and Professor John Milton Berdan of the English Department) to enter the secret "tombs" even though it created a furor among the more orthodox members.

Because of the success the show met when presented at the DKE house on November 26, the performance was repeated on December 4, 1912, at the new Taft Hotel as a benefit for the as yet nebulous Yale Theater.

The Pot of Gold was hardly out of the way when Cole, in spite of his precarious scholastic standing, reserved time to work on *Kaleidoscope,* the annual Dramatic Association smoker, for which he provided music and lyrics. And, as he had done with *And the Villain Still Pursued Her* and *The Pot of Gold,* he also conducted rehearsals, coaching participants in songs whose lyrics he had jotted down on the backs of envelopes while carrying the tunes in his head. "In addition," said poet Archibald MacLeish, who played Butler, a baby, "he also mixed drinks, introducing me to the Tom Collins."

The result of all this activity was a production of unusual polish, of such polish that the more serious-minded enthusiasts of drama became somewhat alarmed lest the smokers, overshadow less frivolous productions. For instance, on April 30, 1913, after the opening, William Lyon Phelps saluted it by saying: ". . . Every serious man and organization often turns to things in a lighter vein . . . and the Dramatic Club is very fortunate in having one man who is a real genius and who writes both words and music of such exceptional high order. . . ." The message? Perhaps no one else should attempt to surpass him.

Jack Crawford, a Broadway playwright who was attempting to establish drama classes at his alma mater, praised the show, then with more forthrightness than Professor Phelps added that "since it would be difficult to equal or surpass this smoker it would be better not to try, lest it lead to more lavish and time consuming productions."

Cole accepted their good wishes and compliments lightly, for he had already made up his mind that, although he was graduating, he would provide a smoker next year.

When graduation time came around, he appeared in the commencement play, George Farquhar's *The Recruiting Office*. Even though he had failed a number of courses in the past four years, the university apparently advanced him credits for his extracurricular activities, making it possible for him to graduate; and as the year drew to a close, he was one of twenty-five senior men chosen to lead the march at Class Day exercises.

In the survey of 292 graduates, Cole was one of 128 who used alcohol (champagne, gin and Scotch); one of 178 who smoked (Fatimas); one of 110 who had been abroad; one of 69 non-church members; and one of the 20 who were to enter law school. Afterward, he reported that he expected to go into "either mining, lumbering or farming." In the class vote, he received the fifth largest number of votes as the person who had done most for Yale. He was voted the most entertaining (beating out Fletcher Van Wie Blood by fifteen votes), the second most original (losing to Ewing T. Webb by five votes), and one of the most eccentric.

CHAPTER IV

If it was necessary to endure Harvard Law School to remain in J. O.'s financial graces Cole was prepared to do so, but his enthusiasm remained at Yale. Even before leaving New Haven, he had arranged with the undergraduates at the Dramatic Association that he and T. Lawrason Riggs (Yale, 1910) would write the annual smoker.

In the fall of 1913, when Cole moved into Craigie Hall No. 404 in Cambridge, he and Riggs, who was doing graduate work at Harvard, at once began to apply themselves to the task of creating the smoker. Riggs was a cultivated, fine-grained, deeply religious and intensely intellectual young man. At Yale, he had been elected to Phi Beta Kappa and had tied for the Greek Prize. Now at Harvard he was concentrating on English literature. Far more mature and defined than his collaborator, he influenced Cole deeply, especially in making unconventional rhymes and introducing all kinds of esoteric allusions into the lyrics. Sometimes the results were forced, but at other times the method produced unexpectedly delightful results.

Whatever this project may have meant to the Yale

Dramatic Association, it had a distinctly negative effect on Cole's relationship to Harvard. His obligation to his law studies certainly suffered. However, that may have been inevitable. In addition to the fact that he made little effort to master the material, there was another difficulty. Cole had little aptitude for conceptual thinking, and the fine distinctions spelled out in court decisions simply did not interest him. From the first, he seems to have realized that there was little hope that he would remain beyond the first semester.

Then, by chance, Dean Ezra Ripley Thayer of the Harvard Law School intervened. Dean Thayer was noted for his humanitarian impulses, and for good reason. Once, for example, having voted to disbar a hard-pressed lawyer who had bilked a client, he made the stipulation that should the money be repaid the disbarment would be set aside. After the meeting he rushed to the lawyer's office and loaned him the money with which to clear himself.

In Cole's case, Dean Thayer chanced to attend an impromptu entertainment at which Cole performed. What he heard reinforced his conviction that the youth was registered in the wrong school. The Dean called Cole in, suggested that he switch to a music course and helped to arrange the transfer.*

In view of J. O.'s sentiment, perhaps it is fortunate that he was unaware of the switch or of the "melopedrama in two acts" called *Paranoia, or Chester of the YDA* that opened at Yale on April 24, 1914. In this production, Cole and Lawrason Riggs shared credit for the book, the music and the lyrics. Monty Woolley was listed as producer-director and Archibald MacLeish played a Nubian slave.

Both Cole and Riggs, of course, were on hand for the performance, which was chiefly distinguished by an original little number called "I've a Shooting Box in

* It has been claimed by some writers that Cole neglected to inform his family of the change. Others have implied that J. O. agreed since the suggestion came from the distinguished Dean Thayer. Actually, only Katie was informed.

Scotland," a song whose lyrics showed a considerable advance over Cole's previous work. It began:

I've a shooting box in Scotland
I've a château in Touraine
I've a silly little chalet
In the Interlaken Valley . . .

The show was unquestionably the best Cole had done. And as the acclaim mounted, he became increasingly dissatisfied with the thought of spending his life in any other way. Nor was he alone in this feeling. The fulfillment that such shows as *Paranoia,* as well as the earlier *Kaleidoscope* and *The Pot of Gold,* provided the youthful members of the Dramatic Association was strong enough so that the boys tried to hold the group together for several years after graduation. Twice (first in Cincinnati, then in Cleveland), these recent graduates convened to entertain the Federation of Yale Clubs. When they went to Cincinnati, Cole sampled the liquor stock in their private railroad car and dashed off a song saluting the city to which they were bound. Later, when the trip to Cleveland came along, Cole was otherwise occupied, but he dutifully composed another salute and dispatched it to the group in a six-page telegram.

In various ways, all during his sojourn at Harvard, Cole persisted in trying to turn it into a little patch of Yale. The fall of 1915, he joined a number of Scroll and Key men from New Haven, including Dean Acheson and T. Lawrason Riggs, in renting a house at 1 Mercer Circle. To care for the place, they hired a man who cleaned, prepared one meal daily and served tea for them and their guests every afternoon at four.

But Cole was too immersed in songwriting to give much thought to anything else. The success of the Yale smokers had given him blazing confidence, and that fall he succeeded in placing two of his songs in Broadway productions. It was an era when scores were assembled rather than written, and even writers of Jerome Kern's stature were subjected to the whims of all-powerful producers. Thus, "Two Big Eyes" (music by Cole Porter, words by John Golden) was interpolated into Kern's score for *Miss Information* and was sung by Irene Bordoni. *Esmeralda,* performed by M. Maurice, "The Waltz King," and Florence Walton, had both words and music by Cole. It was used in *Hands-Up*, described as "A Musico-Comico-Filmo-Melo-Drama." The major part of the score was by Sigmund Romberg and E. Ray Goetz. Neither the shows nor the songs stirred a ripple of interest. *Miss Information* ran forty-seven performances; *Hands-Up,* fifty-two. Cole shrugged off the failures, feeling small responsibility.

Up at 1 Mercer Circle, he and Riggs were deeply immersed in the creation of an American comic opera in the Gilbert and Sullivan tradition. They shared credit (or, as it turned out, responsibility) for music, lyrics and book, although Cole alone attended to the first and Riggs to the last, while both worked on the lyrics. Cole also claimed to have devised the title, *See America First,* one of his early contributions as a phrasemaker.

When the script was completed, Cole insisted upon giving it to a society girl turned literary agent who was the United States representative of the most important Continental playwrights. Her name was Elisabeth (Bessie) Marbury. Cole had met Bessie Marbury during his Yale days and had been impressed by both her social background and success in producing off beat, intimate musicals such as Jerome Kern's *Very Good Eddie.*

Riggs was less enthusiastic, and almost at once it became apparent, even to such neophytes as he and Cole, that Bessie Marbury's production methods were somewhat erratic. Although she had engaged a number of experienced vaudevillians including Clifton Webb and Felix Adler for the cast, the lead was entrusted to a society beauty, Miss Dorothy—Dorothie, for stage usage—Bigelow (who in publicity releases was invariably given her full pedigree, "daughter of Edith Jaffry Bigelow and Poultney Bigelow and the granddaughter of John

Bigelow"). Miss Bigelow's ambition was said to be to become "another Julia Sanderson," in which she was rather handicapped, according to Cole, in not being able to project her voice beyond the third row of the small Maxine Elliott Theater.

The plot concerned a rich American who loves the United States, loathes everything foreign. His daughter adores anything British, abhors the United States —especially after exchanging glances with a duke at the Garden Opera. By stretching the long arm of coincidence, as one critic put it, the two lovers meet in the Wild West. The duke is disguised as a cowhand; the heiress, on her way to an Indian school. During the remainder of the evening, the principals and chorus frolic about the forest, clad in party frocks and knee breeches, singing and dancing such numbers as "The Language of Flowers," "Prithee, Come Crusading with Me," and, perhaps somewhat desperately, "Something's Got to Be Done."

According to Clifton Webb, who made his legitimate debut in *See America First*, it was a college show gone wrong. "I played a cowboy and an autumn flower. Others had roles not so believable," he said. "The set consisted of large graduated poufs and tiers that looked like nothing so much as the Hollywood Bowl. Benrimo, the lighting expert, also helped direct. But mostly, he directed his passes at Dorothie Bigelow—getting nowhere. Nor could he get his mind on his work." It seemed to Webb that Miss Bigelow was holding back, not only from Benrimo but also in her performance. At the final preview, many of her society friends attended. Cole assured Webb that at last Dorothy-Dorothie would give a performance. "That night I concluded she had been studying with Debussy," Webb recalled. "She opened her mouth, made animated expressions, but no voice came out. No matter. Both her entrances and exits were greeted with waves of applause that absolutely stopped the show. Lawrason and Cole were rushing about. Lawrason seemed to have forgotten their reservations about the cast and changes in the book."

The truth is that Cole was so bedazzled by the fulfillment of his dream—having a show on Broadway—that his judgment was beclouded. Nothing seemed good or bad. All he could think of was that at last he was on the Great White Way.

Not so with many others. *Variety* reported that people who attended the preview immediately began thinking up obituary notices.

Opening night, March 28, 1916, was a classic disaster. Dorothy-Dorothie made her entrance. Where there had been show-stopping applause the previous evening, there was only silence. In her agitation, she literally fell on her derrière and the performance deteriorated after that. Out of the shambles, the audience responded only to Felix Adler's vaudeville routines, Jean Cartier's and Clifton Webb's dancing, and a revised version of "I've a Shooting Box in Scotland."

The reviewers generally counseled theatergoers to *See America First* last. Better still, they said, avoid altogether the "newest and worse musical in town." One critic complained that "the two college boys paid rather too much attention to the work of Gilbert and Sullivan and George M. Cohan"—missing the fact that there was a case to be made that they had intended to parody the latter. If so, Cohan also missed the point. Years later, Cole recalled that only Cohan, actress Jane Cowl and playwright Harrison Rhodes sought him out to encourage him.

Rhodes assured Cole that he had talent, but said that if he wished to succeed there was something he'd have to do.

"Work?" Cole asked.

"No," was the reply. "Play hard. Learn about life."

Upon hearing this, Cole, who had viewed the flop as a personal rejection, turned and fled. He felt as if the one thing that he had counted upon to assure his popularity had been destroyed.

After a struggle of fifteen performances, the show closed. "I honestly believed I was disgraced for the rest of my life. I sneaked back to the Yale Club, rushed through the lobby and hid in my room," Cole once told Ed Sullivan.

"Then it was that I decided to join the French Foreign Legion—and I sailed a few days later and joined up." He stated on numerous other occasions that the failure of the show had driven him into the Foreign Legion and his collaborator into the priesthood.

A good story it is, and perhaps even true in spirit, but the fact remains that the show opened on March 28, 1916, and Cole sailed for Europe in the latter half of 1917. Meanwhile, a vaudeville dance team, Fred and Adele Astaire, applied for and received permission to incorporate "I've a Shooting Box in Scotland" into their act.

Cole spent the latter part of 1916 and the early months of 1917 in New York. After the dispiriting experience with *See America First,* he took a flat on East 19th Street. Ostensibly, he was to spend his time studying composition under Pietro Yon, who then was the musical director and organist at St. Patrick's Cathedral. But Harriet Post recalled that the apartment was the scene of one theme party or costume ball after another. As Cole had done in his unhappy childhood, he escaped a miserable present by playing at being someone he was not.

For his part, Lawrason Riggs sent a note to the Yale alumni magazine. "I spent the fall of 1915 in Cambridge, working on the book and lyrics of a comic opera, *See America First,* with Cole Porter, who did the music," he reported. "It was presented in New York during the winter, but failed dismally. Owing to the fact that the composer and I consented to complete transformation of the piece to meet the capabilities of its interpreters and the supposed taste of the public, we suffered, in addition to our disappointment, the unsatisfactory feeling that nothing had been proved as to the worth of our efforts. But we are wiser as well as sadder, and for myself I have done with attempts at dramatic composition, so far as I can foresee."

Finally, in the fall of 1917 Cole sailed on the *Espagna* for France. Another passenger was a young man who was to gain fame as the couturier Main Bocher. Main Bocher's first glimpse of Cole came as the composer climbed aboard ship carrying a small zitherlike instrument. Main groaned. Amateur musicians were the bane of his life. Nor was the situation improved when they were introduced and Main detected that Cole made no great effort to conceal his hostility. During the trip Main developed an appreciation for Cole's abilities as an entertainer, but it took him ten years to feel he had really come to know the personality.

What Cole actually did upon arrival in France has come to be regarded as altogether mysterious. In an article about him in *Town and Country,* Tom Wood commented: "Porter's war record is a case for Scotland Yard. Although he maintains he joined the Foreign Legion as a private, transferred to the Ecole d'Artillerie at Fontainebleau and eventually saw service at the front with the 32d Regiment, French Army. Monty Woolley, who bobbed up in Paris with the U.S. Army, recalls Porter strutting up and down the boulevards in uniforms ranging all the way from a cadet's to a colonel's. Porter, says Woolley, had more changes than Maréchal Foch, and wore them with complete disregard of regulation. One night he might be a captain of the Zouaves, the next an aide-de-camp. . . ." The Yale class of 1913 in an annual report further confused the record with a note that "Classmate Cole A. Porter has joined the American Aviation Forces in France although nobody seems to know in what capacity."

Confusion? Even the records provided by the Ministry for War Veterans and War Victims are inaccurate. They begin: "The Candidate Porter, born June 9, 1899 [Ed. note: wrong] at Peru [United States] son of Manuel [Ed. note: wrong] and Kate Cole . . ."

Actually, Cole's first wartime association in France was with Duryea Relief, an organization which had been set up by an American society woman, Nina Larre Smith Duryea. In line of duty, he visited devastated villages to distribute supplies, but by January of 1918 he had left and was attached to the headquarters of Air Service Lines of Communication of Expeditionary Forces (also known as the American Aviation Headquarters) on the Avenue de Montaigne.

Then on April 20, 1918, he enlisted (number 46,647) in the "First Foreign Regiment at the Central Recruiting Office of the Seine, matriculation list no. 12651—Detailed for pay and rations to the 32nd Field Artillery Regiment—Given the rank of Candidate as a foreigner to take his place August 22, 1918—Detailed for pay and rations to the 15th Artillery Regiment—Arrived and enrolled in the 1st Battery on September 20, 1918—Detailed to the Bureau of the Military Attaché of the United States on January 23, 1919—Discharged on April 17, 1919, by the depot of the 26th Light Infantry Battalion at Vincennes—Stated, at the time, retiring to Paris, 9 Rue Gounod—Stricken from Controls on April 18, 1919."

As had become his custom, first at Worcester Academy and then at Yale, Cole made certain that he enjoyed special privileges in the Foreign Legion. For example, Archibald MacLeish recalled running into him on a boulevard in the spring of 1918 and being astonished when Cole, who obviously spent a lot of time in Paris, invited him to a party "at his house." (That house was the property of a Frenchwoman who lent it to Cole whenever he was in town.) "Of course, I was the most naïve country bumpkin, but I thought it was pretty big high-life myself," MacLeish said. "There were three or four elegant French gals and a couple of Britishers and Cole. I made the mistake of bringing two Harvard characters. We were all pretty dirty. It wasn't exactly the kind of thing you do to a good friend. And I used to have shivers thinking about it. Cole—long before he married Linda—even as an undergraduate always seemed to me the most cosmopolitan figure."

Cole had a simple explanation for his extraordinary freedom. He said that since he was the only American in the regiment, the officers deferred to him, seeing to it that he was always housed with a local priest. "I liked that. The food and lodging were the best to be had," he commented.

As for the Foreign Legion legend, it was romanticized by magazine writers and further distorted by Hollywood writers who fabricated his "biographical film," *Night and*

Day. In the articles and to some degree in the film, he was depicted as a desperately unhappy youth who fled America after the failure of his first musical and joined a group of men who had chosen the Legion as an alternative to suicide. The truth is that he never served in one of its battalions. He was under the control of the Foreign Legion simply because when he joined the French Army during World War I, he was a foreigner serving for pay. Various writers have also endowed him with the Croix de Guerre for (1) personality, (2) comradeship, or (3) just showing up. But the record shows that he was never decorated.

Upon being mustered out, he returned to Paris and once again he turned his mind to music and society. In line with the former, he enrolled at the Schola Cantorum to study counterpoint, composition, orchestration and harmony.

In 1919, Vincent d'Indy, who had helped found the Schola Cantorum in 1894, was regarded as a messiah by young hopefuls. D'Indy, an ascetic gentleman who swept his long white hair back over his ears and turned his haughty back on all that was popular and entertaining, was the stuff of which idols are made. Cole, always ready to ally himself with the latest vogue, was eager to join the throng at d'Indy's feet, and join it he did. One positive result of this move was that the classicist d'Indy succeeded in solidifying Cole's already substantial musical education.

While Cole accepted the discipline of classicism, he could not subscribe to d'Indy's rejection of modern experimentation. As a creative individual, Cole was unable to ignore the new rhythms he had detected in contemporary, especially American, life. He became restive, worrying that he was stifling his imaginative impulses. By limiting himself to the rigid forms of the past, he felt that he would be rejecting everything potentially fresh in his work. D'Indy was not sympathetic.

Cole once told George Beiswanger, who wrote a piece about him for *Theatre Arts* magazine, that he found confirmation for his urge "to escape the stiff four-measure pattern of the then-reigning popular song" when he heard a French soldier singing "Madelon." According to

Beiswanger, "When the Frenchman came to a long note and a rest—introduced to fill out the regulation set of beats—he cut the note short, omitted the pause and proceeded with the song. This bothered Cole Porter at first, then pleased him. He responded to the rightness: the tailoring of the measure to the sense, the fitting of note length and stress to the length and natural accent of the word, the electric distortion of rhythm which is also the heart of jazz and the dance song. . . ." Cole left the Schola Cantorum and set out to satisfy an inner urge by writing popular songs with which to amuse himself and friends.

One of these was a plump, bumptious young extrovert who claimed the whole world as her very most intimate friend. Her name was Elsa Maxwell. Elsa always maintained that her exuberance was overcompensation for being excluded from a posh society party when she was a child in San Francisco. As a young woman, she toured with a Shakespearean company, played the piano in honky-tonks and sang for her supper. Just at the beginning of World War I, she had, through charity work, inched her way into the good graces of some of New York's "400."

Cole first met her shortly after the failure of *See America First*. Elsa attended a party at the home of Mrs. Bridgit Guiness, who lived on Washington Square. She arrived with a ravishing brunette with an ivory complexion and beautiful dark eyes. Beside her, Elsa was dumpy and unprepossessing. Everyone, according to Cole, was entranced by the beauty whose name was Dorothy "Dickie" Fellowes-Gordon. Nobody paid the slightest attention to Elsa until she sat down to the piano to play and sing, "They Call Me Ivy Because I Cling." ("Everyone began to talk about her then—and the fascinating thing is that they're still talking," Cole said in 1957.) After the party, Elsa and Cole became friends.

Now, in 1919, Elsa was living in Paris trying to enlarge her social contacts. In doing so, she promoted Cole and his songs, introducing him to the kind of people he really enjoyed: those who were rich, talented, attractive and on the go.

Another of Cole's friends was the not-very-talented former actress Elsie de Wolfe, who had become one of the first successful female interior decorators. Elsie (later Lady Mendl) was delighted to have Cole entertain her guests with his impudent, suggestive little songs. Occasionally, some Continental (unaware of Cole's private income) would suggest that he arrange for his work to be published. He pretended that such suggestions displeased him, maintaining that he was not interested in *commercial* acceptance. Yet most of those who knew him at the time felt that he was just a brilliant young Midwesterner who was whiling away time waiting to get a break on Broadway.

This was true, but Cole was too proud to admit it. He realized that ninety-nine percent of those who applauded his efforts felt the general public would never take to his songs. It was believed, he later said, that the music and lyrics were charming but "too special" for ordinary people. Elsa was one of the first to take a more positive view. She said the songs were almost too original, but added that the public could be educated up to them. It was a vote of confidence that Cole never forgot.

Probably the most important incident that happened during Cole's postwar days in Paris occurred when along with many other Americans he attended the fashionable wedding of Ethel Harriman and Henry Russell. At the reception, held at the Ritz, he drifted to the piano, soon to be joined by a young woman named Mimi Scott. He played, and they sang. They were a distinct hit.

Among those especially taken by their work was an American divorcée, Mrs. Linda Lee Thomas. Mrs. Thomas, who moved through the loftiest circles of international society, was regarded by many as the most beautiful woman in the world. Cole was enchanted by her beauty. She, in turn, was overwhelmed by his impudent songs, so unlike anyone else's. When she had an opportunity, she sought out a close friend, Schuyler Livingston Parsons, of an old New York family, and asked him whether he knew Cole. Parsons throughout his life had made it a habit of knowing everyone worth knowing. (For instance, Charles Lindbergh was his house guest upon returning to the United States after flying the Atlantic; George Gershwin began composing *Rhapsody in Blue* on Parsons' piano; Gertie Lawrence and Bea Lillie spent their first evening in the United States at his apartment, etc.) Naturally, he knew Cole. Mrs. Thomas said she would be delighted if Cole and Miss Scott would attend a dinner she was giving and do their amusing songs.

When Parsons relayed the message, Mimi Scott wanted to know what Linda Thomas thought they were—professional entertainers? Parsons mollified her and at last they agreed to accompany Parsons to the party.

On the appointed evening, Parsons arrived at Mimi Scott's hotel and waited for her and Cole to put in an appearance. When they did, he was furious. Before him stood two caricatures of cheap music-hall entertainers of the 1890's. Mimi Scott was resplendent in a beaded-jet dress and a hideous picture hat. Cole wore an old-fashioned tail coat and trousers, a shirt with a high celluloid collar and his hair was slicked down and parted in the middle. Recounting the incident in his autobiography, *Untold Friendships,* Parsons wrote: " 'Now,' they said, 'this will put you and your swell friends in your place.' By the time we arrived at Linda's they had lost some of their bravado and when I dashed upstairs and told her what a ghastly trick they had played, she roared as did her guests and even I cooled down enough to be able to introduce them as they made their grande entrée . . ."

Throughout his life Cole eschewed the obvious. Now, his growing attachment to thirty-six-year-old Linda,* an American divorcée who was accustomed only to the most prodigal self-indulgence, alarmed his friends. They feared that he would be caught up in international gambols and his sybaritic tendencies would triumph over his creative instincts.

* Born November 16, 1883.

The Gerald Murphys were among those who deplored the attachment. Murphy, who had sponsored Cole with the DKEs at Yale, felt that Cole's future might be at stake. Sara Wiborg Murphy later recalled Cole as "a natural-born hedonist, which is fine. People like hedonists. But Cole had so much more. He always liked beautiful, expensive things. Not that he thought about money. He never noticed it. He thought everyone had it, because he never had to bother. But he wanted to live like a king—which is all right too. Unless it stops you from working. That's what we were afraid of. Of course, he wanted to marry a very beautiful woman—which he did. Even I have to admit that. She was dull as anything, but she was very beautiful."

Sara Murphy was not alone in failing to appreciate Linda. "Gerald and I always found her stuffy," she said. "Cole was such an affectinate, lovely man. We loved to go out with him alone. He was so bright, so witty. If she came along, it made it sort of heavy going. Some people are like that. Partly it was her great beauty. She was so aware of it. She never moved her mouth or made any false gestures that might cause her to develop a line in her face. Oh my no! But Cole thought she was just wonderful—which was a very good thing if he was going to insist upon marrying her."

Schuyler Parsons, who was devoted to Linda for fifty years, has always maintained that the people who did not like Linda—and there were a goodly number—found her snobbish or dull because when she was bored or didn't like anyone "she could freeze up like an icicle." If so, in that respect she and Cole were very much alike.

Nevertheless, most people were bowled over by her. In 1909, she was purported to be the most beautiful woman in America; ten years later, when her youthful freshness might be expected to have faded, she was widely regarded as one of the most beautiful women in the world. She dressed with superb originality. Her introduction of the simple black dress, accented by one beautiful piece of jewelry, came to be regarded as the height of chic.

Although the camera seldom succeeded in capturing her real beauty, painters fought for the honor to do portraits of her. Not only that, the French, who, then as now, were not always generous in their judgment of Americans, worshiped her. As Baron Nicolas de Gunzberg once explained it, "She had great chic, great beauty and she was always ahead—the French loved her for that, because she always topped them in chic."

Just as no one can adequately account for Cole's musical genius and sophistication, no one can explain the origin of Linda's style. Schuyler Parsons, who first met her when she was a young girl summering with his cousins, the R. Livingston Beekmans, maintains that she always had it. In 1964, he said that he had known many beauties or seen them in the past seventy-three years but "Linda was the equal of any." Tall, with blue-blue eyes, a pink and white complexion and blond hair, she possessed a musical speaking voice and a magical personality. According to no less authority than Bernard Berenson, who kept up a lifelong correspondence with her, she had the most faultless intuitive esthetic sensibility in relation to the first-rate in painting, architecture and sculpture of anyone he ever encountered.

How far all this seems from her early years in Louisville, Kentucky, as one of the three daughters of Mr. and Mrs. William Paca (for one of the signers of the Declaration of Independence) Lee. Although well-born and a banker, Lee had monetary problems that were to exert stress on his daughters' early years. Nevertheless, the Lee sisters were always invited to all the best parties and balls. At one of these, held at Kentucky Derby time, Linda encountered the group who were to take her from Louisville forever.

Linda attracted the attention of Mrs. James Borden Harriman Sr., who came to the Derby in her private railroad car. Mrs. Harriman was charmed by the young beauty, but was puzzled by one idiosyncrasy in an otherwise striking young woman. Eventually, she asked Linda why she always chose to wear the same dress. Linda replied that it was the only ball gown she owned. Her honesty and simplicity apparently intrigued Mrs. Harriman, who thereafter made it a point to introduce her to friends.

In this way, Linda came to be invited to summer in Newport with the Beekmans. Mrs. Beekman was the daughter of General Samuel Thomas and the sister of Edward Russell Thomas. Actually it was E. R. "Ned" Thomas, the "boy banker," sportsman, publisher and playboy, who had fallen in love with seventeen-year-old Linda when they met in Louisville and urged his sister to extend the invitation. In Newport that summer Ned continued the courtship, and in 1901 they were married.

Even the slipper-fitting episode in Cinderella hardly wrought a greater change for that heroine than marriage to Ned Thomas did for Linda. He gave her a cottage in Newport, a mansion in Palm Beach, and a town house at 17 West 57th Street in New York. He gave her a box at the opera, an eight-sail yacht named *The Buffalo Butterfly,* and a collection of jewels including the usual pearls, diamonds and rubies, as well as a diamond pendant and such heavy pieces as a stomacher and two tiaras. (One of the latter was so heavy that when his wife wore it to the opera she and her friends would retire to privacy between acts to remove their heavy "glass hats" in order to give their aching heads a few minutes' respite.) In addition to Ned's gifts, Linda was welcomed by her father-in-law with a $60,000 band of diamonds.

Despite her inexperience and limited formal education, Linda proved perfectly suited to her new role. She managed to run the houses in a seemingly effortless way, accepting occasional crises casually and handling difficult situations with humor. Nor was she intimidated by pretensions of servants, who she always maintained were the world's greatest snobs. An imperious French chef discovered when he attempted to disregard her instructions that she possessed unshakable faith in her own good judgment. When he ignored her, she discharged him and brought on from Louisville a colored cook who had worked for her family. Thomas loyally backed her decision.

One blight marred the early days of the marriage. Thomas had long been identified with horse racing. At the time he wed, he owned a great horse named Hermes. His bride, who had never evinced any interest in racing, gamely attempted to enter into the spirit of the thing, designing colors for the stable and attending the races. But whenever she encountered horses, she fell ill. Today, a physician might diagnose her trouble as an allergy. In any case, succeeding exposures to Hermes and other horses brought increasingly severe recurrences of respiratory troubles. Finally, Thomas, fearing that her lung trouble was developing into tuberculosis, sent Linda and Evelyn Parsons, Schuyler's sister, to Colorado Springs in hopes that the dry air would prove beneficial.

Her absence put a strain on the marriage, although some of their friends felt that it had been doomed from the first because of Thomas' personality. Ned Thomas was a plunger. In Wall Street, at the track—anywhere. An early automobile enthusiast, he racked up a record number of arrests and is said to have been the first man to kill anyone with an automobile in the United States. In the 1907 panic, he lost a personal fortune of $10,000,000. And, in a day when businessmen customarily backed musical comedies in order to meet showgirls, Ned Thomas became an angel.

After 1906, Linda began to spend a major portion of her time abroad. Her husbland lived at the Plaza Hotel and slept in a $10,000 silver bed, but when Linda returned to the United States she stayed with his mother.

Then, in 1908, he suffered a crippling automobile accident. While returning from his stock farm in New Jersey, he broke a kneecap. Linda rushed home to nurse him. For a time, doctors feared that it would be necessary to amputate his leg, but surgeons succeeded in removing bone splinters by performing two delicate operations and the leg was saved, although Thomas limped ever after.

Linda's constant attendance during this period effected a

reconciliation, and at the beginning of December the couple leased a house in Tuxedo, New York. Mrs. Thomas, who was delighted at the resumption of her son's marriage, took Linda and Ned to Europe in 1909, and eventually the three of them spent a pleasant time drifting down the Nile in a yacht. But once Thomas had recovered, the rift between him and Linda increased. Even so, friends predicted that she would never divorce him.

They remained estranged but not separated until 1910, when Thomas was reportedly ordered to leave the Knickerbocker Hotel dining room where he was seen in the company of a woman identified in a newspaper account as Evelyn Nesbitt Thaw. Linda's self-respect now made it necessary for her to separate from him. She moved in with his mother and, eventually, to the Carlton House at 22 East 47th Street.

In 1911, she made an unsuccessful attempt to secure an unconditional divorce. In 1912, she tried once more, naming Teddie Gerrard and "divers women" as corespondents, thereby arousing a question of whom Thomas had been with when he was ordered from the Knickerbocker. The high-spirited Theodora (Teddie) Gerrard was almost a double for Miss Nesbitt. Teddie, who was celebrated for her scandalous "Vampire Dance," was undaunted by the charge. Upon arrival in the United States from England, she gaily greeted newsmen: "Hi! I'm the corespondent in the Thomas divorce case."*

In the settlement worked out on May 30, 1912, Linda received $400,000 worth of bonds and stocks in the *Morning Telegraph* newspaper, an interest in the Astor Theater and other holdings equaling almost $1,000,000. And on July 18, 1912, an interlocutory decree, which was to become final on October 26, was granted. Although Linda was permitted to resume her maiden name, she

* Several years later, Averill Harriman introduced Cole to Teddie at a London party. "Oh," she cried. "I don't know whether I should meet you or not. You see, I was your wife's ex-husband's mistress." Cole promptly kissed her hand.

chose to be known as Mrs. Lee Thomas. In granting the decree, the judge forbade Thomas to remarry in New York State. (Ten days afterward, Thomas married Elizabeth R. Finley at Newport.)

Linda, at this point, decided to reside abroad, dividing her time between Switzerland and a gem of a little house at 3 Rue de la Baum in Paris. There, her reputation as a great hostess quickly spread. Even the French admired her knowledge of wine and food, and it was a fact that she was one of the very few persons Elsie de Wolfe consulted in matters of taste.

She knew all kinds of people, but preferred those who were making or had made their mark in the world. For instance, when Schuyler Parsons turned up in Paris during World War I, Linda invited him to a small dinner. The guest list included the Duchess of Sutherland, Lady Diana Manners, Lord and Lady d'Abernon, Winston Churchill and Charles Grasty, the war correspondent.

Wherever Linda went she was followed by a train of suitors. Some were rich. Some were famous. Some were titled. And some were all three. J. J. Milburn, her lawyer, was a beau, as was Irving Berlin's future father-in-law, Clarence H. Mackay. In quick succession she was courted by a leading nobleman from Italy and one from Spain. Duke d'Aosta was only briefly a suitor. Duke d'Alba, on the other hand, was a serious romantic interest. Everyone assumed that he would marry Linda even though it would have been a morganatic marriage. The Catholic Church, however, intervened and forbade the union because she was a divorcée, albeit the innocent party.

To Yale undergraduates, Cole may have seemed a wordly esthete. To Linda's friends, he appeared to be the bright middle-class son of Midwestern parents. He had affected diamond-studded gold clips on his garters, filled his bathtub with iced champagne and set about teaching himself how to live. Yet he was well aware that although he yearned for beauty and preferred luxury, something was missing.

Linda, who was used to being adored by worldly men,

was fascinated by this talented and outrageously amusing young man, who was eight years her junior. (Not long after they met, Linda began ridding herself of rich admirers and spending more and more time with Cole, because, as they both agreed, there was no one else with whom they could have quite such fun.)

In one of his songs, Cole attributed to a character's lost love the power "to charm the birds off the trees." He himself possessed this quality and he chose to use it over Linda. If his friends opposed her, her friends found him an unlikely suitor. While he was a well-brought-up, mannerly young Yale boy, his worldliness in 1919 seemed to them hardly skin deep. It was true that he longed to learn. He was also alert, but he was a vain man. It was difficult for him to *ask* how to proceed.

Linda, whose detachment shielded a deeply intuitive sensibility, understood his problem and instituted a game. When attending an elaborate social function in which statesmen, royalty, tycoons and entertainers were intermixed, she guided Cole through the intricacies so gracefully that for a long time he was hardly aware of it.

After one of these first parties, the two of them stopped at the Ritz for a drink. There she introduced the notion that the reason they had such Olympian fun together was that they shared a sense of the ridiculousness of it all—since she was only a Kentucky girl while he was an Indiana farm boy.

Later, when Cole reminisced about Paris, he recalled that he could hardly wait for parties to be over. The fun of them lay in discussing everything with Linda. Although he was totally unaware of it, she was grounding him in the rules by which the game is played. On those evenings, one of the world's most sophisticated women and her apt pupil glided through the excitement of the Parisian *haute monde,* playing at "pining for Louisville" and "longing for Indiana."

Where friendship ended and love began, neither was able to say. But friends noticed that whenever Cole was not with Linda he was quoting her. Although she was not especially witty, she was very much alive and vitally interested in everything around her. To him, she was the ideal, the perfect thing—beautiful, amusing, sensitive and endowed with absolute taste. The passion to possess all of this grew. Wherever he went, he wondered how she would have reacted, what she would have thought. What had she said? What was her opinion of this? Of that? What would she say when they talked about it? She was the essence of chic, all that was elegant and knowing and understanding. The qualities that he was striving to achieve seemed always to have been hers. If this was no sweeping passion, it was a very special love.

Yet the rebel who delighted in affronting his conservative Yale classmates, the iconoclast who gloried in treating his war service with the offhand insouciance of a comic-opera plot—this rebellious pixie, when faced with marriage, discovered that he was bound by an unexpected conventionality. Linda, whose money had been shrewdly invested by J. J. Milburn, was far more affluent than he. Despite his iconoclasm toward middle-class mores, he retained enough of J. O. Cole's rigid standards to feel that he must be able to support his wife in the manner to which she was accustomed. He decided to go to Peru and plead with his grandfather to increase his allowance.

It was arranged early in the spring of 1911 that Linda should sail for New York. Not long afterward, Cole followed. Aboard the ship on which he had booked passage were several Americans, one of whom was to play an important part in Cole's life. His name was Raymond Hitchcock. He had been a vaudevillian and now was a Broadway comedian and producer. In 1917, he had begun starring in an annual revue called *Hitchy-Koo*. He was now scheduled to do the 1919 version. Through mutual friends Cole managed to arrange an audition. When the two men met, Cole, who never evinced the slightest confidence in the response his work would evoke, was not reassured by the producer-comedian's taciturn manner. During the ensuing half-hour at the piano, Cole began to perspire profusely as he played a dozen numbers without causing

Hitchcock to applaud, smile or even nod. Fianlly, Cole lost heart and stopped.

Hitchcock stood up. "I'll take them," he said.

Cole asked which ones.

"The lot," Hitchcock said. And that was the manner in which Cole was engaged to do his second Broadway score.

Hitchcock's backers, Charles Dillingham and Abe Erlanger, were not so easily pleased. A number of the songs were thrown out and others added. Then one day, the trio came to Cole to inform him that they had been fortunate enough to acquire an elaborate set of flower costumes which Florenz Ziegfeld had ordered but never used in his *Follies*. Could Cole write a number so the girls could wear them in *Hitchy-Koo of 1919?* Cole could—and did. The result was "An Old-Fashioned Garden."

When Cole's chores were finished, he went to Indiana to petition for an increase in his allowance. But J. O. was angry with him on several counts. The old man had not yet reconciled himself to the fact that once the boy had been educated he had then chosen to go into the theater. To J. O., theater equaled circus and he couldn't see why any educated man would want to involve himself in that. Nor was he pleased that his grandson had chosen to serve in the French rather than the United States Army. When Cole broached the subject of increasing his allowance, J. O. pounded the arm of his chair and shouted his refusal, adding that he had prophesied that no good would come of encouraging this musical nonsense.

Cole returned to New York for the October 6 opening of *Hitchy-Koo of 1919*, his spirits buoyed despite J. O.'s refusal. For his mother had secretly agreed to undertake the increase on her own. It was very much in character for Katie, who felt that she had taken her son as far as she could, to underwrite a marriage which she felt would further help him realize his goals, socially and musically.

Cole had another reason to be hopeful: all portents for the show's future seemed favorable. The ticket brokers' buy of 400 seats a night (at $2.50 and $3.00) provided $30,000, guaranteeing a run of at least four weeks at the

Liberty Theater on 42nd Street.

The competition that season included Alfred Lunt and Helen Hayes in *Clarence;* John and Lionel Barrymore in *The Jest;* and Grace George in *She Would and She Did. Hitchy-Koo* shared its premiere with Ethel Barrymore in *Déclassée* and Sothern and Marlowe in *Twelfth Night*. The *Times*' first-string critic, Alexander Woollcott, naturally chose the Barrymore opening.

At 8:30 on opening night, Hitchcock strolled down the aisle of the Liberty Theater. His tufted shirt, velvet swallowtail coat and beaver plug hat drew immediate laughter that built into guffaws as he warmed to the proceedings by greeting the more celebrated members of the audience with quips and by introducing Elsie Janis and Florenz Ziegfeld Jr. He also confided that personally he had favored presenting "this educational entertainment in schools and Second Presbyterian churches and such instead of a theater," but that Mr. Erlanger had convinced him that people would remember it better for $3 a seat than for nothing.

Next morning the anonymous *Times* critic announced that there was more than a little ground for declaring it the best revue in town, "a statement made in full remembrance of the fact that one of last night's interested spectators was Florenz Ziegfeld, Jr., who has produced a few revues of his own. . . . The music and lyrics are the work of Cole Porter, who has made a particularly clever job of the lyrics and a good tinkling one of the music. . . ."

The show grossed $16,000 the first week. And soon "An Old-Fashioned Garden" began to emerge as a hit. Eventually it sold 100,000 copies of sheet music at a time when success was measured in those terms. Amusingly, to this day the Chamber of Commerce in Peru, Indiana, publicizes "The Old-Fashioned Garden" at Westleigh Farms, and magazine profiles have claimed that Cole wrote the song "near the Front during World War I."

Despite its popularity in the United States, the British never accepted the song, objecting to the mixing of phlox, hollyhocks, violets, eglantines, columbines and marigolds.

What garden, they asked, contained spring and fall flowers abloom at the same time? A question few Americans took time to consider.

It did take American musicologist Sigmund Spaeth to detect a relationship between flowers and bananas. Both "An Old-Fashioned Garden" and "Yes, We Have No Bananas," he said, derive from the early melody "The Quilting Party."

Hitchy-Koo of 1919 was worth noting for another reason, too. Cole always maintained that each score caused some critic to bemoan that he was not up to his usual standard. And in the December 1919 issue of *Vanity Fair*, Helen Wells wrote: "*Hitchy-Koo* has an abundance of haunting songs by Cole Porter, who wrote both words and music. Mr. Porter's lyrics are far above average—one could only wish that this were higher praise—but, as in the case of Mr. Le Baron,* he certainly has not let himself out to his full capacity. Surely he doesn't have to rhyme 'trials' with 'smiles,' for instance. There are thousands of others who can do that for us."

Although he was always sensitive to criticism, Cole was hardly likely to be concerned with such niggling. He was too busy getting back to Paris. Most Americans during the immediate postwar period found it difficult to get passports because of the food shortage. Cole managed, and was off soon after the opening to join Linda.

Then on December 18, 1919, all but their closest friends were taken by surprise when Cole and Linda slipped off to a mayor's office in the fashionable eighteenth arrondissement and were married.

Following the ceremony, the Porters traveled to the South of France, into Italy and as far south as Sicily. Thirty-seven years later, two years after Linda's death, Cole returned to their favorite city, Palermo. From there, filled with nostalgia for this happy time, he wrote to Dr. Albert Sirmay, his friend and chief editor of Chappell and

* Le Baron had written the lyrics to some light music by Fritz Kreisler and Victor Jacobi for a musical entitled *Apple Blossoms.*

Company, Inc. "Sicily is a dream that I remember so well when Linda and I honeymooned here years ago and this Palermo has so many beautiful examples of so many civilizations that one could see and see for months and months. En plus very warm sun, every tree in bloom outside my window as I write you a full moon over the gentle Mediterranean. True Love, High Society, Cole."

In the final months of 1919, he achieved his long-dreamed-of Broadway hit and he won the hand of the beautiful Linda Lee, the first women he had ever wanted to marry. "The gods," as Cole customarily referred to them, seemed to be smiling generously upon him. Yet how infrequently are things what they seem.

CHAPTER V

Every morning at half past seven, Cole Porter leaps lightly out of bed and, having said his prayers, arranges himself in a riding habit. Then, having written a song or two, he will appear at the stroke of half past twelve at the Ritz, where leaning in a manly way on the bar, he will say: "Champagne cocktail, please. Had a marvelous ride this morning!" That statement gives him strength and confidence on which to suffer this, our life, until ten minutes past three in the afternoon when he will fall into a childlike sleep.

Michael Arlen's fanciful word portrait captures the texture of Cole's existence during the next nine years—at least as the public knew it. Upon his return to Paris from his honeymoon, Cole's personality seemed to undergo one of those dizzying switches that earned him a reputation for being complicated and unpredictable. Music, the divine spark which had lit his existence, was downgraded, supposedly because of his fascination with the inner circle of international society of which Linda was so much a part. It was in these years that he began to create the legend of the thoughtless, golden youth who might have wandered out of the pages of Compton Mackenzie or F. Scott

Fitzgerald. And like a Fitzgerald character, he eventually developed an ambivalence toward society and the musical career that he supposedly had spurned. Nevertheless, Cole was by temperament a baroque personality and he now associated with people who appreciated that quality. It was a time to be elegant, witty and selfish.

Not, however, in Peru, Indiana. Soon after his marriage, Katie Porter and his step-grandmother Bessie Cole visited Cole in Paris. Neither had ever before seen anything like the splendor in which he and Linda lived. Katie kept her comments to herself, but Bessie was openly impressed. "It's wonderful the way they do," she told J. O. upon her return to Peru. "Linda has a maid."

J. O. reminded Bessie that she also had a maid.

"Oh, I don't mean a kitchen maid," she said impatiently. "I mean a personal maid. Why, do you know, Linda's maid even puts her stockings on her! Why—"

That was a bit too much for the old pioneer, who interrupted: "Why? What's wrong with her? She sickly or something?"

Whatever J. O.'s reactions, his grandson was helping to forge new conventions. All life long, Cole claimed that he would have wanted to be the best at what he did, whatever his lot. If he had been a bootblack, he said, he would have tried to be the best on the street; if a waiter, then the best in the establishment. Thrown in with a group of hedonists, he set out to become the world's second greatest.

He conceded the title to Linda, who for twenty-four hours had had possession of the Hope Diamond, which was purported to transmit a curse. She had sent it back not because she was superstitious but because she was repelled by its "dirty blue" color.

Linda Lee was original, vital and spoiled. A great friend of hers maintained that she didn't know how to open a door. If by chance no one lit her cigarette, it remained unlighted. Sheets in her home were changed each morning and again following afternoon naps. A woman of rare sensibilities and exquisite taste, Linda found that only the very old and the very new (both irreplaceable) appealed to her. She was an expert on Egyptology. She was a collector of porcelain, of first editions, of French antiques, of Chinese paintings, or of whatever else happened to attract her. Once, when a guest clumsily toppled a delicate crystal from its place on the mantel, he repeatedly apologized in spite of Linda's smiling assurances that he need think nothing of it. When he persisted, announcing that he would replace it, she shook her head. "No," she said with finality, "you can't." By her inflection he knew that there was not another like it in the world.

Linda gave dash to the Porters' life. It was her idea to buy the open Rolls-Royce and have, first, seven little dachshunds and then, later, a bobtailed sheep dog, Major, ride up front beside the chauffeur. She was Cole's authority and when she placed the stamp of approval on anything, that was good enough for him. When she rejected a thing, he rejected it, too. On one occasion, having some spare cash, he decided to surprise her with a smart, custom-made car. When it arrived, Linda seemed delighted with her gift, but she used it only once. Finally, Cole inquired why she didn't like it. Quite seriously she informed him that the springs were so stiff they bruised her sables.

In an era when it was not commonplace for Americans to mingle with the French socially, the Porters were totally accepted. In one respect, they possessed a major advantage. Both had to an unusual degree the ability to charm and interest those who in their opinion seemed worth knowing. On the other hand, they did not hesitate to freeze out anyone who struck them as gauche. One evening, for example, Linda was wearing some dazzling diamond-ruby-sapphire bracelets. A young couple obviously intrigued, danced past the Porters' table several times. Finally the young woman summoned courage to inquire: "Are those real?"

"Real *what?*" Linda demanded coldly.

If she could be icy with strangers, she was always sensitive to her husband's possible embarrassments. Although he was receiving a large allowance, most of it went for living expenses. He could not, for instance, provide jewels comparable to the stomachers and tiaras she already owned. Her solution was to stop wearing the more ostentatious kind.

Cole also enjoyed a special freedom from her household rules. For several years prior to their marriage, she had presided over a staff of servants who ran her home with calibrated precision. Cole, in his early days, was supremely disorganized. After their marriage, Linda did not criticize his habits, but schedules were maintained whether or not he met them. The servants' discipline was at stake.

Guests, too, were expected to be punctual since she had no patience with "being fashionably late." If guests were not on time, festivities began without them. Only Cole was made an exception, and, as Linda said, after all genius had its own dynamics. Soon, though, he too managed to arrive on time.

Following their marriage they lived for a while in Linda's house, then took an apartment at the Ritz and eventually bought their remarkable house located at 13 Rue de Monsieur. At "13" Linda set about arranging a permanent setting for her increasingly beautiful collection of art and furnishings. In the house, she succeeded in creating a unique showplace, yet she did this without for a moment forgetting that whatever a room's esthetic beauty it must be livable and homelike.

Despite the fact that there has been a great deal of comment about the zebra-hide upholstery, those who frequently visited the house knew that this was used chiefly as floor covering. The red lacquer chairs were upholstered in white kid. The much-talked-about platinum wallpaper was confined to one room only. In spite of what has been written—which makes the house sound garish—Linda endowed it with a quiet elegance.

While various Paris residences served as home base, the Porters during the early years of their marriage were forever on the move. They traveled to Venice, Monte Carlo, Rome, London, Biarritz, Seville, Morocco, Berlin, New York and Peru, Indiana. Both were inveterate sightseers and when things became tiresome in one place, they simply engaged a private railroad car and set out on an adventure. The entourage always included Linda, her maid Weston, Cole, his valet Eugene, and a gaggle of friends.

During the 1920's, Europeans found Cole a wonderful drawing-room attraction. As one columnist noted: "What hostess would not bait the rarest fish with the promise of having Cole Porter sing, Elsa Maxwell play, Billy Reardon dance or Viola Tree do her imitations?"

Cole was noted for his wit, his wealth and his wastefulness. When Moss Hart sought him out in the Ritz bar and delivered dancer Georgie Hale's Christmas gift, Cole opened the package at once. He found that it contained garters with solid gold buckles. He removed the ones he was wearing, which also sported gold buckles, and gave them to the bartender.

That incident illuminates in a small way the Porter paradox. In this expatriate period, Cole gloried in his hedonism. Yet hidden beneath it and running parallel to it was a streak of Indiana practicality. Thus, when the story was told, Cole denied it. Later he explained that whenever his extravagances were mentioned, people excoriated him as the greatest hedonist who ever lived. "What they don't understand," he complained, "is that everyone lived like that in those days."

At least all of Linda's favorite people did. At first, Cole sometimes questioned her choice of friends, but eventually he learned that she was highly intuitive about people. Upon the shortest acquaintance, she arrived at amazing conclusions. As it turned out, many of Cole's closest friends—Baron Nicolas de Gunzberg and Duke Fulco di Verdura, to name two—were originally enthusiasms of hers.

Another was Howard Sturges, an amiable bachelor who hailed from Providence, Rhode Island. After graduating from Yale, Sturges had come to Paris to study music. Eventually the studies were dropped, but he stayed on. Upon first meeting him, Linda was taken by his dry wit, kindly nature and whimsical turn of mind. His only defect as a friend lay in his periodic drinking bouts. "They cost me two fortunes," Sturges once said. "Luckily I had a third."

In spite of her annoyance at his drinking, Linda was devoted to him and, eventually, he also became Cole's closest friend. In the meantime, however, Linda had decided to stop the drinking. The next time he disappeared, she set out in her car in search for him. This time she found him actually in a gutter. Loading him into the car, she drove him to a sanitarium where he was dried out. Then, through persuasion, charm and hard-headed, common-sense talk, she succeeded in extracting a promise that he would not drink for a year. He agreed, and thereafter remained sober for the rest of his life. On the anniversay of that date each year, he always presented Linda with some priceless thank-you gift.

Like Sturges, Monty Woolley and Len Hanna spent a great deal of time with the Porters. They were exceptions in that they had first been friends of Cole's. Most of the Yale crowd soon disappeared. A few, such as Arnold Whitridge and his wife (Cole introduced them), the Almet Jenkses and a handful of others, remained on friendly terms. On the other hand, Archibald MacLeish, who was so much a part of the creative ferment taking place in Paris in the 1920's, moved in such a different circle that he was not aware that Cole and Linda were living in Paris.

Cole neither knew nor had any curiosity about the literary crowd. He found Fitzgerald a bore because of his drinking. He never met nor did he make any effort to meet Hemingway, Gertrude Stein, Ezra Pound, James Joyce, John Dos Passos, E. E. Cummings or Glenway Wescott.

After their marriage, Elsa Maxwell was dropped for a brief time by Cole and Linda. Although it was generally agreed by those who knew Elsa then that she gave more pleasure to more people than anyone else (publicity ruined her, is the explanation for the latter-day Elsa), Linda dissented. Initially, she felt sorry for her. Then, when Elsa once airily showed her a huge roll of bills which she described as her bridge winnings, Linda began to suspect her honesty. She became convinced that Elsa had taught Cole to play mah-jongg so that it was easy for her to win. Cole scoffed at the idea, but finally said that even if it were true Elsa had earned the money by being so amusing and by tirelessly promoting his songs. Linda disagreed, but he put his foot down and the two women were reconciled.

Elsa, who was aware of the reason for Linda's hostility, as usual "rose above it" and commemorated the reconciliation by signing a photograph: "To my Beautiful Linda Lee, Elsa—Rat." Thereafter, she was often included in the Porters' social activities.

It was during the spring of 1922 that Cole made one of those moves that established him as a leader of fashion. Upon hearing diva Mary Garden lament the shortness of the spring season at Antibes, Cole ordered an investigation to determine whether there was any reason why it should not be a summer place. There was not. He immediately rented a château, and as soon as he and Linda were ensconced in it, they began inviting guests. Two, Gerald and Sara Murphy, were so taken with the locale they decided to build a villa. So, at second hand, Cole was responsible for the summer season there, although for one reason or another he seldom went back.

Probably this was because of the cataclysmic shift that occurred in the Porters' lives in 1923. That winter they were in New York, living at 735 Fifth Avenue. As was Cole's custom, he entertained extensively in hopes of attracting an assignment. While theater people were delighted to accept his hospitality, nobody offered him a job and, by the end of January, his professional prospects were so poor he was already looking forward to his return to Paris.

Then on February 3, word came that his Grandfather Cole had died at the age of eighty-five. Cole, who had not been close to the old man for several years, found himself strangely untouched, yet he rushed to Peru to comfort his mother. Afterward, he expressed surprise at the romantic touch which J. O. had added to the funeral by requesting only red roses in honor of his first wife, who, he said, had been known as "The Rose of Indiana."

J. O.'s estate, in addition to the Cole-Crane Trust, included extensive acreage and approximately $1,000,000 in cash. Of this last amount, Katie received $500,000, which she split with her son. She and other heirs invested their money in stocks, while Cole used his to maintain himself in the manner to which he wished to become accustomed. Ironically, the prudent investors lost their cash in the 1929 stock-market crash six years later. Only Cole enjoyed spending any of the money.

With his inheritance in hand, Cole was at last in a financial position to afford the long-dreamed-of Venetian palazzo. In his case it turned out to be three, each increasingly grand. In 1923, he rented the Barbaro, which had been the scene of Mrs. Jack Gardner's happy Venetian interludes. The next year, he took the Papadopoli; in 1925, the Rezzonico.

The Barbaro, while it provided momentary fulfillment, was not, from the Porters' point of view, entirely suitable. Plumbing was practically nonexistent. Ventilation was a problem, and the servants were far from united. Nevertheless, once Cole and Linda had met Princess Jane de San Faustino, who led Venice's livelier set, they spent a happy summer there. Princess Jane, as everyone called her, was an American heiress who had married a title. By 1923, she was a handsome widow, made more striking by her black weeds and a Mary Queen of Scot's coiffure. More important, however, she was the acknowledged leader of the fun-loving contingent that had sprung up in Venice following World War I.

Cole, one of the first men to operate a speedboat on the canals, was a particular favorite of Princess Jane's. For him Venice was a succession of days lazed away at the Lido, of elaborate social functions, equally elaborate practical jokes and of experimentation with what at the moment happened to be fashionable and distracting. ("I tried opium once. Found it overrated," he said.)

During the season at the Papadopoli, the guest list, as before, included a constantly changing cast, chosen for charm, beauty, talent and that indefinable electricity that charged social situations. Grace Moore, Artur Rubinstein and Princess Oduskulki, who was the daughter of the great English reformer Wilfred Laboucher, were much in evidence. Drama critic George Jean Nathan, songwriters Irving Berlin and George Gershwin, Lady Emerald Cunard, Tallulah Bankhead, Lady Diana Manners and the John Barrymores visited. (The latter seriously offered to give their daughter, Diana, to the Porters for proper rearing.) And when Lady Cynthia Mosley and her husband, Sir Oswald, whose Fascist leanings were not yet widely recognized, passed through, the Porters entertained them.

While impresario Sergei Diaghilev and his star dancer, Serge Lifar, were guests, Diaghilev suggested presenting a ballet for the Porters' friends. The Porters, he said, would be expected to provide only an orchestra, a fifty-foot statue, and enough candles placed strategically in the trees to light the performance. He estimated 2,500 would do the job. Cole and Linda were delighted.

Preparations began. Eventually, three barges arrived carrying not one but three statues (borrowed from a museum). Three arches had to be built to hold the statues, and the arches required vines as decorations. Now, too, Diaghilev, who loved pageantry, suggested the use of gondolas and liveried gondoliers in black, red and gold.

The night before the extravaganza a violent storm wreaked havoc and the electricity failed, but by the evening of the gala event the weather was once more beautiful. And the scene was adequately lighted by 225,000 candles.

The assemblage was thrilled by the dancing of Lifar and other members of the company. Nor did the fact that a borrowed string of pearls, worn by Lydia Sokolova, broke and scattered about the improvised stage at the edge of the canal detract from the enjoyment. The one disappointment came at the end of the performance when the foreworks that had been planned as a climax, having been dampened by the storm the previous evening, spluttered, smoked and drove the choking guests away.

The Diaghilev ballet, spectacular as it was, was overshadowed by the Red and White Ball, which was given the following year at the Rezzonico.

First, however, the Rezzonico, which the Porters shared with Howard Sturges, deserves a word. Its imposing façade, its impressive entrance, its many huge rooms and its distinctive white candles all contributed to the impression that one was looking at a public museum, which, in fact, it eventually became.

From the first, Cole and Sturges were delighted by the prospect of renting it at $4,000 a month. Linda, on the other hand, had a reservation: she insisted that a clause be inserted in the lease allowing her to install bathrooms. And her unyielding insistence on this point grew into a minor legend.*

Life at the Rezzonico was even more elegant than any small dreamer from Peru, Indiana, could have envisioned. Every afternoon at exactly 4:00 P.M., Linda appeared, clad in a pastel gown, carrying a dainty sunshade, and made her way to an awaiting gondola, where she arranged herself beautifully before it disappeared from view. Then, for an hour, time remained suspended until she reappeared and life resumed.

Even for such ingenious tenants as these, the Rezzonico posed certain problems. The Porter galas have justifiably stood out as among the most original of the era. Yet the first one was a flop. With their good friend Princess Jane, they drew up a guest list of 500. Invitations were dispatched and acceptances ran almost 100 percent. At the appointed hour the canal was jammed with gondolas debarking passengers. Nevertheless, there was a feeling that few people had shown up. A quick check of the guest

* Years later their disappearance proved something of a puzzle to co-producer of *Kiss Me, Kate* Lemuel Ayres and his wife, Shirley. Sturges finally cleared up the mystery. Linda, with her great respect for the past, he said, had had them installed in nooks and closets where they could be removed without damage to the palazzo.

list disclosed that the Rezzonico had simply swallowed them.

Cole analyzed the situation and concluded that the original guest list was not to be revised, yet additional bodies were needed. Consequently, at the next party, gondoliers got up in eighteenth-century costumes and holding candles were stationed at strategic spots about the palazzo, creating the impression of crowds and excitement even though they were not an integral part of the revelry.

Later, Cole hit upon an added refinement. He secured a list of minor government dignitaries from outlying districts and invited them, requesting that each wear any decorations or honors. Naturally, the recipients were delighted at the prospect of an evening amid splendor where the finest cuisine and vintage wines would be plentiful. As Cole had foreseen, two separate parties spun in concentric circles, complementing one another but never meeting. The 500 mingled with each other, the minor officials with other officials.

Though all the Porter galas, fetes and balls were much admired, the Red and White Ball was in a class by itself. In those days, the new society doted on scavenger hunts, murder parties and other antidotes to the stuffy functions that had been *de rigueur* in the early 1900's. Costume balls, of course, were held in high favor, but generally were marred by a few guests who failed to mask. And, even when everyone cooperated, the visual effect was seldom pleasing.

With this in mind, the Porters commissioned the creation of thousands of red and white crepe-paper trousers, hats, blouses, shawls, shirts and skirts. On the evening of the party, dancing was interrupted at midnight. The doors of the large salon were thrown open and guests were asked to create ensembles from the paper clothing that lay on the tables.

When everyone was bedecked, the assemblage gathered in the courtyard, which was bathed in colored lights. There they were entertained by acrobats who cavorted on wires high above the flagstones. And when the entertainment was finished, dancing resumed in the ballroom where the kaleidoscopic swirl of reds and whites created an effect forever imprinted upon the memories of those who saw it.

Cole's private *galleggiante,* or floating nightclub, seating 150, turned out to be a less happy inspiration. At the time, Elsa had been hired to publicize the Lido and Cole decided to give her a hand. Admittance to the *galleggiante* could be gained only by invitation. There was a complete dance orchestra, a chef and a wine cellar. Yet the floating club made only one journey. Guests found that it was practically impossible to maintain their footing on a small moving craft. There was another problem, too. Although Linda had installed bathrooms at the Rezzonico, her husband forgot to include loos on board. By request, the *galleggiante* remained in dock thenceforth.

Despite all these distractions, Cole chafed at the idea that, although he was well into his thirties, he had applied himself to music without seeming to get anywhere. He discussed the problem with Linda and Sturges. What, he wanted to know, was the proper course to take? Unfortunately, neither had any more inspired ideas than he had. But it was more than that, too. Their world, populated with eminent personalities—the amusing, the daring, the titled and the eccentric—for all its frantic activities was as circumscribed as a demitasse cup. He resented it. Later, he was to recognize that, limited though it was, it provided a definite frame of reference. After two monstrous wars and a worldwide depression had destroyed not only this closed society but also the assumptions upon which it was founded, a Porter song could swiftly evoke both the special group to which he had belonged and the wider world in which it had existed.

At the time, Cole was tired of it. To ridicule the excesses good-naturedly, he fabricated an Oklahoma couple, Mr. and Mrs. S. R. Fitch, who were purported to be oil millionaires. It was 1925 and monied American tourists were making a splash with improverished nobility and the international set. The Fitches made their first appearance in the Paris *Herald.* It was in its columns that Elsa read that she had given a large dinner party in their honor the previous evening. Moreover, the guest list represented the *crème de la crème of* English, French and Grecian society with a few White Russians and East Indians thrown in.

Elsa was puzzled as to how the item had found its way into print. Her dear friends, she learned, were immensely rich, refused to be photographed, avoided interviewers and asked only to be left alone while touring the Continent. In studying the details, Elsa somehow detected the fine Porterian point of view. She telephoned him and asked about the Fitches. He protested he had never heard of them, but eventually confessed to planting the item.

As he had suspected, Elsa was delighted at the opportunity to tweak the noses of society columnists who were not always kindly in their references to her. Soon, she and Cole were planting "scoops" about the incredible Fitches in a variety of columns run by reporters who seldom attended the events they chattered about.

The Fitches were omnipresent. They were with the Porters in Venice. They hopped to Hungary, coursed to Carlsbad, made merry in Morocco and remained elusive to everyone except Elsa and Cole.

Plagued by friends who insisted upon an introduction, the conspirators claimed that the Fitches already knew too many people. Finally, the fun grew thin. Cole sent out a photograph of Elsa dressed in a twenty-year-old bathing suit and sporting false whiskers. The caption identified the subject as "S. R. Fitch of Muskogee, Oklahoma."

The secret was bound to get out now. Lady Mendl tipped off Hearst's society columnist, Maury Paul. Paul, who had not run any of the items, warned a former secretary of his who had turned columnist and the story broke. At that point, Cole sent out a final release saying that the Fitches were returning to Muskogee at once because they had grown to loathe every rich American in Europe.

An even more rebellious attitude lay behind another plot

which Cole carried out during the same period. Around 1925 in Paris, he met a young Negro entertainer who hailed from Alderson, West Virginia. She called herself Bricktop and she opened a club where she introduced the Charleston. Cole was delighted by her club and even more by Bricktop herself. In fact, he spent so much time there when he was in Paris that Bricktop reserved a special permanent table for him and his friends.

Cole, in turn, brought lots of customers to the club and eventually hired Bricktop to come to 13 Rue de Monsieur to teach Linda, the Prince of Wales, the Aga Khan, Elsa Maxwell and all his other cronies how to Charleston in the big, mirror-lined room in the basement.

But Bricktop was no paid entertainer, she was a real friend. Soon Cole discovered that she longed to attend a big charity ball that was being held at the Paris Opera. He insisted that she must go. Bricktop made a variety of excuses explaining why she couldn't, then said "they" wouldn't accept her because she didn't have a proper dress.

Nonsense, Cole said. He took her to the great couturier Captain Edward Molyneux and announced that he wanted to order a dress for his friend. When Captain Molyneux inquired what type gown he had in mind, Cole suggested a duplicate of the one that had been made for Princess Marina of Greece, only still more lavish.

Captain Molyneux protested.

Cole insisted.

Bricktop backed Cole up.

Captain Molyneux pointed out that all his dresses were one of a kind, but, as Cole later told Elsa, who told the readers of a national magazine, since Linda was a better customer than most, money talked. The duplicate gown was made.

At the ball, Bricktop created a sensation. The conservatives were outraged. The furor stirred up made her the talk of the town. She became the darling of the rebellious. Her club prospered. As for Cole, he defended her, somewhat irrelevantly, as being "as much a lady as anyone at the ball."

Although Cole never abandoned international society, in later years he maintained that he could hardly recall anything of the 1920's because his attention had always been focused elsewhere.

For her part, Linda looked upon Cole's relatively inactive musical life as a lull, never for a moment entertaining the idea that he would not eventually triumph. She adored his clever, imaginative songs and had supreme faith in her own judgment. Without consulting him, she dashed off letters to Arnold Bennett, John Galsworthy and George Bernard Shaw, urging each to offer a libretto to her talented composer-husband. Money, she let it be known, presented no obstacle. Her letters produced no positive results, except to strengthen Linda's resolve that one day these giants would take her proposals seriously.

The arrival of the great comedienne and popular singer Fanny Brice in Venice during the second year the Porters were living in the Rezzonico probably accounts for Cole's contentment with life in Venice and at the Rezzonico in particular. Fanny, who had sprung from the Lower East Side, was a unique personality, equally at home with socialites, actors, and hoodlums, just as she was adept at singing blues and doing humorous numbers. Both Cole and Linda worshiped her. "She was one of those rare personalities who adapted to any level," Cole said. "Royalty and gangsters were all the same to her."

That summer of 1926, Fanny and Roger Davis, a friend and court jester ex officio (Roger: "Fanny, how long has this terrible flood been going on?") arrived in Venice. Fanny proposed that Cole write some songs for her. Even when he confided that he was thinking of giving up songwriting for painting, she insisted. "This," Cole later wrote, "was the reason for 'Hot House Rose.' When I finished I invited her to the Rezzonico to hear it and afterward she always told friends how wonderfully incongruous it was that I should have demonstrated this song about a poor little factory girl as she sat beside me while I sang and played it on the grand piano that looked lost in our ballroom, whose walls were entirely decorated by Tiepolo paintings and which was so big that if we gave a ball for less than 1,000 people in this room they seemed entirely lost. She never sang the song."

Cole wrote another song for Fanny. It was called "Weren't We Fools?" She intended to use it at her opening when she played the Palace Theater in New York during November of 1927. It was a song of lingering regret over a lost romance, and inevitably caused the listener to think of Fanny's separation and divorce from Nicky Arnstein, although Cole insisted that he had written the number before the divorce. Nevertheless when Arnstein appeared at the Palace for the opening show, agitated friends of Fanny's begged her to drop the number, which they feared would be considered too personal.

The chorus ran in part:

Weren't we fools to lose each other? . . .
Though we know we loved each other
You chose another, so did I . . .

Although never performed in public, the number was frequently done at private parties until the impish Noel Coward ruined its chances of ever being taken seriously when he parodied it by singing:

Weren't we fools to lose each other? . . .
Though we know we loved each other
You chose your brother, so did I . . .

The death of J. O. Cole had brought the Venetian period into being and, indirectly, the death of Cole's father spelled its end. On August 18, 1927, Sammy Porter, who had had scant contact with his son in recent years, died. The next day, the Peru *Daily Tribune* carried a front-page story announcing: "Cole Porter, famous composer of Paris, France, informed of the death of his father, Samuel F. Porter, here yesterday, will sail for America on the liner *Berengaria,* but will not arrive until a week after his father is buried."

The story went on to say that Samuel Porter, who was sixty-nine years old, had died at his country home after a long illness which was the result of a nervous breakdown. The obituary also stated that Sam Porter and his brother owned various drugstores and that they had combined the drug and restaurant business when they opened the Café de la Paix on North Broadway.

As at J. O.'s death, Cole's chief concern was for his mother. He had long ago decided that his father had never appreciated him. Despite the efforts of his cousin by marriage, Louise Bearss, to convince him otherwise, Cole clung to this belief and felt no real grief. When Louise told him how Sammy had surreptitiously shown her the poetry he had written and had been flattered when she assured him that Cole had inherited his poetic gift from the Porters, Cole remained unmoved. In fact, it would be many years before he would accept the fact that, however ineffectual his father may have seemed to him, he had indeed influenced him.

But when the news of Sammy's death arrived, Cole, contrary to the story in the Peru *Daily Tribune*, was in Venice at the Rezzonico. Linda, who was once more plagued with respiratory troubles, was resting in Switzerland and decided not to make the trip to the United States. So as Cole left, he gave Elsa permission to live at the Rezzonico on condition that she do nothing to draw attention to herself. Elsa promised, but on the day of the funeral, her high spirits got the better of her and she tossed an eye-popping party.

News in those preradio and television days did not reach the Porters immediately. When it did, Cole took it calmly, saying, "But that's Elsa." Linda, on the other hand, disregarding her health, rushed back to Venice where she sought out the famed party-giver and wasted only five words: "Get out of my house!"

From then on, the uneasy truce that had been maintained was abandoned. Linda made no further effort to veil her true feelings. Elsa, as was her ploy, rose above it. The only hint that anyone could detect that there had been trouble lay in her failure to mention her "lovely Linda Lee," even when discussing celebrated beauties or distinguished hostesses.

It also marked the end of the Venetian period for the Porters who, for professional reasons, were to spend more time in New York thereafter.

Although the main emphasis in the years between 1919 and 1928 was on Cole's social life, he did not abandon his career. The fact that it went into an eclipse was caused mainly by his voluntary expatriation of himself. As Irving Berlin, with whom he had become friendly after writing *Hitchy-Koo of 1919,* told him, "Producers won't take a chance on you until you settle down at Broadway and Forty-second Street." But for Cole a career was not a matter of geography, time or even a signed contract.

Certainly the signed contract proved no inspiration when he undertook the score for a new version of *Hitchy-Koo,* only to have his work chucked in Philadelphia. Nor was a contract needed to set him to work on "The Blue Boy Blues," "Wand'ring Night and Day," and other songs which English producer C. B. Cochran, whom he knew socially, included in a 1922 revue.

The initial inspiration for "The Blue Boy Blues" came from the letters-to-the-editor columns of London newspapers. At the time the Duke of Westminster, through art dealer Joseph Duveen, had sold Gainsborough's famed *Blue Boy* to railroad magnate H. E. Huntington for $620,000. Duveen, always the showman, arranged for a farewell tour, ostensibly to give the public a last look at a national treasure but actually to increase his own fame by creating a furor. Naturally a vociferous protest developed, including impassioned letters to the editors.

The contretemps delighted Cole, who described the situation lyrically and gave it musical expression in the form of a Negro blues with syncopated comment running beneath the melody. Thus, the form of the Negro's traditional outcry against injustices was used to express the British public's indignation at losing one of its treasures.

The song was a highlight of *Mayfair and Montmartre*, which opened at the New Oxford Theater on March 9, 1922.

As the curtain rose on the scene, first-nighters saw, framed against a setting that reproduced the painting, young Nellie Taylor, dressed in the famous Gainsborough costume. And when she began to sing, they heard:

For I'm the Blue Boy—the beautiful Blue Boy,
And I'm forced to admit
I'm feeling a bit depressed,
The American dollar
Took me and my collar
To show the slow cowboys
Just howboys
In England used to be dressed. . . .

If Mr. Gainsborough knew, I know he'd frown
As the days grow fewer and fewer
I'm bluer and bluer
For I'm saying goodbye to London town.

When the lyrics were finished, the Blue Boy stepped out of the Gainsborough setting and into the American West. There Indians and cowboys tormented the Blue Boy about his suit and manners in a choreographed production number. The effect was stunning.

Yet despite the song's topicality and the superlative interpretation given it by Miss Taylor, it was not long on view. The show failed quickly.

The following August, Cole placed another number, "The Ragtime Pipes of Pan," in Cochran's *Phi-Phi*, but this show also failed, and with it Cole's career came to a temporary standstill.

It was not until a year later that Gerald Murphy came to his rescue. The Murphys, Gerald and Sara, who were dilettantes in the best sense, had once served as apprentices with Diaghilev's ballet company. Now, spending this fall and winter of 1923 in Paris, they naturally were drawn into the orbit of Rolfe de Mare's Ballet Suédois company, then preparing the premiere of "La Création du Monde," for which Darius Milhaud had written the score. When de Mare confided that he needed a curtain raiser, Murphy volunteered not only to write the story and do the sets, but also to persuade his friend Cole Porter to provide the music.

Cole needed no real persuasion, since he was already somewhat bored with international society. With Murphy he turned out a thirty-minute satirical piece called *Within the Quota.* Its tone was set by Murphy's front curtain, which parodied the Hearst press with such headlines as "Rum Raid Liquor Ban," "Ex-Wife's Heart-Balm Love-Tangle" and "Unknown Banker Buys the Atlantic." The story concerned a Swedish immigrant whose adventures with such American types as a shimmying jazz baby, a cowboy, an heiress, and America's Sweetheart were thwarted by social reformers, sheriffs, revenue officers and film censors.

For some reason, at the last moment before the premiere the running order was switched and Milhaud's work opened the program, which was presented at the Champs Elysées Theater in Paris on October 25, 1923. No reason for the change was given, but possibly it was done because in this initial serious work Cole adopted some of the mannerisms of Milhaud's atonal music while retaining the easy appeal that arose from his parody of silent-film piano accompaniment.

The opening night was a triumph. Sophisticated Parisian audiences cheered the work and even Mr. and Mrs. Rudolph Valentino were reported to have laughed at its jabs at screen stars. *Figaro*'s iconoclastic critic wrote an approving review. The *Herald*'s Paris man cabled a rave notice to New York and the one from the *Sun and Globe* translated his praise into sports vernacular and tabbed *Within the Quota* a "satirical touchdown."

As always when his work brought him acclaim, Cole responded with increased creativity. On January 1, 1924, he appealed for the return of Jack Hamlet, "a black and white curly-haired dog with a red collar," who had strayed or been stolen from his apartment. The dog, named for John Barrymore, Cole disclosed, harbored theatrical ambitions. He said that because he was fond of the dog he wanted to give him a part in the new ballet he was writing with the brilliant scenic artist M. Leon Bakst.

Yet when *Within the Quota* failed to repeat its success in the United States, Cole's enthusiasm for ambitious music waned. One critic set the tone when he observed that he hoped the polytonal dissonances were meant to be as funny as they sounded. Cole hoped that he would continue to be given the benefit of the doubt. But in later years, he was to say that his score struck him as mechanical, labored and lacking in inspiration. He had by that time completely forgotten ever starting a second ballet and was unable to recall whether or not he had ever recovered Jack Hamlet.

Later, in 1924, John Murray Anderson signed Cole to do the music for the sixth edition of *The Greenwich Village Follies.* Seldom have two talents been so mismatched.

Anderson leaned toward the big, the gaudy, the sentimental. Later in life, he found his true métier staging production numbers for Ringling Bros. and Barnum & Bailey Circus. He had little feeling for Cole's sly, subtle lyrics. Nor was he able to help the cast, including the Dolly Sisters (The Dollys and their Collies); Moran and Mack, "The Two Black Crows"; Vincent Lopez and His Orchestra; and dancer Robert Alton to put across Cole's songs, which included "I'm in Love Again." Eventually, he substituted the work of Owen Murphy and Jay Gorney. This edition ran only 127 performances. Later, Cole was to see "I'm in Love Again" develop into the first of his delayed hits, but when the show closed in 1924 he was filled with gloom. It was at this point that he consulted Linda and Sturges, seeking advice on how to avert the dead end to which his career seemed headed.

The only offer that came his way during 1925 was to contribute three songs to the original play which Monty Woolley was directing for the Yale Dramatic Association's Christmas Tour. The play, *Out o' Luck,* was a World War

I drama concerning the exploits of ten American doughboys and a French girl. The action included a home talent show for which Cole wrote the songs.*

Not until the close of 1927, after Cole had returned to Paris from his trip to Peru, did any other offer come his way. Then Edmond Sayag, manager of Des Ambassadeurs nightclub, decided to produce a United States-oriented revue. He signed Fred Waring, Morton Downey, Frances Gershwin (George's and Ira's sister), Buster West (the comedy star), Evelyn Hoey (a blond singer), Georgie Hale (an actor-dancer) and plenty of beautiful American chorus girls.

It was Hale who persuaded Sayag that the score for the revue should be composed by Cole. Hale then prevailed upon Cole to attend rehearsals and give the staging the same attention he had lavished on the Yale smokers, contending that recent failures had grown out of inept handling of the material.

Cole welcomed the opportunity to work, and by opening night in mid-May of 1928 he had a twenty-four-song score for which Sayag felt justified in charging the stylish audience $70 per ticket (dinner and show, but no champagne, included).

The audience was dazzling. Elsa gave a party honoring the Grand Dukes Dmitri, Michael and Alexander. William Randolph Hearst, Jr., and his bride entertained a large party. Linda, having recovered from a respiratory attack, returned from a trip to Italy and was widely admired for the chic of her sapphire-blue satin dress which had been designed especially to show off a Cartier ornament, a "huge lapis-blue scarab set with two old faience turquoise Egyptian wings, held together in a setting with long diamonds."

* "Butterflies," "Madamezelle" and "The Opera Song." The last was introduced by John Hoysradt, who sixteen years later also introduced "What Am I to Do?" in *The Man Who Came to Dinner* on Broadway. Since the character Hoysradt played was based on Noel Coward, Cole signed the piece as "Noel Porter."

Cole's satisfaction in the success was decreased when the management began wrangling with performers over the new tables that had been crowded into the playing area. To complicate matters, the show was broken into three segments and several cast members left. He was still committed enough, however, to write a number for Clifton Webb when Webb and Dorothy Dickson joined the cast. This song, "Looking at You," was an immediate success and traveled so well that it was eventually used in the London and New York versions of *Wake Up and Dream*.

For all practical purposes, the success of the Des Ambassadeurs revue marked the end of Cole's professional stagnation, which had extended from his marriage through 1927. During those eight years, he had made periodic attempts to work, each of which was stilled by failure. Smarting from these rejections, he had assumed the pose of an oh-so-bored playboy who was reluctant to accept a job lest he be needed for further work just at the moment when he was about to be off for Antibes or Biarritz or Morocco. It was an excellent ploy. Reporters were fascinated by it and it was a face-saver.

Yet by the time Linda and Cole arrived at the old Ritz in New York during the winter of 1927, it had become a burdensome pose and Cole was ready to drop it. At last he had reached the point where he was willing to put himself into the hands of a professional whom he would allow to guide him. Consequently, he invited Louis Shurr to lunch. Shurr, a New Yorker by birth, had decided to become a theatrical agent before he was out of his teens and by 1927 had managed to make himself something of a power. His stable of clients included such high-voltage names as Grace Moore, Irene Dunne, Jeanette MacDonald, Marilyn Miller, Bert Lahr, Victor Moore, William Gaxton, Jack Pearl and Cilfton Webb. But what interested Cole was Shurr's knack for finding not just a job but the *right* job for anyone who came under his aegis. At lunch Cole wanted to know what Shurr could do to help him.

Shurr, great admirer of Porter songs, said he was confident he could get him a good assignment almost at once. As a first step he set up an audition with Vinton Freedley and Alex Aarons, two young men who were covered with glory as producers of George Gershwin musicals.

Cole eagerly agreed to audition at a Broadway theater. There climbing into the orchestra pit, he seated himself at the piano and played and sang his entire repertoire, ranging from risqué to romantic to sentimental to patter to blues numbers.

The response was disappointing. Aarons felt that the songs were old-fashioned compared to Gershwin's. Freedley, for his part, considered them too unusual and esoteric to fit into a book musical.

The persistent Shurr urged Cole not to lose heart and promised that he would set up a number of other auditions before the month was out. Before he could do so, he was approached by E. Ray Goetz, a flamboyant bon vivant and dilettante who had made something of a reputation as a songwriter, a playwright and a producer. At the moment, Goetz was attempting to arrange for Gilbert Miller to produce a Gallic musical, starring Goetz's wife, Irene Bordoni. The title of the show was *Paris* and Goetz thought that Richard Rodgers and Larry Hart would turn out the type of numbers that were needed. Shurr agreed that Rodgers and Hart would indeed be ideal were they not already engaged in converting Mark Twain's *A Connecticut Yankee in King Arthur's Court* into a musical comedy. Why not, Shurr asked, sign up both Rodgers and Hart in a single package?

How?

Hire Cole Porter.

Goetz thought Cole's American and Parisian background suited him admirably for the task, although he reserved the right for other composers' works to be interpolated, and eventually he and Walter Kollo turned out some numbers themselves, including "The Land of Going to Be."

For Cole, working with Goetz turned out to be his Broadway education. Despite Goetz's dilettantism, he was a producer who fully understood the mechanics of assembling a Broadway musical of that period. In addition, he was unflappable in the face of a crisis.

Not that *Paris* made any creative demands upon Cole. His numbers were spotlighted in revue fashion and had for the most part been written earlier. The story was such that this was easy to do. It concerned a Boston boy (Erik Kalkhurst) who falls in love with or into the clutches of a continental actress (Irene Bordoni) to the distress of his society-matron mama (Louise Closser Hale). In the ways known only to musical comedy, Mrs. Hale is transformed from a dowager into a fiftyish flapper and helps foil her son's romance with the result that Miss Bordoni ends in the arms of her leading man (Arthur Margetson). Librettist Martin Brown's greatest achievement, it seemed to reviewers who tried to summarize the plot, was somehow to introduce Irving Aaronson's Commanders, an eleven-piece orchestra, into the hotel-room set.

When the production opened in Atlantic City, New Jersey, on February 6, 1928, the score included "I've Got Quelque Chose," "Two Little Babes in the Wood," "Don't Look at Me That Way," "Vivienne," "Which" and "Let's Misbehave." "Let's Misbehave," which was hailed out of town, was eventually replaced by "Let's Do It." In opting for the latter, Cole discovered that there was infinitely more humor in a provocatively insinuating proposal than a direct proposition.

Paris moved from Atlantic City to Philadelphia, where it sold out for five weeks at the Adelphi Theater, then moved to the Lyric for another seven before it wandered west to Chicago and then back to the Music Box in Manhattan, where it opened on October 8, 1928.

No New York reviewer went so far as to place this modest little entertainment in a class with *Showboat,* as one Philadelphia writer had. In fact, few even implied that its plot was no better than it should be, but the production had no trouble competing at the box office with Lynn Fontanne in *Strange Interlude,* Mae West in *Diamond Lil,* Blanche Yurka in *The Wild Duck* or with

"The Scandolls" in George White's *Scandals.*

Paris was good news, and the best news of all was Cole Porter. As *The New York Times* noted, three of Miss Bordoni's songs were grand and it could not be a coincidence that those three were written by Cole Porter.

Cole, significantly, had missed his triumph. By the time the show opened, he had come to expect so little at the hands of Broadway that he had returned to Paris. However, when he read the review of the customarily caustic critic from *The New Yorker,* he must have suspected that his problems were over. After entering minor reservations about the plot and the Goetz-Kollo songs, the critic commented: ". . . When it came to Cole Porter's songs, however, I cared for no one's opinion but my own, an ecstatic one. 'Babes in the Wood,' 'Don't Look at Me That Way,' and 'Let's Fall in Love'* are up to Mr. Porter's best, and there is no better. No one else writing words and music knows so exactly the delicate balance between sense, rhyme and tune. His rare and satisfactory talent makes other lyrists sound as though they'd written their words for a steam whistle."

With such a reception, it was inevitable that Cole would be back soon with brighter, more ambitious and altogether better songs.

* "Let's Do It."

CHAPTER VI

The success of *Paris* brought Cole long-awaited but often postponed recognition as the creator of daring lyrics and deft melodies of unique character. The extravagant response to them heated up his enthusiasm and soon scores came bursting forth like Roman candle displays.

He contributed two songs to the Paramount film, *Battle of Paris,* starring Gertrude Lawrence.

He wrote the score for *Wake Up and Dream,* a revue which was produced both in London and New York.

He quickly followed that with scores for *Fifty Million Frenchmen, The New Yorkers* and *Gay Divorce.*

More importantly, whatever the worth or lack of it in any of these shows, at least one of Cole's songs from each production helped to solidify his growing reputation.

Wake Up and Dream, an elaborate revue produced in England by C. B. Cochran, had 24 settings and 500 costumes for its English cast—Jessie Matthews, Sonnie Hale, Tilly Losch, George Metaxa, Toni Birkmayer and William Stephens—to struggle with. Since there had been no time for an uninterrupted dress rehearsal before opening in Manchester, the premiere promised to be just that. The situation was so grim that Cochran stepped to the footlights on opening night and told the audience:

"Circumstances have been against us. I'm afraid you will be disappointed with our performance tonight. Later we shall have a fine show."

For his part, Cole remained aloof and unruffled by the chaos, keeping so much to himself that Jessie Matthews, who starred in both the London and New York productions, scarcely ever met him. He confined his worries to how the Lord Chamberlain would react to the racy lyrics of "Let's Do It" (which had been lifted from *Paris).* When that gentleman met Cole, shook his hand and congratulated him on his splendid research, Cole relaxed, interpreting the reaction as an omen of impending triumph.

Which is what it turned out to be. The *Morning Post* compared the audience at the London Pavilion on opening night March 27, 1929, to those of "the old diamond horseshoe days at Covent Garden." Appropriately, too, the reporter added, since Mr. Porter's music has already been voted as being "on a much higher plane than any other American composer."

Cole saved most of the reviews, but characteristically the only one that elicited any response was that of the London *Times,* which read in part: "Its music, except when it borrows in passing from the gayer masters, though cheerful enough, is strangely characterless." Besides this comment, he penciled: "So nice!"

Three days after the premiere, he and Linda returned to Paris, confident that *Wake Up and Dream* had scored a success, and their optimism proved justified by an eventual run of 263 performances.

Soon Cole began work on *Fifty Million Frenchmen,* his first major bid as the composer of a complete score without a collaborator. Almost at once, trouble set in. In fact, if the production proved nothing else, it destroyed the theatrical bromide that when a show is right everything falls neatly into place.

Upon arrival in New York from Paris, Cole was disappointed to learn from E. Ray Goetz that Irving Berlin had been obliged to bow out as co-producer. (Berlin was too busy.)

Berlin suggested Sam H. Harris. Harris was unavailable.

Finally Warner Brothers offered the money with Goetz billed as producer. Goetz agreed.

In return, Cole and librettist Herbert Fields (son of Joe Fields of the vaudeville team Weber and Fields) violated the Dramatists Guild rule forbidding members to sell film rights without permission of the Guild's arbitrator. Eventually, Fields and Cole were fined $1,000 and suspended for six months.

Rehearsals were difficult to coordinate, since Fields' book proved to be so sprawling that director Monty Woolley and his assistants were forced to drill different groups on stages of the Lyric and Knickerbocker theaters, in the lounges of the Selwyn and Apollo theaters, at the Metropolitan Opera House and at the Mecca Temple.

When the day arrived to entrain for Boston, there was more trouble. The sets, designed by architect Norman Bel Geddes (who had never designed scenery before), were so cumbersome that seven railroad cars were needed to carry them, and even so some pieces had to be left behind.

In Boston, the stage of the Colonial Theater proved to be too small to accommodate the sets that had been brought from New York. The opening was postponed while Bel Geddes worked to simplify his creations. After twenty-four hours, the production was hung, then another five hours were consumed synchronizing lights.

The opening was postponed twice more.

Amidst all the uproar, final dress rehearsal ran from Wednesday evening until 7:00 A.M. Thursday, after which everyone went home for four hours, arose, returned to the theater and resumed rehearsal until one hour before the premiere.

Cole responded with detachment. On opening night, he was near the front door, dressed in white tie and tails and greeting his friends with the unnerving aplomb that was to become a central part of his legend.

Hidden away was all the anxiety and hard work which he seldom acknowledged. Caught off guard, however, he did admit he had written six numbers for every one used.

Lyrics, he said, gave him more trouble than music. His goal was to catch an idea and a title. The title suggested a musical phrase which he repeated two or three times during the chorus. The next step was to work out a line with a kick which generally came before the title of the song at the end of the chorus. Although the song did not always develop in the above way, he generally followed that pattern, he said.

The first performance went well, and next morning Boston critics were encouraging. They found amusing the idea of an American playboy attempting to exist without funds in Paris for a month in order to win a bet. They also praised Cole's work as fresh, inventive and tuneful. But that same morning, Florenz Ziegfeld, Jr., popped up to predict a flop. He warned Goetz that there was not a single singable song. Goetz was amused. But Cole, who always attributed the wisdom of Solomon to any producer, no matter how musically illiterate, was so unsettled by Ziegfeld's judgment that he quickly agreed to play and sing several numbers on Alexander Woollcott's *Town Crier* radio show, hoping the influential Woollcott would urge his listeners to attend the musical.

Finally on November 27, in the midst of the stock-market collapse, the $254,000 production—which needed to gross $30,000 a week to break even—opened in New York to mixed notices. Walter Winchell, one of Porter's earliest enthusiasts, and Gilbert Gabriel, who called the show "the best thing in seven years or so," led the cheers. John Anderson noted Cole's growing fondness for the animal kingdom and suggested that he must have been scared by a box of animal crackers when a baby. J. Brooks Atkinson, as he billed himself, thought the score pleasant, and Richard Watts announced that although the lyrics were the most delightful in town there wasn't really an outstanding song hit in the show.

All in all the critical response was tepid enough that on December 19 Irving Berlin generously set forth his views in a paid advertisement: "The best musical comedy I have seen in years," he announced. "More laughs than I have heard in a long time. One of the best collections of song numbers I have ever listened to. It's worth the price of admission to hear Cole Porter's lyrics."

Audiences agreed, enjoying Genevieve Tobin's and William Gaxton's way with "You Do Something to Me," Betty Compton's "Why Shouldn't I Have You?" "Paree, What Did You Do to Me?" and "You've Got That Thing," as well as Evelyn Hoey's "Find Me a Primitive Man."

Yet it remained for Helen Broderick to stop the show. In two-a-day vaudeville, as half of the team of Crawford and Broderick, she had exhibited the flair of a stellar comedienne and several producers had offered her roles on Broadway. Helen took them whether the scripts were good or bad and, until *Fifty Million Frenchmen,* all had been bad.

After one failure, Helen amused Broadway by demanding of a critic whom she met in a hotel lobby whether he knew why critics were like eunuchs. He cautioned her to remember she was a lady, but Helen was not to be silenced. "Critics are like eunuchs," she said, "because they tell you how to do things they can't do themselves."

There is a belief that to insult reviewers is a sure way to win good notices, but nobody ever suggested that was the reason Helen made a hit playing hardboiled Violet Hildegarde in *Fifty Million Frenchmen.* Her headlong pursuit of shocking sensations, whether French postcards or a bootlegged copy of James Joyce's *Ulysses,* brought roars of laughter. Her song, "Where Would You Get Your Coat?," delivered in front of a drop was the type of material any vaudevillian knew how to put over. Then, in Act Two, she had "The Tale of an Oyster," the saga of a social-climbing marine mollusk, which was to gain latter-day popularity on a limited scale but failed to get over with 1929 audiences and was finally dropped. Nevertheless, the show launched her legitimate career and solidified Cole's place in the theater as it racked up a run of 254 performances.

At a time others were feeling the economic stress of the Depression, Cole was riding a private boom. On December

30, little more than a month after *Fifty Million Frenchmen* opened, Arch B. Selwyn imported *Wake Up and Dream* from London, bringing along Jessie Matthews, Tilly Losch and William Stephens. New to the cast were Jack Buchanan and a Canadian girl singer, Frances Shelley.

The critical reaction was, for the most part, mildly disapproving. Paradoxically, however, the show further established Cole as a songwriter of distinction. Walter Winchell was so taken with "What Is This Thing Called Love?" that he hailed it in his column as a new kind of love song. Although *Wake Up and Dream* ran only 136 performances, Winchell's campaign on behalf of that one song left Cole considerably better known than he had ever been before.

With two shows launched, Cole, Linda and Mrs. Herman "Dumpy" Oelrichs, a fun-loving, gravel-voiced society woman, set out on January 1, 1930, for Venice by way of Hollywood, China and Japan. In the Hawaiian Islands Cole composed "Let's Go Places," which he sent back to Goetz suggesting that it be included in *Fifty Million Frenchmen*. The song never made the show, but press agent Dick Maney succeeded in garnering so much newspaper space with it that as Cole moved through China, the Malay Straits, Nangpo Colony and Siam, he sent back songs from each to help publicize the show.

Visiting Japan in May, the Porters attracted unwelcome publicity when, impatient with miserable train service, Cole leased an entire private train to take him and his party to Kyoto. Headlines reported the "American millionaire's" extravagance, and, with the Depression at home in mind, the Porters and Mrs. Oelrichs fled the Japanese spotlight.

But even unpleasant headlines couldn't dampen Cole's *joie de vivre* for long. In Ceylon, he encountered animal trainer Clyde Beatty and mischievously proposed that Beatty deposit a baby elephant on Monty Woolley's doorstep. But Linda reminded her husband of his recent headlines and for once he was dissuaded from carrying out a costly practical joke.

After arriving in Europe, the Porters spent a few weeks

in Venice and Paris, then returned to New York where Cole took up work with Herbert Fields and Ray Goetz on *The New Yorkers*. The show was to be based upon an idea developed by Goetz and cartoonist Peter Arno. At first, they had intended to satirize gangsters in a book musical, but somewhere along the way the story was jettisoned. Just as *Fifty Million Frenchmen* had evolved into a musical tour of Paris, *The New Yorkers* became a picaresque tour of New York.

The cast that Goetz assembled promised excitement. There were Clayton, Jackson and Durante (with Jimmy Durante providing a couple of songs for himself), Fred Waring and His Pennsylvanians and three glamorous leading ladies: Kathryn Crawford; society girl Hope Williams; and Ann Pennington of the dimpled knees who, according to *The New York Times,* once advocated "facial expression" as an aid in achieving stage success.

The rehearsal and out-of-town tryout periods were relatively uneventful, although the opening in Philadelphia was delayed four days during which Cole fended off boredom by writing "Take Me Back to Manhattan," a bit of private relaxation that was deemed amusing enough to be added to the score.

At the New York premiere on December 8, 1930, the Broadway Theater saw an assemblage of denizens of Park Avenue who fully appreciated such humor as Hope Williams' description of it as "a street where bad women walk good dogs." They liked Cole's contributions too, especially the bitter, beautiful "Love for Sale," the simple, sentimental, deeply felt "I Happen to Like New York" and the jaded, witty "The Great Indoors."

None of the major critics exactly denigrated the score, but most seemed to agree with Atkinson of the *Times,* who opined that with a couple of exceptions the tunes and rhymes held to the average of song-and-dance shows.

The New Yorkers played only 168 performances. Nevertheless, again it greatly added to Cole's stature, just as his fifth production in three years was to do. Called *Gay Divorce* (altered to *The Gay Divorcee* for films), it was produced by Dwight Deere Wiman and his partner Tom Weatherly as Fred Astaire's first solo starring venture after his sister and dancing partner, Adele, retired to marry an English lord.

The story concerns a young Englishwoman who attempts to win a divorce by hiring a gigolo to compromise her. Astaire was to play the part of a man sincerely in love with her who passes himself off as a gigolo. Cole, who always maintained that he had "no book sense," was wildly enthusiastic about this one, so enthusiastic that he began writing the score before he was under contract. Once he had finished a few numbers, he played them for Astaire. Having heard the first, "After You, Who?" Astaire announced he would do the show.

It was for *Gay Divorce* that Cole began his practice of composing a song to make use of a singer's natural assets and bypass his weaknesses. The song he wrote for Astaire was "Night and Day." In this case, Cole wrote the music before the lyrics (generally he decided upon the rhythm, wrote the words and then the music) and sat down at the piano to try out the melody. As he played, Monty Woolley arrived, listened and announced that he had no idea what Cole was trying to do but that it was terrible and he should give it up.

Next day, Cole left for a weekend at the Vincent Astors' in Newport. On the train, he worked on the lyrics, but, perhaps disheartened by Monty's reaction, he found himself blocked.

All weekend he remained stymied. Then on Sunday, he joined his hostess and Schuyler Parsons for luncheon. The then Mrs. Astor, who enjoyed dining without interruptions from servants, had arranged for the three of them to take luncheon from trays on a porch. Despite the fact that a rainstorm was in progress, they held to the plan. But as the meal progressed, Mrs. Astor became unnerved by the noise caused by a broken eaves spout and said, "I must have that eave mended at once. That drip, drip, drip, is driving me mad!"

Cole leaped up at once, saying, "I think that will work!"

He immediately tried it out on the piano where for the first time the completed version of "Night and Day" was played and sung. "Drip, drip, drip" became "the drip, drip, drip of the raindrops," the portion of the lyrics which no amount of thought or consultation of thesauruses, rhyming dictionaries or phrase finders had turned up.

When Astaire heard the song, he doubted whether he could sing it. Cole insisted he try, saying it had been written for his voice. Unconvinced, the star approached coproducer Tom Weatherly, saying his voice would crack if he sang it. Weatherly shared Astaire's doubts and asked Cole to throw it out. But Cole felt sure he had caught hold of something unique and insisted upon hearing whether the star's voice would adapt to it. Despite Weatherly's warning that he was killing the show by holding on to a song nobody liked, Cole remained unmoved.

Gay Divorce opened at the Ethel Barrymore Theater on November 29, 1932, with Claire Luce playing opposite Astaire. The plot, despite the ministrations of director Howard Lindsay, seemed old hat. And one critic wrote that whenever Astaire paused, he seemed to be looking anxiously toward the wings as if awaiting the appearance of his sister, Adele. It was clear, too, that while reviewers considered Cole's contributions workmanlike, he was no longer the man of the hour. There were partisans for "Mister and Missus Fitch," a song based on the imaginary Oklahoma couple, "I've Got You on My Mind," which detailed all the reasons why a person isn't the right love object but mysteriously has that magnetic appeal, and "I Still Love the Red, White and Blue," rendered by Luella Gear with stirring and sardonic effect.

"Night and Day" was dismissed by the critics. Song pluggers tried to interest orchestra leaders and singers in it, but there was a great deal of resistance from them, too. They said the song with its forty-eight instead of the usual thirty-two bars was "too long." Some called it a "tapeworm song." They also claimed that the four notes above the octave made it difficult to sing. When Cole told a reporter that he had been inspired by a Mohammedan priest calling the faithful to prayers in Morocco, Tin Pan Alley took the position that he ought to have left it there.

In fact, as Cole and Linda sailed for Paris, Cole was convinced that the song was doomed to quick failure, but Linda predicted that it would eventually win popularity. "Someday, darling, it will be a big hit," she assured him. He was not optimistic, as yet not having grown accustomed to the idea that his greatest hits generally were to be ignored or dismissed when first heard. The closing of the show after 248 performances killed any lingering hopes he held for the song.

Thus, the five productions in three years left Cole feeling mildly uncertain whether or not his newfound popularity was already on the wane. In need of distraction, he accompanied Ray Goetz and Herbert Fields to Vienna to see Fritz Kreisler's new operetta. To Dr. Albert Sirmay, his friend-editor-counselor at Harms, Inc., he wrote, "music nice—libretto awful." He said that the performance had lasted three hours and forty-five minutes, but that the only joys were a new waltz and the orchestrations of Robert Russell Bennett.

Upon returning to 13 Rue de Monsieur, Cole was delighted to find a letter from Dr. Sirmay praising *Gay Divorce* and replied that he would put it in his scrapbook alongside one from Irving Berlin, "for certainly no two letters could I respect more or be happier to have."

Albert Sirmay, a jolly erudite Hungarian, was already a friend and as the years passed was to become a valued adviser, a devoted musical secretary and a discerning editor. Born in Budapest, Dr. Sirmay was educated at Budapest's university and its Royal Academy. As a young man he wrote hundreds of popular songs and contributed scores for ten musicals produced in such places as Vienna, London, New York and, of course, Budapest. After coming to the United States in 1923, he chose to concentrate upon his work as an editor for music publishing houses.

When Dr. Sirmay urged Cole to return to New York, Cole replied that he was afraid he could not come back soon since Max Gordon had not showed up with a contract. In addition, *Stardust*, the show he was to have done with Ray Goetz and Herbert Fields, seemed to him likely to "be produced in heaven," because of a new tobacco tax that had ruined Goetz's backers. Nor was he hopeful about the project upon which he was working with Gilbert Miller. They were adapting a play, *The Spell*, into a musical called *Yours*, but the rate of progress made Cole suspect that it would never be anybody's.

CHAPTER VII

At the time Cole was speculating on his next assignment to Dr. Sirmay, Charles Cochran already had decided to engage him to write the score for a musical version of James Laver's novel *Nymph Errant*. Laver, Keeper of the Department of Engravings, Illustrations, Designs and Paintings at the Victoria and Albert Museum, had written what was then considered a shocking story of the misadventures of an English girl attempting to rid herself of her virginity. Cochran's plan was to persuade Gertrude Lawrence to play the heroine and to entrust the libretto to Romney Brent, who had written a farce called *The Mad Hopes*. Brent, a Spanish-American who was at the time appearing in the London version of Noel Coward's *Words and Music,* was far better known as an actor than as a playwright; but Cochran felt that Brent's flair for writing smart dialogue made him just the man to tackle the new project.

Brent agreed to work up an outline. Eventually it was finished and forwarded to Paris. Cole expressed interest and suggested a conference at 13 Rue de Monsieur on January 29, 1933. Brent subsequently said that at the initial meeting, he had been struck by how much Cole resembled a Boston bull puppy. "He had that kind of little, round face, you know, the way the folds of the mouth went back and the very black eyes. He wasn't handsome, but he had a very pleasant face, that winning smile and those expressive eyes."

Brent was even more awed by the splendor in which the Porters lived, but most of all he was surprised at Cole's deep professional humility. "After all, he was *Cole Porter.* He had written four or five big productions. But he was so easy to work with, this man. He could tell me—I'd never written a musical—a few things. And I would toe the mark. With pleasure, I would have. There was none of that."

What there was was an overwhelming sense of style and drama. For instance, during the initial luncheon Cole suddenly recalled that it was "the great Katie's birthday" and seemed overcome with guilt at having forgotten. Explaining the situation, he summoned a servant, asked that pencil and paper be brought, after which he spelled out a sentimental message, saying that he and Linda sent deepest love to "dear ma" and begged her to let them know how she was. Next day, Brent said, Cole's question was answered by return cable. It read: "Okay. Kate Porter."

After their conference, Cole agreed to undertake the assignment if Brent were willing to go to Carlsbad with him and Linda. There, Cole proposed to take "the cure" while the two of them worked. Naturally, Brent agreed.

On the morning of departure, he arrived at Gare de l'Est. "This I had never seen before. I'd seen it in movies, but I'd never met anyone like them in private life. Linda was standing there, her English maid behind her. All Linda's bags matched. Cole was standing there. All his bags matched too. His valet stood behind him. And here I came with an old torn suitcase.

"Linda was charming with her gentle Southern accent. There was nothing dead about her. Nothing of the bitch about her. She was lovely looking, with her aristocratic air. Beautifully bred and terribly nice. She was a darling."

When the Porters' party got on the train, there were numerous bedrooms reserved: one for Linda, one for Cole, one for Brent, as well as a sitting room, and assorted sleeping and work rooms for the servants.

Even before they were settled, Cole summoned Brent to his bedroom saying that he wanted to discuss the production, but before they began he asked his valet to fetch "the little bag." It was placed before him and opened. To Brent's astonishment, he saw that there were numerous small compartments, all of which held bottles or tubes or boxes of one kind or another. Without any kind of apology or reference to what he was doing, Cole proceeded to analyze the outline while at the same time he popped pills into his mouth, sprayed his throat, applied a variety of lotions and generally ministered to his health. When he finished, he rang for the valet, motioned toward the bag and then returned to the discussion. Brent, who had not yet become familiar with his collaborator's disdain for "middle-class" reticence about physical functions, was astounded.

Since it was off-season, Carlsbad was quite deserted, the very reason the Porters had chosen to come at this time. Aside from Brent and their close friend Mary Cass Canfield, they saw no one.

Each morning, Cole and Brent would take a long walk while talking over the development of new scenes. But first they would go to the pump room where Cole drank great amounts of the chemical water before starting off on one of the bypaths.

They would stroll along deep in discussion until a small toilet was sighted, at which time Cole would suddenly excuse himself, hang his cane (each guest carried a cane to signal others that the toilet was occupied) outside the door and disappear.

Time passed. He would reappear. He and Brent would take up their discussion of the scene where they had left off. Eventually Cole would once more ask to be excused. "This happened about four times each morning," Brent said. "Cole was a first-rate hypochondriac. He really had nothing wrong with him. He was a man of forty-three or so, full of piss and vinegar, but he thought he was sick and that this was doing him a world of good."

During their daily discussions, Brent would suggest that he write dialogue to a certain point in a scene and let Cole take over. Cole always insisted that the scene be written out completely before he began converting the dialogue ideas into lyrics. "In order not to make the songs seem intrusions, the music began long before the song came into the scene. The music was there a long time before Gertie Lawrence began singing. That was Cole's idea and he was one of the first to use it."

After they had returned to the hotel, Cole would write between 10:00 A.M. and 1:00 P.M. During those hours, some of his most brilliant music and lyrics were completed at one sitting. Since Brent had written the scene the previous evening and had given it to Cole that morning, he knew that there had been no opportunity to work out the song previously.

He found Cole a delightful collaborator, although possessed of a social quirk that was unnerving. The Porters, Mary Cass Canfield and Brent customarily dined together and then spent the evening chatting or playing card games. If they were simply talking, Cole would sometimes arise abruptly while someone was in the middle of a sentence and leave without so much as a word of explanation. Sometimes he would be gone half an hour, sometimes an hour and sometimes longer. Eventually it began to seem to Brent that this occurred most often at times when he was talking and it disturbed him sufficiently that he asked Linda whether he was unconsciously offending her husband.

"Good God, no, Romney," she said. She explained that Cole had always been that way, that he would think of something or feel bored and saw no reason not to leave. "He wouldn't think of being rude to you consciously," she assured him. "That's the way he is and I've learned to accept it."

Following their stay at the spa, Cole spent ten days getting into top shape by rowing down the Danube, after which he and Linda rented an English cottage at Winkfield Green near Cochran's home at Bray. They invited Brent to be their guest, and in this setting the work on the production went ahead.

There were several panic-filled weeks when it was discovered that Cochran had not been able to persuade Gertie Lawrence to commit herself to the show. Nevertheless Brent brought choreographer Agnes de Mille to Cochran's attention and she was signed. At last, after a great deal of equivocating, Miss Lawrence signed too. Cole was ecstatic; she was one of the legendary superstars whose artistry and personality assured the success of almost any project with which she chose to associate herself, even though her singing voice was only adequate.

On September 11, 1933, Manchester took on a carnival-like atmosphere with the arrival of *Nymph Errant*. Crowds lined both sides of Quay Street that night, cheering all arrivals at the premiere, including the critics. Many of the women who attended sported Mediterranean tans and most of the men were in white tie. Noel Coward was cheered lustily. Douglas Fairbanks Jr., who was romantically involved with Miss Lawrence, drew an even greater response. Cole, on the other hand, was hardly recognized.

Next day, even the *Telegraphs*'s "own correspondent" attributed the music to Romney Brent, while the *Daily News Chronicle*'s man announced that the music was imitative and owed much to Noel Coward.

Despite some negative responses to the book by the critics, Cole sent a note to Dr. Sirmay telling him that the libretto was, in his opinion, the best he had ever had. Fox Pictures also liked it well enough to buy the rights (and the financially pressed management was happy to receive the $25,000 fee), although no picture was ever made. (In later years, Cole gave the back of his hand to public opinion and to Fox by announcing that the score which neither Broadway nor Hollywood utilized was the best he had done. It may be assumed that he arrived at the evaluation as a result of the score's being shunned, just as "Love for Sale" became his favorite song because of its "stepchild status" in relation to radio.)

During the Manchester tryout, the management found

itself in an embarrassing predicament. At the end of the first act, the heroine is attending a costume ball and has a number requiring legato singing, at which Miss Lawrence was notably weak. Because all of them were fond of her, Cochran suggested that it might be more fitting for Cole to tell her privately that she was not up to the number. Cole suggested that Brent do it. And Brent passed the responsibility back to the producer. Finally, Cole solved the problem by pretending that he was dissatisfied with his writing and that he felt the song was psychologically wrong for the character. When he so informed Miss Lawrence, she readily agreed to the suggested change and Cole wrote a new title song to show her off to best advantage.

Brent often found himself marveling at Cole's tact, since the songwriter had a reputation for snobbishness. "In the theater, he was entirely democratic," Brent said. "He never gave the impression that he felt these were not gentle-born people and, of course, not rich the way he was. He was a gentleman, but he could talk to the stagehands as if he were one of them. He was liked very much by everyone. The people in Cochran's office loved him. After a secretary took a few messages and did a little dictation for him, he sent her flowers. It was the gesture of a gentleman who liked to give happiness. Nor did he speak spitefully of anybody. He could have—people in the theater often do—but I never heard him make an unkind crack. He had a strong ego. He knew he was very talented and he used his talent to the best of his ability to be the famous person he was."

Both Brent and Cole marveled at Gertrude Lawrence. Afterward Cole maintained that her indefatigability accounted for the fact that she became a superstar. After rehearsal, he said, she would insist that Agnes de Mille coach her so that she could incorporate dance steps in a number. Although she could have faked it, she often worked for hours until the exhausted Miss de Mille would say that the number was good enough.

"Not good enough. We'll do it again. Not good enough at all, dear," Miss Lawrence said. That attitude, Cole thought, eyplained why when she entered the Savoy Grill, a mass of people arose and applauded, a response that Cochran told him was unequaled since the days of Patti.

The London premiere on October 6, 1933, was regarded as the top social event of the "Little Season." Ambassadors from Spain, France, Germany, Brazil and America were in the audience and there were the usual figures from the international set.

The story of the schoolgirl who arrives home—after adventures in such diverse locales as a Turkish harem, the Folies de Paris, a nudist camp and a desert sheik's tent—only to have her dotty aunt rebuke her for being ten minutes late, delighted first-nighters. Cole's lyrics were admired for the "witty inference of every intonation and a sting in every verse's last line." The press, however, was generally restrained in its praise despite Miss Lawrence's way with that delightful song, "The Physician" and the minor felicities of "When Love Comes your Way" and "How Could We Be Wrong?" There were cheers, too, for Elizabeth Welch, an American Negro singer and actress, who belted out the bluesy "Solomon."

Naturally, there was a supper party afterward in honor of the Porters. Lady Cunard was the hostess and the Duke di Verdura, Lord Arlington, the Alistar MacIntoshes and Mr. and Mrs. Evelyn FitzGerald were among those present. For people such as these, *Nymph Errant* was a triumphantly witty show, but for the general English public there was not enough interest in the amoral dalliances of a schoolgirl, even a schoolgirl played by their beloved Gertie, and the show managed only a six-month run.

Not quite a month after *Nymph Errant*'s opening, on November 2 to be exact, Fred Astaire and Claire Luce captivated London with their performances in *Gay Divorce* at the Palace Theater. Critics this time saluted Cole's lyrics as original, cerebral, witty, amusing, and admirably suited to his stars.

Cole's fame now had reached the point where he was the target of a number of litigiously inclined persons who were convinced that he was pilfering their output. Soon after the opening of *Nymph Errant,* Cochran received a letter that was to foreshadow some less mad and some even madder:

Dear Sir,

Since last April I have been annoyed by a man giving the name of Mr. Noel Coward of England.

I have written several plays and I am also composing music.

Starting on December 1st, I have been told through the Psychial [*sic*] Research Society of England and America, that my music and plays are being stolen through Electric Transmission.

At the present time I have under way an opera which Mr. Coward said that he and Mr. Cole Porter were going to steal. I have the material copyrighted here in America and would like to know how to protect my rights in England.

Mr. Coward also told me that the music I had been composing he is using in his play called, *Conversation Piece*. This, you know, cannot go on.

This matter has been taken up by the music publishers of America, and I should like for you to speak to Mr. Cole Porter regarding this matter about an opera, and have him get in touch with me before difficulties arise creating a scandal here and abroad.

Yours very truly,

It was signed with an actual name and a pseudonym. Cole's impulse was to regard it as the work of a practical joker or a deranged mind. In this case nothing developed. Several years later, an accuser no less mad was to cost him thousands of dollars in attorney's fees.

CHAPTER VIII

Despite all predictions to the contrary at the time of the Porters' wedding in 1919, their marriage was working well. Linda—beautiful, charming, individualistic—was accustomed to exercising quasi-royal prerogatives. Cole—witty, talented, original—was used to getting his way. The prospects for such an alliance would seem dim. But Cole and Linda not only loved one another, they were also devoted friends.

What at first might have seemed a weakness, their separateness, turned out to be one of the marriage's strengths. A great deal of freedom went hand in hand with a great deal of trust. After thirteen years of marriage, each could be counted upon to support the other fully and lovingly whatever the situation. Passion wears out, but respect and mutual dependence do not.

Togetherness was not then a popular catchphrase, but had it been both Cole and Linda would have regarded it as not altogether civilized. It was something quite alien to their station in life and to their set. They were dependent and devoted, yet fully capable of exercising free choice. If Cole scheduled a jaunt, Linda was free to attend or not as she chose. There were walking trips through the Dolomites, cruises down the Rhine or Danube or Nile, skiing parties in the Alps and all manner of other distractions.

Sometimes Linda chose to go along, say, to Switzerland, not to ski perhaps but to enjoy the good Swiss air. At other times, she exercised her option to remain in Paris. Although she could have pleaded "health problems" on these occasions, she did not. She was enough of an individualist to feel that she owed it to herself never to subject herself to unnecessary physical hardships or so much as a moment's boredom. This was a special marriage which for all of the Porters' idiosyncrasies served their emotional needs and thus was to endure, with only one serious disruption, for thirty-five years.

At the time Vinton Freedley first attempted to contact Cole Porter to persuade him to do a new show in 1934, Cole was floating down the Rhine in a *faltboot*. Freedley's successful partnership with Alex Aarons had come to an end in 1933 when George and Ira Gershwin's *Pardon My English* had turned out to be a disaster. Depressed by this and in bad health (doctors never decided whether he had had a heart attack or suffered a heat stroke), Freedley, while confined to a wheelchair, had himself pushed aboard the *Majestic* and set out for Europe determined to turn a long-supressed ambition into reality: to produce a Cole Porter musical. "I'd always admired Cole," he said. "I wanted to do a show with him. But Alex thought Cole was old hat—even before he was new hat."

Freedley's idea was to do a show centering around the confusion and fun involved when a gambling ship is wrecked. To insure humorous treatment, he sought out librettists P. G. Wodehouse and Guy Bolton. Bolton, who was living in England, had tax problems that made it difficult for him to leave the country. Wodehouse refused to leave France. And Cole was floating down the Rhine, stopping, as he later said, "only at Ritz cities" where he and a companion ravaged for plovers and Royal Tokay. ("A small adventure, but a pure one," Cole observed.)

Freedley eventually arranged a meeting between the writers, resulting in an outline for *Hard to Get,* as the show was called, which was turned over to Cole. Not too many weeks after that, Cole turned up at Freedley's hotel in London with a bagful of songs, songs that Freedley "fell in love with" at first hearing.

At this initial meeting between the two, Cole also played several bars of background music which he had written for *Nymph Errant* and suggested that these contained the potential for fuller treatment. Freedley agreed and the rights were obtained from Cochran for $5,000. The music was developed and won wide popularity as "I Get a Kick Out of You."

Not long after Cole's visit, the Wodehouse-Bolton script arrived and Freedley read it with increasing despair. He had always admired Wodehouse and Bolton, but there was, he felt, as tastelessness about his piece of work that no amount of rewriting would eradicate. While he was wracking his brain to find a solution to the problem, an unconnected disaster solved it for him. One morning he read in a newspaper that a pleasure ship, the U.S.S. *Morro Castle,* had burned off the coast of New Jersey, taking 134 lives. This, Freedley felt, made it mandatory for him to junk the plot line and come up with a new one. Wodehouse and Bolton were no longer available. After some thought, Freedley suggested that Howard Lindsay, who had contracted to direct the show, write a new script, but Lindsay felt directing by day and writing by night would be too demanding a schedule.

Cole, meantime, was finishing the score in Hollywood. At Freedley's suggestion, he investigated available writers there and later in Paris where he and Linda spent a few weeks before returning to New York for rehearsals. No suitable candidate was unearthed, and finally Lindsay reluctantly agreed to undertake the task if a co-worker could be found for him. How Lindsay's collaborator was located is impossible to say. The only indisputable fact seems to be that the suggestion came from Neysa McMein, a clever magazine illustrator who enjoyed great popularity among literary and theatrical figures. Miss McMein at one time claimed that the name of the collaborator, Russel Crouse, was spelled out for her on her Ouija board.

A newspaper account said that Cole had gone to her country estate to visit the eight cats that Miss McMein was keeping for him and that he had mentioned the search for a writer to work with Lindsay. On the following Monday, Miss McMein was reported to have called Cole at 7:00 A.M.

"Russel Crouse," she said and hung up.

Another version had her phoning Cole to say, "I dreamed about Russel Crouse last night. He's your man."

In view of this story, the whimisical Crouse later wrote: "That makes me the original dreamboat, I guess, although I feel more like Cleopatra's barge."

In any case, Cole called Freedley and gave him the name. Freedley called Crouse, an ex-newspaperman who was working as a press agent for the Theater Guild, and a meeting was arranged between the two potential collaborators. They clicked and Lindsay took Crouse to Cole's apartment to hear the score.

What Crouse heard was "I Get a Kick Out of You," "Blow, Gabriel, Blow," and "You're the Top." Later, he recorded his reaction: "All I can say is that no doubt Ludwig van Beethoven, Johann Sebastian Bach, Wolfgang Amadeus Mozart, Richard Wagner, Johannes Brahms, Felix Mendelssohn, Claude Debussy, Frédéric Chopin, Giuseppe Verdi, Jacques Offenbach, Johann Strauss, Joseph Haydn and Francis Scott Key could have marched into the room and I wouldn't have looked up."

Cole's response to Ethel Merman, who had been cast in the leading role, was roughly comparable to Crouse's reaction to the score. Upon hearing her siren song blasting a brassy comedy line across the proscenium or pushing a quiet sentiment to the highest reaches of the second balcony, he placed her among the living divinities. Although she had been seen only in *Girl Crazy* and a couple of other shows, from the beginning he referred to her as The Great Ethel, The Great Merman or La Merman. He deferred to her, delighting in a personality that was customarily assured and direct, as he could seldom be. Her no-nonsense recognition and appreciation of her talent, her lack of middle-class modesty, her free-wheeling directness and her longshoreman's vocabulary—all of these appealed to him. "She's too honest to be anything but herself," he said.

Probably the situation that expressed the admiration he felt for her better than anything else was his willingness to submit the score of his show for her father's and mother's approval. And when they vetoed two numbers, he discarded them without protest. Even more significantly, Ethel's complaints about "Blow, Gabriel, Blow" resulted in Cole's rewriting it. In doing so, he paid her the highest compliment. For he thoroughly disapproved of rewriting songs. In most cases, he simply threw them out and supplied new ones. Brash William Gaxton wanted him to rewrite "Easy to Love," expressing doubts about its construction and saying that he could not hit the high notes. Cole simply replied that it was a superior piece of work and refused all efforts to get him to change it. Rewriting, he said, ruined songs. The result was that "All Through the Night" replaced "Easy to Love."

Inconsistent? Objectively, yes. By his own lights, no. Miss Merman was an artist and a friend, Gaxton was not. Artists and friends deserved special treatment. And, it might be added, a friend had to be guilty of an enormous breach of confidence before Cole would change his original assessment of him or her.

When the time arrived for rehearsals to begin, Lindsay and Crouse assembled Miss Merman, Gaxton, Victor Moore, Bettina Hall and a group of lesser players to tell them the plot. Actually, Lindsay ad-libbed the outline of a superlative musical comedy which held listeners spellbound. As Crouse later commented, "To me it was a better speech than the Gettysburg Address." Ever after, both Lindsay and Crouse wished that they could recall the complicated story line.

Ten days after that first meeting, with great difficulty and skipping all scenes that gave them any real trouble, the writers finished the first act. At the reading by the cast, any missing scenes were skipped with Lindsay saying vaguely, "Oh yes. That's such and such scene. We're working on that."

Time passed, but try as they would the authors could not come up with an opening for the second act—that moment when the audience either settles back in its seats and decides the show is a good one or chalks it up as a near miss.

Finally, Crouse telephoned Cole and announced that unless he could provide the opening there would be no second act. Next morning, Cole appeared with the slyly satiric "Public Enemy Number One," which turned out to be the rousing kind of number needed. He also provided a sea chanty, "There'll Always Be a Lady Fair," to divert audiences while scenes were being shifted. Deeper along in rehearsals, the capture of the Lindbergh kidnapper Bruno Hauptmann made it necessary to change a part of the "I Get a Kick Out of You" lyric. One passage:

I wouldn't care
For those nights in the air
That the fair
Mrs. Lindbergh went through . . .

was changed to the famous five-rhyme:

Flying too high
With some guy
In the sky
Is my i-dea of nothing to do,
Yet I get a kick out of you!

As the rehearsal period progressed, scene designer Donald Oenslager reminded the producer that unless the set for the final scene was ordered at once, it would not be finished in time for the Boston opening. Freedley had no vague idea where the action took place and was certain that Lindsay and Crouse didn't either. As Oenslager became increasingly insistent about having an answer, he solved the dilemma by saying: "Donald, give me an interior with exterior feeling."

The tempo was frantic. Confusion reigned. There are even conflicting stories as to how a title was found. In an early interview, Cole said that when Bill Gaxton was asked whether he minded making an entrance two minutes after the curtain went up, he replied, "In this kind of spot, anything goes!"

"Title," said Cole.

On another occasion, he told a reporter that Gaxton was discussing the show with the doorman and remarked that they didn't even have a title. The doorman, according to Cole, answered, "Well, today anything goes!"

Title!

Either incident may have happened, yet the fact remains that Cole had used "Everybody knows, anything goes" as part of a song in *And the Villian Still Pursued Her* at Yale in 1912.

Musical productions were scarce during the deep Depression. Even mildly entertaining shows were hailed. The fresh, tuneful show that opened in Boston on November 5, 1934, dazzled the town. The book still had to be tidied up and Cole's "Waltz Me Down the Aisle" was discarded.* These were all the changes that were made. And on November 21, 1934, greater fame still came to Cole with the explosion of *Anything Goes* at the Alvin Theater. Tickets brought $50 each. Newspapers described the event as the greatest gala since the Depression began. One society columnist reported that even those sitting in the balcony were resplendent in chinchilla. Everyone connected with the production was applauded for bringing a bit of relief to the grim Depression days at hand.

As was her custom, Linda presented Cole with a cigarette case commemorating the occasion. The Porters

* It later turned up in *Jubilee,* was thrown out and finally was converted into "Wunderbar" for *Kiss Me, Kate.*

and their friends sat in the first three rows and he applauded as enthusiastically as anyone else. During the intermission, he called out to a friend, "Good, isn't it?"

At the postpremiere party given by Freddy Frelinghuysen, Cole's spirits went into orbit as the telephoned reports of reviews credited him with making a humorous comment upon a world where "good's bad today, and black's white today, and day's night today . . . ," a world of turmoil and change.

He was also hailed anew for having devised another heretofore unheard-of type of love song. They rhymed superlatives of "You're the Top" with its references to the Louvre Museum (for the film version his college-professor cousin suggested changing it to the Field Museum), to Dante and Durante might have seemed unlikely to appeal to the hoi polloi—but they did. Radio censors might insist that in "I Get a Kick Out of You" singers get no kick from champagne (instead of cocaine)—but still the expression was several light years from the usual archaic poesy of the conventionally cast love song.

Cole himself recognized that it was his good fortune to come along at the time he did. Born twenty years earlier, he said, he would have found himself an Indiana banker. In speaking to interviewer Herman Motherwell prior to the critical acclaim accorded *Anything Goes*, Cole pointed out that Victor Herbert (whom he admired) would never have approved of the descending chromatic melody and the even, fluid harmonies of "All Through the Night"; the strange Latin rhythm of "The Gypsy in Me"; the every-other-word accent, which he would have thought misplaced, in "You're the Top"; the perfectly good melody of "I Get A Kick Out of You" made nervous with rhythm in scoring; or "Anything Goes" getting its *fuoco* from "intrusion by saxes where he would simply have told the drummers to bang the drums. . . ."

Brooks Atkinson wrote that while the emotions of "I Get a Kick Out of You" were less exalted than Shelly's "To a Skylark" the style was equally perfect.

In his assessment for the New York *Daily Mirror*,

Walter Winchell noted: "King Cole Porter, as he is affectionately called by this department, was host again last night. . . . Cole Porter to use his own theme is 'tops.' He is the Kern of the music masters, if you will pardon my prejudice—or the Roosevelt* of the lyrists. At any rate, Porter's bitter and pungent patter at the Alvin is a positive panic. The fooling and the fun were fervently fondled by the first fans."

A month later the columnist recorded his feelings about the show once again. "There is no other ditty around right now with such contagious lyrics and most of us who crash the sin saloons threaten orchestra leaders that unless they keep playing the Cole Porter score and have somebody sing the words that they will rate scallions. . . . That's the swell kick one gets from being a professional baddie—you play the part and have more fun than a crib full of quintuplets. . . . and so booo! I'm Hauptmann!"

That same week the New York *Sun-Record* nominated as "the most exciting lyric ever composed for a popular song" the words of "You're the Top." Soon Cole was receiving an average of 300 parodies each month of "You're the Top" and "Anything Goes." Winchell ran the better ones in his column. Radio stations used the parodies until Cole finally forbade any except his original lyrics. Amusingly, the edict backfired. Scheduled to appear on a network radio show, he turned up at the studio with freshly composed lyrics, only to be politely informed that no substitutions were ever allowed. Cole replied that he knew that. It was he who had forbidden use of imitations, but continuity acceptance refused to allow him to sing those that he'd written especially for the show.

Such an outburst of enthusiasm for these show tunes naturally produced strong detractors. One, Guy Bolton, according to Oscar Levant in his *Memoirs of an Amnesiac,* was still offering detailed reasons why the lyrics had been overrated some thirty years after the Broadway production

* Early in FDR's Administration, the columnist was pro-Roosevelt.

closed. At the time it opened, F.P.A. (Franklin P. Adams), the columnist and critic, gazed into his clouded crystal ball and predicted that the songs would never become popular. The tunes, he complained, were impossible to whistle. (What the public wanted, according to Adams, were songs like "Toyland, Toyland," "Nancy Brown" and "I've Got Bells on My Fingers." Who, he demanded, could remember the words to "Anything Goes"?)

Less than two months after the show's premiere, *Time* (in its January 7, 1935, issue) gave the answer: everyone who mattered.

"So popular are composer Porter's lyrics that it is now considered the smart thing to know them all by heart, to rattle them off loudly whenever and wherever the tune is played," *Time* reported in their story on the New Year's dance that Mrs. Franklin Roosevelt staged for her sons Franklin Jr. and John at the White House. Typically, Mrs. Roosevelt was amused by Cole's lyrical report on the topsy-turvy world conditions:

So Mrs. R., with all her trimmin's
Can broadcast a bed for Simmons
'Cause Franklin knows
Anything Goes!

Time dubbed Cole "The Man of the Hour."

Then, in a rash of other magazine stories, various writers announced that he was forty-three, forty-two and forty-one years old; "small," "smallish" and "elfin"; "slender" and "round-faced"; "urbane" and a man "given to roaring enthusiasms." One reporter observed, "He is Broadway, but of the Broadway Brahmans." Another noted that he looked "party-fatigued and sleep weary"—as well he might, had he attended the "four or five parties each night" mentioned by a newspaper interviewer, and then slept only "from sun-up until 10 A.M.," as another claimed.

For still other reporters, Cole listed his likes and dislikes. He liked: cats, parties, swimming, scandal, crime news, people, tabloids, films and Peru, Indiana. In music, he preferred Stravinsky, Bach, Mozart, Gershwin and Rodgers.

He disliked or was indifferent to: baseball, steam-heated rooms, golf, poetry, Belgium, pressed duck and English railway hotels. And he might have added being interviewed. Karl Bernstein, who acted as press agent on many of Cole's shows, said later that he behaved in the same way in regard to *Anything Goes* as to his final show, *Silk Stockings*. "He was self-contained, aloof and above the fray." Bernstein recalled. "He wanted no publicity—unless you could convince him that it would help the show. He never wanted his picture taken—but once you persuaded him to allow the photographer in, you had no trouble keeping him in front of the camera. In fact, just the reverse."

Certainly, he became one of the best publicized celebrities in the United States directly after the opening of *Anything Goes*. So much so that RKO-Radio Pictures capitalized on his name in publicizing the film version of *The Gay Divorcee* despite the fact that only "Night and Day" was used from the Porter score.

Fox Pictures got into the act too, announcing that they had hired Cole to do the songs for *Adios Argentina*, which, according to *Film Daily*, Cole would compose in the East, recording the numbers in a variety of ways and sending them to California for acceptance or rejection. What *Film Daily* didn't say was that Fox was obviously impressed enough with his new eminence to announce the studio was also preparing *Nymph Errant* with Alice Faye as the English schoolgirl.

Neither project reached production. (Eventually, however, "Don't Fence Me In" emerged from the *Adios Argentina* score; and shortly after Cole's death, 20th Century-Fox once again announced *Nymph Errant*, this time as a vehicle for Julie Andrews.)

A project that had long been simmering came to a boil

when Cole lunched with Moss Hart on the day following the opening of *Anything Goes*. Hart, who had come to the fore in 1930 when he and George S. Kaufman lampooned Hollywood in a farce called *Once in a Lifetime,* had had a couple of hits since. He had first met Cole at the Ritz bar in Paris when he delivered a pair of garters with gold clasps—dancer Georgie Hale's Christmas gift—to the songwriter. The next evening, Hart dined with the Porters and the two men talked about doing a show together. Now in 1934 the time seemed to have arrived, except that Cole was committed to producer Max Gordon while Hart was with Sam H. Harris. Cole solved that problem by suggesting that Gordon and Harris become co-producers. Hart's only other objection lay in the fact that he had promised himself to winter in some sunny clime. Why, he asked, not go to Morocco to write the show?

Cole had a better idea. Bali, Or the South Seas—or Africa—or the world!

The two would-be collaborators betook themselves to a travel agent and before the afternoon was out had arranged for a world tour.

Linda was delighted.

Howard Sturges was eager to accompany them.

Two days before sailing, Cole suddenly realized how much joy the trip would give his pal Monty Woolley. At that moment, Woolley was a guest of the Herman Oelrichs. Although it was past midnight, Cole went to their home, was admitted and went to a guest room where Woolley was slumbering. Shaking him into consciousness, Cole announced that he had just forty-eight hours to pack for a world tour.

When the party left New York, it included Cole and Linda, Hart, Sturges, Woolley and a travel writer named Bill Powell. They sailed on the Cunard White Star liner *Franconia.* There were 250 aboard, but it is safe to say that the contents of Cole's luggage were unique. Among the special equipment he had brought were a metronome, a typewriter, a small piano-organ, twenty-four black pencils, a quire of music paper, recordings of the songs of *Anything Goes,* a phonograph and three cases of Grand Chambertin '87.

At presailing festivities, Cole entertained a sizable number of theatrical and society figures as well as the press. To the last named, he poked gentle fun at the Cunard release which stated that he was going around the world by way of California to put "the rhythm of the Equator" into his next show. "I find on reading Cunard literature that I am to get inspiration in out-of-the-way places; I suppose this is really what I am after. I will look. Mr. Hart will look for a musical comedy somewhere between Hawaii and Tahiti and Samoa and the Fiji Islands, and perhaps we will capture something of Bali, although I have never seen Bali before," a *Herald Tribune* reporter quoted him as saying. Then he added, "Most of the music in that part of the world is played from memory. If I can write it down fast enough, I may get another 'Night and Day' out of it."

While Cole was holding his press conference, Howard Lindsay and Russel Crouse had sequestered their bon voyage gift into his stateroom. She was an ugly carved statue with a bulging figure. The perpetrators of the joke expected him to have her tossed overboard as soon as the ship reached the high seas. Not at all. Cole ordered native costumes for her at each port and threw an elegant cocktail party in her honor.

Not everything was play, even though he and Hart had pledged not to work until they had reached Panama. The voyage was to be fun, fun, fun and Moss Hart confessed that he had presumed that nothing constructive would be accomplished. What he failed to realize was that both he and his collaborator were compulsive workers. By the time they arrived at the Canal Zone, Cole had finished a song and Hart had completed a scene.

Later, Hart was to admit to envying Cole his attitude. The latter could and did work hard, but he never allowed work to interfere with his joy at being alive or his need to involve himself in the life that was swirling about him. Hart was astonished when Cole composed songs on the sundeck, flying over Africa, climbing among Indian ruins and "never once, come weal or woe, did it interfere with his personal life."

When the ship stopped briefly on the West Coast, the Porter party visited Hollywood where MGM gave a dinner for Linda; Fox gave one for Cole; and in the afternoon the Irving Berlins gave a party for both of them. When Mrs. Berlin brought over the legendary Louis B. Mayer, who was purported to be terror personified to those working in films, Cole burst out laughing, thinking he looked exactly like a shark. Mayer took umbrage at the reaction and informed him that MGM had got along without Cole Porter for years and would continue to do so. Cole stood his ground, and a few days after leaving Hollywood he received a cable from Mayer offering him a job. He ignored it. This was followed by another and another until at last the offer became too attractive to resist. Cole wired acceptance to work on an original film musical.

In the South Seas, he found life consistently interesting. To a photographer who took his and Hart's picture wearing flower necklaces, he suggested the caption: "Just an old Hawaiian lei." From Pago Pago, Cole wired Tallulah Bankhead, who was appearing in a revival of *Rain* on Broadway: "It may be raining on Broadway, but it's dry as hell here." And as a dedicated sightseer, he made it a point to view a cannibal who was under arrest for eating a missionary.

At one point, a slight contretemps developed between Linda and Moss Hart. Although the rest of the party had taken to polo shirts, shorts and sandals, Hart continued to dress in what she considered too formal attire in the wrong situations. One morning, in a moment of excessive high spirits, she went to Hart's stateroom, gathered up his wardrobe and pitched it overboard. Hart was beside himself. Cole announced that Linda would replace it. Hart didn't want it replaced. Eventually Linda turned on the charm and replaced the wardrobe. Good feeling was restored.

At another point during the voyage, Linda chanced to remark that she had always longed for an audience with the Sultan of Zanzibar but understood that it was almost impossible to arrange. The impossible was a challenge Cole welcomed. He immediately went into action, contacting both Lady Cunard and Duff Cooper.

Then, on April 10, he casually showed Linda a cable from the Castle Mail Steamship Company. It was addressed to the Cruise Director, RMS, *Franconia.* Kilindini Mombasa (East Africa). "For your information we beg to advise you that we have received the following cablegram from our Zanzibar agents, Messers Smith, MacKenzie, Smith and Co.: 'Advise Cruise Director, Franconia, audience Sultan arranged for Cole Porter party. Private secretary will meet them on board at 10:30. Yours faithfully."

The invitation was RSVP and the requirements were specific. For Linda, wardrobe was no problem; for the men it was another matter. They were to wear white suits, white topees, white shoes and black ties. Cole had a white suit. Sturges had a natural pongee that would do. Woolley had a tan and white seersucker. And at one stop, a tailor whipped up white suits for Hart and Bill Powell within two hours. Linda selected a white sports dress, a white hat and pearls. The pearls, Powell later noted, "made the Sultan sit up and take notice."

At 10:30 on the appointed day, the Sultan's equerry Saunders-Jones, an Englishman with an Oxonian accent, arrived in the royal launch, which was manned by an old salt with a beard and a red fez. The sailors wore khaki shorts and blue skating caps, which Cole said made them look more like chorus boys than a crew.

The palace turned out to be a dazzlingly white, two-story, rambling stucco structure guarded by a lone, red-fezzed sentry. Once they entered it, a robed attendant took their topees and they ascended the carved, solid-ebony staircase that led to the throne room on the second floor. This room ran across the front of the palace and had dead-white walls on three sides. The fourth was given over to French windows which opened onto a veranda. Through the window the Sultan's two yachts could be seen.

To Cole, the Sultan's throne on a dais opposite the windows was the most interesting feature of all. It was only a large chair upholstered in vermilion velvet. Behind it, adding to its regal appearance, was a huge wooden carved back decorated by a lion and a unicorn. And above it were three elaborate chandeliers which lighted the throne, a painting of Queen Victoria and one of King Edward VII.

The equerry informed the party that His Highness' full title was Seyyid Khalifa Bin Harub el B'assaidi, KCMG, K.B.E. He said that since Zanzibar had become a British protectorate the Sultan was a figurehead, a person whose opinion was always sought during weekly meetings of the governor, the financial adviser (the Sultan's fortune was largely in cloves) and the Sultan's equerry, even though one and all understood that this request for the Sultan's point of view was merely a formality. As a token ruler, he was destined to appeal to Cole's theatrical sense of the ridiculous. Yet when Cole saw the little throne facing the French windows, he was moved to wonder whether the Sultan didn't secretly harbor a wish to escape.

When His Highness appeared, he turned out to be a coffee-colored, affable, middle-aged (fifty-seven) gentleman who sported a spade beard. His eyes were partly gray, partly brown. Linda thought he was dashing, but Cole claimed to have detected a bored look.

During the audience, the Sultan, who had been educated by an English tutor, informed them that although he was in the midst of a three-day fast and could not join them, he wanted them to partake of a local delicacy—sherbet. (The equerry later told them that it was a tribute to Lady Cunard for the Sultan to have received them; during this semiannual ritual he was "more elusive than your Miss Garbo.")

His Highness inquired after Lady Cunard and Duff Cooper and informed his guests that only that morning he had received a ping-pong set from England, a gift from Lady Cunard. ("He seemed disappointed that none of us challenged him to a game," Cole said.) Then the Sultan announced that he had a special treat for them. With great ceremony, two servants carried in an ancient victrola, wound it up, set the needle and the party sat in silence as the beaming host watched them listen to a very scratchy recording of Irene Bordoni singing "Night and Day."

During the trip back to the *Franconia,* Linda asked Saunders-Jones how many wives the Sultan had. It turned out he had only one. Linda inquired what she was like, but Saunders-Jones could not say. He had never seen her. The whole adventure was of the kind Cole pursued relentlessly and never forgot.

When the party finally returned to New York four and a half months and some 34,000 miles later, Cole had amassed most of the songs needed for the new musical, *Jubilee.* One number had come from the audience with the Sultan of Zanzibar, one from a native dance witnessed in Martinique; a third was inspired by the music of Bali. In Kingston, Jamaica, while on a guided tour, he heard a strange sound. He asked the guide what it was. A kling-kling bird, was the answer. And where was it? In the divi-divi tree.

"Song title!" cried Cole—and that's what he made it.

When the ship docked both Cole and Moss Hart were to be met by their respective mothers. Hart, during the tour, had often entertained the group with stories of his mother's ingenuousness. When he suddenly had become affluent, he had simply led the family away from their grimy tenement apartment and installed them in a luxurious one in Manhattan. His mother, who had always had to watch pennies, could hardly understand her good fortune. When he told her to name anything in the world she wanted, she considered the offer carefully and then chose a charge account at Macy's.

Quite by accident, on the day of the *Franconia*'s arrival, Mrs. Barnett Hart and Mrs. Samuel Porter fell into conversation, discovered each other's identity and spent an enjoyable half hour matching stories about their talented sons. So enjoyable, in fact, that in the taxi that was taking

Mrs. Hart and her son uptown, she commented with some surprise: "You know, that Mrs. Porter—she's very nice, very, very nice for a country woman!"

During the world tour, Cole had taken time from playing and writing the score for *Jubilee* to turn out additional lyrics for the London version of *Anything Goes* which C. B. Cochran was producing. Fearful that the topical allusions of "You're the Top" might lose impact on English audiences, Cochran wanted substitutions made. Cole agreed and set about converting the Bendel bonnet into an Ascot bonnet; a dress by Saks into one by Patou; and the eyes of Irene Bordoni into those of Tallulah Bankhead.

The same sort of alterations were performed on the title song. For the United States Cole had twitted the Roosevelts, the Rockefellers and Mrs. Ned McLean. For England he restrained himself, mentioning none of the royal family but only Parliament and the Chancellor of the Exchequer:

But while we hope for days more sunny
The government gets our money
'Cause Neville knows
Anything goes!

Finally on June 14, 1935, the London production opened at the Palace Theater. Critics were less than impressed by the improvised quality of the book, which seemed to have lost its topicality. But the major problem revolved around the casting of Jeanne Aubert as Reno Sweeney. Even in her native language Miss Aubert was no Merman, but in English the thick Gallic accent rendered the lyrics of "I Get a Kick Out of You" and other numbers unintelligible. Even Jack Whiting's personal triumph as Billy Crocker (a character named for one of Cole's pals from Yale) was not enough to save the show. Especially since Sydney Howard failed to bring to "Public Enemy 13" the helpless, lovable quality which made Victor Moore's characterization unforgettable.*

Cole, meanwhile, had gone to the West Coast where he and Moss Hart intended holding auditions for *Jubilee.* They put up at the Beverly-Wilshire Hotel and he informed the manager that he would need the services of a top-flight secretary who was capable of screening all callers. The manager, aware of Cole's uncompromising standards, knew just the person—Sylvia Lewis. Miss Lewis, a former newspaperwoman and public-relations representative, was at the time part owner of a secretarial service, but she took this assignment herself. "I was with him only a short time," she once said. "But I never forgot the experience. He was egocentric, difficult, demanding to work for in the sense that everything had to be done well. He was also charming. If he had never written a lyric or a note of music, he would have been a fascinating personality. Cole Porter was far harder to know than Moss, but it was worth the effort. He recognized quality in others as he recognized it in himself. And when he got it, he was so appreciative. He got me. It may sound conceited, but I think he recognized that just as he was top-flight in his field, I was in mine."

Disappointment was in store for Cole when he set out to secure the services of a number of performers who turned out to be under contract to film studios, but still he remained in an expansive mood as one piece of good news after another rolled in about *Anything Goes.* To help him and Hart cast the show, Cole enlisted the aid of Louis Shurr, who was now operating both in New York and Hollywood. Shurr managed to line up an impressive list of talented personalities for auditions, and everyone was happy.

The premise of *Jubilee* concerns a king of a mythical country who is about to celebrate his diamond jubilee. Not

* The same problem plagued Hugh O'Connell, who played the part in the West Coast company. In the Gaxton-Whiting role, a young song-and-dance man (later Senator from California), George Murphy, proved moderately successful.

only the king but also the queen, the prince and the princess are eager to cut loose and have some fun. They decide to do so—and disappear. What they do is the basis of the book.

For the prince and his American showgirl inamorata, Charles Walters and June Knight were signed. A character comedienne, May Boley, delighted Cole by her playing, combining sympathy and satire, of the Elsa Maxwell character. Both Cole and Moss Hart were enthusiastic about Melville Cooper for the vacillating king. Yet their major enthusiasm was reserved for Mary Boland, a former stage star who had been appearing in films but was willing to undertake the part of the vulgar queen. Looking over the assemblage of talent, Cole became so euphoric in his estimation of its box-office potential that he decided to break his rule against investing in his own work. He sank $18,000 in the show.

He had good reason to feel optimistic. He was a man who behaved gracefully both in defeat and success and now he was having a gratifying taste of the latter. On the basis of his past achievements, MGM volunteered to provide a major portion of the backing for *Jubilee* without even hearing the score. What, he must have asked himself, could go wrong?

In addition to the excellent cast lined up in Hollywood, the producers had signed Mark Plant, Montgomery Clift, Jackie Kelk, Margaret Adams and Derek Williams. The scenery, which was to be provided by Jo Mielziner, promised to be some of his most eye-catching and there were not one but two costume designers.

Rehearsals moved along uneventfully even though production director Hassard Short and dialogue director Monty Woolley frequently clashed and Woolley was eventually sacked. Characteristically, in such professional matters Cole remained aloof and impersonal, taking neither side of the quarrel even though Woolley was a personal friend. For Cole the show came first.

On the surface everything else functioned smoothly. Even the ambitious Sapphic-ode number, spoken in Greek as June Knight danced (causing the male chorus singers to exclaim over her beauty while the females hurled epithets at her) presented few problems. And when another number proved to be a dud, Cole turned out a complicated octette "Mr. and Mrs. Smith" for the second act.

Still, there were mysterious forces at work. Spiteful little tricks were being played on various members of the cast: a ripped shirt here, a missing prop there . . . nothing to speak of really. And then on the day the company was to leave for Boston came the deluge of threatening letters. Mary Boland received one, as did Max Gordon and Sam Harris and Moss Hart and Cole. Letters that warned them that they were leaving Manhattan at the risk of their lives. Cole suggested that the producers take an ad assuring rivals that the show wasn't all that good. He refused to view the situation more seriously even after they arrived at their Boston hotels and received second letters threatening death if the recipients stepped inside the theater.

Miss Boland, understandably somewhat jittery about her return to the theater after three years in Hollywood, suddenly began to come unglued. A twenty-four hour guard was assigned.

At that point, June Knight, who had hitherto been unmolested, received a letter that left her in such a state of nerves that she canceled an interview with Marjorie Adams of the Boston *Globe*, causing cynics to suspect a publicity stunt.

Ignoring the crisis, Cole applied himself by writing a new song. Leaving the theater in the afternoon of the day preceding dress rehearsal, he went to his room in the Ritz-Carlton, locked himself in and composed the music and lyrics for "Gather Ye Autographs" (which was not inspired by the letters). By 6:00 A.M. the next morning, he had completed the song. By 7:00 A.M., it was sent off to orchestrator Robert Russell Bennett. By 3:00 that afternoon, it was in musical director Frank Tours' hands. By the time dress rehearsal was called, a somewhat ragged rendition of the number was ready.

Not so Miss Boland. Early in the morning, she had

begun bolstering her courage by taking an occasional nip. As the day progressed, she grew more and more certain that she was a sniper's target and took more and more nips. That night, she managed an unsteady entrance only to find herself in a very unqueenly position. Helped up, she made it to her dressing room and did not return. Thus, the $150,000 production was forced to do without its star and box-office insurance at the final dress rehearsal. Understudy Olive Reeves-Smith walked through the role.

While everyone else sank into gloom, Cole greeted threats and mishaps alike with ever-increasing glee. Associates in all his ventures were always mystified by this seemingly ambivalent attitude. On the one hand, he was devoted to the theater. Yet he always showed a chortling lack of concern about mistakes. "He was always delighted with calamities," his friend R. C. Kelly once said. "A missed cue, a blackout that didn't happen, only caused him to hope they'd fix it some day. I've seen Moss practically tear the back end off the theater when something went wrong, but Cole would lean back and laugh instead of hitting the panic button."

This, of course, did not prevent him from being demanding, caustic and insistent about getting the musical effects he wanted from arrangers, conductors or singers. The last were expected to possess perfect diction and to perform the songs as written. (In the late 1940's, he once sent Frank Sinatra a telegram asking why Sinatra sang his songs if he didn't like the way they were written.) For the rest of the production, Cole displayed a more relaxed standard, as if it really did not matter that much, which in his eyes it may not have since his work seemed easiest when the characters and situations were unimportant enough to leave him relatively unhampered.

By opening night in Boston, the repentant Miss Boland had pulled herself together and, despite all the stresses, the performance went more smoothly than anyone might have had reason to hope. The only incident to mar the occasion was a minor fire in the wardrobe room.

Audience reaction was favorable and the reviews

encouraging. But the authors and producers were far from sanguine. At the request of Moss Hart, Cole turned out a new number in eight hours. All of it except one adjective, that is. That one eluded him. As usual in such a situation, he sought the aid of friends, after trying various rhyming dictionaries, thesauruses, etc. Finally, architect Ed Tauch suggested "gossamer." The line became "A trip to the moon on gossamer wings." The song, of course, was "Just One of Those Things."

Finally on Saturday, October 12, 1935, *Jubilee* opened at the Imperial Theater in New York. Once again the jinx was working. Because of inadequate police protection, autograph-seekers and celebrity-chasers gained control of the situation and 100 of them managed to crash the theater, refusing to leave until additional police arrived to help escort them out.

The Porters were cheered by the crowd as they appeared, even the unfriendly elements succumbing to the resplendent Linda, who was dazzling in a new diamond and aquamarine necklace which Cole had designed to commemorate the occasion. As usual, she had presented him with a special cigarette case.

The show, which Moss Hart had facetiously described as "a cross between *The Merry Widow* and *As Thousands Cheer,*" was a satiric operetta with a far more cohesive book than most of the productions with which Cole had associated himself. It follows the four members of the royal family through various amorous involvements. The queen falls in love with a Tarzan-type swimmer (Mark Plant) whom she meets at a Greek masque given by an Elsa Maxwell-like party-giver. The princess becomes involved with a supersophisticated director-actor-writer. And the prince is bewitched by an American dancer. Along the way there is ample opportunity for satiric jabs at modern mores both in the United States and abroad.

Although the critics made minor complaints on the count that the libretto and lyrics suffered from too many inside jokes, all but one of the daily reviewers praised the show. Burns Mantle of the *Daily News* led the cheers and stirred up a furor by breaking his review in the final Sunday edition whereas other critics held their notices for the Monday paper. By so doing, he gave even wider circulation to his uncontained enthusiasm—enthusiasm which led him to call this the best musical since *Show Boat*.

Today, legend has it that "Begin the Beguine" was overlooked. This is not strictly true. It received neither more nor less attention than "Our Crown" or "The Kling-Kling Bird in the Divi-Divi Tree." It did receive more attention than "Just One of Those Things," which, with few exceptions, was ignored. "Begin the Beguine" simply did not excite the public in 1935. A year later, Artie Shaw's recording started it on its way to enduring popularity.

Backstage on opening night the principals had received yet another batch of threatening letters, although no actual trouble occurred. But on November 13, fires broke out at three different times, resulting in $20,000 worth of damage to the scenery. The evening performance had to be canceled. This latest fire made it evident that the show was plagued by an arsonist. Consequently, two guards were stationed backstage at each performance. Harris also hired a private detective agency. (Why neither the city nor the insurance agency intervened is a mystery.) When the detective had gathered sufficient evidence to identify the culprit, that fact was made clear to the guilty party. Thereafter, all problems ceased.

Who was it? Libel laws prevent identification. However, there were several children connected with the production, and who can say to what lengths a disgruntled stage mother may be prepared to go to revenge lack of appreciation of her child's abilities?

Two days after the fire, the Porters sailed for Bermuda where, with their guests Mrs. Herman Oelrichs and Moss Hart, they occupied the Vincent Astor house for three weeks while Cole prepared himself for his first Hollywood assignment.

Jubilee, which opened so auspiciously, closed after only 169 performances. On January 6, 1936, Miss Boland missed a performance because of "severe abdominal pains," according to newspapers. Soon she was to miss more. Not long after, her agent instituted a campaign to secure her release so that she could return to Hollywood where a "picture offer" awaited. Since it is possible to hold a star to her contract but impossible to force her to give a good performance, the release was granted. Once she left, box-office receipts dropped precipitously. The show closed. Cole lost his entire investment. Never again could he be persuaded to invest a penny of his millions in a Broadway production.

To him Miss Boland had been guilty of a breach of confidence he could not forgive. He was repelled at the thought of anyone squandering talent, associating as he did acceptance with success and rejection with failure—so much so that he ever after found it difficult to say a kind word about her. When a friend informed him that she was writing her autobiography and noted that he hoped Cole would like the book, Cole shot back: "I'd have to like the *book* better than I like her."

CHAPTER IX

"Hollywood? It's rather like living on the moon, isn't it?" Cole inquired of a reporter who had asked him how he liked the film capital. He quickly added that he had been warned that nobody talked about anything except motion pictures, but luckily he didn't want to talk about anything else. It was an old ploy, this alternately tweaking the nose of authority and then flattering it. And it worked just as well on the reporter as on Mrs. Cornelius Vanderbilt, whom Cole customarily and mischievously addressed as "Mrs. Corny."

The Porters rented the Richard Barthelmess house, arriving in December 1935. It was the kind of house that was considered fitting for a great star in the 1920's and '30's. It had the inevitable swimming pool and tennis courts, although the taste was somewhat more restrained than in the abodes of some of Hollywood's elite.

Cole immediately became an enthusiast of Southern California. At this period, he took what he called "sun coloring" seriously, dousing himself with an evil-smelling concoction of oil and vinegar which he found an effective tanning lotion and wearing a reflector around his neck so that he tanned evenly under the chin.

Linda was not so enthusiastic. The climate proved to

have a deleterious effect on her respiratory system, which was giving her trouble, and the film colony never fascinated her as legitimate theater stars had. However, there were plenty of congenial friends about. Howard Sturges was there. Dr. Albert Sirmay visited, as did R. C. Kelly, Cleveland columnist Winsor French, pianist Roger Stearns and many others.

For French and Stearns, the Porters provided a guest house, including every detail from liquor to postage stamps. In his room, French was amazed to find a typed list of the private telephone numbers of Hollywood's biggest stars, none of whom he knew.

According to French, each evening around 10:00 P.M. Cole sat down to write a song. When his work struck him as worthwhile, French reported to Cleveland readers, ". . . it was his unfortunate habit to drift toward the house I shared with Roger Stearns so they could sit down to the piano together and spin his latest brainchild into an endless duet. On one occasion, if anyone cares, I listened to 'Rap Tap on Wood' for not less than six hours."

Cole's songwriting for the film industry made it easy for him to adjust to Hollywood. For Linda there was no simple out. Her idea of an amusing time did not coincide with what went on in Hollywood social circles. Even when Mary Garden turned up and was tendered a dinner by Adrian, the costume designer, Linda found the evening trying. According to a columnist, the high point occurred when finger bowls were placed in front of the guests. In each bowl a gardenia floated, beneath which lay an unopened oyster shell. Each guest was given a sharp knife to pry open the shell and discovered a Japanese cultured pearl. "The celebs got a thrill out of making the discovery," the columnist reported. Whether Linda's distaste for Hollywood intensified her dislike of pearls or vice versa, she eventually sold hers.

Nor did she enjoy Hollywood's custom of combining business and social affairs. Since there seemed no other alternative, she gracefully acquiesced, but the strain was always there, as on one evening when their guests included columnist Louella Parsons and her husband, Doc Martin. Doc had had more than a few too many drinks and before leaving he proceeded to be sick in a corner of the Porters' drawing room. Cole, who had had almost as much as his guest, ordered Doc out of the house, despite warnings of others present to remember Miss Parsons' power and her reputation for being a tough in-fighter. But Cole remained adamant. The Martins left. So did many of the Porters' diffident film-star guests. Miss Parsons, however, proved herself far less vindictive than rumored, always printing favorable squibs about Cole and maintaining friendly relations with him until his death.

Such incidents only increased Linda's reservations about the West. She was repelled by the hard-drinking film colony, holding with the European conviction that strong drink destroys one's ability to savor fine cuisine. A light drinker herself, she abhorred dining with guests in various stages of intoxication. Eventually she set a two-cocktail limit before dinner. Cole, who preferred three, deferred to her wishes. (Strangely, even after her respiratory problems made it impossible for her to spend time in California, he continued the two-drink rule in his home, although in a restaurant his guests could have as many cocktails as they desired.)

Another custom which left Linda dissatisfied with the conversational quality was the after-dinner problem created by the ladies' disappearing for long periods into the powder room to gossip. She studied the situation carefully and decided there was only one civilized course of action. She locked the main powder room. Anyone who insisted upon going was sent to an upstairs guest room. Each went alone and then returned to join the party.

In addition, Linda was not always happy with the level of talk. When it wasn't devoted to films, it was often peppered with scatology and obscenity. No prude, she nevertheless found it tiring. During one dinner, it seemed out of hand. At last, she turned to a vivacious former dancing star who was the chief offender and said quietly, "My dear, I've heard all those words before. I've even done most of them, but I'd prefer not having to dine on them."

Despite her reservations, Linda realized that her husband reveled in the atmosphere and, for a time, she thought of buying a house in California. She and Cole considered the Barthelmess place and eventually rejected it. The second year they were there she spent considerable time looking at estates in the company of a guest, Baron Nicholas de Gunzberg. (Both Porters had known him since the middle 1920's. Linda had immediately become friendly with him. Cole had been put off by the Baron's somber, White Russian manner, considering him gloomy, but in Hollywood he decided that the Baron was not at all glum and boring, and the two became lifelong friends. The Baron afterward maintained that it had taken Hollywood to make Cole appreciate him.) Among the estates that he and Linda looked over was Valentino's Falcon's Lair, but neither it nor any other pleased her. At one point, architect Ed Tauch was commissioned to draw up plans to build, then Linda's health problems became so severe that she decided she could never endure the climate and the project was abandoned. Even so, Cole was reluctant to give up his sojourns there.

Probably no other facet of his life is so fully documented (unfortunately) as his experience in writing his first full score for a film, *Born to Dance*. After each significant meeting, he would dictate his impressions to his social secretary, Miss Margaret Moore, who had accompanied the Porters to the West Coast.

The diary, in slightly abridged form, not only provides a clear picture of the industry, but also illustrates Cole's ability both to laugh at and cooperate with business associates. It begins:

> FRIDAY, December 20, 1935: Went to Sam Katz's [executive producer] office. He could not have been more charming and told me that unlike other productions on the MGM lot, my picture would not be the result of havoc, as most of them are. After having explained that he had engaged Jack McGowan and Sidney Silvers to

construct the book of my picture, he called them in and they told me the idea of their story.

The idea was based on the recent escapade of Jack Barrymore and Elaine Barrie. Sam Katz explained that what they wanted to do was to have Clark Gable play the Jack Barrymore part, and Jean Harlow the Elaine Barrie part. I held out for more singers in the principal leads, and they finally decided that if the girl playing the love interest opposite Gable could sing, the trio would be a very strong box office draw.

When the conference was over, Sam Katz said, "Come back in a few weeks." I left feeling that once we started all would be peaceful.

MONDAY, January 6, 1936: Dined with Sam Katz in the commissary on the MGM lot. Present: Sid Silvers, Jack McGowan, and a new author named Hatch . . . a certain Mr. Pye . . . another gentleman whose name I did not catch, but obviously an assistant to Sam Katz, and Alex Aarons, whom I had known in New York, but who now is also working for Katz.

After dinner we went to Sam Katz's office for a conference. Immediately I was told that all idea of the original story, and of having Clark Gable and Jean Harlow, had been discarded. Sam held forth that it was dangerous to have two principal leads who could not sing, play in a musical, and suggested that whatever story we decided upon should be done by singing and dancing people. I remarked that this had been my contention when the first conference took place, but that they had persuaded me that the box-office draw of two such great stars as Gable and Harlow would give the picture importance, which would make up for their not singing. So I found myself holding up for their ideas at the first conference, and they holding up for mine at this second conference. Soon it became evident that the authors had no story in mind at all. . . .

Then someone said, "I have a great idea for the beginning of a picture. Why not show in an opening chorus a long line of people waiting to see the body of a dead movie actor, and then take up the separate lives of the people who are waiting in line." This was met with great enthusiasm for a few minutes, and then suddenly the whole crowd turned on the suggestion.

Several other suggestions were presented. Finally Jack McGowan said to me, "Cole, why don't you write an opening chorus, and it may be we can get a story from that?" . . .

Then, one by one each of the people at the conference took me in the other room, patted me on the back and told me not to worry. As a parting shot, Sam Katz said to the authors, "Try to think of a story within a reasonable time, and when you get it, let Cole know." The authors then gaily suggested to Sam Katz that they all have a vacation in the desert, and he said, "Yes, boys, by all means."

Then Sam Katz drew me aside and said, "Now, Cole, don't worry about authors, because I can spend $200,000 on authors in order to give you the right script. Goodbye, Cole, come back in a few weeks."

This was the end of the conference.

MONDAY, January 13, 1936: Present: Eric Hatch, Alexander Aarons, Jack Cummings. They came up to the house for lunch, as a result of having called me up and told me that at last they had a great idea for my picture.

On arrival, Jack Cummings took me aside and told me that McGowan and Silvers had been thrown out of the picture, as they were exhausted from just having finished *Broadway Melody*.

Jack Cummings is to be the producer of my picture, and he is another member of "The Family." "The Family" means that he is related to Louis B. Mayer, as is practically every other person you meet on the Metro lot.

The idea of the picture was this—a boy and a girl on rival newspaper syndicates try separately to win the

Pulitzer Prize for the best-written newspaper story of the year. They are in love, but in competition, and finally together write a story which wins the prize.

Cummings suggested that we show relief maps of two hemispheres, and that, say, we were going to cover a story in Tibet, an electric line would take us from the newspaper office across America, over the Pacific into a certain spot in the Himalayas. This method of presenting sketches to be used throughout the picture.

As it was explained to me, I liked it much better than anything that had been suggested so far, and we parted very exhilarated.

TUESDAY, January 14, 1936: Sam Katz telephoned me and asked me to be at his house at 2:00 P.M. for a conference. I went there and found Cummings, McGowan and Silvers. Before we started, Sam drew me aside and told me that Hatch had been thrown out of the picture. He then announced to us all that he had just had a meeting with Louis B. Mayer, and that Mayer definitely wanted my picture to be a revue, in order to utilize all of the stars on the lot. Then there was a long discussion as to whether or not to use *As Thousands Cheer*, which Metro owns. Once more they all suggested to me that I write a new "Man Bites Dog," which was the opening sketch in the stage production of *As Thousands Cheer*. I killed this as soon as possible, knowing I could not possibly top Irving's [Berlin] number.

By this time all thought of *As Thousands Cheer* had disappeared, and Sam said, "I don't think we should use *As Thousands Cheer* at all. I think we should make this the *Metro Revue*, and all we need is a central idea to start if off."

Silvers, thinking of the days when he used to be a stooge for Phil Baker in vaudeville, suggested we open by showing him in the box of a theater watching a stage performance. No one liked this idea, and for half an hour there was complete havoc. Then I suggested that it might be interesting to base our revue on the different sections of a newspaper. If this device were taken, all we would have to do would be to plant the newspaper in the beginning, then turn the pages to find our different sketches. They all leaped at this, as if I had suddenly discovered radium, and Sam suggested that after such a great idea I should go to the desert and take three weeks' rest. Silvers and McGowan then asked it they could go too. . . . I insisted that we begin work on this revue immediately, and here in Hollywood, as time was flying, so it was decided that tomorrow Silvers and McGowan come to the house at 2:00 P.M., and we talk all afternoon—every afternoon. They wanted to come in the morning at 11:00 and remain all day, but I firmly announced it was too long a session for me, and that I did my best work alone. . . .

WEDNESDAY, January 15, 1936: Present: Jack McGowan, Sid Silvers.

They appeared immediately after lunch and announced that, after thinking the matter over, they did not like the revue being based upon the different sections of a newspaper. They began to discuss the Eric Hatch idea of the boy and girl rivalry on a newspaper, and decided they did not like that either. Then McGowan suggested we do a picture based upon the pursuit of John Barrymore by Elaine Barrie, and give up all idea of writing a revue, but instead do a straight musical story.

I suggested that Sam Katz's reason for wanting me to do a revue was to utilize all the stars on the lot. Then Silvers asked me, "Do you *want* to do a revue?" I said, "No, I don't believe I do, unless we can find a revolutionary idea, but I have great respect for Sam Katz, and as long as he clings to a revue so much, I want to give him a few days before I tell him definitely that nobody has been able to present an idea good enough to warrant doing one." At this Silvers and McGowan yelled with joy, and said, "We don't want to do a revue either and we had hoped you would say yesterday that you didn't, when we all met. . . ."

THURSDAY, January 16, 1936: Present: Sid Silvers, Jack McGowan.

Arrived 3:00 P.M. I asked them whether or not they had found overnight, any idea for a revue, and . . . they had not thought of pictures since they left the house yesterday. . . . McGowan then brought up a play that he had written in New York last year for Harry Richman called *Say When*, and asked me whether I would like to use it. I could not remember it well, after so long a time, so he told me the story of *Say When*. I asked whether Metro owned this, and he said no, but he thought if I asked for it they would buy it from him.

By this time we realized it was entirely useless that we ever meet again, and I made an appointment with them to go to Sam Katz's office tomorrow and tell him the way we feel about his revue. On the way out they both asked me to come to their office about half an hour before the appointment so that we could all say the same thing.

Then they said good-night.

FRIDAY, January 17, 1936: Went to the office of Jack McGowan and Sid Silvers at 11:30, and they were both in a state of jitters, and also rather terrified at the idea of announcing to Sam Katz that we did not want to do a revue, but I told them not to worry, that I thought I could explain our reasons without upsetting him too much.

So at 12:00 we went to the office of Sam Katz. In came Jack Cummings, who had obviously been ordered to listen in. I explained to Sam that after a great deal of conversation amongst us about some angle for a revue, we could get no further, because in our hearts none of us wanted to do a revue, and that the boys had contributed nothing to me and I had contributed nothing to them. I told him I felt guilty accepting so large an amount of money per week and not being able to work on something about which I was enthusiastic. Told him what I could do well would be a Cinderalla story on a low-comedy premise, with Eleanor Powell in mind. I could see that he was very disappointed, but was somewhat assuaged by my suggestion, in that it included the person of all who he is trying to make an important star—Eleanor Powell. So he very nicely said, "Then boys, we will give up all idea of a revue, and all you have to do is find what Cole is looking for." McGowan suggested a musical, based upon a six-day bicycle race. Silvers did not like this, and thought a radio story would show off Powell to her greatest tap-dancing ability. . . . Suddenly Silvers thought of a musical play that he, McGowan and Buddy De Sylva had worked on four years ago, about two sailors and the hostess of a lonely-hearts club. McGowan brought up the objection that De Sylva would probably have to be paid about $5000 for his rights in the property, but Sam waved that aside saying, "Oh, that's all right, boys; don't let that stop you." As they explained it, it sounded amusing and a good vehicle for Powell. . . .

[A telephone call interrupted the meeting and eventually Cole took the phone.]

During the telephone call, Sam must have found time to think, because the minute it was over, he said, "Now boys, I like this idea for your picture very much, but why couldn't you lay it in Honolulu instead of New York?" The boys explained to him that this was impossible. So he said, "Well, anyway, give me one character and one scene that I have always clung to: the character, a female wharf rat who can sing torch songs; and the scene, two battleships, one full of boys and one full of girls, to be used as a setting for a comedy lead-up to an important marital [march] song." This did not seem to upset anybody, and as I left, Sam said to McGowan and Silvers, "You boys go away now and try to bring me back an idea in two weeks."

That was the end of this conference.

On the way home in the motor, I figured out, by computing the salaries of the writers engaged on this picture so far, that it had cost MGM $29,000 to decide not to do a revue.

TUESDAY, January 21, 1936: Jack McGowan telephoned. I asked him whether they had gone away and he said no, because Sid Silvers was ill, and he wanted to make an appointment with me to go see Sam Katz to find out "where we were at," that he and Sid Silvers were to see Buddy De Sylva to find out whether Buddy would sell his rights to this idea for a picture for $5000. He replied that he had just talked to Buddy, but Buddy wouldn't sell for less than $12,000. $12,000 seemed very expensive to me. *2:00 p.m.* Sam Katz telephoned me to say that he had arranged for the release of Laura Hope Crews for the Boland part in *Jubilee*. I said, "Sam, how about my picture?" and he said, "Don't worry, my boy, we will find an idea in a few weeks. In the meantime, take advantage of California and get a lot of health."

THURSDAY, January 23: Sam Katz telephoned, saying, "Cole, I have great news for you. I bought the idea for that picture from Buddy De Sylva and it only cost me $17,500." That was all.

TUESDAY, January 28: I came in and found that Jack Cummings had telephoned, so I gave him a ring and asked what he wanted. He replied, "I only telephoned to find out how you liked California," I said, "How about my picture?" and his reply was, "I don't know anything about your picture, I just got back from Palm Springs, I've been there for the last ten days, why don't *you* go there?" Then he rang off.

WEDNESDAY, January 29: I found a message to call up Jack McGowan. I called him and asked why he had telephoned. He said, "I just wanted to call you up to tell you not to be discouraged, and to say that if you wanted Sid or me to see you, we could come over anytime and say hello. I said "Have you worked out any story yet?" He replied, "No, nothing yet." So I told him that it might be better that we not meet until they had found at least some outline of a story. This seemed to delight him and he rang off.

FRIDAY, January 31, 1936: Sam Katz telephoned and said, "Have you seen the boys lately?" I said, "No, Sam, I haven't, but I talked to McGowan on the telephone and asked him whether he and Sid Silvers had as yet found a story, and he said, no, they had not. I suggested that we not meet again until they had."

This pleased Sam very much and he said, "That's absolutely right, Cole, it would only be confusing to you, so just let them alone until they find a story, and in the meantime have a good time and get the benefits of California. Goodbye."

WEDNESDAY, February 12, 1936: Sam Katz telephoned and said, "How are you, Cole, and do you still like California?" I told him I did, and then he added, "I think the boys have really gone to work and they might have something for you by the end of the week. Goodbye, Cole."

FRIDAY, February 14: Sam Katz telephoned again to say that McGowan and Silvers wanted to meet me sometime on Monday, so we made an appointment for 2:30 Monday, February 17.

MONDAY, February 17, 1936: Conference in the office of Mr. Sam Katz. Present: Sam Katz, Jack Cummings, Jack McGowan and Max Gordon listening in. (Max Gordon is being paid $2500 per week for 12 weeks to listen in at conferences.)

Once we were settled in our very comfortable chairs, Sam said to Jack McGowan, "Now, Jack, tell Cole the story you worked out." Then Jack began, "Well, we open our picture with a shot of the New York harbor, where three sailors (Alan Jones, Sid Silvers and Buddy Ebsen) are being given an important letter by the captain of their boat, to deliver to an admiral in Washington." Then he stopped a moment and said, "Hell, Sam, that's all wrong." And Sam said, "Yes, that isn't the opening that you told me the other day at all." There was a short silence until Jack said, "I'm sorry, Cole, but I can't remember any of it. Sid is in bed with the flu and you'll have to wait until he gets out, and then we'll tell you the story."

So Sam suggested that Jack McGowan give me a list of the characters they plan to have in this picture. As the list progressed, I was suddenly very surprised to hear that there would be a troupe of Japanese acrobats in the lonely-hearts club, but as the scene of acrobats with Silvers was described it sounded very funny. Sam didn't laugh with the rest of us, and I couldn't understand why, until he said, "Jack, you can't make those acrobats Japanese, on account of the danger of political trouble; make them Arabs!" Jack said, "Sam, they're supposed to be spies." To which Sam retorted, "Then make them Arab spies."

When we had discussed the characters a bit, Sam said to me "Now, Cole, my boy, Sid will be out of the hospital by the end of the week, and I will give you a ring and you can talk with him before we go away. I said, "Sam, what do you mean, 'go away'?" He replied, "Well, I am taking the boys and their wives, on Saturday, for a little trip to Panama. We will get back about the tenth of March and by that time I think we ought to have an outline of the story."

Jack McGowan had been very silent during the last few moments, and suddenly he leaped to his feet saying, "I have a great idea. Instead of making them sailors on a battleship, why not make them sailors on a submarine?" This caused great enthusiasm, especially as we had all been secretly thinking that his picture was going to be singularly reminiscent of FOLLOW THE FLEET, but

Sam didn't like this idea at all, and he said, "You know, Max, I always wanted to have a scene showing two battleships, one covered with boys and one covered with girls." Jack Cummings immediately stifled him by saying, "Sam, we can get just as good an effect if you have those three sailors on a submarine, because we can get the entire Atlantic fleet to put on a parade for us and have the submarine at the tail end of it." This calmed Sam, and from now on, it's agreed that the three sailors will be "three sailors on a submarine. . . ."

TUESDAY, March 3, 1936: The following radio was forwarded from Sam Katz's secretary to me: "Advise Cole Porter our story line complete. Stop. Our opening song must approximate traditional stirring Navy song to be sung by male chorus in beginning and reprise for finale. Stop. Cole Porter can begin working on this now and try to have same ready for us on our return. Regards."

TUESDAY, March 10, 1936: Arthur Lyons telephoned saying RKO wanted to borrow me from MGM and start me working within two weeks on the next Fred Astaire picture, and asked if I was interested. Of course I was interested, and when about ten minutes later Sam Katz telephoned and said, "Hurry out to the studio, I want to read you the story we have for you," I was very downhearted, thinking that I had to throw up a great job for a mediocre picture. But once I arrived in his office and sat with Max Gordon and Jack Cummings, as Sam read the scenario and a great deal of the dialogue of the picture which McGowan and Silvers are writing for me, all qualms left and I realized that I had fallen on a wonderful film.

When it was over, I played the opening number (which he had wirelessed me about) and they were so delighted with it they all kissed me. Then I played another number which I had just finished, "It's De-

Lovely," and they were equally enthusiastic about it and spotted it immediately in the story.*

We went into details about what I would have to write, and in checking up on the musical numbers, I found that there will be a total of seven numbers at most, three of which I have written.

We discussed casting, and I heard to my great joy that the picture will be played by Alan Jones opposite Eleanor Powell, Sid Silvers opposite Una Merkel, Buddy Ebsen opposite Judy Garland, and Frances Langford to play the jilted society girl.

At the end of the conference, Sam said to me, "You will notice there is no mention of one battleship covered with boys and another battleship covered with girls, but Jack McGowan and Sid Silvers are doing their best to work it in."

THURSDAY, March 12, 1936: Conference in the office of Sam Katz. Present: Sam Katz, Jack McGowan, Sid Silvers, Jack Cummings.

McGowan read aloud the outline of the story and the dialogue that they had finished so far, and once more I was convinced that they have presented me with a great picture.

I played them all the numbers which I had finished, including a new one that I wrote last night for Frances Langford. It's called "Goodbye, Little Dream, Goodbye." This number seemed to have much greater success than I could have ever expected. They sang it over and over again, and at the finish Sam Katz said to me, "You know, Cole, that song is beautiful, it's—why it's Jewish."

FRIDAY, March 13, 1936: As the result of "Goodbye, Little Dream, Goodbye," Major Zanft asked me to come to see him at his office. He told me that

* This was later thrown out.

people in the Katz unit had dined last night with the powers at Paramount and they raved so over this new song that Paramount had asked him to offer me $50,000 for two months' work on the next Crosby picture. . . .

Arthur Lyons called me up to tell me about the excitement "Goodbye, Little Dream, Goodbye"* had caused on the MGM lot, and added that the Katz outfit had hinted to him that they would like to have me back next year for the same length of time, but for $100,000 instead of the paltry $75,000 that I am struggling along with now.

MONDAY, March 16, 1936: Conference in the office of Mr. Sam Katz. Present: Sam Katz, Jack McGowan and Sid Silvers.

I arrived to find Jack and Sid very excited over having thought of a title for our picture, to wit: *Great Guns*. I didn't like it, nor did Sam, especially, but the boys were so enthusiastic that we let them rave on.

They also had an idea that the reprise of the opening song of the picture should be used as the entrance for Langford, which would mean throwing out "Rolling Home." I said nothing about this, but after they left I told Sam I was going to fight them on it.

THURSDAY, March 19, 1936: Conference in office of Mr. Sam Katz. Present: Sam Katz, Max Gordon, Jack Cummings, Jack McGowan, Sid Silvers.

McGowan read aloud a lot of new dialogue, and it was grand. Then I played them a honky-tonk-waltz clog, "Hey, Babe, Hey!" and it was a thundering success.

Then Sam led in a tubercular-snore specialist, who proceeded to amuse us a great deal with a new routine showing the different ways of saying "yes."

Then a boy of sixteen was led in, a waif from West Virginia, who performed on the harmonica, and gave one of the greatest performances I had ever heard,

* This was later thrown out.

especially when he used his nose instead of his mouth. After the two performers had left, Sam explained that he was using them in the boys' next picture and wanted me to hear them.

We all parted very exuberant.

TUESDAY, March 31, 1936: Conference in office of Mr. Sam Katz. Present: Sam Katz and Max Gordon.

I played them a new rhythm song which I had just finished for Eleanor Powell called "Rap Tap on Wood."

Sam Katz was so pleased with it that he began talking to me about planning from now on to come back every year on January 1 and work for him until June 1, and he added, "Next January will be especially interesting for you, because that is when we are going to shoot your present picture." This scared me a little bit, knowing as I do so well how quickly songs date.

THURSDAY, April 2, 1936: Conference in the office of Mr. Sam Katz. Present: Sam Katz, Max Gordon, Jack Cummings, Jack McGowan, Sid Silvers.

I played the authors "Rap Tap on Wood," and they were delighted with it. So that means another number in the bag.

Then McGowan read aloud the love scene leading up to what I thought would be "I've Got You Under My Skin," but as he read it, I realized that this song would be entirely unfitting. So I left, promising to write another one.

MONDAY, April 13, 1936: Conference in office of Mr. Sam Katz. Present: Sam Katz and Max Gordon.

I took in a number on which I had been working very hard for the past week, called "Who But You," and played it for them. Even as I was playing, they walked away from the piano and looked out the window, and at the finish of it they told me it was absolutely no good.

Then the authors came in and read me some new material, which was excellent. Sam suggested that I play them the number that I had brought in, but I refused, as I knew there was no chance of its going over his head. So we discussed putting back "I've Got You Under My Skin." They all decided they wanted that song, but when I left I knew it was wrong, and much too romantic a number for this character to sing.

TUESDAY, April 14, 1936: Conference in the office of Mr. Sam Katz. Present: Sam Katz, Max Gordon, Jack McGowan, Sid Silvers, Jack Cummings and Seymour Felix (dance director).

I played them a song which I had resurrected and rewritten last night, called "Easy to Love," The response was instantaneous. They all grabbed the lyric and began singing it, and even called in the stenographers to hear it, their enthusiasm was so great. When the singing was finally over, Seymour Felix got on his knees in front of Sam Katz and said, "Oh, please Mr. Katz, let me stage that song when the picture is shot."

So left once again very happy.

MONDAY, April 20, 1936: Present: Sam Katz, Jack McGowan, Sid Silvers, Jack Cummings.

I took in "I've Got You Under My Skin" and they all liked it very much. Sam Katz asked me to get hold of Frances Langford at once and coach her for the song so she could come out and demonstrate it as soon as she was ready.

WEDNESDAY, April 22, 1936: Conference in office of Sam Katz. Present: Sam Katz, Sid Silvers, Jack McGowan, Jack Cummings, Roy Del Ruth (who was to direct the picture).

McGowan read the entire script, and I played all the numbers finished up to date. Del Ruth, who is supposed to be a very taciturn person, was most enthusiastic and told us he thought we had a great picture.

FRIDAY, April 24, 1936: Conference in office of

Sam Katz. Present: Sam Katz, Sid Silvers, Jack McGowan and Jack Cummings.

I took in the verse to "Easy to Love" and they seemed to feel that it would fit perfectly.

Then the discussion began as to who would play the lead. . . . After I returned home, I began thinking about James Stewart as a possibility for the male lead. I talked to Sam Katz about this on the telephone and he thought the idea was most interesting, if Stewart could sing. The next day Stewart came over to the house and I heard him sing. He sings far from well, although he has nice notes in his voice, but he could play the part perfectly.

MONDAY, May 11, 1936: Conference in the office of Sam Katz. Present: Sam Katz, Jack McGowan, Sid Silvers, Jack Cummings, Roy Del Ruth, Seymour Felix, and a strange man, whose name I did not get.

Frances Langford came in with her manager, and sang the concerted number which I had just finished, "Love Me, Love My Pekinese," and "I've Got You Under My Skin." The concerted number was received with great enthusiasm, and as for "I've Got You Under My Skin," as sung by Miss Langford, it was what is called in Hollywood "colossal."

Then Sam said, "Now, Cole, I want you to write a skating waltz. We haven't enough beauty in this picture and I want to sign Sonja Henie for an ice ballet." I said, "But, Sam, where can you put it?" He replied, "Well, instead of taking the male lead and the Broadway star to a nightclub, we will take them to a skating rink. The only difficulty about the whole thing is that Henie wants too much money; she wants $100,000, and we only want to give her $50,000." I said, "Sam, how long will the sequence take?" He said, "Oh, two minutes."

I left this conference, feeling very happy about the picture as a whole, but definitely worried as to Sonja Henie and the skating waltz.

WEDNESDAY, May 13, 1936: Sam Katz telephoned me to say that Del Ruth had been to see him and wanted me to throw out the opening to the picture, "Rollin' Home." Sam asked me to think this over and let him know.

FRIDAY, May 15, 1936: Jack Cummings and Sid Silvers came to the house. They looked rather embarrassed, and I knew there was bad news in store for me. The bad news was that they had all met and decided my opening was no good. After questioning them a little bit I found out *why* they found it no good, and saw an easy solution to adapt it to all their wishes, so the opening stays in.

SATURDAY, May 16, 1936: Sam Katz telephoned me, saying. "Cole, I have a great script for next year when you come back to me. It is by Bill McGuire, who wrote *The Great Ziegfeld,* and it is a wonderful story." Then he began to describe the story, and it became more and more complicated, and when he finished I had no idea whether it was good or not. But it was nice to know that Sam was thinking seriously of the future.

SUNDAY, May 17, 1936: Sam Katz telephoned; said he had Al [Alfred] Newman for my orchestra director, and Eddie Powell to make the orchestral arrangements. This is a great break for me, as they are the two best men in their lines in Hollywood.

I had been worrying ever since a few days ago about Sonja Henie and the skating waltz, so I asked Sam the news, and he said, "No, Cole, that's out, she won't come down on her price."

TUESDAY, May 19, 1936: Present: Jack Cummings, Roger Edens, Eddie Powell, Al Newman, Sid Silvers, and the head of the music department (whose name I do not know).

They all came to the house. I plied them with whiskies

and sodas, and then played the entire score. Even if the score had been awful, none of them would have known it, as they all felt so well, but they left saying it was the greatest thing they had heard in years.

WEDNESDAY, May 2, 1936: Conference: In Roger Edens' Office. Present: Sam Katz, Seymour Felix, Mr. Pye (the art director), Sid Silvers, Jack McGowan, Roy Del Ruth, Al Newman, Eddie Powell, Commander Haislip, Virginia Bruce. Virginia Bruce gave us an audition of "I've Got You Under My Skin" and "Love Me, Love My Pekinese." She sang them very well indeed and, after she had left, they definitely decided to use Bruce. . . . Then I played the finale to them, "Swingin' the Jinx Away," and it went with a bang. So my troubles are nearly over.

Just as I was leaving, somebody came in and said, "Sonja is making her tests," so I said, "Sam, are you going to use Sonja Henie after all?" He said, "Well, Cole, we haven't quite decided yet, but if her tests are good, I think we will take her, although I still think $100,000 is too much money." So I shall have to begin thinking about the skating waltz again.

Then Sam took me to his office and gave me the McGuire script, about which he telephoned me a few days ago. I left the studio very happy about the picture, as the enthusiasm from everybody is so great. They start shooting on June 15 and it is practically sure that they have the Pacific fleet. . . . Del Ruth says the picture should be ready for release on October 1.

TUESDAY, May 26, 1936: Sam Katz called me to the telephone while I was in the midst of an excellent egg, and said, "Cole, can you take a great shock?" My reply was a groan, and then he said, "Your finale 'Swingin' the Jinx Away' is out." When I recovered sufficiently to speak I said, "Sam, I know this is wrong," and he said, "Everybody had decided the lyric is wrong and the tune hasn't enough drive," so I gave him a "goodbye," and hung up the telephone. I called Sid Silvers and Jack McGowan immediately and they were outraged. It seems that all this developed from Mr. Del Ruth and Mr. Seymour Felix having planned elaborate production effects on the water, which they felt could not follow my number, even if the tune were any good, and they had decided it was not. One of the details of the production was to be a fleet of motorboats covered with girls.

I called up Sam Katz in the evening and told him I still felt that my tune was right, and that my lyric was right, in that it established the swing as a national institution, and that if he would only arrange for a curtain back of the singer this number, showing the Capitol of Washington, those concerned with the production of it could go anywhere afterwards, as long as it was America. Also pointed out that the song would have value on account of the elections next autumn. By this time Sam completely agreed with me regarding the lyric, but still thought the tune was not any good. So I called up Silvers and McGowan again and told them what had happened. They recounted their interview with Sam Katz in the afternoon. It seems that Del Ruth and Felix had turned him to such an extent against the finale that he was not at all sure that any of my tunes were any good, or that I had ever written a good tune. So they had to get up and give an audition and sing every hit I have had since I started writing.

WEDNESDAY, May 27, 1936: Jack Cummings telephoned me and asked if I would come out to the studio and discuss the finale with them all. I refused, saying that as far as I was concerned the finale was the best I could possibly do, and that furthermore it seemed very topsy-turvy that a director and a dance director should dictate to me what I should write, and pointed out that if this occurred in the theatre and the director and the dance director announced that they could not produce a number which I had written, we always got a new director and a new dance director. Then I rang off.

In the evening Linda and I dined with Sam Katz at his house. It was a very pleasant dinner with excellent Chinese food, followed by beautiful singing by Igor Gorin. There was no mention made of the finale until we left, and then Sam came out to the car with me and said, "Well, Cole, old boy, you were right; I had two piano arrangements made of your finale, and after hearing it several times, I think the lyric is not only right, but you have written a great tune, so your worries are over." But in the meantime, I called up Arthur Lyons [Cole's agent] and told him to cancel any arrangements with Sam Katz about making my contracts for next year. We shall not go into that until all my work has been accepted and approved on this job.

FRIDAY, May 29, 1936: Miss Moore telephoned me at the swimming pool to say that Jack Cummings wanted me to come out and discuss the finale with Del Ruth and Eddie Powell. So I called up Jack and said, "Has Del Ruth teamed Eleanor Powell with him against me on my finale?" and he replied, "Well, he is very set against it and Eleanor says she can't dance to it." I made an appointment to go out to the studio at four in the afternoon. Then I began telephoning. First I telephoned to Roger Edens and to Eddie Powell, and asked them to be there. Then I telephoned to Silvers and asked him if he could possibly go to the studio quickly and persuade Edens to get busy with Eleanor Powell and try to work out some routine for the number. At 4:00 I arrived at Sam Katz's office, and he took me for a long walk to a large rehearsal hall, where I found Del Ruth, Seymour Felix, Sid Silvers, Roger Edens, Eddie Powell, Nathaniel Finston (head of the music department at MGM), Eleanor Powell, her mother and an upright paino. When I came in I realized there was battle in the air. Then Sam said, "Now, Cole, my boy, Roy Del Ruth will tell you what he thinks of the finale." Everybody became very silent and Del Ruth began. He said, "This is not personal at all, but I definitely do not like your finale. I think it is a great letdown after your other numbers and will ruin the picture. It seems to me the lyric is entirely wrong, and as far as the tune goes, it reminds me of everything I have ever heard since I was a small boy. I had hoped so much that you would write a hit song that had the brilliance of 'Broadway Rhythm,' our great number in *Broadway Melody*." When he had finished, I said, "I understand your point of view perfectly, but I disagree with you in every way. I think my lyric is excellent and applies completely. As to the tune, you tell me it reminds you of everything you've ever heard since you were a little boy, which is exactly what I wanted to do. For weeks, I studied all of the American folk songs and tried to write a melody which would be essentially American, not fashionable jazz, but a spirited folk song, such as the 'Arkansas Traveler.' " Then I asked Eddie Powell what he thought of the number in regard to its orchestration, and he said, "Well, as far as I go, it's a great chance for me, because it is obviously written for orchestration and military band, and I can easily make it much more brilliant than I made 'Broadway Rhythm' last year, because it lends itself to scoring." Then Finston got on his feet and said, "Mr. Del Ruth, I am sure you are wrong about this number. You say it won't be a 'hit song.' I will bet you on the other hand that the orchestras throughout the country will take up this song to such an extent that you will curse Cole Porter for having written it."

At this moment Eleanor Powell stood up and said, "Nobody has asked my opinion, but the number suits me perfectly. In fact, I already have a routine which I would like to show you." At which she took the middle of the floor, her accompanist went to the piano and she proceeded to do one of the most exciting dances I have ever seen in my life. When this was over, Sam Katz said, "Well, Cole, my boy, I guess you were right, if the number suits our star, and Eddie Powell says he can arrange it even better than 'Broadway Rhythm,' I think there should be no more discussion about it, so the number is definitely in."

Then Seymour Felix took the floor and he said, "But, Mr. Katz, how am I going to bring on my motorboats filled with girls after that lyric?" Sam completely lost his temper and said, "I don't want your motorboats filled with girls. I want this number to lead up to our star, and if you want to use girls, the only way I will allow it is if you can shoot them out of cannons. And by the way, that would be a swell effect."

But Felix was not to be downed. He said, "But the number is corny. I have always hated that old-fashioned one-step rhythm and you are going to kill your picture if you leave it in." Then Sam exploded, and by the time he finished, there was very little left of Mr. Seymour Felix.

When I realized that the battle was over and that there was nothing more to discuss, I said good-night to everybody. When I shook hands with Del Ruth he smiled and said, "Well, Cole, thanks for everything."

Then Sam stood up and addressed everybody, saying, "Ladies and gentlemen: The discussion is over, the number is set for the finale, and we are going to have a swell picture. It is going to be a million-dollar picture, maybe it will cost a million and a half," and he beamed with satisfaction.

When I got home I telephoned Sam Katz and said, "Sam, is this settled definitely or not, because it's very worrying when people change their minds as often as they have about this number?" He said, "Cole, my boy, just put it all out of your mind; the number is in." Then I said, "But I am still worried about Felix. Felix dislikes it so much that I'm afraid he won't do a good job on it." To which Sam replied, "Don't you worry, Cole, my boy, I already have another dance director in mind."

TUESDAY, June 2, 1936: Sam Katz telephoned and said, "Cole, will you do me a favor?" and I said, "Probably; what is it?" and he said, "Will you come out and play and sing your score to Louis B. Mayer and

[Irving] Thalberg tomorrow afternoon," I said, "Why?" and he answered, "Well, Cole, my boy, after all, they are *slightly* interested." So I agreed to do it; however, with dread.

WEDNESDAY, June 3, 1936: After a stiff whisky and soda, and my arms full of books which Miss Moore had prepared, containing the lyrics in the order which they come in the picture, I left for the studio. A few minutes later I was in Louis B. Mayer's office. He was there, also Sam Katz, Jack Cummings, Roger Edens, Sid Silvers, Mrs. Koverman, (L.B.'s secretary and an angel), Eleanor Powell and Virginia Bruce. Suddenly the door opened and in crept Thalberg, looking more dead than alive, and obviously angry at being disturbed to hear this score. I passed out the lyric books and began. By the time "Rollin' Home" was over, I realized that the atmosphere was friendly. When I finished "Hey, Babe, Hey!" there was a wild applause and L. B. began jumping around the room whispering to people. I attacked "Entrance of Lucy James" next, and it was during this that Thalberg suddenly became a different person and began smiling. Then the door opened and in walked Eddie Mannix (general manager of MGM), and L. B. said, "Cole, you've got to repeat 'Hey, Babe, Hey!' for Eddie," which I did, and they all sang it. From then on it was clear sailing and the moment I finished the finale, Thalberg leaped out of his seat, rushed over to me, grabbed my hand and said, "I want to congratulate you for a magnificent job; I think it's one of the finest scores I have ever heard." He was followed by L. B., who came up and put his arms around me and said, "Cole, how about coming into the next room and signing your contract for next year?" to which I replied, "No, L. B., I don't understand money matters."

Then Mrs. Koverman said, "Gentleman, I think this is worth a celebration. What do you all want to drink?" So we ordered big whiskies and sodas, and everybody stood around the piano and sang the entire score again. It was completely jubilant.

Then L. B. addressed the house and said, "Now, Sam, this material is so fine that I don't want you to take any chances with it. I want every lyric heard, and in order to assure that, I want you to make rushes of these numbers and then show them in theaters as shorts to find out whether the audiences can understand every word. And another thing, this finale is so brilliant that I want you to go to town and spend $250,000 on that number alone." When everybody had hugged and kissed everybody else, I went over to Sam Katz's office with Jack Cummings, to see the model for the lonely-hearts club and the drawings for the finale. The model for the lonely-hearts club was so beautiful that I wanted to join the club at once. As for the finale, it's staggering.

While this was going on, more whiskies and sodas were brought in for everybody and I motored home, exhausted and just a little bit tight.

On arriving home I found that the minute I left L. B.'s office, he telephoned to Arthur Lyons to come to the studio and arrange my contract for next year.

TUESDAY, June 9, 1936: I signed for $100,000 for one picture beginning December 1, 1936.

Thus ends one of the few diaries Cole kept.

Given Cole's "no praise-no good" psychology, it is easy to see why, in the face of studio enthusiasm, he took to Hollywood and eagerly looked forward to an early return. Having taken a stand against the know-nothings and thereby having won the support of Mayer, Thalberg *et al.*, he envisioned a long and productive career alternating film and stage scores. He was convinced that he had done a good job and could do it again. Then, too, the studio's excesses and eccentric behavior amused and pleased him.

By mid-June, he left Hollywood for New York by way of Callander, Ontario, where he had gone to view the Dionne quintuplets. But even before arriving at the Waldorf-Towers, he was already looking forward to an early return to the West Coast. He was particularly bemused by his first exposure to Metro-Goldwyn-Mayer's battery of anonymous press agents, who were turning out reams of fact and fantasy designed to make *Born to Dance* synonymous with the best of Cole Porter. What pleased him was that they didn't pester him to set up interviews as theatrical press agents did, but stories poured forth just the same.

He was amused at the piece which catalogued the four months of preparation that had gone into the finale. He liked the item reporting that he had insisted that MGM hire a Navy man to check naval terms in his lyrics. (It quoted him: "Research is absolutely essential to lyric writing. One of the first songs I wrote, 'An Old-Fashioned Garden,' was criticized in England because I had the wrong flowers growing together. Since that time I have been extremely careful. I took a course in anatomy before I wrote the lyrics for the doctor song ('The Physician') for Gertrude Lawrence and I studied all manner of insect and animal life before I started on the words of 'Let's Do It.' " He liked, too, Frances Langford's by-lined piece giving him credit for getting her to entertain at a birthday party which resulted in her signing a Hollywood contract.

Not that all the stories that poured forth pleased him. He was annoyed to read that he was earning $10,400 per song for *Born to Dance* as compared to $1,250 for *Jubliee* and $3,500 for *Anything Goes*. All these figures, the press agent told a reporter, were "mere pittances" compared to the $18,000 per song he would receive for his next MGM assignment.

Cole's attitude toward money was always complicated and ambiguous. By inclination and by association with old society he had come to regard discussion of one's earning power as a violation of good manners. Yet he avidly read stories about the enormous fees being paid Kern, Gershwin, Berlin and other contemporaries, and he soon began to want the reassurance of a comparable fee for *his* services even though he prohibited publication of the amounts involved. He generally contented himself by saying that the offers were "too attractive to resist." Strangely, he had no objection to being described as "rich" but shied away from "wealthy," which he thought pretentious sounding.

There were a few stories emanating from Paramount, too. The studio was busy giving *Anything Goes* the treatment at the same time *Born to Dance* was being filmed. For *Anything Goes,* Ethel Merman was swaggering through her original role, joined by Ida Lupino, Charles Ruggles and Cole's less than favorite performer, Bing Crosby. Cole had nothing against him personally, but he didn't like the singer's style. Crosby, it might be said, subtracted a dimension from "You're the Top" by crooning it. Not that Crosby's crooning the tune made a great deal of difference since only "You're the Top," "I Get a Kick Out of You" and "Anything Goes" (with additional cleansed lyrics by Cole's distant cousin Ted Fetter) were retained in the film. Instead there was a clutch of new songs by Leo Robin, Richard A. Whiting, Frederick Hollander, Edward Heyman and Hoagy Carmichael.*

Cole viewed the mutilation of his original score as one of the breaks good or bad that come with a career in show business and, as a practical man of the theater, he readily agreed that Paramount be allowed to put up half the backing for his new Broadway show, *Wait for Baby!* which was to be produced by Vinton Freedley, to have a book by Lindsay and Crouse; and to benefit from the free-swinging style of Ethel Merman. Other cast members included Jimmy Durante, Bob Hope and Polly Walters.

Cole had hardly finished the title song, based on the catchline from Maxwell Anderson's and Laurence Stallings' *What Price Glory?*, before the title was changed to *—But Millions!* over which everyone became terribly excited for a couple of days before turning on it and

* The release was called *Anything Goes,* but when it was later sold to television just at the time Paramount was remaking it, the title was changed to *Tops Is the Limit.*

settling upon *Red, Hot and Blue!*

Rehearsals were distinguished only by a hilarious, maniacal struggle between La Merman's and Durante's agents. Neither group had specified in the contract that his client was to have a preferred left-hand top billing. Nor would either agree the client of the others should have it. For a time it appeared that one or both stars might withdraw. Eventually, however, the controversy was settled when Cole suggested that the billing be as crossed-purpose as the argument:

VINTON FREEDLEY

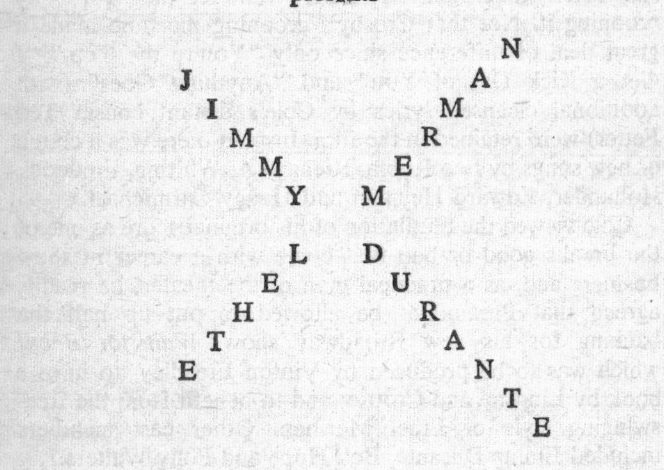

in

RED, HOT AND BLUE!

All went smoothly prior to Boston, and on October 6, the day of dress rehearsal, Cole was confident enough about the job he had accomplished to do, for him, an almost unheard-of thing—praise his own work. Chatting with a newspaper reporter, he extolled the orchestrations and said that this work was superior to that of *Anything Goes* because he had become familiar with La Merman's voice and knew exactly how to use it to achieve impressive effects.

In discussing the songs, he was happy that a number written for *Born to Dance* had found a place in *Red, Hot and Blue!* This song had had its origin during the 1935 trip around the world. Linda and he had heard so much about the beauty of dawn over the Rio harbor that they had decided to rise early to witness it. On deck of the ship, they encountered Monty Woolley, who had spent the night "lifting a few" while awaiting the sunrise.

As dawn broke, Cole cried: "It's delightful."

Linda added: "It's delicious."

And Monty chimed in: "It's de-lovely."

The three phrases which helped to make "It's De-Lovely" a hit song.*

Another happy inspiration was "the touching ballad" he had written especially for Jimmy Durante. This whimiscal bit, called "A Little Skipper from Heaven Above," told the seriocomic story of a female sea captain who masqueraded as a male and eventually had to confess to her crew that she is going to have "a little skipper from Heaven above."

Whether Cole sincerely believed what he said or was attempting to do a bit of public relations work for his numbers, his optimism was not to last long. Audience reaction was spotty both to his songs and to the book. The low comedy plot concerns a rich widow (Merman) conducting a lottery run by an ex-convict (Durante), which she decides to throw to her lawyer (Hope) whom she loves, but who loves the memory of a girl (Polly Walters) who as a baby branded herself by sitting on a waffle iron when he tried to kiss her. The action, of course, finally brings the widow and the lawyer together.

* Cole also told the story, substituting mangosteen melon for the Rio harbor. Upon hearing Monty's remark, agent Robert Raison commented: "With friends like that, who couldn't write hit songs?"

Notices were mixed. With her tongue deep in her cheek, Elinor Hughes of the Boston *Herald* noted there was enough libretto for two shows and suggested that the first act be given one evening and the second act the following evening. "Eugene O'Neill and Noel Coward have tried that and succeeded," she twitted.

During the Boston engagement, relations became increasingly strained. Until this show, Cole had always taken great pride in his reputation for civilized behavior during tryouts whenever a producer suggested rewriting or eliminating a number. This time, he seemed far from his usual amiable self.

Although he agreed that The Great Merman needed a new song, he appeared short-tempered and preoccupied. So much so that when he passed Russell Crouse several times without speaking, Crouse began to wonder what he had done to offend him. Happily, that question was answered when Cole suddenly smiled at him and called out, "In my pet pailletted gown!" Cole had found the phrase that completed the lyrics of a new song, and Crouse knew that Cole's coolness had been only concentration in finding the right words for the new number.

That song was "Down in the Depths on the 90th Floor," and many of those who saw Miss Merman perform the number, standing alone in the spotlight wearing the $1,000 gold-pailletted evening dress, consider it one of her finest achievements.

As exchanges grew more acrimonious, Cole suddenly packed up and returned to New York without saying goodbye to anyone except Miss Merman. Freedley in high dudgeon blasted his desertion before an all-important conference over "Ridin' High" which, he declared, the new arranger Robert Russell Bennett felt needed work. Freedley also claimed the right to make suggestions to Cole as well as to the authors of the book and implored him to "play ball with us for another ten days." At this point, the New York opening had been postponed and a full-fledged disaster seemed to be in the offing.

Cole was not intimidated. He wired Freedley at his home

in Pomfret, Connecticut, that he was "hearing indirectly" that the new scoring of "Ridin' High" had been abandoned. "I have lost all heart and have stopped work. Please address further complaints to Dick Madden.* Cole Porter."

Freedley promptly sent a blistering wire to Madden. In part, it read: "Staging a musical comedy without a composer is not easy. He is acting outrageously to the authors and me. Why can't he take it like a man and not hide behind your skirts? If he does not do something drastic, he has another *Jubilee* to his demerit. Can he afford this?"

The wire produced no reaction, but when the New Haven *Register's* critic singled out the songs as disappointing and announced that Cole could "do better," his professional pride forced him to make peace with Freedley and return to do additional work on the show.

The arrival of *Red, Hot and Blue!* at the Alvin Theater in New York on October 29, 1936, was marked by additional flourish on the Porters' part. Cole attended the premiere with Mary Pickford on one arm and Merle Oberon on the other. Linda not only gave him a commemorative cigarette case, but also received one which Cole had had the Duke di Verdura of Verdura, Inc., create for her. It was a beautiful platinum box, the bottom of which was inlaid with green-gold zodiac signs, while the lid was a sunburst of rubies, encircled by diamonds and sapphires—a $10,000 bauble.

Among the first-nighters was chief of the G-men J. Edgar Hoover, and despite his well-known reluctance to lend his endorsement to anything, reporter Michael Mok succeeded in getting a quote on the show: "It's a bright entertainment, put over with lots of style, and there's quite a lot of truth in the cracks," Hoover observed.

The critics disagreed. Richard Watts, of the *Herald-Tribune,* voiced a complaint that was eventually echoed by Walter Winchell, Norman Winter and Ira Wolfert, among

* Dick Madden was Cole's lawyer.

others: "When I say it is disappointing what is meant is merely that it isn't up to the usual Cole Porter standard, which is so high that even his lesser scores are an event. Furthermore, when the incomparable Miss Merman sings a song she does it so magnificently that you immediately are lured into the belief that it is something of a masterpiece. It is only very careful second thought that leads you to the realization it is less than a classic. . . ."

Eventually, *The New Yorker*'s critic Robert Benchley worked a variation upon that theme: ". . . Miss Merman is her usual dynamic self, and I have an idea that one or two of Mr. Porter's songs benefit greatly by her powers of projection, although on a second visit to the show, I was convinced that Mr. Porter's score is much better than I thought the first time. . . ."

Only George Jean Nathan, of the major reviewers, gave Cole a rave notice. And even this was of little comfort, since it was Cole's contention that his good friend Nathan wouldn't recognize "The Star-Spangled Banner" when he heard it unless he saw everyone else standing up. (Later, when he mentioned Nathan's musical weakness to a *New York Times* reporter, the reporter asked whether he minded being quoted. "Not at all," he replied, "as long as you include George's name.")

Despite the mild reviews, the show played to standees the first few weeks and managed to run until April 10, 1937. At that point, Paramount Pictures investors, convinced that the production could not get through the summer, persuaded Freedley to close in New York and send the company to Chicago.

There the reception was little short of astonishing. All the songs that had been patronized by New York reviewers were hailed. Ashton Stevens of the Chicago *Herald-Examiner* found them "diabolically dulcet"; the *Daily News*' Robert Pollak announced that the show was "studded with tunes that only Mr. Porter can write"; and the Chicago *Daily Tribune*'s Charles Collins recommended "those words of Cole Porter's worth hearing for their ingenuity and wit." Columnist Lloyd Lewis in the *Daily*

News hailed "It's De-Lovely" as ". . . probably the best Cole Porter has written since 'Night and Day' and would have been well worn considering how long ago *Red, Hot and Blue!* started in New York, had it not been a stout as well as intriguing composition."

Ironically, the enthusiasm of the Chicago reviewers failed to put the show across. It closed after a couple of weeks.

Red, Hot and Blue! had two major effects upon Cole, one favorable, the other questionable. The latter developed in the wake of the unfriendly New York notices. After reading the reviews, Cole consciously set out to write in a more popular style. To strengthen the show, he turned out a new song for Miss Merman. It was a pseudohillbilly number, "The Ozarks Are Callin' Me Home." In it, he attempted to capture genuine nostalgia, but to save the song from falling into cheap pathos he detailed a list of horrors—paw givin' maw her daily lickin', granmaw wrasslin' 'round with a big black bear, etc.—for which the unhappy heroine yearned. As someone once pointed out, this made a devastating comment upon the kind of life she was leading in the city. After finishing it, Cole announced that it represented a decision on his part to write songs with wider appeal for "common people and less of the brittle, bright poesy with which I've been associated."

The more favorable development was the strengthening of the Merman-Porter association. The more often he worked with her, the more convinced he became that she had no peer on the musical-comedy stage. Her clear, direct attack upon the songs inspired him; that and the way she would deliberately flat for comic effect, and all the other wonderful humorous invention she brought to each problem. He was dazzled, too, by the uncomplicated, forthright manner in which she handled problems and people, perhaps because he found that kind of directness so alien to his nature. When anything minor went wrong, Cole laughed and walked away. That was his way. When things went wrong for Miss Merman, she made sure that they didn't go wrong again. For instance, in *Red, Hot and Blue!*, she sang "It's De-Lovely" with Bob Hope. After the show had been running for some time, she was puzzled by laughter at an unexpected moment. The cause of the titters turned out to be Mr. Hope, who had casually lowered himself into a reclining position. Miss Merman was furious and after they made their exit offered to further flatten his ski nose with the heel of her shoe if he ever did it again. Cole applauded that directness—in others.

Not unnaturally, La Merman responded to his enthusiasm. In one signed article published in 1936, she let the world know that she was flattered when he named her his favorite singer. "And I'll return the compliment," she added, "by saying that I'd rather sing his songs than those by any other writer."

Cole had little time to brood about the eventual success or failure of *Red, Hot and Blue!* or of *Born to Dance*, which was about to be released. As for the latter, it set the critics dancing in the streets, as they used to say. Eleanor Powell was applauded. Cole's inspiration in casting Jimmy Stewart provided the latter with an opportunity to make a decisive bid for stardom. Frances Langford, Virginia Bruce, Una Merkel, Buddy Ebsen and Sid Silvers were all praised. "I've Got You Under My Skin" with twenty-five airings immediately leaped to second place in the list of songs played most often on the radio; "Easy to Love" with eleven credits was twelfth; "Swingin' the Jinx Away" with six exposures was twenty-sixth; while "It's De-Lovely" with twenty-four airings held third place.

But Cole never tarried in New York for the film's opening. A month after *Red, Hot and Blue!* premiered, he flew to Hollywood via TWA to join Linda, who had gone ahead to open the Barthelmess house for the second year. With him was Howard Sturges, Cole's valet, George Steel, a dog and a cat.

In an interview with a reporter who saw him off, Cole expressed fondness for pancakes, white flowers, the color red, Cézanne, traveling, Oriental music, "Love for Sale" and jigsaw puzzles. He said that of all the places he'd seen he liked South Africa best. "It's a healthy place," he observed. "If I had a son, I'd send him there. It's full of opportunities." As for himself, he hoped upon finishing the film to take a trip to China.

"The film" about which he spoke was to be based on the 1928 Broadway hit, *Rosalie*. In its original version it had had seven songs by George Gershwin and eight by Sigmund Romberg, but apparently on policy film companies never used the scores they bought and this time Cole turned out eight new songs for the movie. In his opinion the title song was the dreariest he ever created, a conviction he held to even after it earned widespread popularity. He often told how he had written six versions before coming up with one that he took to MGM, where L. B. Mayer listened and then suggested that he forget he was writing for Nelson Eddy and dash off a good old-fashioned honky-tonk number. Cole left in a rage, raced home, turned out a new version in three hours and took it back to the studio. Mayer accepted it and "Rosalie" eventually sold more than 500,000 copies of sheet music.*

Nelson Eddy, who played a West Point cadet to Eleanor Powell's princess from Romanza, harbored no doubts about the number "Rosalie," but he was less agreeable about "In the Still of the Night," insisting that it was improperly constructed and therefore impossible to sing. Cole decided to take the song to L. B. Mayer. As he played it, Mayer, who was sentimental, was so moved that he burst into tears. After recovering his composure, he

* Upon being congratulated by Irving Berlin, according to a letter Cole wrote bandleader Paul Whiteman (*Esquire,* November, 1965), Cole informed Berlin that he wrote the song in hate and still hated it. To which the pragmatic Berlin replied, "Listen, kid, take my advice, never hate a song that has sold half a million copies." Dr. Sirmay, who was familiar with all versions, cites this as a case where a songwriter was not the best judge of his work. He says the final version is far superior to the others.

summoned Eddy to his presence and announced Eddy *could* sing it—and Eddy did.

During this period there was a temporary estrangement in Cole's domestic life. After finishing *Rosalie,* he signed for a new film to be made the next year although Linda had pleaded with him to give up Hollywood and concentrate on Broadway. Hearing what he had done, she said no more about it but quietly packed up and went to their Paris house without him.

Cole lingered before joining her there while his new valet (the old one was ill) made up his mind whether or not to continue in the job since *his* wife wanted to remain in California. Eventually, the valet decided to go. This was Paul Sylvain—gentle, intelligent, kindly—who from the beginning was totally devoted to Cole's well-being.

After a brief stop in New York, Cole joined Linda in Paris. She was still angry over his film contract and he refused to make any concessions. The strain grew deeper as days passed, and Linda quietly but firmly went her own way. Finally, Cole decided to accompany Howard Sturges and Ed Tauch on a walking trip.

They visited Munich and went to Salzburg for some musical evenings before beginning the walk. On July 15 they set out and the tour proved no disappointment. Several times Cole wrote friends telling of the exhaustion that followed several hours of hard climbing and listing such simple delights as the comfort of a warm hut or the smell of schnitzel cooking. On August 16 the party attacked the Dolomites. And by the 18th, he was writing that if he lived through the tour he would feel fine. That day he had just hiked four hours before breakfast.

All this strenuous activity so conflicts with the sybaritic Cole Porter of later days that friends sometimes doubted he had ever made the trip. But prior to 1937, he frequently took them as part of his puritanically oriented health regimen whose origins seem to reach back to Indiana and the days of "the viler the remedy the quicker the cure."

On August 26 the party took to more conventional travel, viewing castles in Copenhagen; and on the 27th, they went to Elsinore where Cole witnessed a performance of *Hamlet* and posted a card to Dr. Sirmay:

Then on to Oslo to see the Viking ships, to Stockholm to inspect palaces and to Helsinki where Cole was equally interested in reindeer for lunch and a "chic little Greek Catholic church!" These were the impressive, beautiful and esoteric things that continued to fascinate the inveterate sightseer until the end of his life.

Finally, from Paris on September 13, 1937, Cole wrote Dr. Sirmay requesting that he keep himself free to work on the Clifton Webb show after September 27. Dr. Sirmay, he said, would be constantly needed. On October 4, he bade the still angry Linda goodbye and sailed on the *Estonia* for New York to work on the new score.

The show's title turned out to be somewhat prophetic: *You Never Know.*

CHAPTER X

Two weeks after he wrote Dr. Sirmay to be prepared for his arrival, Cole was in Oyster Bay, Long Island, anticipating a relaxed weekend at Countess Edith de Zoppola's house. According to another guest, the Duke di Verdura, almost from the moment Cole arrived, he began trying to organize a riding party and spent an unusual amount of time on the telephone making arrangements. At last he was successful and several of the other weekenders set off with him for the Piping Rock Club in Locust Valley.

At the stable, as the group prepared to set out, Cole spied a horse that struck his fancy. The attendant tried to discourage him from choosing that particular mount because it was known to be skittish, but Cole insisted. Soon after the party set out on the bridle path, as they came up over a hill, Cole's horse was frightened by a clump of bushes. The animal shied and reared. Cole did not pull the reins too quickly, as was rumored. The skittish horse simply reared and fell backward. Tragically for Cole, he failed to kick the stirrups free. The frantic animal attempted to rise, fell back and rolled, crushing one of Cole's legs. Then it partially regained its feet, tried to shake itself free, staggered and went down again, falling on the opposite side. This time the horse rolled and pulverized Cole's second leg before it freed itself.

In a matter of seconds the accident was over and it had happened so swiftly that Cole hardly realized he was hurt. When Benjamin Moore, another member of the riding party, reached him, Cole was conscious and assured Moore that he was fine. It never occurred to him that he might be seriously injured. But Moore took one look, cautioned Cole not to move and dashed off to summon help. As Moore disappeared, Cole dismissed his friend's concern and calmly took out the ever-present pencil and notebook and, so he insisted later, finished the lyrics to the title song of *You Never Know*.

At the clubhouse, Moore excitedly placed a call for an ambulance. None was immediately available. He then desperately sought and got one from the Locust Valley Fire Department.

Once Cole was in the ambulance, he went into shock. For the next couple of days he was by turns unconscious and delirious. Dr. Joseph B. Connolly, who was in charge of the case, minimized publicly the seriousness of the accident. The official version was that the songwriter had suffered multiple fractures in both legs, that there had been no other injuries and that the patient was resting comfortably.

Nevertheless, word of the catastrophic nature of the accident spread. The following evening Cole had been expected at a party in honor of George Gershwin which was being held in the April-in-Paris Room at Leon and Eddie's nightclub on West 52nd Street.The party was being given by Henry Fitz of Chappell and all composers and lyricists who were under contract to the publisher were invited.

Cole's failure to appear caused Fitz's assistant, Selma Tamber, to put in a call to find out why. "When Vincent Youmans and Jerome Kern and all the rest heard what had happened, the deadliest pall came over the party," she recalled. "Strangely enough, Cole with all his sarcasm and sense of humor and high-handedness was greatly beloved.

They had such respect for the talent of the man. The party broke up very early."

Until that moment, Cole had been a symbol of the invincible youth who rode unscathed from one triumph to another. Now in some mysterious way, even though the details were lacking, his colleagues seemed to realize that the golden period had come to an end.

The following day, Cole's secretary, Margaret Moore, assured reporters that her employer was "very cheerful, all things considered." The rest of his staff also played down the extent of his injuries in their reports.

When John Smith, his chauffeur, called Ray Kelly, a friend of Cole's who had expected to dine with him the evening after the accident, and said something had happened, Kelly asked what. Smith said Cole had broken both legs. "That sounds like a calamity," Kelly later recalled saying, but Smith would neither confirm nor deny the accuracy of that estimate.

Privately, Dr. Connolly had contacted Linda at 13 Rue de Monsieur and advised immediate amputation of both legs. Linda insisted that any decision be postponed until she arrived. She then contacted Kate Porter at once and explained her theory that the loss of Cole's legs would so crush his spirit that he would never recover and that every effort must be made to save them. Kate agreed. Despite widespread criticism by friends, Linda held firm to her decision.

Two days after the catastrophe, Elsa Maxwell and Clifton Webb visited Cole at the hospital, where they found him under heavy sedation. Even so, he made a visible effort to play the gracious host. Upon sight of Elsa, he whispered, "It just goes to show fifty million Frenchmen can't be wrong. They eat horses instead of ride them." (Elsa, touched by this show of spirit, reported the remark in a letter published in *Harper's* magazine, although for some reason she signed it with the pseudonym of Mrs. Rochell Potts.)

After greeting her, Cole turned to Webb and said,

"Don't worry. The show *will* be finished." At the moment he had in hand only "You Never Know," "At Long Last Love" and "From Alpha to Omega."

One of Linda's first moves after arrival was to bring in Dr. John J. Moorhead, a noted bone specialist. Dr. Moorhead, apprised of Linda's and Kate's views that amputation would prove psychologically devastating to the patient, examined the legs, talked to Cole and frankly told the women that under ordinary circumstances he would agree with Dr. Connolly's recommendations. At the moment, he reserved judgment, but if a high fever were to develop, amputation would be necessary.

In the meantime, he explained candidly and in detail to Cole the extent of the injury and possible alternative treatments. "Then," as Cole later remembered it, "he smiled in the way doctors always do when they're about to say something unpleasant and asked, 'Do you have courage?' "

Cole said he didn't know.

Dr. Moorehead said that this was an opportunity to find out. If Cole wished, the doctor said, he would attempt to rebuild the shattered legs. Progress would be slow. There would be great pain, great discomfort. Discouragement would plague them. They might even fail, but there was also a chance of achieving their goal. He likened the task to assembling a jigsaw puzzle.

Cole agreed to accept the agony and the setbacks in hopes of saving his legs. Once that decision was made, his outlook apparently improved. Until the accident, he had ruled as despotically as an emperor, whether in Paris, Venice or New York. And, despite Cole's lighthearted air, Clifton Webb, who visited him often, sensed an underlying despair. Webb sought out Linda and told her that in spite of her own precarious health, she must summon up the strength to get Cole out of the hospital and back to New York. She agreed.

On November 29, Cole was admitted to Doctors' Hospital in Manhattan. There, Dr. Foster Kennedy was called in as a consultant by Dr. Moorhead. Miss Moore, Cole's ever loyal secretary, told curious reporters that her boss was "doing very nicely."

At that moment, in the hospital, Cole was undergoing almost unbearable pain. Yet he failed to admit his misery even when it became so intense that his eyes would involuntarily roll back in his head and great rivulets of sweat would pour down his face. In fact, his stoicism was so great that his bravery earned him the immediate admiration of nurses and doctors, who so often witnessed the spectacle of the debilitating effects of excruciating pain. Even at his worst moments, he refused to dramatize his situation or to complain about the unremitting torment and the helplessness of his predicament.

Surgery was performed in an attempt to relieve some of the pressures and minimize nerve damage. Then, on December 8, he underwent a second operation, this one to repair nerve damage. Afterward, his legs were wrapped in vaseline gauze and placed in plaster casts. To help guide them, Cole's doctors requested that he keep notes on the various sensations—pain, itching, twitching—that he experienced during the day. They hoped to draw upon these sensations to learn what unseen injuries had been incurred and how much damage had been done and to utilize his information as a guide in rebuilding the legs.

"I never lost heart," Cole once explained. "I made an adventure of it." Yet occasionally the mask slipped. On one occasion, for instance, Dr. Moorhead asked what sensations he had to report.

"There are at least a thousand little men in these legs and they're all carrying sharp knives. They're jabbing all over. I'm in great pain," Cole reported.

Dr. Moorhead casually nodded and remarked, "Well, you're entitled to that."

Suddenly, the perfect patient vanished. In his place was five feet, six inches of fury who ordered the doctor from the room. Somewhat later, Cole was contrite and apologetic, but he remained angry at himself for losing control.

Indicative of his struggle to treat his tragedy lightly was the game he played with Elsa, naming his left leg Josephine and his right Geraldine. Each, according to its responses to treatment, was given a personality. Josephine was a docile creature who gave as little trouble as possible. Geraldine, on the other hand, was "a hellion, a bitch, a psychopath." She was, they agreed, a potential murderess. Yet when the doctors broached the subject of doing away with her, Cole's refusal was prompt and final. He loved Geraldine no less than Josephine.

Indomitable though his spirit may have been, no human being could endure such a continuous onslaught of pain. As he suffered one sympathetic ailment after another, an increasing amount of sedation was prescribed. There was one kind of painkiller, then another and another and another, until at the height of his suffering he was taking over a dozen types of sedatives. Even though they were of various kinds, the quantity became so great that his doctors grew concerned over the possibility that he would become addicted.

As his condition slowly improved, they attempted to avert this by gradually taking him off the various drugs. Finally, Dr. Moorhead discontinued everything except one-half of a belladonna tablet, and Cole took up yoga in an attempt to regain self-control.

On January 17, 1938, he was honored at a surprise party which Elsa tossed in the Perrouquet suite at the Waldorf-Astoria. The purpose: a "coming-out party" for Josephine and Geraldine in honor of having their casts removed. The fact that such removal was impossible and would be for many months perturbed no one. Everyone had only one goal: to cheer up Cole.

Elsa arranged that Imogene Coca, June Sillman, Mary Jane Walsh, Grace Moore, Maxine Sullivan, Evelyn Laye, Adele Dixon and Jack Buchanan appear in musical number and skits, one of which satirized the "Meadowlark hunting set." And among the 500 guests who gathered to honor the ailing songwriter were Mrs. Vincent Astor, Colonel Theodore and Mrs. Roosevelt, Mrs. William

Randolph Hearts, Mr. and Mrs. Benjamin Moore, Mrs. William Woodward, Count and Countess Castlebarco, Mr. and Mrs. Alfred Lunt, Mr. and Mrs. Artur Rubinstein, Mr. and Mrs. Richard Rodgers, Mr. and Mrs. Gilbert Miller, Gertrude Lawrence, Countess Dorothy di Frasso, Ina Claire, Dorothy Fellowes-Gordon, Duke Fulco di Verdura, Baron Nicolas de Gunzberg, Prince Serge Obolensky, and George Jean Nathan, Rodman Wanamaker, Clifton Webb, Condé Nast, Frederick Lonsdale, George Abbott, Marc Connelly, Frank Crowninshield, and Cecil Beaton.

Afterward Cole said that he was so filled with morphine he hadn't the foggiest notion of what was taking place, but admitted he had enjoyed the attention. Later when he was told about the party, he said, "Apparently everyone had a wonderful time. I'm sorry I missed it."

In the days that followed in his Waldorf apartment, Cole was often wheeled to the twin pianos, one of which had been raised by wooden blocks, making it possible for his wheelchair to be shoved close to it. One of Cole's legs was placed on a hassock, the other on a piano stool. In this way, many hours were spent playing the classics.

But X-rays soon revealed that further surgery was necessary, and on February 3 Cole underwent still another operation on his right leg. Next day, *The New York Times* reported his condition "favorable," and not long after he was released from Doctors' Hospital. He decided upon a month's vacation in Cuba, taking a friend, Ray Kelly, and his valet Paul to help him get about. Between them Kelly and Paul took to sweeping Cole up and carrying him wherever he wanted to go—into nightclubs, aboard ships, planes, etc.

In Havana, Cole whiled away the days spending long hours on the beach, baking his legs in the sun and laving warm salt water over them. Then, later in the afternoon, after a nap, he and Kelly would make their way to the Florida Bar, a favorite of Cole's since it was there that his beloved daiquiris had been invented.

In the hospital and out, under sedation or without it, tunes kept rolling through Cole's mind. Soon after the accident, Dr. Moorhead, a Porterphile, began urging him to go back to writing, not only because he admired Cole's songs but also because he believed that it was the only possible way for Cole to avoid an emotional collapse. Cole agreed to try and was pleased to discover that for him concentration on music was almost as effective as sedation.

When Dr. Moorhead was not urging him to work, Elsa was telling him: "Rise above it! Never look back! Have no regrets! Look to the future!" Cole tried. As he had promised Webb he would, he struggled to finish the score of *You Never Know* so that it would be ready for rehearsal in early February.

Upon return from Cuba, he was eager to hear the full orchestrations of the show. Because it was impractical for him to go to the theater, on February 28, 1936, the Shubert brothers, who were producing it, sent eighteen musicians to Cole's Waldorf-Towers suite. A six-hour session ensued. Libby Holman, Lupe Velez, Toby Wing and Webb performed the entire show. To Cole's drugged brain, it seemed his best score.*

The libretto is based on Siegfried Geyer's romantic comedy *By Candlelight,* which had been produced with only small success in 1929 in spite of a cast that included Gertrude Lawrence, Leslie Howard and Reginald Owen. Now Rowland Leigh, an English screenwriter, had adapted it.

In New Haven, on March 5, *You Never Know* drew the largest opening night crowd since pre-Depression days. Webb and Libby Holman, handicapped by mediocre material, found themselves overshadowed by Lupe Velez,

* Twenty years later when he was once more thinking clearly, he he wrote me after I had seen a revival of the show at a summer theater: ". . . Why anyone ever dug up *You Never Know,* I shall never know. It was the worst show with which *I* was ever connected."

a mercurial beauty whose tantrums and peccadilloes earned her enormous amounts of tabloid coverage as "The Mexican Spitfire."

Upon first encounter with her, most people were charmed by the extravagance of her personality. In New Haven, for instance, she regularly made the trip from her theater dressing room to the Taft Hotel wearing only slippers and a voluminous mink. Other conduct was not so attractive. On sight, she felt an antipathy for Libby Holman. In New Haven, during curtain calls, the two engaged in a tussle with Lupe blacking Libby's eye.

The production itself was chaotic. After New Haven, it moved to the Shubert Theater in Boston, where on March 9 it opened to an audience that seemed so intent upon saluting the beleaguered composer's courage that even Mrs. Calvin Coolidge, the former First Lady, came out of retirement to attend. The production was still chaotic.

By the time the show reached the National Theater in Washington, D.C., on March 22, changes were still being made in both the book and the score. Robert Katscher had added a song and Rowland Leigh had written additional lyrics. Backstage relations had, if it were possible, deteriorated. Lupe Velez's hatred of Libby had become so passionate that she often threatened to "keel her." The stage manager took the threats seriously and insisted upon escorting Libby from her dressing room to the stage, which further infuriated Lupe. Webb, who said he thought the ruckus was pure publicity, did invite Lupe to supper after the show to attempt to calm her. The conversation started off quietly enough. Then, gradually, Lupe grew hysterical and showed Webb the ring with which she intended to murder Libby. Eventually, she regained control of herself and Webb decided to give her a straight talking-to. "Lupe, you must not say such things. One day you'll turn them all against yourself," prophetic words in light of her eventual suicide.

The production became less chaotic, and by the time the show reached the Forrest Theater in Philadelphia on April 2, Webb felt that sixty percent of the script worked, even though J. J. Shubert kept saying that he couldn't understand what the show meant and suggested that they drop the idea of an intimate musical and add some chorus girls. "He wanted to put in the old trout from *Blossom Time*," Webb recalled later. "I persuaded them to call in George Abbott to doctor the show and bring it up to par. It was agreed."

Pittsburgh followed Philadelphia, then on April 30, the company opened in Detroit to a good reception. In Chicago, the notices were mixed. Libby left the cast. In Des Moines, Iowa, the audience response was not discouraging and the critics were kindly.

Arrangements for the final date of the spring tour had been in preparation since the day the show went into rehearsal. This three-day engagement at English's Theater in Indianapolis, Indiana, was sponsored by the Indianapolis Civic Theater, and Governor M. Clifford Townsend proclaimed May 23, the opening date, Cole Porter Day.

The Civic Theater originally had hoped Cole would attend. Upon learning that his health would not permit his presence, the committee delayed making the news public, fearing that this disappointing fact would dim enthusiasm for the project.

Even though Cole was absent, his mother appeared at all the events to acknowledge the tribute to her son, and Harvey Cole, a cousin, represented him officially. In addition to the Governor, William H. Long (mayor of Indianapolis), Walter C. Boetcher (mayor of Peru), Mrs. J. O. Cole (Cole's step-grandmother) and Mr. and Mrs. Omar Cole (his cousins), as well as other relatives participated.

Cole sent telegrams to the dignitaries and an overall message to "everybody else who had anything whatsoever to do with this truly wonderful but I think undeserved honor to me and my family. . . . Seven months ago I had my legs knocked from under me by a very unkind and inconsiderate horse. Tonight, I find my wind knocked out of me by so much attention, and even if I were actually with you I should still be speechless.

"Luckily my mother, who, like all good mothers, has so often borne the brunt of her son's misdeeds, is here to face the music for me and I wish her much joy and happiness. It's probably the only sensation that can compare with my own deep gratitude to you for this signal honor."

Although it is impossible to be certain, undoubtedly the message was written by one of Cole's representatives and simply approved by him. Certainly, it does not seem couched in his style.

There was another message, too. This one, addressed to the head of the Civic Theater, Wallace O. Lee, is more typical of its author:

> Dear Mr. Lee:
>
> Of course it's something to be a Hoosier who becomes a New York and Hollywood celebrity; but when a New York and Hollywood celebrity becomes so celebrated that he's known in Indiana, too, he touches the mantle of fame itself. Mr. Cole Porter of Indiana, New York and Hollywood and several continents receives honor from his native state for being an honor to it.
>
> (signed)
> Booth Tarkington

The following day the Indianapolis *Times* finessed an embarrassing situation. Their reporter filed a glowing account of the ceremonies, and their drama critic credited Cole with the good things in the show and blamed its deficiencies on others.

Thus, the tour ended—or almost ended. When accounts were finally settled, the Civic Theater found itself in the red. Their representatives had blindly signed a contract obligating them to guarantee the Shubert producing firm an amount almost equal to the maximum possible gross on the first-night theater party which they sponsored. As a result, when Wallace Lee sent Cole a scrapbook and medallion as a memento of the occasion, he politely suggested that Cole intercede with the Shuberts, asking them to subtract the amount saved in federal-tax monies from the Civic Theater's indebtedness to them.

Cole's response, contained in a letter dated June 17, in which he thanked the Civic Theater for the medallion, clearly delineated a little-known side of the songwriter.

> As regards the Shuberts, and your funds deficiency, I regret that I have no authority and can do nothing to help you. I have suggested numerous times, to the Shuberts, that they communicate with you in regard to this matter and if they have failed to do so, I can offer no further solution.
>
> Goodbye and again many, many thanks.
>
> Sincerely,

A more emotional nature might have offered to make another attempt or have sent a check to help the organization out, but that was not Cole's way. It illustrates the accuracy with which George Cukor depicted him when he once said, "Beneath that social exterior and that fancy-schmantzy way of talking, he was a tough businessman."

Ultimately the show in that version did not reach New York, but it did get there the following fall.

Yet in his private struggle, the courage that Porter displayed combined with natural charm to sweep away all annoyances. Linda, who had firmly opposed his undertaking additional film work after finishing *Rosalie*, had been considering delivering an ultimatum in the fall of 1937: that he choose between films and his marriage. When the accident occurred, the idea of a divorce was forgotten. Although still angry, she rushed to Cole's side, just as a quarter of a century earlier she had rallied to aid the injured Ned Thomas. She told their mutual friend, Winsor French, "It's too heartbreaking. You don't desert a sinking ship."

Linda, despite suffering severely from a respiratory condition at the time, gallantly rose above their small differences to provide the emotional support that her husband desperately needed. There was an obligation and she was determined to fulfill it with dignity and grace, qualities which she had in abundance. That year, for example, when a close friend died in Boston, Linda wanted to attend the funeral. Air travel was not yet popular so Cole arranged for a doctor friend of theirs to travel near the compartment that Linda and another friend of the dead woman were sharing. All went well on the trip to Boston, but on the return trip the doctor was summoned to Linda's compartment. Seizing the usual heart and lung remedies, he rushed into the room. There sat Linda calm, collected and healthy—trying to comfort her hysterical friend. "I think this can be said of Linda—that she always rose to occasions," Schuyler Parsons later observed. "She knew how worried Cole was over her making that trip and how ill he was and she was bound she would be fit and well when she got back to New York."

Cole evoked sacrifices from less expected places, too. After he had been ill for some time, Dr. Sirmay noticed that Dr. Moorhead never missed visiting his patient and inquired when he planned to go on vacation. Dr. Moorhead replied that Cole's legs were in such wretched condition that he would not be able to leave. He told Dr. Sirmay, it had become his goal in life to save those legs. To fulfill his exacting assignment required his being alert to the slightest clues as to where trouble might be developing. By all reasonable medical evidence, he admitted, a double amputation should have been performed immediately, *but*, he added, an extraordinary temperament necessitated an extraordinary wager to win all—or to lose it.

At this point, enter the Spewacks. Quiet, retiring, Russian-born Samuel Spewack had in early youth gone to work for Herbert Bayard Swope's *World* and had distinguished himself for his sometimes ingenious, sometimes impertinent but always thoughtful dispatches from foreign lands. His wife, Bella, was Hungarian-born and she had a warm, wild exuberance that either exhilarated a person or drove him mad. She was likely to describe a woman as "almost as badly dressed as I am."

She made snap decisions which seemed destined to be wrong but turned out to be correct. Luckily, she was blessed with an instinct for musical theater and she had the drive and the single-mindedness of an automaton. For a bedridden, agony-wracked composer, Bella was an angel in disguise.

By 1937, Sam and Bella had written a series of Broadway plays, the most successful of which was the Hollywood farce *Boy Meets Girl*. The project which they brought to Porter was at first called *I Am an American* and then changed to *First in the Hearts*. It was based on their play *Clear All Wires,* a farce and/or satire on Americans in diplomatic service. For the lead they hoped to secure Charlotte Greenwood.

Cole found the material agreeable and worked hard not only on the new score but also on maintaining his private humor. When a visitor arrived he joked and played and sometimes even descended to the level of donning funny hats. What he refused to accept, at least what he refused to express, was the slightest degree of self-pity. His pain was unrelenting, but as far as possible he ignored it.

Occasionally this was impossible and the façade cracked, as, for instance, on the night when he had had too many drinks in an attempt to blot out the gnawing ache in his legs. Finding the pain still plagued him, he asked Ray Kelly to bring him his pills. Kelly refused to allow him to mix alcohol and sedatives. Cole insisted, became abusive and finally demanded the bell that he might summon Paul to bring the medicine. Kelly again refused. After an ugly exchange, Kelly, who also had had too many drinks, stood up and said, "Porter, I'm leaving." With that he walked out, leaving Cole without the bell. As he walked down the hall, he could hear Cole berating him.

The following day, Kelly neither called nor appeared at the apartment, although it had been his custom to see that Cole took his daily drive. Then, late in the afternoon, Kelly's doorbell rang. When he answered, he was handed a large box from the Waldorf Florist. Puzzled, he opened it. Inside the huge package was one large, very dead lily.

Attached was a card which read: "So sorry. Please call and have dinner with me. Cole."

On June 9, 1938, his forty-seventh birthday, Cole suffered a setback, after slipping on a marble stair and breaking his left leg again, making it impossible for him to continue going out socially as he had begun to do. Travel was, of course, out of the question, so the Porters rented a place at Lido Beach, Long Island. Oliver Jennings, a friend from college days who lived there, located it for them and Linda efficiently organized the household so that her husband might have minimal discomfort.

Naturally, the legendary Porters were the object of a great deal of speculation and almost as soon as they moved in a small mystery developed around them. Neighbors noticed that a truck from the Waldorf-Astoria appeared at the house twice weekly. What odd, exotic delicacies, the Long Islanders must have wondered, were being delivered? And how disappointed they would have been to discover that the truck picked up soiled linen on the first trip and brought it back freshly laundered on the second, an arrangement Linda had made to insure the standard of workmanship to which her husband was accustomed.

The small staff included a general maid; an excellent cook; John Smith, the chauffeur; Weston, Linda's maid; and Paul, Cole's valet. Cole was ever after to recall the kindness shown him by Paul during those first days of illness, as well as that of Dr. Moorhead and Ray Kelly.*

For entertainment, word and card games were played. Kelly is recalled by those who knew him at the time as something of a wizard at the former. Among the other players were Jennings, Neysa McMein, painter Ben Baz, and Elsa. Jennings later remarked that Kelly was the equal of any player, so good, in fact, that Jennings always wondered whether he hadn't at times helped with lyrics.

This summer of 1938 was a fateful one for Cole—and

* In his will he left Paul's twin daughters $75,000 and Kelly and his four children the rights to one-half of his copyrights.

the new show he was working on always occupied a special niche in his affections. The vicissitudes that *You Never Know* encountered in tryout had somewhat shaken his faith in himself, which was inevitable since by this time his legs had been broken and reset seven times, and his emotions as shattered as his bones. Describing his state of mind, Cole likened it to being married seven times to the wrong woman. Luckily, he had the Spewack show to concentrate on. Vinton Freedley was once again the producer. There were parts for Victor Moore, William Gaxton and June Knight, the girl from *Jubilee.* Freedley was also hopeful that they might persuade Mae West to undertake the role of the ambassador's wife.

Miss West was approached and expressed interest, but apparently she wasn't kidding when she said, "C'mup 'n see me sometime." She insisted that Cole come to hear her sing. It was explained that because of his disability he couldn't get about, but the great comedienne remained adamant. Reluctantly the idea was given up. Then, fortuitously, the Spewacks ran into Sophie Tucker coming out of a delicatessen. Bella called Cole and told him to relax, their problems were solved.

Meanwhile, one tune after another emerged from Cole's drug-stimulated brain. As he viewed the completed work, he was seized with euphoria. If the score approached the excellence that in his judgment it possessed, he could count on an active creative existence whatever his physical prognosis. Freedley, the Spewacks and the stars were as enthusiastic as he was.

During the last part of August, Cole returned to town. His left leg was still in a small cast below the knee; the right, encased to his hip. Linda, at this point, slipped, fell and fractured her arm; and thereafter, they referred to themselves as "Mr. and Mrs. Bones."

At about the same time that Cole returned to the city, Clifton Webb arrived from Europe to begin rehearsals for the rewritten *You Never Know* and received a nasty surprise. John Shubert, during Webb's absence, had done away with all of George Abbott's revisions, added a bar scene, a swimming-pool scene and engaged young lovelies for the chorus. "They were paying me more than they had paid Jolson," Webb said. "But I couldn't speak the lines and I knew we were dead before we opened out of town."

Cole, at this point, turned his back on *You Never Know*. When the company opened in Hartford, Connecticut, on September 14, Libby Holman was once more playing her original part. Paul and Grace Hartman, dance satirists, had been added, but it was to no avail.

On September 21, the show came to the Winter Garden in New York. Patricia Coffin, then a columnist for the *World-Telegram*, reported next day that although Cole was unable to go to the posttheater parties, he and Linda attended the opening whose audience she described as ". . . a chatting, smoking 'mélange' of bejeweled, befurred and perfumed women wedged between the black and white phalanx of their escorts. . . ."

The press reaction was mild. Cole's songs—"At Long Last Love," "From Alpha to Omega," "What Is That Tune?" and "You Never Know" failed to get across. Critic Euphemia Van Rensselaer Wyatt summed up the venture by remarking that *By Candlelight* ". . . was a dull event with Gertrude Lawrence and Leslie Howard . . . [and it] had managed to take the bright edge off Cole Porter's music; to blur the comedy of Clifton Webb and to still the vibrations of Libby Holman."

After a month four chorus girls were dropped as an economy measure and some of the cast members accepted salary cuts, but such measures failed to help. Fourteen weeks after opening, the show had run its course. The night before it closed, J. J. Shubert appeared in Webb's dressing room. "Clifton, if we put things back the way they were, don't you think we could get a run out of it?"

"Not with me," Webb told him—and that was the end of it. It was also Webb's final appearance on Broadway.

Word was out that Cole Porter was through. He was no longer chic in many circles. At the time, for instance, producer Max Gordon was negotiating with what were then two bright young writers, John Monks, Jr., and Fred

Finklehoffe, co-authors of *Brother Rat*. They had written a libretto which Gordon hoped to produce and he suggested Cole as the ideal composer. Finklehoffe and Monks were having none of him and suggested instead an unknown whom they predicted would soon be better than Cole. "Fine. When he is bring him around—until that time I'll wait," Gordon said.

He is still waiting.

When rehearsals began for the Spewack show, which was finally called *Leave It to Me,* Cole was too sick to attend, but followed developments closely from home. There were several problems. Sophie Tucker, who had never worked in a musical play, had trouble learning to relate to other actors. Victor Moore was his usual gloomy self. He was convinced, as always, that not one of his lines was funny and nothing could persuade him that they were. During the run of *Anything Goes* he had resolutely maintained that Cole, Lindsay and Crouse were hiring claques to produce the theater-rocking laughter he inspired. Now he suspected Cole and the Spewacks were about to do the same for this show. In addition, June Knight was unhappy.

From the moment she signed, it was apparent that she was dissatisfied. On the way to Cole's apartment to sing "My Heart Belongs to Daddy," she kept begging agent Louis Shurr to persuade the composer to give her "Most Gentlemen Don't Like Love." Shurr explained that it was suitable for a sophisticated, mature woman, but that with her the idea was to capitalize on her youth and natural sweetness.

Miss Knight had made a personal success in Jubilee and Cole was of the opinion that she had that "x" quality which creates a top star. But as rehearsals progressed, she quibbled and complained about so many things that finally Shurr went to her recently acquired millionaire husband, Arthur Cameron, and put the question to him: Did he or did he not want his wife out of the show? Cameron did.

Since rehearsals were well under way, a replacement had

to be found immediately. One of Linda's friends suggested a protégée of hers, a girl with "a thrilling voice." Cole agreed to hear her. After the audition, he told Linda: "Her voice *is* thrilling. What your friend neglected to mention is, her protégée is a midget."

With the show two weeks into rehearsal, Shurr arranged for producer Laurence Schwab to bring an unknown girl named Mary Martin to audition for the role. Schwab had discovered this girl in an amateur contest at the Hollywood Trocadero and had put her under contract. Previously, she had taught dancing and since winning the contest had occasionally appeared in nightclubs and on radio.

As they walked in, Mary Martin later said, she saw a sea of faces, "the most conspicuous belonging to a small man lying in a bed which had a piano hanging from the ceiling above it."

That was Cole. The others included Victor Moore, Bill Gaxton, Vinton Freedley, the Spewacks and some of Cole's personal friends. Bella Spewack took one look at the auditioner, who wore a funny off-face hat and "strange clothes," and could not imagine *her* playing the part. Cole thought she looked altogether too wrenlike. Someone asked her what she proposed to do, and she said she'd sing four songs. After the second, Cole told her the audition was divine. Nevertheless, Miss Martin insisted upon singing all four. After she'd finished, Cole again told her she was divine.

"It was the strangest audition," Bella Spewack said years later. "Cole said, 'divine'. But he always said divine. I didn't know whether he meant it. So I asked her to audition in a theater so I could listen from the balcony. But before she could answer, Cole said, 'Deck her out,' and I knew he meant he liked her."

In later years, few people believed Cole's contention that Mary Martin had not been aware of the implication of a few lines in the song when the show opened in New Haven. She herself has said that it was "more than a few."

Actually, because of the impact of her debut, the part she played has been enlarged in memory. She did not really figure importantly in the plot. She was directed to be herself and to sing the song with an innocence that was real and that she was encouraged to project to the fullest. She never had time to read the script or to stay for a complete rehearsal. "I didn't really care," she said. "Because I was in a Broadway musical. My life's ambition."

At the premiere in New Haven on October 13, 1938, she made her entrance and spoke innocently her first and only line of dialogue, "I want to renew my subscription." The audience reaction to that statement startled her. Yale boys howled and whistled and stamped and applauded. At the moment everyone there except Mary Martin knew that she had been the mistress of the publisher (Bill Gaxton) and that she was now saying, "I want to be your mistress for another year."

"When Mary delivered that line, she was so shocked at the reaction she turned around to look at them and see what she had done wrong," Bella Spewack said. "And they loved her all the more for it."

When it came time for her song, she did it just as she always had. Although she hadn't understood the meaning of some of the lyrics, there hadn't been time to go into all that and it didn't seem important anyway because everyone was forever telling her how wonderful she was and encouraging her to sing the song exactly as she had the first time. Sophie Tucker especially told her to be sure to keep her "eyes up to heaven" as she naturally did, but Miss Tucker also showed her the exact words and phrases when the eyes must look straight up. (It wasn't until Miss Martin was asked to sing the song on radio and found some of the lyrics had been changed that she asked, "Why?" And even in 1965, she *still* thought of the song as she did the first time she heard it.)

Cole was too ill to attend the New Haven opening, but Linda went. Immediately after the curtain fell, she called him to say that in Mary Martin they had a bright new star to add to the established contingent.

From New Haven the show went to the Shubert in Boston. There, one day, the cast was astonished to see Cole wheeled into one of the theater's boxes. Despite Dr. Moorhead's objections, he had insisted upon being on hand to make any necessary changes. "Right then and there," Sophie Tucker said, "everyone made up their minds that we were going to give this man a hit."

The plot of the show concerns Alonzo Goodhue (Victor Moore), who is assigned to an ambassadorship in Moscow, while longing for his Topeka, Kansas, home. His wife (Sophie Tucker) is annoyed because they weren't assigned to London and blames it on the fact that they have only five children instead of nine like Joseph Kennedy. A Chicago correspondent tries to help Goodhue get recalled by writing antagonistic speeches for him, having him boot a Nazi in the stomach and take a potshot at a Russian nobleman, but every seeming faux pas turns into a much-admired act. At last he's recalled when he offers an international peace plan which would end war.

The Boston critics generally admired the show, even before changes were completed in the second act. Amusingly, Elinor Hughes, after praising the undertaking, wrote: "We offer as a brief suggestion that the song 'My Heart Belongs to Daddy' and the scene built around it haven't much place in the show; *Leave It to Me* doesn't need a strip tease to make it funny." Several days later, finding the number was still being performed, Miss Hughes lunched with Freedley and urged him to cut out that dirty song in an otherwise clean show. Freedley said he liked it and she pressed her point, saying that the show was too good to need blue material to put it over.

Every evening, Cole studied the performance and made notes for himself and others. On a day when the company had given matinee and evening performances and rehearsed new material after the latter, an incident occurred that Richard Halliday, Mary Martin's manger-husband, felt had an everlasting effect upon her.

At 3:00 A.M., her telephone rang. It was Cole, who said, "I didn't hear the word 'maul' in the lyric tonight." Then he hung up. Miss Martin was flabbergasted, but from that time on she made certain that audiences understood every word in every lyric she ever sang.

It was just this perfectionistic attitude which Cole brought to all his work. Never would it have occurred to him to wait until he saw the singer at the theater next morning, if the call would improve the delivery of the song.

How did the new star react to Cole generally? Assessing him later, she said that she felt he was a taskmaster. She knew that he had definite opinions about how numbers should be done and he had the perfectionist's habit of demanding the best of everyone.

In Boston, Louis Shurr was astonished to find that Miss Martin was doing a swing version of an operatic aria in the first act. It was interpolated—a number she had performed in her nightclub act with great success. When Shurr asked Cole whether he was going to allow this, Cole said he wanted to avoid trouble at all costs. Shurr then asked whether he could talk to Freedley. Cole said he could, and Shurr pointed out to Freedley that it was hardly helpful to the show to have Miss Martin appear as an operetta singer in one act and a courtesean in the second. Freedley, according to Shurr, said that it didn't bother him; when she sang the aria, he went to the men's room. "Don't you think the audience feels the same way?" Shurr asked.

Obviously they didn't. The number stopped the show every night, but Shurr proved to be a persuasive figure because on the following Saturday the number was deleted.

On November 9, 1938, *Leave It to Me* arrived at the Imperial Theater in New York, where it played to a dazzling group of first-nighters, who cheered it. Its acceptance also proved a needed shot in the arm for Cole. Following his dazzling performance in writing the score for *Anything Goes* in 1934, there had been a steady decline in the quality of his work, reaching its nadir in *You Never Know*. With *Leave It to Me*, the resurgence of creative power, coupled with his courageous behavior in the face of misfortune, gave the critics an opportunity to salute him, which everyone from Robert Benchley to George Jean Nathan did. Not that he became sacrosanct. Richard Watts agreed with Benchley and Nathan, but added: "Of course,

Mr. Porter still appears to feel that no score of his is official without reference to Elsa Maxwell, and I still do not see why he was so grimly determined to get into his lyrics a sock at Heywood Broun. In one way at least the songs are almost revolutionary, and I'm not referring to the fact that here is one musical comedy to my knowledge that used the Internationale as the first-act finale. The startling thing is that Mr. Porter makes no reference to Lady Mendl."

The songs that critics liked most were "My Heart Belongs to Daddy," "From Now On," "Most Gentlemen Don't Like Love," and "I'm Taking the Steps to Russia." Walter Winchell was one of the few who thought "Get Out of Town" good enough to rate a mention.

Cole flourished as one good notice after another came in. Although his health was still precarious, his ambition now became unlimited. Once more musical acceptance proved itself a succor to his spirit.

CHAPTER XI

After recovering from the initial shock of the accident and after the legs had seemingly been saved, Cole still faced the problem of learning to live with what he regarded as a temporary disability. He was to try to solve the problem in a variety of ways, even after osteomyelitis, an infection of the marrow of the bone, complicated his progress and made full recovery an almost impossible goal.

To help him along, Dr. Moorhead originally had urged that as soon as he was able to travel he go to Cuba; now, not quite two years after the accident, the doctor again prescribed a vacation in some sun-drenched country where, as Cole put it, "They could set me out in the sun like a potted plant."

Cole agreed to go, but complicated plans by scheduling an arduous journey which many full-bodied men would have hesitated undertaking and by insisting upon learning to speak Spanish fluently before setting out. The latter was accomplished in a single month. With Ray Kelly to keep him company and to help the faithful Paul in moving him about, Cole set out for the Machu Picchu ruins in Peru.

In order to reach the site, Cole, whose legs were still in braces, had to be lifted to the back of a horse, after which the tension-filled group slowly wound their way around the dusty, sinuous mountain roads. There were sheer drops on each side, and once they faced a precarious-looking wooden bridge which made Kelly and Paul suggest turning back. Cole refused and insisted upon going forward even though one misstep could have proved fatal.

Upon arrival at the ruins, the party was confronted by the most primitive accommodations. The rooms were barren. Dining conditions were meager and there were only outside bathing and toilet facilities. Both Kelly and Paul expected an explosion from the man who sometimes sent back a daiquiri three times so that it be not too sweet, not too sour, but just right.

In Machu Picchu, there were no such demands. Cole fell into the spirit of the place and enjoyed roughing it, even insisting upon having a photo made of himself bathing from a basin on a tree stump so that he could send it to Linda. Each morning, too, although still getting about with canes, he doggedly set out to see the ruins. Before leaving the area, he had managed to learn the history and significance of most of what he had seen.

Upon returning to New York, Cole was hardly given a moment to think about the condition of his legs. In his absence, Linda had gone to Paris, closed 13 Rue de Monsieur, and disposed of the contents of their wine cellar because of the threatening international situation and because Cole's health made the possibility of their doing any large-scale entertaining in Paris remote. In a move designed to please her husband, she also shipped their furnishings from Paris to California. Although she doubted that she could live there, she was willing to make another attempt, taking two Barthelmess houses. The larger was for the two of them; the smaller Malibu beach house was for him to use as a studio and a place where he could bake his legs in the sun. She was functioning now not only as a wife but, like Katie, was also deciding what was best for Cole's happiness and Cole's career and she was seeing to it that whatever he needed was provided.

In addition to working and traveling, Cole found many minor ways to distract himself from his pain. One was the distinct style of apparel he developed to clothe himself in Hollywood. In New York he had always worn, and continued to wear, dark suits and formal wear. His only Eastern idiosyncrasies in dress were an ever-present untrimmed red or white carnation as a boutonniere and the absence of an overcoat or hat. (He claimed that since he only walked from his heated car to a doorway and back again he had no need for a coat.)

In Hollywood, his wardrobe was, in a word, wild. His sport jackets were plaids and stripes and anything but conventional. Still talked about is the coat that came into existence because he called his tailor one morning and instructed him to bring out some samples so that several sport coats could be made up. Instead of a number of swatches, the tailor carried one large piece of material upon which many squares in a variety of colors and designs had been printed. Cole took one look at the conglomerate cloth and cried, "Make it out of that!" The tailor protested, but Cole had his way. Afterward, he always referred to it as his "Joseph coat" or his "coat of many colors." It caused so much startled comment, with its riotous patches of plaids, stripes, blue and reds, that Cole excitedly ordered several others made for friends. As usual, when he found something that he liked, he could always think of at least ten friends with whom to share his enthusiasm.

He began wearing white socks at this time, too, but for a practical reason. When asked why he wore them with his dinner jacket, he said it was because his grandfather had always worn them. Actually, the socks contained no dye that might cause infection in his legs and at the same time, attracted the attention of passersby who might otherwise bark his shins. But to make such a simple revelation would have been unthinkable to a man as fastidious and imaginative as Cole.

He also amused himself by investing a good deal of time and thought in his friends, sometimes, it seemed, almost to the exclusion of the rest of the world. For instance, columinst Leonard Lyons ran into him at the old Hollyoood Trocadero one evening that summer just before the time when bombs began to fall on Warsaw. Everywhere, no one seemed to think or talk about anything else, and when Cole stopped Lyons and asked, "Have you heard the news? Did you hear?" Lyons assumed he meant the war had begun. Cole shook his head. "So you haven't heard," he said. "Monty got the part!"

"That's the kind of a friend he was," Lyons recalled many years later. "On the day World War Two began, the big news to him was that Monty Woolley had been given the leading part in *The Man Who Came to Dinner.*"

Another incident involving Monty happened shortly after the show had opened. Monty, who was riding high as the irascible Sheridan Whiteside, decided to throw a party. For years, he and Cole had competed to see who could pull the most embarrassing practical joke on the other. Now Cole had a new idea. Since Linda was not attending the party, he called Billy Rose, producer of the circus musical *Jumbo,* and inquired whether Rose could introduce him to a bearded lady who would accompany him to Monty's party. Rose could and did.

When Cole called to make the arrangements, he announced that they need not dress formally. The bearded lady expressed disappointment, saying that she had a beautiful gown, and Cole hastily agreed she should wear it. Then she added that she had to be home early in order to cook a duck dinner. Again he agreed and the bargain was made.

Upon the appointed day and at the appointed hour, the bearded lady met him in "an exquisite lavender dress," her beard hidden behind a long white veil. At the Ritz, she excused herself and disappeared into the ladies' room, soon reemerging with a flowing white beard hanging down the front of her dress. Cole proudly offered his arm and escorted her into the party where, according to actor David Burns, he introduced her to everyone, saying, "I want you to meet Monty's sister."

Finally as the time came for her to leave and she graciously bade everyone goodbye, Cole felt elated. She had been the hit of the party. He escorted her to the street and hailed a taxicab for her. As she got in, she said, "I want to thank you so much. This reminds me of parties when I was a little girl." That remark depressed Cole and set him to wondering whether she had always had the beard or whether it had suddenly grown later in life as the result of a glandular disorder.

When the Porters had left New York for California, Ray Kelly once again had gone along with them to lend a hand in helping Cole get about. Kelly, who loved the water, spent much of his time at the beach house and he was later to say that the best escape for Cole was work. According to him, Cole worked constantly and while composing carried about with him a little soundproof room that no one could penetrate. "It was a small house, this one in Malibu," Kelly said. "And although I thought I knew Cole well before, I got to know him even better there. In such confining quarters, I learned that he worked like a fiend, all hours of the day and night. A great many times I'd think I was talking to him and then suddenly it would dawn on me. He hadn't heard a word. He had music or a lyric or something going through his mind. To test him I'd say, 'A big black gorilla is coming through the window.' And his head would go up and down. Yes, that's right. He hadn't heard a word."

Sometimes, Kelly recalled, in this period Cole would blot out pain by writing a song in his head after he had had several drinks. When he had finished it, he would play it to Kelly. Next day, he might ask what he had been working on the night before. This happened so frequently, in fact, that for his birthday on June 9, Kelly bought him several reams of manuscript paper. "I did it in self-defense," he said. "Because I'd try to hum back what he'd been doing and he'd say, 'No, that's not quite it. It's something like it, but you've forgotten something.' " There were, according to Kelly, countless songs lost in that manner.

What Cole was working on that summer was the 1940 edition of *Broadway Melody*. Once again, Eleanor Powell was to be the top female star and Fred Astaire the male lead. Together, they appeared in an intricate and impressive dance—in fact, a tour de force—to "Begin the Beguine," for which MGM had purchased film rights as a part of the *Jubilee* package. Five new Porter songs were used too, of these "I Concentrate on You" gained widest popularity.

That summer of 1939, Cole heard once more from agent Louis Shurr, who explained that producer-songwriter-scriptwriter B. G. De Sylva had an interesting project for Cole. Actually, De Sylva had called Shurr the previous day in a highly disturbed state over the ecstatic notices that his picture *Bachelor Mother* had received. What irritated De Sylva was that he had obtained the rights to the story when he negotiated his release from Universal Studios. He had then secured the services of Ginger Rogers, director Garson Kanin and writer Norman Krasna. Yet in the reviews Miss Rogers fared handsomely and Kanin and Krasna were hailed for "doing it again," while De Sylva was ignored.

To remedy the situation, Shurr suggested that De Sylva make the kind of success in New York which Hollywood couldn't ignore. De Sylva liked the idea, but how? Shurr said he had a client, Bert Lahr, whom MGM was dropping upon completion of *The Wizard of Oz*. Did De Sylva know of a property for him? De Sylva did—a story called *DuBarry was a Lady*, which Herbert Fields had sold to Paramount and was in the process of getting back. De Sylva said that he and Fields would tailor the story to Lahr's talents. "But who will we get as the leading lady?" he asked.

"Write it for Ethel Merman—and I'll get you Cole Porter," was Shurr's reply. He then called Cole and outlined the plan, omitting all motivations, and asked him to see De Sylva. Cole agreed. There was an immediate rapport, but after De Sylva left, the businessman in Cole took over. "I want to do the show. But who will pay me?" he asked. It was very much like him to demand an advance of a few thousand before proceeding. His personal fortune notwithstanding, he always negotiated in a businesslike way.

"You want an advance now?" Shurr asked. "I'll get one for you." De Sylva provided it, and Cole was ready to go to work.

For the second lead, Shurr suggested a girl who had just been released by Paramount and was appearing in San Francisco with Jack Haley. De Sylva, who was working with Herbert Fields in Santa Barbara, was cautious about signing anyone without much stage experience, but after going to San Francisco to see her perform he changed his mind and asked Shurr to have her audition for Cole.

She was dubious about the idea, telling him: "You know, Louis, I don't sing too well."

He assured her that given her personality, figure and looks, her voice was not too important. "You'll be a sensation on Broadway," he promised. And when Cole saw Betty Grable, he agreed at once.

During the fall *DuBarry Was a Lady* was readied for rehearsal. The story concerns a washroom attendant (Bert Lahr) who is possessed of a passion for a singing star and tries to eliminate competition by putting a mickey in his rival's drink. He becomes confused, drinks the mickey himself, passes out, and suddenly is back in the court of Louis XIV where he is the King and La Merman is DuBarry. Once started, the story had seemed to write itself. Cole dashed off the score without difficulty, and on November 9 the production opened at the Shubert in New Haven. From the premiere to closing night, houses were jammed. Reviewers' enthusiasm was extravagant. Word of mouth was rhapsodic.

After five performances, the company moved to Boston for a November 13 opening. Box-office activity was brisk. Nevertheless the hardworking press agent planted stories that Cole and De Sylva were "frantically trying to clean up the show" to avoid censor trouble. No such artificial box-office stimulants were needed.

Unhappily relations backstage were strained from the first. And all those involved were uneasy, despite the New Haven and Boston triumphs, about how New York would take to this high-class burlesque show. In addition, there was trouble with Phil Regan, a former New York policeman. Regan had been hired without having auditioned after De Sylva saw him in a motion picture.

From the first rehearsal, Cole had predicted that nobody would hear the lyrics beyond the third row, but De Sylva and director Edgar MacGregor reassured him, saying Regan was "holding back." When Cole suggested that the singer let them hear how he sounded, Regan replied that the songs were written for a baritone whereas he was a tenor. To Regan the solution was simple: Let Cole rewrite the songs. Cole was not sympathetic.

Finally, during the tryout, it was decided to replace Regan, but the Singing Cop was not letting that happen without a fight and he induced newspaper friends to enter the fray. One controversial Boston columnist, who admitted not having seen the show, cast Cole as chief villain in refusing to alter a song ". . . even so slightly as to give Regan a chance to hit a high one in the song 'Do I Love You?' " Even so, the harassment was to no avail; Regan's contract was bought up for $6,000 and Ronald Graham was brought in to replace him.

Shortly after, Louis Shurr decided that Betty Grable would elicit a stronger response with a different dancing partner. He suggested Chuck Walters, who was hired, and the ovation the Grable-Walters combination received the first time they appeared together proved Shurr's hunch was correct. If the show accomplished nothing else, it once and for all made it unnecessary to identify Miss Grable as "Jackie Coogan's ex."

While these cast changes were being made, De Sylva asked Cole to write a song with a "low-level sentimental appeal." Cole turned out a number that had it both ways—a humorous ditty of a love-hate relationship—instead of the expected sentimental song. He called it "Friendship" and the surprised audience demanded so many encores that on one occasion Miss Merman and Lahr performed the final one holding sheets of paper upon which new lyrics had just been typed. When the audience still refused to let them go, Lahr begged off by announcing that was all the lines there were and urging, "Come to Philadelphia. There may be some new ones there."

Cole wrote another song for the show while out of town, and he told readers of *Life* magazine about it soon after. There, in a series of pictures of him in various degrees of distress under the headline: "I Had a Song to Write for the Matinee and I Had a Terrible Headache," he had endorsed Bromo-Seltzer. That product had made it possible for him to write "Give Him the Oo-La-La."

People familiar with his reputation for fastidiousness were amazed that he would lend his name to commercial exploitation. Asked why he did it, he once said, "Why not?" On another occasion he said, "Everyone was doing it." And there is probably more than a grain of truth in that answer. Although Cole was a rebel of sorts, he was undoubtedly impressed when Queen Marie of Rumania endorsed products. On the other hand, he was a man who would never settle for the obvious and it seemed to delight him that friends expressed consternation that he should so exploit his fame.

In Philadelphia the show broke the record set by George M. Cohan in *I'd Rather Be Right* and before its New York opening Walter Winchell reported that "they were offering $70 for a pair of opening night *DuBarry* ducats around the Stork Club."

Unhappily, first-nighters at the 46th Street Theater failed to respond. With some astonishment, Cole saw that whereas audiences in New Haven, Boston and Philadelphia had frequently interrupted proceedings with applause. New Yorkers were frigid. Even "Friendship," with its bitchy humor cutting the sentiment, a quality that seemed surefire for the Broadway-type sophisticate, failed to earn its customary number of encores.

Next morning when Paul brought the newspapers, Cole's fears were confirmed. The lyrics, he read, were no more inspired than the book. Atkinson characterized them as "slatternly." There were numerous kind words for Betty Grable, who became the toast of the town with her dancing and singing of "Ev'ry Day a Holiday"; for Bert Lahr; and of course, for The Great Merman.

"Friendship" and "Well, Did You Evah!" gained widest popular acceptance; but "But in the Morning, No!" probably offended more reviewers than any other song Cole ever wrote. ("Dirt without wit," sniffed *The New Yorker*.) Among the others, "It Ain't Etiquette," "Do I Love You, Do I?" "When Love Beckoned," and "Katie Went to Haiti"—especially the last two—contained more appeal than was evident on opening night.

Second-nighters, ignoring the negative reviews, laughed and applauded as lustily as out-of-towners had. The show played to 98 standees on Saturday night, outgrossed any other show in town during its second week, and eventually racked up a run of 408 performances.

With the production launched, the Porters flew to Peru, Indiana, to spend the holidays with Katie and returned to New York to prepare for a trip to the South Seas. In speaking to a reporter about his globe-trotting, Cole alluded to his reputation for being easily bored and complained, "I don't know why they say I'm bored. I like anything as long as it's different."

One thing he did not like was being interviewed. It put him on the defensive. With some writers he clammed up. Columnist Louis Sobol, for instance, tried desperately to establish a rapport and succeeded only in eliciting grunts. Next day the exasperated Sobol had the last word in his column, informing readers: "For terseness only one national figure was more of a problem to newspapermen, the late Calvin Coolidge."

On January 20, 1940, Cole and Linda, Winsor French, Bill Powell, Roger Stearns and Leonard Hanna sailed on the S.S. *Kungsholm* for Cuba (Cole: "Heaven must be awfully like Havana."), the Panama Canal Zone, Mexico and the South Seas. The Canal was a must for Cole since he was about to begin work with Herbert Fields and Buddy De Sylva on another rowdy show, this one to be called *Panama Hattie*.

A most significant decision was reached on this trip.

Linda had for some time felt that both she and Cole suffered from rootlessness since the closing of their Paris house. She had looked at places in Calfiornia and found nothing. She had investigated Long Island but uncovered no house that suited her. Newport had been considered and rejected. But during the cruise, French suggested Williamstown, Massachusetts, and Linda was intrigued. Cole opposed it on the grounds that possible gasoline and tire rationing made it an impractical location, but Linda was not convinced.

On a teeming June day in 1940, she met French to go house-hunting in Massachusetts. Of the places shown them by the local real estate agent that morning, none seemed suitable. They decided to lunch and then look at one other possibility—Buxton Hill. As they drove up the long, winding drive to it, a rainbow suddenly appeared over the handsome fieldstone house with its picturesque overhanging eaves. Linda, who was always mildly superstitious, decided it was a good luck omen. Still, she was practical enough to rent the house semifurnished for a season before deciding whether or not to buy.

Cole, meantime, unable and unwilling to undertake still another adjustment in his life, refused to be a part of the negotiations and distracted himself by driving across the northern United States, zigzagging back and forth across the Canadian-United States border and stopping on occasion at such well-known resorts as Banff on Lake Louise and at other such little-known spots as Eureka, Montana.

By August 3, he was in Los Angeles installed in a house he had rented from film star Richard Cromwell, where he was awaiting the arrival of Dr. Sirmay to consult with him on the songs he was writing for *Panama Hattie.*

His state of mind was slightly unsettled with worry about European friends in the war, the fate of the Paris house and, most importantly, Linda's insistence upon taking the Williamstown place. But as fully as he could, he practiced the same stoicism with which he met his illness.

His relationship with Dr. Sirmay was now closer than

ever. Dr. Sirmay, who at times functioned as an editor and at times as a musical secretary, was always a friend—a friend who was convinced that Cole was a genius. "Like all geniuses," he said, "Cole had no consideration for anybody in work. He had no consideration for anybody's sleep. He called me at three o'clock, at four o'clock in the morning if he wanted to announce to me something he had thought of. Because he was a very late sleeper, at four or five he'd go to bed. Later, he changed his habits, but in his glorious years he wrote during the night. And always when he finished he wanted to hear what someone thought. Never did he talk about himself, praise himself. Never did he have the attitude other songwiters had that 'I have written this wonderful song,' that never came out of his mouth. If I praised him, he would smile and ask, 'You really mean it?' Of course I was a very close critic and if I said it, I meant it."

This time in Hollywood (Dr. Sirmay had first come West to assist Cole while he was working on *Born to Dance)* Cole wanted Dr. Sirmay to take down the melodies as he dictated them. "You know, Cole was a highly educated musician. So he helped himself by dictating. He was a left-handed writer and it was not easy for him to write down music. But he gave me everything worked out to perfection. Occasionally I corrected a bar or two that I disliked, but I was an intimate adviser."

Under this setup, Cole and Dr. Sirmay worked for a couple of weeks before Cole was due to depart for New York and rehearsals of *Panama Hattie* in which La Merman was to make her debut as a solo star. Involved in the production was De Sylva, who was to produce and co-author the work with Herbert Fields; the cast included Arthur Treacher, Betty Hutton, Phyllis Brooks, James Dunn, burlesque comic Rags Ragland and child actress Joan Carroll.

The story concerns Panama Hattie (Merman), who runs a nightclub in the Canal Zone, falls in love with a Philadelphia Mainliner who is serving as a government official (James Dunn), foils a plot to blow up the Canal, is ridiculed by the official's small daughter (Joan Carroll), tries to drown her sorrow with booze, makes friends with the little girl and marries the man she loves. Although the show was generally regarded as glorified burlesque, there was genuine enthusiasm for it.

In New Haven, it earned unanimous raves and large attendance. So much so that when *Pins and Needles* followed *Hattie* into the Shubert, *Variety* blamed its mediocre business on the fact that "*Hattie* had milked the town the week before."

In Boston, the production earned such a tumultuous response that De Sylva, envisioning big success, enlisted the aid of Louis Shurr and press agent Nat Dorfman in tossing a gigantic opening-night party. Irving Berlin had come up to see the show and assured everyone it was a big hit. Ann Corio and Arthur Treacher satirized the striptease to amuse guests. Cole, using only one cane now, arrived with what a columnist called "Boston's loveliest and most important people in tow." Almost everyone was optimistic—almost. Betty Hutton was near tears, having won only three ovations. Once again the notices were excellent, although Elliot Norton thought the show ran a bit long and seemed thin in spots. Nevertheless, it drew so many customers in its two-week stand that a third week was added. During the break-in, it grossed $90,000.

At the premiere on October 30, 1940, at the 46th Street Theater, the usual smart opening-night audience saw Ethel Merman assert her claim to consideration as a leading musical comedy star and the daily reviewers all agreed that she had made it.*

They liked *Hattie* better than they had *DuBarry*. And the song that was overwhelmingly their favorite was the

* Nobody saw fit to mention—nor was there any reason why anyone should have at this point—that the dancing girls included June Allyson (who understudied Betty Hutton), Betsy Blair, Doris Dowling and Vera-Ellen. For Miss Allyson, the opportunity to play the Hutton part one evening earned her the starring role in *Best Foot Forward* late in 1941.

schmaltzy "Let's Be Buddies," charmingly performed by La Merman and eight-year-old Joan Carroll. Not everyone raved, however. Novelist John O'Hara, working as a drama reviewer for a newsweekly, brutally attacked Cole, writing: ". . . In the carping department belongs Mr. Porter's music. Who'd have thought we'd live to see the day when Cole Porter—*Cole Porter!*—would write a score in which the two outstanding songs are called 'My Mother Would Love You' and 'Let's Be Buddies'? And written straight too; no kidding. In 1940, Cole Porter writing 'My mother would love you . . . and come to think of it so do I.' Ah, well, he had a bad riding accident a year or two ago. This ought to teach him to stay in his Brewster-Ford and away from horses."

After another excursion to bake his legs in the tropical sun off South America, Cole once again gravitated toward work as a means of taking his mind off his personal problems. Before going to the West Coast to begin doing the songs for *You'll Never Get Rich,* which was to star Fred Astaire and Rita Hayworth, he talked with Herbert Fields and his sister Dorothy about writing the score for a show of theirs which Vinton Freedley was hoping to produce. Now that B. G. De Sylva had impressed Hollywood enough to go there as the head of Paramount, Cole felt free to return to Freedley's auspices. Nothing definite was settled, however, and when Cole arrived in Los Angeles on the Union Pacific Streamliner, he told reporters that he intended to remain at least three months, working on his new film.

He was particularly looking forward to the assignment, he said, because among male stars Astaire occupied a position comparable to the one held by Ethel Merman among the female contingent. Although, of course, Cole didn't point it out, there was an élan, a life-style of Astaire's that was similar to his own. In addition, Cole, who frequently liked one partner in a marriage and not the other, was as fond of Phyllis Astaire as of Fred.

To anticipate working and actually *doing* the job proved to be two different things. Cole found writing songs for a plot that utilized military life as the background for the familiar Hollywood triangle was surprisingly difficult. Even his enthusiasm for the cast—Astaire, beautiful Rita Hayworth and humorist Robert Benchley—could not carry him through the assignment with ease. He had been accustomed to the lavish and Olympian rites of production as practiced by MGM, whereas Columbia Pictures was budget-minded and practical. Cole was amused but slightly disconcerted too when studio head Harry Cohn insisted upon submitting the songs to clerical workers to pretest their appeal. Cohn's methods coupled with the absence of real creative inspiration, to say nothing of the unexpectedly lengthy ASCAP strike against radio, combined to depress Cole.

In this mood, he wrote Dr. Sirmay on June 23, 1941:

> Dear Doctor: I am sending you the proofs of "Dream Dancing" and "So Near and Yet So Far," which I have corrected the best I can. But, oh God! How it bored me. Two more proofs have just arrived and as soon as I can bear to, I shall correct them and return them to you. Thank you so much for the clippings. It is heaven here and it seems incredible that people are willing to stay in New York when it is so simple to come to California. Why on earth do you do it? I'm working very hard and believe I have some good new numbers. In any case, it's a most interesting job."

Two days after he wrote Dr. Sirmay, he moved from a period of depression to elation. For Herbert and Dorothy Fields arrived to confer with him on the proposed Broadway musical. It was to be called *Let's Face It*. Cole thought the first act good and the second "a pip." To add to the happiness of the occasion, they also informed him that Danny Kaye, who had scored in *Lady in the Dark*, was ready to sign for the show.

The next week he was unsettled again by being faced with a new adjustment. With the United States at war, Paul felt a loyalty greater than that to "my boss, Mr. C. P.," as he often referred to him, and enlisted in the Seabees.

Sadly, Cole packed up and returned East, where he finally hired a bang-up waiter from the Waldorf-Astoria to serve as his valet. This was Wilhelm, totally efficient, totally ruthless in his attitude toward other employees. Instead of requesting things from the maids and housemen, he would imperiously snap his fingers, point and bark. This attitude caused untold resentment among the staff, as well as Cole's secretary, Miss Moore, who was not used to being ordered about by anyone except the Porters, and who resented it even when they did it. Wilhelm's attitude, however, did ensure Cole maximum comfort.

By now, Cole had become such a stickler for neatness and organization that Linda sometimes jokingly referred to him as "Craig's wife's husband," but even he found Wilhelm's efficiency so unrelenting that he was somewhat disconcerted. Cole would ring. Wilhelm would appear.

"Wilhelm, I think—" Cole would begin.

Wilhelm would interrupt, "I have it right here in my pocket, sir."

"Please!" Cole would cry, half in real, half in mock irritation. "At least give me the opportunity of telling you what I want."

With the valet problem solved, he moved on to Buxton Hill, which Linda had now purchased. Although Cole was still disapproving of Williamstown, he was not to hold out against it for long. While he had been doing his picture in Hollywood, she had been transforming it into a country retreat of the kind she felt sure he would respond to.

She had filled it with all her treasures—the pale Aubusson carpets, her paintings, her Egyptology collection and other furnishings from their Paris house. The antique Chinese wallpaper, which had come from Knole Castle in England and which depicted exotic birds flying through bamboo jungles, fitted perfectly into the tremendous drawing room. She had constructed a free-hanging staircase and she managed to erect a greenhouse of sorts as well as a swimming pool down beyond the silver birches and weeping willows at the far end of the meadow.

Cole's first glimpse pleased him. The stately house overlooked a formal garden that joined an enormous spread of velvety meadow which trailed off into the birches and weeping willows above which rose the distant purple-peaked Berkshires was to his taste. It was a view of which he was never to tire.

What delighted him even more, however, was the small carriage house which Linda had thoughtfully and imaginatively converted into a work cottage. Here, as she always had done, she provided him with a place where he could create, an area removed from the main household. Characteristically he named it "No Trespassing."

After a few days at Buxton Hill, Cole once more had made another of his dizzying switches in attitude. After opposing Linda's every move in connection with the project and maintaining a policy of noninvolvement as she struggled to obtain war-scarce materials to install the swimming pool and make other improvements, he fell in love with it and thereafter could not sing her praises too highly.

Not only was Buxton Hill beautiful, but it was also comfortable. Linda saw to it that he had no adjustment to make. There was no one to make him uncomfortable with either ill-advised compliments or sympathy. Although Cole made it a policy not to complain about his physical condition, his reactions sometimes revealed his true feelings. Always aware of his unprepossessing looks, after the accident he found it difficult to accept well-meant compliments about his person. When an English actress, Constance Collier, thought he was looking particularly fit and commented, "Cole, my dear, you're looking so well you're positively handsome," Cole bridled: "I don't wish to look handsome, but I do want to be neat." And it was a fact that he was compulsively neat, a state which his physical suffering never affected.

Actually, he preferred that no mention be made of his health. Although he was still suffering agonizing pain from osteomyelitis, he wished to suffer in silence. Unpleasantness of any kind, physical or emotional, he did not regard as a suitable subject for conversation. Of a well-known writer who often discussed his psychological crises in detail, Cole said: "He tells me rather more about himself than I care to know." He operated on the assumption that it was a sign of the highest cultivation never to depress friends with personal problems. The only hint of his own suffering during this period came from his unobtrusive extraction of a pill from his pillbox and a discreet nibble at the medicine.

Friends soon learned an inquiry about his health almost always brought the same response: "Very well, thank you. Now tell me the dirt." Occasionally, someone would persist in discussing his problems, but to do so was to risk receiving a calculatedly rude response. Once, a long-time friend, Mrs. Harrison Williams, the perennially best-dressed woman, stopped by this table at Le Pavillon and expressed concern over his well-being. Cole as usual said he was very well indeed.

Yes, she persisted, but how were his poor legs.

Cole eyed her coldly and snapped, "Fine. How are yours?"

At Buxton Hill there were no such incidents, and Linda invited a succession of guests—including writer Anita Loos, Howard Sturges, Winsor French, glamor girl Jean Howard, Baron de Gunzberg and Duke di Verdura—who were the type of electric personalties that Cole enjoyed.

It was a happy time for him, endowed with a tranquillity he had seldom achieved since his accident. Upon arising for breakfast, he would find the previous day's *New York Times, Herald Tribune, Daily News* and *Mirror* laid out for him.

His first move always was to seize the *News,* turn to Dick Tracy and check new developments. Dick Tracy, he said only half-facetiously, was the most important thing that had ever happened to him.

When he had satisfied himself on that score, he picked out his favorite paper, the *Mirror,* and turned to his favorite columnist, Walter Winchell. That done, he began at the front of the paper and read the new "dirt." Other papers were read only for their amusement sections, unless there was news of some World War II battle of particular importance which he was following.

Breakfast and the newspapers finished, he set out to work in the cottage, continuing until lunchtime, after which he might relax or might continue working. Whichever he did, he always broke in time to enjoy another of his folk heros—NBC's *Stella Dallas*. Cole discovered her quite by accident. He found it impossible to listen to even the simplest pop song without unconsciously beginning to analyze it. So he twisted the dial searching for talk programs and happened upon poor Stella; her daughter, Lolly-Baby; a society woman who was always referred to as "the mad Ada Dexter" and a variety of other characters. Eventually, the Porters and their circle took Ada, Lolly and Stella to their hearts, but Cole remained the first and chief fan, refusing to miss an installment unless it was absolutely necessary. Once, because he was motoring from California to New York by way of Peru, Indiana, to visit his "ma," he delegated Linda to write down everything that transpired. Upon arrival at the Waldorf-Towers ten days later, he eagerly inquired what had happened to Stella. Linda said nothing of consequence and Cole crowed with delight. On the West Coast, Stella's broadcast time fell during luncheon and guests were forbidden to speak. Even such spellbinders as Orson Welles and Lady Mendl submitted to the edict. Those who failed to obey were not asked again.

At Williamstown Cole took a drive every afternoon. Often his destination was the farmhome of a woman painter who was just getting started. One year he bought twenty canvases from her and sent them to friends as Christmas cards. One of the larger works he gave to Ethel Merman. It was a farm scene with red roosters and a lot of other things which La Merman felt didn't particularly match the décor of her apartment. She gave it away. Five years later, when he asked how she was enjoying her Grandma Moses, she realized what she had done. Worse than that, she couldn't remember to whom she had given it.

Much of the time that first summer, though, was spent in working on the songs that he was writing for *Let's Face It,* his twelfth show in thirteen years. After weeks of intensive application, he felt his work was finished and sent it off to New York.*

The libretto was based on a 1925 farce, *The Cradle Snatchers,* in which three divorcées took up with gigolos. To modernize it under wartime conditions Dorothy and Herbert Fields transformed the gigolos into soldiers. In addition to Danny Kaye, the soldiers were Benny Baker and Jack Williams; their sweethearts were Nanette Fabray, Mary Jane Walsh and Sunnie O'Dea; the divorcées, Eve Arden, Vivian Vance and Edith Meiser.

During rehearsals, Cole was accompanied by Dr. Sirmay, who found that Cole was reluctant to speak up, either because of self-control or because of a reluctance to offend. He was not, however, above inquiring what Dr. Sirmay thought of some dubious bit of business, orchestration or effect. Then standing up and calling out, "The Doc says you shouldn't do it that way! He doesn't like it," he would proceed to explain how it should be handled.

When he had sat down again, Dr. Sirmay would implore him not to expose him in this way. Cole would apologize, but a few minutes later he would be on his feet once more informing the assemblage: "The Doc doesn't like it!"

Although Cole was noted for the icy calm with which he approached his productions, he began viewing *Let's Face It* with increasing alarm as the weeks went on. In Boston, at the end of the dress rehearsal of the $80,000 show, during which he had fidgeted nervously, he got up and bolted from the Colonial Theater.

Dr. Sirmay, who had sensed his desperate mood, rushed after him, calling for him to wait. Cole hesitated, and Dr. Sirmay wanted to know where he was going in such a

* The score was surprising in one way: Cole agreed to allow songs by Kaye's wife, Sylvia Fine, and Max Liebman to be interpolated.

Two forceful personalities, Cole's grandfather, J. O. Cole, and his mother, Kate Cole Porter.

Cole at 21 months (above)
and (below) at an impish 3½ years.

Above, Cole tunes his violin for a photographer. Below, he poses with schoolmates, including Desdemona Bearss, at right.

COURTESY WORCESTER ACADEMY

At Worcester Academy (1905-1909) Cole, right, poses with classmates in Sheridan's *The Rivals.*

At Yale (1909-1913) Cole (second from right) poses with members of the Whiffenpoofs.

In 1919, in Paris, Cole married Linda Lee Thomas, regarded as one of the world's most beautiful women.

"Just before breakfast" was the message Cole sent Linda on these postcards from Munich. At top with Monty Woolley and (bottom) with Howard Sturges.

Elsa Maxwell, above, was one of Cole's earliest fans. At left, Cole with Betty Shevlin Smith in a Paris nightclub in the 1920's.

In 1926 Linda
posed for this study
by Steichen. Below,
Linda, Cole, and
dancer Billy Reardon
at St. Moritz.

Cole and Linda's Palazzo Rezzonico in Venice, where they lived during the 1920's.

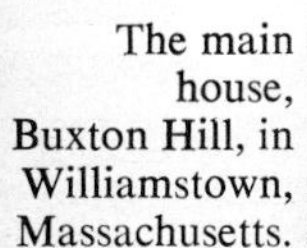

The main house, Buxton Hill, in Williamstown, Massachusetts.

The view toward the pool area as seen from the big house in Brentwood, California.

THEATER COLLECTION, NEW YORK PUBLIC LIBRARY

Anything Goes, with William Gaxton, Ethel Merman, and Victor Moore (1934), was Cole's biggest hit up to that time. It also began a long association between Cole and La Merman.

Valet Paul Sylvain and a chauffeur carry Cole into the premiere of Noel Coward's *Set to Music*. (1939).

Cole posing on a horse near Machu Picchu, Peru.

Ethel Merman in the title role in *Du Barry Was a Lady* (1939).

COURTESY WARNER BROS.

Cary Grant played Cole in the 1945 pseudo-biographical film of Cole, *Night and Day*.

Cole confers with Dr. Albert Sirmay, his musical editor and friend.

COURTESY DR. SIRMAY

CULVER PICTURES, INC.

Kiss Me, Kate (1948), Cole's masterpiece, with Patricia Morison and Alfred Drake.

Cole with Bella Spewack, with whom he collaborated on *Kiss Me, Kate.*

Two of Cole's
closest friends,
Howard Sturges
and Jean Howard.

High Society, with Grace Kelly, Frank Sinatra and Celeste Holm, was Cole's next-to-last film.

COURTESY METRO-GOLDWYN-MAYER

On Cole's birthday, June 9, 1960, representatives of Yale convened at his Waldorf-Towers apartment and bestowed an honorary degree upon him.

Below, Cole sits in his favorite red chair at his cottage "No Trespassing" in Williamstown, Massachusetts.

COURTESY OLIVER JENNINGS

hurry. Cole said he had to rush to tell everyone in New York not to come to the opening. "I don't want them to witness my disgrace," he explained.

Eventually, he was persuaded to return to his hotel and restrain himself until he saw how the show played before an audience. Luckily, he did. At the premiere the performance roused wave after wave of laughter and applause, the next morning Elliot Norton announced in his review that the show was hilarious, while Leo Gaffney in the *Daily Record* said, "Because he writes his own lyrics, Cole Porter has a way with a song unmatched in the American scene . . ."

When *Let's Face It* arrived at the Imperial Theater on October 29, 1941, the reviews were excellent, although Richard Watts was sounding his usual lament: "It's not that the score is one of Cole Porter's most sensational . . ."

Cole agreed. Certainly, he did not expect that 303 performances would elapse before theatergoers tired of his brain child. Nor would he have believed that twelve years later *Theatre Arts* magazine would cite it as an example of what George Jean Nathan meant when he wrote: "The best musical comedies . . . are those in which sense is reduced to a minimum, the worst, those which aim at rationality. The critical insistence upon books that lean to some intelligence and realism has done much to debilitate musical comedy. . . . What we want . . . is a return to the old-time razzle and dazzle and the incredible."

The writer in *Theater Arts* then added, "This rare and difficult dramatic form which carries absurdity to a logical superlative has enlivened the hearts of many theatergoers in musicals like *Let's Face It*. . . ."

CHAPTER XII

What lay behind Cole's panic?

Poor health is part of the answer. Advancing age is another factor. And there was also his feeling of aimlessness and alienation.

Take his health, for example. During the tryout period he suffered increasingly severe pain because of a bone growth which caused constant pressure and constant pain in his left leg. Thus on October 19, ten days before *Let's Face It* opened at the Imperial Theater, he quietly signed himself into Doctors' Hospital for further surgery, and he was not released until the middle of November. Even then his left leg was encased in a cast for another six weeks.

For some time he had also been aware of a feeling of aimlessness. Customarily, when hospitalized he worked eagerly on a new project. This time he did not. Upon emerging from the hospital, he told reporters that he had done nothing while ill. "I think," he said wearily, "I'm turning into a bug."

He also felt out of step with the period. The war years, with their big, primary emotions, were not a comfortable milieu for him since they provided little time to examine the different shades of emotion which he so expertly delineated.

Although he took interest in the big battles and contributed generously to war relief, he was not stirred to action the way his friend Irving Berlin was. He admired Berlin's patriotism and defended him when others criticized him for self-promotion in doing the *This Is the Army* show.*

On the other hand, while praising Berlin's contributions to the war effort, Cole rebelled against wartime rationing. He cadged sugar, butter and gasoline stamps shamelessly; delegated friends to search out hard-to-find items; and took to chewing Chiclets only when they became almost impossible to obtain.

Nor was he cheered by the thought that *You'll Never Get Rich* was a success. The picture opened at Radio City Music Hall while he was still hospitalized and most reviewers recommended it and the seven songs, of which "So Near and Yet So Far, "Since I Kissed My Baby Goodbye" and "Dream Dancing" registered most strongly. But Cole, a severer critic, regarded the songs, as less than his best, feeling, for example, that the lyrics of "Dream Dancing," smoothly evocative though they might be, were ones that any Tin Pan Alley songwriter might turn out. Nor was he pleased with the way the songs were used in the picture.

Partially, too, his panic may have been due to the realization that he was now fifty years old. For all his

* Cole's letter was written in reply to one about Berlin: "Dear Little —Mouse: I can't understand all this resentment toward my old friend, The Little Grey Mouse. It seems to me that he has every right to go to the limits toward publicizing the music of his Army show, as every cent earned will help us win the war. If I had my way, he would have been given the Congressional Medal for years, because even you must admit he is the greatest songwriter of all time and I don't mean Stephen Foster. It's really distressing in these days of so much trouble to know that envy still runs rampant even on that supposed lane, Tin Pan Alley. I am sure you will agree about this, dear Little —— Mouse, Love, Rat Porter."

experience and success, it was becoming increasingly difficult for him to muster enthusiasm for his projects. Although he always presented a smiling countenance for the public, his private depressions were increasing. Unhappily, too, Linda's health was precarious enough to worry him and make it impossible for her to give him the emotional support she had previously provided.

In spite of this, when a friend suggested that Cole might profit from a few sessions with a psychiatrist, both Cole and Linda ridiculed the idea.

"It's unfortunate they felt that way," the friend said. "They were both intelligent people but from their point of view psychiatrists might have been witch doctors. Linda, of course, was such a vital, outstanding person—both as a beauty and a human being—that she needed none. She understood herself and she understood Cole completely. She knew when to treat him as a husband, when as a naughty boy and when as a genius. But being ill herself left each of them wrapped in despair."

For a couple of months, Cole stayed in New York and waited for his depression to lift. It did after he received word that he was wanted by Columbia Pictures for another film. Although he was not eager to work for Harry Cohn again, he agreed to take the assignment, only to find upon arrival in Hollywood that the film had been postponed while the writers tore up the story and manufactured a new one.

"My situation is such a muddle I shan't even write you about it. Gregory Ratoff [the director] is full of charm and could not be nicer, but he is much madder than any hatter *I* have ever met," Cole told a friend in a letter. "So far I've written three very good numbers, it seems to me, and a fourth I shall probably throw out although Ratoff likes it."

At last on July 22, he brought Dr. Sirmay to California for three weeks to help work over the songs he'd written, six of which were eventually to find their way into the Columbia Picture *Something to Shout About,* starring Janet Blair, Don Ameche and Jack Oakie. The only number to register with audiences, however, was "You'd

Be So Nice to Come Home To," which struck just the right note of longing for millions of war-separated couples.

Meanwhile, a project for which he had been waiting when *Something to Shout About* came along began to jell. Herbert and Dorothy Fields called it *Jenny Get Your Gun* and their idea was based on a couple of newspaper clippings which they thought would make a nifty musical comedy plot. One item concerned three cousins, who happened to be complete strangers to one another, inheriting a ranch. The other told of a person whose Carborundum filling in a tooth served as a radio transmitter. A girl with a radioactive tooth sounded like a perfect role for Ethel Merman, and she thought so too. So the Merman-Porter combination was reunited for the fifth time. Cole was delighted, once more affirming that La Merman sounded like a brass band going by and adding that he was old-fashioned in that he liked a singer who could sing. Having worked with her four times previously, he was now convinced that her best notes were A flat, B flat and C natural. Therefore, he would be careful to construct his lyrics so that these notes coincided with important words.

Since Buddy De Sylva seemed permanently settled in Hollywood, everyone naturally assumed that this would be a Vinton Freedley production, but Freedley was less than enchanted with what he read and heard. He asked for changes which neither the Fields' nor Cole were willing to make. "All his suggestions were bad ideas," Cole said. And the more he thought about it the more convinced he became that Freedley regarded him in the same way he had that neophyte who had come to an empty theater, manuscripts in hand, climbed into the orchestra pit and pounded out an audition for the producing team of Freedley and Aarons in 1928. The upshot of all this was that Cole suggested taking the show to another management. The Fields' agreed.

The question arose as to whom they should approach. Cole suggested a young shirt-sleeves showman named Mike Todd, who had had the wit to convert *The*

Mikado into *The Hot Mikado* and to cast it with colored performers. Such audacity was enough to intrigue Cole, but he found the young producer's behavior on opening night even more appealing. According to legend, Todd had only one fifty-cent piece in his pocket when the Shubert brothers offered him an astronomical sum for a half interest in *The Hot Mikado*. Fully aware that should the critics turn thumbs down on his offering he would be without funds or earning power, he flipped the coin to come to his decision, looked at it and turned down the offer. That kind of bravado Cole found exhilarating.

He picked up the telephone, called Todd, suggested he and the Fieldses do an audition and was met with the kind of response he had dreamed about. Todd bought the show without hearing a joke, a tune or a lyric.

A friend once said that Cole liked anyone who happened to be slightly crazy, and Todd qualified. He was imaginative, shrewd, ruthless and more than a little eccentric. He had fought his way to Broadway via the Chicago streets, the carnival lot, the clout and the con, with an unwavering eye on the main chance.

As Cole did with each successive producer, he endowed Todd with omnipotence. "He hypnotized himself," Elsa Maxwell said. "He had to. You have to when you put your shows in their hands." Baron de Gunzberg noted that Cole spoke of "my producer" almost as "my Father Confessor." This state of obeisance continued as long as the producer seemed to remain omniscient, but once a failure occurred Cole was likely to move away.

To support Miss Merman in *Something for the Boys*, as the show was eventually called,* Todd hired a deadpan nightclub comedienne, Paula Laurence; comic Allen Jenkins; a saucy little dancer, Betty Bruce; and a strong-voiced leading man, Bill Johnson.

Upon hearing the score, Miss Merman assured Cole that he had turned out the best group of songs anyone had ever written for her, which, as Cole later observed, just goes to

* Original titles: *Jenny Get Your Gun* and *The State of Texas.*

prove that none of us knows. Nevertheless the production was geared to the escapist appetites of wartime America and it served its purpose admirably. Stager Hassard Short put the emphasis on high-spirited clowning, and the scenery and costumes were designed for maximum splashy effects.

Audiences cheered the show in Boston, as did the critics. Cole was delighted with it. Upon its premiere at the Alvin Theater on January 7, 1943, *The New York Times'* man described the production as "lavish to the point of good taste."

Miss Merman was the recipient of outright love letters, although some critics felt she had to keep moving to stay ahead of Miss Laurence and Mr. Jenkins. There were a few reservations, but even the astute Louis Kronenberger, who was then writing for the newspaper *PM,* was willing to go along with the raucous carnival, while putting his finger on a question that was troubling Cole. "This is the third time that Mr. Porter and Miss Merman have teamed up for success, and *Something for the Boys* more than sustains the level of *DuBarry Was a Lady* and *Panama Hattie.* If it doesn't come close to *Anything Goes,* it is because Mr. Porter isn't the composer he once was. For Miss Merman is no less a wow."

In the six months prior to *Something for the Boys'* opening, no musical comedy had succeeded on Broadway, but this show was sold out from opening night until well into the following year, eventually racking up 422 performances. Privately, though, Cole's personal friends deplored the low level of invention by all hands including Cole. They missed the sense of style that had once pervaded every Porter song, since there was no denying that the complexity of sentiment as well as of rhyming was for the most part missing. "By the Mississinewah" left the audience gasping with laughter, but it was largely the Misses Merman and Laurence who supplied the fun.

After promising Mike Todd a new show for 1944, Cole once more left for Hollywood where he was scheduled to compose the music for a film called *Mississippi Belle.*

Linda agreed to give the California climate another try, and, as a consequence, Cole took a new house from William Haines, a former film star turned interior decorator. Located at 416 North Rockingham in Brentwood, it suited him as well as a leased house could, although he had written into his lease that changes could be made with the understanding that he would restore it to its original condition upon vacating it. He set about enclosing the rear porch as a dining room, building a pergola and ordering a swimming pool constructed (in spite of wartime shortages) in anticipation of entertaining that he and Linda would do.*

During this and the following season, the Porters saw long-time friends and made numerous new ones. Fanny Brice was there, as were Sir Charles and Lady Mendl, Clifton and Maybelle Webb, Anita Loos, the Ronald Colmans and many others.

Cole's old friend Dorothy di Frasso brought *her* friend Benjamin Siegel, whom some people were unkind enough to call "Buggsy" (although not to his face), and Cole was delighted. As a man who got away with breaking small rules, he was always fascinated by those people who seemingly got away with breaking the big ones.

Always on hand too were the bright, beautiful young people. A prime favorite was Merle Oberon, with her beautiful almond-shaped eyes and air of mystery. Others who decorated the dinner parties were Virginia Bruce, Claudette Colbert, Joan Crawford and, occasionally, Garbo.

Soon after the Porters arrived in Hollywood, they began meeting Miss Garbo at social gatherings. Like the rest of the world they were fascinated.

Cole, who referred to her as "Miss X," loved her

* When the pool was finished, it was discovered that the diving board at the deep end interfered with serving of outdoor luncheons. What to do? Someone suggested removing the board. Cole would have none of that. "Switch the ends around," he said airily—and that was what was done.

mystery. It was inevitable, too, that she should further interest him since she was a new experience: someone who turned down his invitations. And even when she promised to attend a party, she could not always be counted on. Even so, they understood one another. After a time, it became the custom to sit down to dinner whether or not she had arrived. Often she would appear after a course or two had been finished, murmur something about having lost her way, and take up whatever course was being served.

In any case a strange friendship grew, which Cole enjoyed and did not attempt to explain. On one occasion, for example, she visited him and as they sat beside the pool, she suddenly asked whether he was happy. He considered her question for a moment and said that he thought he was. At that Garbo stared off into the distance and murmured, "How strange that must be!"

In her, Cole, who was often accused of being remote, found a match. The last time he saw her, which was at a New Year's Eve cocktail party in 1958, she came up to him as he was about to leave, kissed him on each cheek and demanded, "Why are you always so unfriendly?"

Another favored guest was Orson Welles, who usually brought along the lovely Rita Hayworth, who sat silently by, adoring Welles as he talked.

Constance Bennett was a frequent guest, too, and she had enough beauty and charm to be invited back even though she had a habit of begging her host to let her write lyrics to his music.

Errol Flynn was always welcome and always entertaining with his outrageous stories of past and present peccadilloes.

Joan Blondell was a special favorite, but Dick Powell was only tolerated as long as he was Joan's husband. Cole liked her even better after she divorced Powell to marry Todd.

Linda, who found many stars too narcissistic to be of interest, always insisted that Clark Gable be included on the guest list when he was on the Coast. He had won her heart when she had complimented him on his beautiful teeth, only to have him spontaneously remove his front bridge.

One of the people the Porters liked best was Samuel Stark, a former actor who had settled in California and gone into the jewelry business. As someone who shared Linda's love of beautiful things and Cole's sense of humor, they found in him a real friend.

At this time, Cole undertook two typical Porter projects. Although he already spoke French, Spanish, Italian and German, he now proposed to master Russian. Surprisingly, in view of the fact that he possessed perfect pitch, he found some of the sounds difficult to master. The grammar, on the other hand, seemed to him rather easy and he approved of the fact that there were no articles and there was no verb *to be.* "I have a feeling I shall not get very far in this," he admitted, "but that which I do learn will be enjoyable when I take that big country place in Crimea."

He also decided to study astronomy, noting that almost every song of his contained some reference to the moon or the stars. Consequently he hired a UCLA professor to lecture him, Linda, Sturges, Sam Stark and various other friends one evening each week. In the beginning the group was large, but one by one the auditors dropped away until only Cole and Stark were left. Then Stark found the mathematics too difficult. Cole said that explained why Stark wasn't a better musician, to be a good musician, he claimed, you had to be a good mathematician. He studied on alone.

When he discovered that the professor had a Latin-American wife, Cole invited the two of them to dine and, in planning the party, assumed the girl was Mexican. That evening there were flowers from Mexico, a cactus centerpiece and a program of Mexican recordings on the phonograph. Instead of the customary daiquiri, he ordered Mexican glasses, salt, lime and tequila. When drinks were poured, Cole turned to the professor's wife, smiled and said, "Now, you make a toast."

The puzzled woman timidly asked what the drink was.

"Tequila," said Cole, and asked how to drink it. To his dismay, she informed him that she was from Colombia and had never heard of the drink.

In June of 1944, Linda and Cole went to Mexico where they joined Mike Todd and the production staff of the new show which Cole planned to write for Todd. Almost immediately various members of the party, including Cole, contracted dysentery. Then his general condition became run-down and the osteomyelitis flared up. After two weeks, he returned to New York and entered Doctor's Hospital for further surgery.

Although he generally delighted in shocking people, he was astonished—and upset—to read in Danton Walker's column that he had been kicked out of Mexico for disgraceful behavior. For once, he was in no mood to rise above inaccuracy, and dispatched his lawyer to Walker's office to protest that the item was untrue, that Cole was undergoing surgery and wanted a retraction. To which Walker blithely replied, "If it isn't true, why is he upset?"

By September Cole was back at the Waldorf-Towers, working hard on the Todd musical and feeling somewhat anxious about money. Medical expenses, rising taxes, the cost of remodeling the California house and having the Williamstown sun porch enclosed as a gift to Linda set him to wondering whether he was overspending.*

Finally the new Todd musical was ready for casting. They now called it *Mexican Hayride*. Comedian Bobby Clark was signed to star. For a leading man they chose Wilbur Evans. For the female lead, they cast a beautiful blonde who was equally at home in comic and romantic roles. She was the sister of Gypsy Rose Lee and after having run through six other names she now called herself June Havoc. Following a career as a baby headliner in

* Wartime taxes were beginning to assume enormous proportions, and he had just learned that Secretary of Treasury Morgenthau had assessed him $90,000 for his first-quarter payment.

vaudeville, she had become in swift succession a marathon dancer, a nightclub performer, a summer-stock actress and finally Gladys Bumps in the original production of *Pal Joey.* A series of film roles had followed, and now, in *Mexican Hayride,* she was cast as a lady bullfighter who tosses the ear of the bull she has just dispatched to a fugitive from justice (Bobby Clark) rather than to the person intended. He then becomes goodwill ambassador for a week, which gives him easy access to all kinds of nefarious schemes, including fixing a national lottery.

Although Bobby Clark, with his painted-on eyeglasses, his cigar and his double-time skitter, brought great invention to the part, and Miss Havoc and Evans labored spiritedly, both the book and the songs were seriously wanting. To a friend, Cole wrote prior to the opening: "That thing *Mexican Hayride* still stinks, but many shows that stink play on when they play the Winter Garden because of sidewalk business."

In an attempt to get the show into shape, the Boston opening at the Shubert Theater was postponed until Christmas night. Whatever the dissatisfaction of those responsible, the production contained enough razzle-dazzle during those austere days to draw a large advance and largely tolerant critical notices.

On January 4, 1944, Cole reported: "This show has in it forty-five minutes of unadulterated boredom which we are now trying to eliminate. This forty-five minutes of unadulterated boredom still exists after we cut out twenty minutes from the show. So you can see what a job we have ahead of us. The only really great thing about the opus is the production which is out of this world. But after all, it would really help us quite a lot if we had the show billed as 'Scenery and Costumes of *Mexican Hayride.*' "

During the stay in Boston, Cole apparently decided that there was not much he could do to increase the show's chances of scoring a success. Although he traveled back and forth between there and New York several times, he claimed that there was little he could contribute and he spent most of his time reading his "pet book, *Goodnight, Sweet Prince.*" He also found time to attend the wedding of the former Lady Sylvia Ashley and Lieutenant Edward John Lord Stanley, and to give the bride away.

Despite Cole's continued disenchantment with this $225,000 production, Bill Doll, the show's agent, managed to create the impression among New York newspaper readers that the show was a full-fledged hit in Boston. At the time of its New York opening, it had amassed a couple of hundred thousand dollars in advance sales.

At the Winter Garden premiere on January 18, 1944, the show played well and earned pleasant notices, although most reviewers were of the opinion that the book and songs left something to be desired. Nevertheless, Bobby Clark's low-clowning style pleased everyone. And Miss Havoc had everything, according to the *Journal-American;* was a lovely, bewitching darling of a comedienne, according to the *World-Telegram;* and was in top form, according to the New York *Sun*. In addition, Evans, Corinna Mura, Luba Malina, George Givot and Paul Haakon were cited as star material.

Of the songs, Cole's personal favorite was the Mexican-flavored "Sing to Me, Guitar," which Miss Mura performed. Miss Havoc sold "Abracadabra" and "There Must Be Someone for Me" through sheer personality and refusal to be downed by relatively pedestrian lyrics. Along with Clark and Givot she stopped the show with "Count Your Blessings," in which Cole allowed Bobby Clark to insert his own jokes.

The popular hit of the show was "I Love You," sung by Evans. Cole had written it as the result of a twenty-five-dollar bet he made with Monty Woolley. Monty contended that Cole's talent lay in the offbeat, the esoteric, maintaining that he could never take a cliché title such as "I Love you," write lyrics which included the banal sentiment, "It's spring again/And birds on the wing again . . ." and come up with a hit. Cole accepted the challenge and eventually the song topped the Hit Parade for many consecutive weeks. ("Some people felt," Cole said, "that the superior melody overcame the ordinary lyric.")

The second week of its run, *Mexican Hayride* played to

100 or more standees at every performance and it was doing equally good business in the seventeenth week. Then on July 19, Miss Havoc left the cast, ostensibly because of an injury incurred from a fall during the show. Actually, she had been offered the starring role in *Sadie Thompson,* the musical version of Somerset Maugham's *Rain.* Cole reacted exactly as he had when Mary Boland abandoned *Jubilee*—he added Miss Havoc's name to a list of performers who were never again considered for a Porter show. The production eventually ran 481 performances. although it was his first show since *DuBarry Was a Lady* not to be done in London.

The previous year Cole had written nine songs for the film *Mississippi Belle.* This had not been accomplished without difficulty, and less than a month after *Mexican Hayride* opened he was requested by Warners to do more work on that score.

The producer of the picture was Arthur Schwartz, a respected Broadway composer, but from the beginning there was apparently an unconscious rivalry between the two men. And this season the friction increased until it reached an intensity heretofore unequaled in Cole's professional life. The more Cole thought about it, the more convinced he became that the property was being ruined by Schwartz because of the latter's desire to express his personality. Privately, he maintained that Schwartz was trying to duplicate his picture, *Cover Girl.*

After fretting about the situation for a while, Cole asked for a meeting with Jack Warner; Warner's assistant, Steve Trilling; and Schwartz. When they met, Cole complained that nine of the thirteen songs he had written had been tossed out and five replacements were requested. He said that he had been under the impression that he was writing a score for *Mississippi Belle,* but obviously what was wanted was *Mississippi Cover,* in which case they ought to replace him.

The more unpleasant he became, he said later, the pleasanter everyone else was, and the upshot of the meeting was that ten of the thirteen songs were retained and Cole was to supply two new ones.

Cole left the studio proud that he had behaved well, but not convinced that he had accomplished his goal. He was soon to have proof that he had. Upon arrival at home, he received a call from Jack Warner asking him to do another picture the minute he finished *Mississippi Belle.* "Thus," he gloated, "once more we prove the fact that if you hit Hollywood people in the pants they always like you better."

Having called their game, Cole now proceeded to indulge in a bit of private mischief. "Don't tell on me," he wrote to Dr. Sirmay, "but I've written the lyric and also the refrain of 'So Long, San Antonio,' and also changed a bit of the music to make a new ballad for A. Schwartz. It's entitled 'So Long,' but in this case 'so long' doesn't mean goodbye, but leads to the inevitable honky-tonk conclusion, so long will I love you. Ain't I clever?"

But Schwartz was by no means vanquished. When Cole handed in "So Long," the producer called up to say how much he liked the number and then went on to suggest several changes in the melody. "Instead of jumping in my car and rushing out to Warner's to bump him off, I controlled myself and said, 'Well, perhaps you're right.' Of course, I shall make no changes. . . ." Cole thought he deserved a halo for his patience.

The first week in June Dr. Sirmay wrote to say that Billy Rose was making a new effort to persuade Cole to do the songs for his upcoming show. "He is so eager he'd move heaven and earth to get you and make you happy," Dr. Sirmay noted, adding that Rose would not expect Cole to write those portions of the production which he disliked.

Since it had now become apparent that there were too many problems attached to *Mississippi Belle* for it to go into immediate production, Cole agreed to provide the light music for *The Seven Lively Arts,* for which Igor Stravinsky was to do the *scènes de ballet.*

As soon as Cole returned to New York he began attending auditions along with Rose and director Hassard Short and dance director Jack Donohue. Their goal was to find six unknown girls and a young man, each with an outstanding personality and a voice. "The result instead of being discouraging is extraordinary," Cole wrote Sam Stark. "There is so much talent in this country that it makes you want to sit back and glow. We have found one girl called Mary Roche, who has the personality of a young Mary Pickford. She has a lovely voice and it is schooled and she can dance. There are others who have walked in about which we're not sure, but all of them reek of talent and ambition. As I sit there, I feel proud of my country."

Cole especially enjoyed these encounters with the young, feeling that they kept him in contact with the viewpoint of the upcoming generation. He expended great effort in attempting to prevent himself from settling back and accepting the comfortable attitudes of his own age group. Margaret Case Harriman pointed out in her profile of him in *The New Yorker* that he had written his first hit, "An Old-Fashioned Garden," in 1919 and "Make It Another Old-Fashioned, Please" in 1940. "The way Porter has kept abreast of the phrase 'old-fashioned'—from nosegay to a national institution—is one indication of his agility in marching with the trend. His relation with the public has been a timeless one, unconnected with the calendar except in the number of emotional careers his songs have punctuated."

Among those signed for *The Seven Lively Arts* were Dolores Gray, Billie Worth, Paula Bane, Nan Wynn and Bill Tabbert; with such headliners as Beatrice Lillie, Bert Lahr, Benny Goodman, Alicia Markova, Anton Dolin and Doc Rockwell, the vaudeville monologist.

Cole went to Williamstown in the middle of September to finish work on the songs for the show, which was to be the story of young people who are drawn to New York in hopes of pursuing careers in the arts. Just as in *Mississippi Belle,* he found that he was having difficulty in writing songs which met his standards, except for a comedy number for Bea Lillie entitled "When I Was a Little Cuckoo."

Nor was his state of mind eased by having Rose decide

to throw out the book and turn this gigantic production into a satiric revue for which George S. Kaufman, Moss Hart, Robert Pirosh, and Charles Sherman were to write sketches and Ben Hecht was to provide a running commentary on the seven arts: theater, ballet, opera, concert, radio, music and modern painting. There were 150 performers, a 40-piece orchestra, 40 stagehands, costumes by Valentina and Mary Grant and nine carloads of scenery designed by Normal Bel Geddes—according to the publicity releases. In any case, whatever the exaggeration, there was so much scenery that two carloads were left behind when the show departed for Philadelphia.

On November 24, 1944, the production opened to a sold-out eleven-day engagement with an estimated $40,000 in mail orders returned. The grapevine had predicted a total washout, but the Philadelphia reviewers were overwhelmed by the sheer size. Although the performance staggered and lurched, the Philadelphia *Record* had no doubt that it would emerge as one of the great revues of the decade. The *Inquirer* was even more enthusiastic although the show had run until 12:15 on opening night at the Forrest. Cole was treated handsomely as were most of the participants.

Behind scenes neither the production staff nor the stars were fooled by the enthusiasm. Bea Lillie was unhappy over the relatively short out-of-town break-in for the show, and many others were also dissatisfied. Cole found Rose difficult to work with—an even shrewder and more ruthless businessman than Todd, but lacking Todd's understanding of creative talent.

At the charity preview in New York on December 7, Bea Lillie did not appear, claiming a sore throat, although *Variety* noted that insiders suspected that she was unhappy with Rose.

For the gala opening, Rose staged a spectacular party for the 1,600 persons in the audience, making this the most lavish premiere in many years. In an effort to appropriate Ziegfeld's mantle, Rose arrived at the theater with Eleanor Holm Rose on one arm and Billie Burke Ziegfeld on the other. Seats sold for $24 each and white-gloved waiters poured champagne before the show, at intermission and after the performance. In the lounge there was an exhibition of modern paintings.

Next morning, Cole read the gloomy news. The show had everything but style, taste and real wit, according to the critics. Several of them liked "Ev'ry Time We Say Goodbye," "Frahngee Pahnee" and "Is It the Girl?" but even those who liked the songs were parsimonious in their praise.

Cole began 1945 by undergoing his thirty-first operation, one which put both legs back into casts. While he was immobilized, Rose attempted to shave running costs by cutting twelve instruments from the orchestra. Cole was in despair. For the rest of his life, he was to think of *The Seven Lively Arts* (179 performances) as his unhappiest experience in the theater.

CHAPTER XIII

While Cole was preoccupied with *The Seven Lively Arts*, one of his least expected successes was in the making, giving him a much-needed boost in morale. During World War II, Hollywood studios turned out a succession of star-laden films—grab bags of song, dance and low comedy. Warner Brothers hired Walter Gottlieb to produce one such vehicle, using as background the famed servicemen's canteen, where motion-picture stars entertained the boys. The film was called *Hollywood Canteen*.

Its songs were gathered from any available source, including unpublished numbers that languished on the shelves of Warner's music publishing firm. Among these was "Don't Fence Me In."

Gottlieb later said he was mildly surprised to learn that Cole was the creator of the song, and when he inquired into its background he found that it was being held as the theme song for a musical biography based on the life of cowboy-humorist Will Rogers. Gottlieb thought it excellent material for another Rogers—Roy, whom he had borrowed from Republic Pictures for *Hollywood Canteen*. Warners agreed and the song was recorded by Rogers, the Andrews Sisters and Bing Crosby. But just as the picture was ready for release, the studio legal department discovered that the number actually belonged to 20th Century-Fox.

How had this come about? In late 1934 and 1935, Cole had written it for a film (called *Adios, Argentina* or *Argentine Nights*) which producer Lou Brock proposed to do at the old Fox studios. Brock, in fact, had found a poem called "Don't Fence Me In," which had been written by a Montana cowboy. He had brought the poem to Cole's attention and suggested that the songwriter buy the rights and use the idea.

Cole agreed that it was a great title, contacted the author, Bob Fletcher of the Missoula [Montana] Power Company, and managed to acquire all rights for $150. From the poem, he eventually used only the title and a couple of phrases. After finishing the score, he left on a trip around the world and promptly forgot all about the songs, since the picture was never produced.

Exactly how the song got from Fox's inventory into Warner's is unclear. However, Jack Warner personally called Darryl Zanuck, head of 20th Century-Fox, explained that the song was already included in his picture and asked to buy the number. Zanuck gave it to him without charge, and eight years after it had been written "Don't Fence Me In" finally reached the public in December, 1944. By January 3, 1945, columnist Sidney Skolsky reported that it was "the most instantaneous song hit Cole Porter ever had. It's first on the Hit Parade, first in sheet music which is enormous and it's the first-selling record with Bing Crosby and the Andrews Sisters."

Cole's comment upon hearing about the song's resurrection was a sigh, followed by, "Oh, that old thing." He expected no reaction to it and gave it little thought since he was now preoccupied with regaining his health and writing new numbers rather than resurrecting old ones. Nevertheless, he was to hear much more about it.

By March 21, Bing Crosby's recording had sold 1,250,000; the Andrews Sisters had sold more than 1,000,000 copies; and there was a 1,200,000 sale of sheet music. Such success was bound to draw unwanted attention. While Cole was still in the hospital, a well-known New York eccentric, Ira B. Arnstein, who for the past twenty years had been suing one after another of America's leading songwriters for plagiarizing his work, got around to Cole. In mid-February, he filed a suit in federal court, charging that Cole had lifted four songs—"Don't Fence Me In," "I Love You," "Begin the Beguine" and "You'd Be So Nice to Come Home To"—from his (Arnstein's) "A Modern Messiah" (unpublished), "La Priere," "The Song of David," "I Love You Madly," and "Sadness Overwhelms My Soul."

To make certain that the public understood the scope of the conspiracy against him, Arnstein, according to newspaper reports, passed out mimeographed sheets detailing his charges to reporters. His most damaging claim: that he had been blocked for the past ten months in his efforts to bring suit because Cole had hired away or intimidated any lawyers to whom Arnstein spoke.

Finally on May 7, the $1,000,000 plagiarism suit brought against Cole by Arnstein was called.

Arnstein testified that Cole had stolen his songs.

Sigmund Spaeth testified that Arnstein was prepared to sue anyone who used A, B, C, D, E, F, and G notes.

Monty Woolley testified he was with Cole when "Night and Day" and "Begin the Beguine" had been written. He further testified that he had seen none of Arnstein's published or unpublished tunes lying around.

Professor Samuel A. Baldwin testified that certain portions of Cole's songs bore resemblance to certain portions of Arnstein's.

Deems Taylor, president of ASCAP, testified that he found no similarity.

Cole testified he had never heard of Arnstein or his tunes before the suit was filed.

The jury dismissed the plagiarism charges as being without merit after deliberating one hour and fifty minutes. Thus ended a case which occupied the court for two weeks. Over the previous twenty years, *Variety* estimated that Arnstein had caused publishers and songwriters to spend

$250,000 to defend themselves against his charges.

Cole's lawyers, John F. Wharton and Samuel J. Silverman, were more seriously worried over the fact that a precedent had been set for allowing copyright-infringement cases to be settled by a jury rather than by a judge who could ponder the briefs, analyses and charts in privacy. The jury, the lawyers felt, had to rely upon recollection of exhibits and testimony. This might, they feared, result in a miscarriage of justice.

Meanwhile, Walter Winchell picked up and printed a story that Cole had bought the lyric "Don't Fence Me In" from a cowboy named Fletcher. Then Kate Smith honored Cole on her radio program, saying: "Mr. Cole Porter has done something special with this song which breathes the yearning of free men. . . . It's one of those things I have liked, and this morning because I'd like to thank him for you, for our fighting forces, for myself, I have made up my mind to send him a memento, a Gruen Curvex watch, with a special inscription from all of us to him, because he gave us 'Don't Fence Me In' "! Undoubtedly, it was fortunate that Miss Smith did not divine Cole's intentions of spoofing such numbers when he wrote the song.

Winchell followed up with a story that Fletcher had written to Miss Smith to complain, saying that he didn't mind losing the royalties since he'd sold the poem, "but in lieu of this he thinks he should have the watch."

Cole responded by hiring lawyers to contact Fletcher, Miss Smith and others. Fletcher denied having written the letter, Miss Smith denied having received it and eventually it was discovered that Winchell's informant was a United Artist's flunky whom the columnist paid $60 a week to feed him gossip.

In 1934, Cole had written Dr. Sirmay that a major studio proposed to pay vast sums for the right to make a film based upon his life. The picture had been suggested by Irving Berlin, who called Cole one day to say that he had awakened at 3:00 one morning and had been struck by the idea that the agonies Cole had suffered with his legs and the achievements he had scored in spite of his suffering would be an inspiration to servicemen who were facing similar problems. (At that time, the war was expected to last for several years.) Berlin then called Jack Warner, related the idea to him, and Warner, who also thought the movie would be a wonderful morale booster, approached Cole.

From the first, the songwriter was inclined to go along with the project, but Linda loathed the idea. Finally she agreed after stipulating that both she and her husband must be allowed to pass upon the merits of the script and that she be allowed to approve the actress who played her role. The deal was made.

Ironically, Arthur Schwartz, with whom Cole had quarreled bitterly over *Mississippi Belle*, was assigned to act as producer. Cole did not protest. Then, one screenwriter after another attempted to devise a story line without success, causing Orson Welles to comment that he could understand that. "What will they use for a climax?" he asked. "The only suspense is—will he or won't he accumulate ten million dollars?" And it is true that one despairing writer gave up, commenting: "No struggle anywhere all the way down the line."

Shortly after Cole was released from the hospital in March of 1945, Arthur Schwartz, director Michael Curtiz and several Warner Brothers writers flew to New York to secure Cole's approval on their script.

Cole canceled one appointment and everyone was filled with foreboding when the time came to see him next day, but as they walked into his apartment, he waved the script at them and called out, "I like it fine."

He had really roared with laughter as he read the complicated contrivance that they had manufactured. Later, he confided to a friend, "It was the strangest feeling—as if reading about someone I knew slightly." Publicly, he said, "It ought to be good. None of it's true."

With filming in the offing, he set out for his Brentwood home, planning to stay nearby during shooting and to take the opportunity to bake his legs in the California sun. He had been disabled for six years now and he had begun to realize that he would never fully recover.

The effect of the constant pain that he endured was becoming apparent in the way he responded to small annoyances. It was harder these days for him to shrug off an inaccurate column item or the seeming irresponsibility of a producer. Whereas he had always prided himself on his reputation for being an easy man to work with, he now approached his co-workers with a discernible edginess. He had engaged in a full-fledged feud with Arthur Schwartz. Billy Rose had seemed to him cold and ruthless, and the experience was one upon which he looked back with anguish. On a more personal level, he was dissatisfied with his valet, with his cook, with his life.

His artistry suffered no less than his business relationships. At the peak of his form, his lyrics for *Anything Goes* had made a witty, disenchanted comment upon the mixed-up state of the world in 1934; "You're the Top" had dazzled with its casual mixing of slang and erudite allusions in rhymed superlatives; "I Get a Kick Out of You," with its five internal rhymes, had given notice of his unrivaled technical dexterity as a lyricist. The hypnotic spell of the "Night and Day" melody and the beat of "Begin the Beguine," as well as the daring length of both, had set him apart. Now, although displaying his customary bravado in public appearances, in private life his feeling of despair made it impossible for him function on that former high level.

In "Count Your Blessings," he had settled for a simple listing of romantic twosomes—with no wit, no gags and no tag. So it was, too, with "Abracadabra," the lyric of "I Love You" and most of the rest of the *Mexican Hayride* score.

The Seven Lively Arts work had consolidated his decline; except for "Ev'ry Time We Say Goodbye," the score was lyrically and melodically uninspired. No one was more aware of this than Cole. Nor was anyone more aware that his greatest recent success was written two years before he suffered the accident. One evening in conversation with public-relations man Stanley Musgrove, Cole observed that there was no doubt that he had just begun to hit his stride when the accident occurred and that since that time there had been a noticeable decline in the quality of his work.

That summer he wrote little, but he did keep an eye on the progress of his life story and he persuaded Jack Warner to hire Monty Woolley as technical director. Warner was also happy to honor Linda's request that Alexis Smith play her part. In regard to the leading role, when Cole mischievously asked that Cary Grant, under contract to Columbia, be given the job, nobody expressed any opposition. Jack Warner personally opened negotiations with Harry Cohn, head of Columbia Pictures, who insisted that Warner come over and have breakfast with him before he'd agree to a deal. The request threw Warner into a rage, but he finally went, only to have Cohn brag that Jack Warner had come over and got him out of bed to have breakfast.

In that way, Warner's secured the services of Cary Grant rather than some more suitable actor such as Fred Astaire, whose style and outlook would have approximated Cole's. Grant, on his part, took the assignment seriously and spent evening after evening dining with Cole to study his speech mannerisms and personal idiosyncrasies.

Monty by this time had been added to the cast, but since he was playing himself the script portrayed him as a professor of Cole's rather than an upperclassman. Such liberties bothered Monty not at all, but he roared and swore and complained to Cole that the Yale Yard was proportioned incorrectly and that too many lettermen were being used. Cole gleefully backed his charges.

Plans were made to secure all the stars who originally performed the numbers to repeat them in the picture. Then, the front office accountants began totaling up costs of the film—including the $150,000 that was to go to Grant and the $300,000 to Cole for rights to the story and music—and it was found that the film would require capitalization of at least $4,400,000, an astronomical figure for that time.

In an attempt to shave costs, it was decided that Mary Martin should recreate "My Heart Belongs to Daddy," but that Ginny Simms would serve as a kind of all-purpose performer, singing numbers introduced by Irene Bordoni, Ethel Merman and Virginia Bruce, to say nothing of those of William Gaxton.

That year the memories stirred by the film made Cole feel more and more the contrast between the old freewheeling days and the present. It also frustrated him to be forced to rely so completely upon others. One evening he invited Sam Stark to dine and during dinner announced that he wanted to drive an automobile again. Would Sam teach him?

Stark asked what Linda thought of the idea.

Cole replied that he was determined to learn no matter who opposed him. If Stark refused to help, he'd sign up with a professional school.

Stark agreed.

Linda was soon apprised of what was transpiring. She called her husband and pleaded with him to give up the lessons. She also appealed to Stark to discontinue the project. Sturges, too, attempted to dissuade Cole via long distance, and Monty Woolley, who was on the scene, called Stark, argued with him, cursed him and demanded that the lessons stop.

But Cole was not open to either persuasion or coercion. During the lessons, he questioned Stark in minute detail about the car until he understood the mechanism perfectly. At first he kept to the lonely side streets of Brentwood, but finally he announced that he was ready to take to the busy streets. By the time he returned East that fall, he had passed his test and was confident of his ability to handle the car even though his legs were still in braces.

When he demonstrated his new-found skill, Linda at once recognized what an importance this mastery of the automobile represented. She wrote Stark thanking him for being such a good teacher. "He [Cole] is an expert. I am amazed. It is so good for him to have that freedom to drive his own car. It is the beginning, I hope, of simplification of his life. He has far too many people around him, waiting on him, and actually messing up his life. He sees it now. Much love, Linda."

That same fall, at Cole's instigation, Miss Moore wrote the International Red Cross in an attempt to gain information on the whereabouts of Paul Sylvain. Cole was dissatisfied with his current valet and was hopeful that Paul had survived the war and was willing to return to his service.

The Red Cross suggested that a detailed letter be sent to the Bureau of Naval Personnel. This produced an address and on October 15, Miss Moore wrote Paul asking whether he would consider returning to New York. "Mr. Porter has asked so many times about you, and he said to me a short time ago, 'Please write and find out how Paul is, he was so good to me when I was first ill.' He had another serious operation on his leg last December—and I pray this will be the last one—for you know how many he has had on both legs. Weston and all your friends want to be remembered to you, and above all, Mr. Porter sends his very best to you."

The letter produced the desired results—Paul returned to the Porters and remained with Cole until his own death.

Sometime after that fall Orson Welles approached Louis Shurr saying that he had a great idea for a musical show to be called *Around the World*, based on Jules Verne's classic, and that he hoped to interest Cole in doing the score. Shurr said that the composer was available and he would speak to him on Welles' behalf. Cole was eager to work with Welles but he was troubled by the fact that he owed a show to Mike Todd. Would Welles consider writing the book and directing, but letting Todd produce?

Eventually Cole, Welles, Shurr and Todd lunched at Henri Soule's Le Pavillon and Shurr set a deal for Welles to be paid $2500 a week and expenses to remain in New York for three months while working on the book of *Around the World.*

After a couple of weeks, Welles informed Shurr that he felt Todd had lost interest and suggested that other arrangements be made. It developed that Welles was correct and Shurr moved him into his office while he scouted new producers. But for each one Shurr found, Welles offered an objection until it became clear that he wanted to produce as well as write and direct the show.

Cole agreed to this, and was filled with admiration as he watched the former boy wonder call Sir Alexander Korda by telephone and ask for the rights to the story, which Korda owned, as well as $100,000 in cash. In return, he promised to appear in a film.* Korda accepted the proposition.

Welles then called Harry Cohn and ad-libbed the plot of a film** in which he and Rita Hayworth would appear and which he would direct. Cohn was interested. Welles said that he needed $100,000 for the Broadway show he was producing. Cohn advised him to call his brother, Jack, who made the deal.

During the second week in January, Cole and Welles were hard at work solving creative as well as production problems attendant to the gigantic undertaking. Although there were financial difficulties, Cole felt no obligation to help solve them. He considered six months' work on the score as his investment—worth at least $100,000.

As Welles first planned the production, there were to be twelve musical numbers in the thirty-two scenes, including a spectacular aerial ballet which closed the first act. Because of the complexity of the production, which utilized a full Japanese circus and forty tons of sets, costumes and props (including a 1,600-pound mechanical elephant), Welles considered opening his extravanganza in New York and dispensing with an out-of-town tryout.

But as casting proceeded, one actor after another gave him new ideas for new scenes. By the time Arthur Margetson was chosen to play Phileas Fogg, Alan Reed to

* The film turned out to be *The Third Man.*

** The film turned out to be *Lady from Shanghai.*

enact Dick Fix and Mary Healy to appear as the Hindu girl, the script had swelled to forty scenes. When the actors began to work their way through the accumulated maze of light, music and prop cues, somebody suggested a title change: "Welles-a-poppin'!" The gag quickly traveled the theatrical grapevine, eventually appearing in *Variety.*

Cole, who was not always elated by spectacle, was optimistic in spite of the apparent chaos. He had during January and February been following developments, attending rehearsals and taking a hand more directly than in any production since his accident. Then, suddenly, he was incapacitated by a serious flare-up of his osteomyelitis.

He agreed, though, when Welles decided that an out-of-town break-in was essential to get the show into running order. It was booked to open at the Boston Opera House on April 26, 1946.

By the time the company entrained for Boston, Cole had recovered sufficiently from his illness to accompany them. Then, because of the complexity of the production, which made the backstage area look like a Rube Goldberg machine, the stagehands were unable to complete hanging the scenery and to have the production ready for the premiere. There was a postponement, which Cole viewed as a good-luck omen since several of his biggest hits had been delayed for the same reason.

On April 28, however, the critics wrote either outright pans or suspended-judgment reviews. This time Cole could not view the matter with his usual detachment. He attributed the pans to the fact that the show had had to open in a rough state because the production was underfinanced, to the fact that Welles had offended W. R. Hearst by making *Citizen Kane,* to anything except the truth—which was that the physical production was too unwieldy to fit easily upon any stage. He had had too many flops in recent years to be able to accept another. In a somewhat pathetic letter to Sam Stark, Cole rationalized: "I can't give you any news of the show yet as in Boston we are the prey of drunken stagehands and drunken electricians. Even when they are sober most of them are ninety years old. They all hate the show because there are so many light and scene changes and they are used to nice comfortable operas where there are two sets and no light changes whatsoever. We open in New Haven next Tuesday night, or at the latest next Wednesday night after which we shall know more—what with a new gang of mechanics.

"Orson Welles has been a tower of strength. The whole company loves him and rightly so because he never loses his temper or his power to surmount almost impossible difficulties, so if the show flops, I shall at least have had a great experience with a wonderful guy."

The New Haven engagement for *Around the World* turned out to be something of a booby trap. Financial troubles were increasing, and these took on a tragi-comic aspect when a costume company snatched back its own work and—by mistake—the work of another costumer only a half hour before the opening.

Following the overture, the old-fashioned movies that were to introduce the show failed to materialize. The stage manager stepped out from behind the proscenium arch, apologized for the recalcitrant machine and asked indulgence to allow the show to begin again. Once more the machine failed. This brought forth Welles, who ad-libbed: "This just goes to prove what many of us have felt right along. Movies are not here to stay." He then described what the audience was to have seen.

Problems multiplied. Alan Reed, who had taken the Fix role to demonstrate his capabilities as a comedian, withdrew, saying that the role had been transformed into a straight villain. But Welles stepped into the part and proceeded to burlesque the villainy, with hugely comic results. During his first performance, he entered the barroom scene and demanded: "Straight formaldehyde with a black widow spider ridin' the olive." He tossed off the concoction with gusto, only to find that his false whiskers had dropped to the bar. "Mighty powerful stuff, that liquor," he said. "Burns whiskers right off'n a man's face."

The impromptu ad libs and mishaps began to work a

fascination on New Haven audiences. By the end of the week attendance built to capacity. Cole still hoped that they had a show, although he was somewhat discouraged to see that after undertaking the Fix roles, Welles was concentrating upon the book and gradually dropping his songs. After four of them had been dropped, he did not argue or fight with Welles about it. He simply lost interest in the project. On May 31, the day *Around the World in Eighty Days* was set to open at the Adelphi Theater in New York, Cole took a plane to California.

The cast faced a stifling May night. The theater was not cool, but the notices were. Welles, Margetson, Mary Healy and Julie Warren—in fact, all the actors—were praised but the book was criticized for being disjointed. Cole was charged with having written an undistinguished score (one of the kindlier descriptions of it). The production lingered for seventy-four performances, and then Welles gave up.

With the closing, word went around Broadway that King Cole had lost his touch. Consensus was that he would not be heard from again. His kind of wit, style and chic were alien to the times, it was said. What audiences wanted now were songs with the common touch, a genre with which Cole was not entirely at home. Even his popular songs—"Night and Day," "Begin the Beguine," "Just One of Those Things"—were an acquired taste. The odds were that he was through.

Just as "Don't Fence Me In" had come along to revive Cole's reputation after *The Seven Lively Arts* fiasco, *Night and Day* now served as a forceful reminder of what great delights he had provided over the years.*

On August 1,1946, the *Night and Day* film had its Hollywood premiere, and that evening, instead of attending the opening, Cole gave a small dinner party. His guests, who also did not attend the opening, were Ann Warner,

* Seemingly everyone forgot the initial reactions to the song "Night and Day." At that time one critic wrote that Cole had attempted to write a new "What Is this Thing Called Love?" and had failed.

wife of the head of the studio that had produced the picture; Cary Grant, star of the film; George Cukor, Jean Howard and Sam Stark. Following the opening, Jack Warner dropped by for a drink.

When asked what he thought about the film, Cole resurrected a line he had used first on *See America First.* "It's a dream," he said. When persistent questioners pressed him as to what kind of a dream, he replied, "I'd prefer not to say."

The success of the picture, ironically, increased his fame at a time when he felt himself creatively at an ebb. But as always public approval proved a balm to his ego and he flourished, enjoying doing the kinds of things that people hesitated to suggest. By the end of September, he had appeared as a special guest on Louella Parsons' radio broadcast, had granted several interviews and was a regular on the Brentwood-Bel Air A-party circuit.

When it came time to leave California, Cole decided to motor through the Southwest and persuaded Sam Stark to accompany him as far as New Orleans. On November 9, they left Brentwood, arriving in Las Vegas in time to go nightclubbing with Jean Howard Feldman, who was there to divorce her husband, agent Charles K. Feldman, and with Michael Pearman, a friend since the days when Pearman had appeared in the chorus of *Jubilee* under the name of Buddy Birmingham in order that his proper English family not discover what he was doing.

Next day, Cole, such a resolute tourist that he sought out places that Babbitts might avoid, inspected the Hoover Dam Power Plant and on the 11th arrived at the Grand Canyon. Then on to Phoenix and on the 13th to Tombstone, Arizona, where a young reporter from the Tombstone *Epitaph* requested an interview. Cole imperiously waved him away, announcing, "No interviews."

The persistent youth explained that he was just starting on the paper, that this was one of his first assignments and . . .

"No interviews. No interviews."

Then he added the magic words that he had only recently graduated from Yale . . .

Yale?

"Sit thee down," Cole interrupted to say.

From Tombstone, Cole and Stark moved on to El Paso where a Southern Methodist convention was in progress and no reservation for them could be found at the hotel of their choice. Cole insisted that he had made one. Finally a manager appeared, recognized him and confessed that they had thought he was Paul Porter of the OPA, whose job it was to check on the rental charges during the war. They had not held any rooms, he said, but he managed to arrange accommodations at a motel.

"It was okay," Stark recalled, "but it wasn't a first-class place. The first thing Cole said was, 'There aren't any towels.' I pointed them out. He said he needed more. He said call them up and say you want some billowy ones. I tried to tell him this was just a little motel. But he was on the phone ordering White Rock and asking for real bubbly White Rock. When he got off the phone, I told him they were going to say that there were two madmen occupying these rooms. You're ordering service as if you're at the Waldorf. He didn't understand what I was talking about."

In Del Rio, Texas, there was once again room trouble. Originally they had intended to go the northern route, but plagued by rain, Cole had called the weather bureau to demand, "Where is the sun?" Told that it was shining in Texas, he had changed his routing and reservations had become shaky. In Del Rio, it appeared that there was nothing available anywhere. Finally, a small double room was located in a clean but old motel. The frames of the beds were wrought iron, the lamps had come from a dime store and the telephone was attached to the wall. Cole found it quaint.

That night, as was his custom, Stark set about washing his shorts and his socks. Cole looked at him as if he were performing some odd ritual and inquired what he was doing. Stark said what he always did—his washing. Cole thought he'd try it too. Stark offered to do it for him, but

Cole insisted upon doing it himself. Then, having finished, he rushed to the telephone and placed a person-to-person long distance call to Linda in Williamstown, Massachusetts, to inform her that he had saved fifteen cents by doing his own laundry.

From Del Rio, they moved to San Antonio where Cole shocked Stark by the cold manner in which he refused a dinner invitation from the hotel manager. When Stark said he thought Cole had been unnecessarily rude, Cole disagreed. "If I'd accepted," he explained, " there would have been a son or a niece or someone who wanted to be a singer."

While in San Antonio, they hired a car to visit the Alamo, a site which greatly impressed Cole, so much that even after he became exhausted and had to return to the car, he insisted that Stark continue the tour so he could tell him about it.

Hurrying through Houston and the Louisiana bayou country, they arrived in New Orleans and checked into the Hotel Pontchartrain on November 17. There they remained for four days during which Cole submitted to interviews, dined at famed restaurants and continued his sightseeing and sightseeing and sightseeing before he took off for New York and Stark returned to California.

Cole was hopeful that his return to New York would bring solicitations for a new Broadway show, a film—anything. Offers had rarely been so scarce. Luckily for him, both his and Linda's health was for the moment good. For the first time in years—from December of 1946 through April of 1947—the Porters resumed attending formal dinners. "This is all so new to me after so many years of regretting due to my work, my legs or Linda's larynx," Cole wrote Stark. "But I like it and so does Linda. But underneath my liking it I am constantly conscious of being a waster, and to such an extent that my first prayer every night is for work. This work, this job, this contract does not arrive and until it does, picture me as basically bored. Isn't it tragic to lose the power of enjoying doing nothing? I am surrounded by all the creature comforts and major amusements, but it is not enough."

In this note to Stark, a devout Catholic, Cole speaks of his prayers. It was a typical ploy to adapt his personality to that of friends. Thus, Stark came to believe that Cole was basically deeply religious and had seriously considered becoming a Catholic convert in 1944 or 1945. According to Stark, Cole talked it over with Linda, who encouraged him to take the step, although she maintained that it was too late for her.

Most of Cole's other friends were led to believe that he was an agnostic who might have wished for the support and comfort of some religious conviction but who was unable to summon up belief.

Nor is religion the only area where this man of many facets can be found. There are as many as three or four versions of various incidents that occurred during his lifetime. Friends tell each with absolute authority, secure in the knowledge that Cole told them the real dirt. In conversation, it is not unusual for one acquaintance to attribute some attitude to Cole which brings an incredulous smile from another of his friends who has heard another version. This brings the question: "Are you sure he wasn't putting you on?"

Of course, no one could ever be certain that he wasn't. In fact, the better one knew him, the less sure one was.

Although he often complained about the dullness of society, he found it an enjoyable contrast to those years when on account of his "ridiculous legs" he had had to turn down all invitations. Even so, both Porters agreed that they must proceed carefully. A smoke-filled room invariably left Linda feeling ill next day. Too much dissipation was likely to bring Cole another attack of osteomyelitis.

As he described their modus operandi, they would attend a large formal function at, say, Mrs. William Randolph Hearst's one evening, dine simply with a couple of friends at Le Pavillon for an evening or two, then another large function, say with the Duke and Duchess of Windsor, after which they would spend several evenings at Le Pavillon again.

Le Pavillon, which Cole facetiously called his "little boarding house, simple but good," was by all odds his favorite restaurant in the United States. The old Ritz, the Colony, or in a pinch Dinty Moore's, L'Aiglon or Gallagher's Steak House, would do, but for regular dining, Le Pavillon won out over all others. Both the food and the service were as Cole liked them, and the owner Henri Soulé understood his preferences and catered to them.

Nor can Le Pavillon's clientele be ignored. It was made up of the kind of people whom Cole liked best—beautiful, elegant, well-dressed, well-born and rich. This liking for the rich was instinctive. Cole did not climb. He did not have to, but he preferred the rich and the well-born. Once he complained, "How do you avoid name-dropping if those are the people one knows?"

He also enjoyed the flurry that his appearance at the entrance of Le Pavillon caused. On one occasion he was dining with MGM's Harry Krebs when Peggy Hopkins Joyce set down her champagne glass and drifted over to his table. "Cole!" she effervesced, and then she noticed the French ice sitting in front of him. "Oooooh!" she cried. "May I have it?" Cole said she could. She thanked him effusively and returned to her friends. Cole laughed and signaled a waiter with whom he held a whispered conference. A few minutes later, Krebs was startled to see a gallon of French ice being delivered to the actress' table.

On January 16, 1947, the Porters dined with the Duke and Duchess of Windsor. Cole had known and liked the Duke when he was still the high-stepping Prince of Wales. At the time, the Prince, an aficionado of American music, had been one of the earlier admirers of Porter tunes.

Once, Cole went to have cocktails with him in London. It was an informal and pleasant occasion. During the visit, the Prince said, "Come into the other room, I want you to see a picture of Mum." Cole followed, expecting to see a small framed portrait, only to be confronted by a life-size painting of the Queen of England.

In later years, Cole found the Duke a delightful companion with whom to discuss music. The Duchess fascinated him the way all movers and shakers did, as well as for her infinite chic. But in a moment of candor, he said of the Duke, "They had to get rid of him as King. He's simple. If he came here and I gave him a set of drums, he'd beat them all evening and be perfectly happy."

When social life became obtrusive, the Porters would go to Williamstown, sometimes accompanied only by their servants and their dogs. Cole owned two schipperkes, Pepin le Bref IV (given him by Merle Oberon) and Peppi's consort, Berthe.

Linda had a small Manchester terrier, Gracie, upon whom she showered great affection. Always a matchmaker, Linda, when she saw Sam Stark's dog, Teddy, decided that Gracie loved him. At the time, Stark was living in Dana Point, California, a small town in the Southern part of the state. He was confused one day when the telephone rang and someone asked for Teddy Stark.

Instead of saying Teddy was his dog, Stark asked who was calling.

"Is Teddy Stark there?" the caller repeated.

"Who wants to talk to him?"

"Western Union."

"This is Teddy," Stark said.

The caller then read the message: "Love to you, darling. Gracie Porter."

"Oh! That's another dog," Stark exclaimed.

The caller, who was the manager of the little railway station, muttered that he thought dog telegrams were a damn-fool waste.

Stark was amused and wrote the story to the Porters. Thereafter, both of them expended great energy in concocting messages with difficult words which would trip up the agent.

The high point of the old fellow's irritation must have been reached after Stark had presented Linda with some then-rare dripless candles. Both Porters were enthusiastic about this new discovery. Cole ordered an enormous amount to be sent to friends all over the world. Linda ordered more for herself. The candlemakers, swamped with orders, complained. Stark wrote the Porters saying that the candles were in short supply. Soon after, he received Linda's reply in a call from the station manager, who read the following message in a choked voice: "Dear Sam. Love, love, love. How can I get more? Love, love, love. Linda."

At approximately the same time, Stark met a girl whose mother suffered from arthritis which had settled in her hands. The doctors prescribed that she use her hands for cooking and sewing to strengthen them. Consequently, she busied herself making homemade fudge. Some of this was given to Stark, who, recalling how Cole loved homemade candy, sent him a box. He also sent a note explaining that the old lady who had made it would be thrilled by a signed letter from Cole saying that he had enjoyed her candy.

About a week later, the candy maker was ushered into Stark's drawing room by his Filipino servant. She clutched a sheaf of papers and was obviously distressed. When Stark had succeeded in calming her, he discovered that the papers contained a list of thirty or forty of Cole's friends that had been typed by Miss Moore. In addition, there were detailed instructions. Two pounds were to be sent to a woman in France and were to be in a pink box; one pound to a man in Cleveland, in a blue box; and on and on and on. Stark assured his visitor that he would take care of the problem. Then, he sat down and wrote Cole a letter saying that he had practically given the woman a nervous breakdown, that she made the candy in her kitchen as therapy and was not equipped to set up a shipping service. Soon, he received a reply from Cole, explaining that he had sent the orders "because I thought she would be flattered."

February, 1948, brought good news. Ray Kelly, who had been so kind to Cole at the time of his accident, visited for five days. While there, he had announced that his wife, Virginia, was expecting a third child in April. The plan was to call the child Cole Howard Kelly. "The betting is that it will be Cole Kelly, but I have only faint hopes," Cole noted. "Every time I am a prospective godfather it turns out to be girl." It was a boy.

In March, Cole wrote Stark suggesting that he fly East and accompany him back to California by boat via the Panama Canal. Cole was due in California to turn out the score for the MGM film based on S. N. Behrman's *The Pirate*, which had been a great Broadway success for Alfred Lunt and Lynn Fontanne. Now Metro proposed to turn it into a musical for Judy Garland and Gene Kelly. Vincente Minnelli was to direct, Arthur Freed to produce, and Gene Kelly and Robert Alton to devise the choreography. Although a full score was not demanded, Cole was glad to find that someone at last thought him employable.

On April 13, Stark, Cole and Cole's valet, Paul, went to Jersey City, New Jersey, to board the *President Polk*, reaching Havana two days later. There, a chauffeur provided by ASCAP took them sightseeing, including to a back-country sugar plantation, which so interested Cole that a luncheon was arranged, for which a table proved readily available but a tablecloth was obtained only after much scurrying about. The chauffeur, sensing Cole's enthusiasm, offered to arrange for them to attend a native dance.

The dance was held at a primitive nightclub which turned out to have a dirt floor. The drinks—rum and Coca-Cola—were dispensed from a thatched hut. At sundown about 100 people had gathered. All were barefoot, and when the band began beating out the rhythm, the crowd moved to the dirt floor. Cole excitedly reached for his notebook and jotted down musical phrases, *bon mots*, rhythmic patterns and anything else that might eventually prove useful. His enjoyment was supreme until someone pushed through the crowd and requested his autograph. Suddenly, the magic vanished. He wanted to get out at once.

When they reached the Panama Canal Zone, Cole and Stark hired a car and drove to Old Panama. That afternoon, they sipped cocktails at Kelly's, which had served as the inspiration for *Panama Hattie*, after which they drove to the Union Club for drinks and dinner. In Cuba, Cole, who could tolerate only minimal heat, had insisted that they buy the silk pleated blouses that were to be seen everywhere in Havana, even during evening hours.

They were wearing these blouses when they entered the Union Club. Although everyone else was more formally dressed, the headwaiter showed them to a table near the dance floor and the waiter served them cocktails, but when Cole requested a dinner menu, the headwaiter rushed up to say that he was sorry but that they did not serve anyone without coats. Cole inquired whether they served out of doors. They did not. Behaving with a sweet reasonableness that he was not always able to manage, Cole shrugged and said that in that case there was nothing to do but leave. As they were about to drive away, the headwaiter came running toward their car, shouting, "Oh please, Mr. Cole Porter. I did not know it was you. The lady from the boat recognized you. Please come in. For you, I will get a coat."

Cole and Stark stepped out of the car and returned to the club where each was given a white jacket and black snap-on ties. During dinner, Cole whispered, "Don't look now, but two of the orchestra are without their coats."

Several months later when Stark received an itemized statement for his share of the trip from Cole's accountant, there was a $13.75 charge for dinner and coat rental from the Union Club.

From April 20 to 23, they spent their waking hours drinking and playing backgammon. This game was one of Cole's chief delights at this period of his life. Each morning, the steward was instructed to arrange the chairs and table. The two men then took their places and began to play. Nearby stood Paul, ready to fetch drinks and other refreshments.

The *President Polk* was a small ship, and early on Cole had decided that he did not find the other passengers interesting. Although he kept pointedly to himself, this did not deter some of his shipmates from stopping to watch the game and question him about it. Cole made up a name for it, denying that it was backgammon. When anyone insisted, he would move the disks in a crazy pattern to confuse the onlooker and then would proceed to throw pieces overboard, swearing that this was according to the ancient game's tradition.

Several sets were lost in this way and whenever such a scene occurred, Stark snatched up Cole's gold cigarette case, fearing that he would get so carried away that he would toss it overboard, too.

The last night of the voyage, Cole and Stark shared a bottle of Cutty Sark. When it was finished, a note was drafted: "Playing backgammon April 26, 1947, on the *President Polk*." They signed their names, corked the bottle and tossed it overboard. Although instructions asked that anyone who found it communicate with them, the note was never answered.

At 8:00 A.M. on April 27, the *President Polk* docked at Wilmington, California, and Max Aydt, who with his wife Helene watched over 416 North Rockingham, was on hand to drive Cole and Stark there.

Stark then went on to his home in Dana Point and Cole began making changes in the score for *The Pirate*. Late in the schedule, Gene Kelly came to the house to beg Cole to write a clown number for him and Judy Garland. Cole promised to try. Finding himself without inspiration, he consulted the thesaurus and discovered many amusing words. Still, he was at a loss about what to do with them. Nevertheless, he was able to work out a melody. When he played it for Gene Kelly, the actor detected a certain melancholy quality which he related to the sadness of all great clowns.

Responding as always to encouragement, Cole wrote the lyrics overnight and took them to producer Arthur Freed. Freed listened to the words and music of "Be a Clown" and pronounced it the best number Cole had ever written.

Buoyed up by their enthusiasm, he appeared at MGM to hear Kelly and Judy Garland record the number. Miss Garland made no secret of how she felt about it. She did not want to sing it. "She pointed out that there were hardly any laughs where I had attempted to provide an infinite number. It was very embarrassing to have it pointed out," he once said.

Of the other songs "Mack, the Black," "Nina," "Love of My Life" and "You Can Do No Wrong" failed to stir much excitement among the public. In fact, after the picture was released Cole received no further film offers for some time.

That summer at a party given by Lady Mendl in Hollywood, Cole encountered Alexander Steinert, whom he and Linda had known in Paris in the 1920's while Steinert was studying at the Schola Cantorum. Later Steinert had worked with George Gershwin and had finally gone to the West Coast for film work. Upon meeting him again, Cole said that he needed advice. Could Steinert recommend anyone to come to 416 and play four-hands with him? "I don't play well," he said, "but I'd like to take it up again."

Steinert said that since he was unemployed he'd be glad to come. "After that we did a considerable amount of piano playing. I was fascinated because Cole's taste ran true to form. He liked any music that was stylized or classical. He didn't go in for the heavy romantic music. It would be Scarlatti, it would be Haydn, a couple of things of Bach's. And he would get so excited about it."

One afternoon, Steinert arrived earlier than expected. When Max let him in, Steinert walked into the drawing room. There on a low table was an array of cotton, forceps and other surgical instruments—a rather grim sight. "My lord!" Steinert cried. "What is that for?"

Cole shrugged. "My flesh and bones don't like each other," he said.

Generally he made no reference to such matters and they were not so serious as to curtail his social life. On August 15, he gave a luncheon for Dolly O'Brien and Clark Gable, who were involved in a hectic romance that had gossip columnists speculating whether Dolly would or Dolly wouldn't. The other guests included Mrs. Irving Berlin, Constance Bennett, Ethel Barrymore, Frances and Sam Goldwyn, Fred and Phyllis Astaire, George Cukor, Colonel

Coulter, Sammy Colt and Sam Stark. This luncheon took on significance because several guests insisted that Dolly decided at the party that she would not marry The King.

Two weeks later, Cole went to a private screening of *The Pirate* attended by Arthur Freed, Judy Garland, Vincente Minnelli and Irving Berlin. Berlin and Freed assured Cole that it was a great picture. Cole's response: "We shall see." He wanted to believe them, he needed a hit, but he had been dispassionate enough about his work to doubt that this small clutch of songs he had turned out would produce any vast impact on the great unwashed public.

On September 5, he left California by plane, stopped over for a few days in Indiana with the ailing Katie and then proceeded to New York to search for a new show. His agents had managed to turn up a variety of offers, but Cole was in a quandary. He often lamented that the burden of his professional life lay in his inability to judge the possibilities of a libretto. This self-assessment was not an example of false modesty. For instance, among the projects offered him was a musical comedy treatment of *The Taming of the Shrew*. The idea had originated with an eccentric young stage manager, Arnold Saint Subber, and a brilliant young costume designer, Lemuel Ayers. Through agent Dick Lamarr of the A&S Lyons agency, Bella Spewack had received a call.

"What did I think of the idea of *The Taming of the Shrew* as a musical?" Bella Spewack remembered being asked. "I said, 'It's a lousy play. I read it in high school. One of the worst Shakespeare wrote.' I went over next day and said, 'If you're thinking—you know—of just musicalizing Shakespeare, that's for high school. I want a show that's a six-sixty ticket.' Saint fell to his knees and hugged me around the legs and said, 'Please, you're the only one that can do it. I know it. I know it.' I said I'll think about it and if I get a notion how to make it a Broadway show I'll call and tell you. It took me six weeks. Then I came with the story idea and it was exactly the show as it was. Then came the business of composers. Now the boys came over to the flat Sam and I had on Fifth

Avenue. They had Burton Lane. Burton Lane came to see me and said maybe in a year he could get to it. We didn't click. I said, 'Just forget it.'

"Then they came and said they had this fellow from the Hasty Pudding show. And I said to them, 'I'm too old.' I was forty-seven and I thought I was old. I said, 'I'm not going to any Hasty Pudding show. I'm not discovering anybody. I have to have somebody of my standing.'

" 'Who?'

" 'Cole Porter.'

"They said, 'He hasn't had a hit in three years. The last show he did was a flop.'

"I said, 'Get out of this room and never come back.'

"They said, 'How do you get him?'

"I said, 'I'll get him.' So I called and made the arrangements.

"Cole said, 'Tell me about it.'

"I told him. Then he looked very sad and said, 'I don't think I could do it.'

"I said, 'Cole, it's so simple. Don't be frightened by Shakespeare. It's just a story about a girl getting married to a young man who wants to marry her. Forget the rest.'

"He said, 'Well, let me think about it.' "

Privately, Cole felt the project was too esoteric, too high-brow for the commercial stage. Instead, he encouraged a soap-opera writer named Elaine Carrington to develop an idea she had. Miss Carrington was ambitious to move out of soap operas into musical comedy which, in turn, was to serve as a stepping stone to straight comedy. Her subject was the annual Miss America Pageant. Cole could see all kinds of possibilities in the idea and requested an outline of the first act.

When it arrived, he was down in the depths on the forty-first floor. As a soap-opera aficionado, he recognized the real McCoy when he read it. He was also enough of a showman to realize that what amused him for fifteen minutes daily would never stand up in the hard, hard world of Broadway. Reluctantly, he bowed out of the project.

Bella Spewack continued to call, and more because he had no other promising leads than because of any real belief in her idea, he set up another appointment. His practical sense told him he was wasting time. Shakespeare revivals never played long; who could hope to titillate the tired businessman with a Shakespearean idea?

Bella could. "I came back a second time and he asked me to read the play to him. He said Linda had read part of it to him and he hadn't understood it. I can't read. But I *read.* He asked me again. The third time he asked me to draw the set. He was so wicked really. So mischievous.

"I didn't give up. I said, 'Look, all this crap with three men wanting to marry Bianca is Tom, Dick or Harry. The pedagogue—that's out. It's a story about this theatrical couple playing *The Shrew*, who have been divorced!' He asked me to lunch to talk about it and said, 'Oscar Hammerstein thinks I ought to do the thing with Elaine Carrington . . .'

"I said, 'Look, Cole, this will be wonderful, but it's up to you now.' I don't know. He was so sensitive and insensitive at once. I don't know why."

Bella still persisted. She browbeat, flattered, nettled, needled and persuaded him and she kept telling him that the project contained the seeds of a hit until Cole glumly inquired how he could expect audiences to understand something that he didn't. Bella had no answer for that, but the sparring continued until shortly before Christmas when Cole, Linda and Sturges flew to Indiana. Upon returning to New York, Linda had another respiratory attack and Cole began being bothered by his legs again. As often as he was able to meet with Bella, they tentatively worked on the show although no agreement was to be made until he felt surer of the project.

Then in February he suffered a severe setback in his right leg. It was serious enough for Dr. Moorhead to predict that the leg would not return to normal for several months and Cole again found himself living with "old-fashioned pain." Each Tuesday, Wednesday and Thursday morning, he visited the doctor for treatment which was so excruciatingly painful that he frequently lost consciousness.

In addition to his physical illness, he was also plagued by new tax problems which made it impossible for him to spend more than six months a year in California henceforth. With these disappointments pressing him, he felt that his single blessing was the prospect of the new show. Bella, having worked with him before, realized, as many of Cole's friends did, that it was easier to interest him in specifics and in small problems than in larger ones. Consequently, she approached him in that way. "I wrote out suggestions for song titles to stimulate him—and it just came like an avalanche once the initial strivings were over. He started writing. There was one song I never heard though. The boys wouldn't let me. 'What the Servants Saw Through the Keyhole.'*

"He signed with the producers on March thirty and we signed our collaboration contract later. There was nothing in writing between us. We had no lawyer—and you know I don't think I could do that with anybody else. It was just his word."

In that manner, the perfect musical was born.

* "What Does Your Servant Dream About?"

CHAPTER XIV

Kiss Me, Kate is essentially one of the theater's thrilling stories of triumph achieved in the face of seemingly insuperable odds.

Cole was considered passé by investors who preferred to place their money on currently successful favorites. His health was uncertain and, worst of all, he was plagued by self-doubt.

The Spewacks were better established as playwrights than as librettists, and, in any case, some people felt they were not suited to adapt Shakespeare.

The director, John C. Wilson, was better known as a producer, while one of the producers was an established costume designer and the other was an excellent stage manager.

There was no first-magnitude star to attract money men.

And worst of all, Shakespeare was considered box-office poison.

Still, between February and May of 1948, Cole turned out the major part of the *Kiss Me, Kate* score—some twenty-five songs, of which seventeen were eventually used—and the experiment was in progress.

Sometimes the work was easy. Once, for example, Cole asked Sam and Bella Spewack the name of a poem which contained the line "I have been faithful to thee . . ." The Spewacks added "Cynara" and told him it was by Ernest Dowson. A week later, he played a song suggested by the poem. It was the cynical "Always True to You in My Fashion."

It was not invariably so simple. Cole's faith in himself had been shaken. After Dr. Sirmay praised "I Hate Men," calling it a little jewel, Cole remained skeptical. Upon hearing "Where Is the Life That Late I Led?" Dr. Sirmay told him it was wonderful, but Cole still wondered whether it was any good. Over and over, he needed reassurance.

In addition to his own difficulties, he worried about his mother and Linda, who were in precarious health. And to complicate matters further, his faithful secretary, Miss Moore, suddenly died.

As always when there was a disruption of schedule, Cole found it difficult to work well. Luckily for the project, he soon found a charming blue-eyed social secretary, Mrs. Everett W. Smith. Mrs. Smith, who had formerly worked for Eleanor "Cissy" Patterson, Mrs. William Rhinelander Stewart and Mrs. Lytle Hull among others, turned out to be as adept at handling Cole's business affairs as his social engagements. Since she was also fiercely loyal, she was soon giving him the same security that he had had with Miss Moore and work went on.

Another mishap to his right leg at the beginning of April tired his spirit. In a letter written to Sam Stark early in May, Cole described what he had been through. "Yesterday I had a blood transfusion. I feel like a boxer, but now it is nearly over I must admit that this three weeks has been complete agony. There was an ulcer and abscess due to the bang Peppi gave me when he ran the length of the hall and jumped on me with charming enthusiasm. These [the abscess and the ulcer] appeared close together just over a large nerve center. This started all the nerves in my leg raising terrific hell and the pain has been so great that the drugs have had practically no effect. Also due to the bump, part of my shinbone is exposed and the surface was scratched. The skin around the bone is gradually covering it and will within a few weeks cover it entirely. But I have learned my lesson and from now on will always wear a guard on my right leg. . . . My show is very exciting. I've written 15 songs and have about five more to do. You'll like this score. It's so simple it sounds as if it had been written by an idiot child. . . ."

While he was experiencing all these troubles, the songs Cole turned out included "So in Love," "Another Op'nin', Another Show," "I Hate Men," "Too Darn Hot," "I Sing of Love," "We Open in Venice," "Tom, Dick or Harry," "Where Is the Life That Late I Led?" "Always True to You in My Fashion," "Why Can't You Behave?" and "We Shall Never Grow Younger." This last was so touching that it caused almost everyone connected with the show to burst into tears when it was auditioned. Yet it was quickly discarded. "Too sad for a musical," was the verdict.

Occasionally, Bella Spewack's honesty nettled Cole. When he wakened her at 2:30 A.M. to play his latest song, "Why Can't You Behave?" the exhausted Bella was not happy to hear "his lovely, velvety small voice" singing the new number at that hour. She let him know it, saying that the song was a "lay-me-down" piece which would make it difficult for her to get the book moving following it.

Whenever Cole was angry at her, he addressed her as "Madame Spewack," which he did that night, but next morning he apologized. Too many drinks, he said.

The Spewacks originally were to accompany him to California to collaborate, but his illness caused his departure to be delayed so long that they decided to finish the script in New York and mail him a copy. After reading it, he sent them a wire: "The best musical comedy book I have ever read arrived this morning. Congratulations. Cole."

Soon after, he forwarded a new song, "I Am Ashamed That Women Are So Simple," from California. Its lyrics were made up entirely from Shakespeare's lines. Although the score was already large, the producers and the Spewacks decided that room must be made for it. But Bella wrote a letter begging him to write no more songs.

She might have saved ink. Cole was bothered that the gangsters had no exit line at the end of a scene. Agent Robert Raison asked Cole, "Why not let them sing?" He suggested a low-comedy number. The idea amused Cole, who turned out a song on the struggle of underworld types with the intricacies of verse. He called it "Brush Up Your Shakespeare" and sent it along to the producers with a note predicting that Bella would probably cut her throat.

Now that the score was finished he busied himself in other ways. He approached opera star Jarmila Novotna to play Kate, but the diva was not interested in attempting musical comedy.

When Mary Martin appeared in Southern California with the national company of *Annie Get Your Gun*, Cole invited her and her husband-manager Richard Halliday to 416 North Rockingham and played the score of *Kiss Me Kate* for them. Both of the Hallidays liked it.

Several talks were held, but somehow one of those inexplicable misunderstandings occurred. Miss Martin later confided to Bella Spewack that when she asked to take the music home to study it, Cole replied that it was impossible since these were his only copies. She interpreted this to mean he didn't really want her.

On his part, Cole became convinced that she was unenthusiastic about his score and prepared himself for a turn-down. "When she refused to commit herself, I knew we'd lost her," he said.

Richard Halliday in 1965 recalled the negotiations in still a different way. "One day the phone rang and it was Richard Rodgers saying that they had bought a new property, *South Pacific*. Would Miss Martin wait until she heard the music before making a decision. We knew the property. We had read it only the same week, and had tried to buy it only to find Rodgers and Hammerstein had already made the deal. Rodgers mentioned Pinza. We heard three musical numbers the day after arriving East, and within hours enthusiastically agreed. The combination of the nurse (which Oscar Hammerstein said he'd wanted to write for Miss Martin since 1942), the modern story,

Pinza and the three songs had the stronger appeal."

When Cole's suspicions were confirmed, he fell into a deep depression which he described as "glooming." Nor was the word from New York good. The inexperienced team of Ayers and Saint Subber was undergoing difficulties in persuading backers to share its enthusiasm.

One person who was excited by it was John C. Wilson, a friend of the Porters from Venice in 1925. Wilson, who had produced and directed a string of Noel Coward successes, was eager to direct this show. He also felt that Lily Pons would make a marvelous Kate. Miss Pons, whose health was at the time uncertain, was living in Cannes. Wilson went there to persuade her. She said she was flattered, but that she couldn't consider a rigorous Broadway schedule.

Wilson then flew to California to continue scouting. There, among others, he saw a young actress who for three years had been mired down in B pictures. She looked the part. She said that she could sing a little, but her agent doubted that she had the flamboyance to carry the role.

Wilson told Cole about this girl, Patricia Morison, and Cole suggested that she come to his house. When they met, he was captivated by her manner. He gave her three songs to work on and told her to call when she was ready to audition. "If she can sing, our problems are solved" he told Wilson. "We'll create a great new star."

Two weeks later, Miss Morison sang for him. Although her voice was somewhat uncertain, Cole was so impressed by her presence that he suggested she take singing and acting lessons, even taking a hand himself by counseling her that in the Kate scenes she should walk like a spider whose legs and arms were attached at her solar plexus. He also hired Constance Collier, who was doing Shakespearean coaching, to work with the newcomer.

Several weeks passed before Miss Morison again auditioned for Cole, this time at the Wilshire-Ebell Theater. Cole then and there told her that as far as he was concerned she was his choice for the part.

Alex Steinert once said of Cole: "He never had to fight

anyone. He won his battles without fighting. He knew the Spewacks had someone else in mind, but didn't want to antagonize them. So he sent Pat to New York for a benefit and to visit the Spewacks and they fell in love with her."

From the beginning, Alfred Drake had been marked for the Fred Valenti-Petruchio role.

Concurrent with all this activity, Earl Wrightson, Christina Lind, Lorenzo Fuller, Lisa Kirk and pianist Joe Moon were auditioning for potential backers. Guiding the money-raising activity was Selma Tamber, who later served *Kate* in various capacities. "*Kate* was a rather fantastic story, you know," she once said. "Nobody would give us a penny. Not a penny. Cole was a has-been. He had done nothing. He had written nothing. Lemuel Ayers? Lem Ayers was only known as a tremendously talented designer, tremendous. He had done *Oklahoma!*, he had done so many marvelous things. Saint was known as a stage manager. Period. We couldn't get the money. We did audition after audition without success. I don't know. I just don't think anyone believed in Cole at that time. No one certainly believed in Saint Subber and Lemuel Ayers. We had one audition at Fairfield Osborn's house—he was Shirley Ayers' father. He's the head of the New York Zoological Society. We had one great audition at his fantastic house and we had invited all the great wealth that existed. They came from somewhere and they were all very, very high. We'd do the audition and the next day I would do the telephoning. This time I didn't get one penny. Not one penny. They had been so drunk, some of them, that they hadn't any idea what they'd heard. It was brutal trying to get that money. Howard Cullman put nine thousand dollars in. And he got some of his friends to come in, but we scrounged for money and we couldn't get it."

On his return from Hollywood, Cole conscientiously began turning up for backer's auditions, always on time, always a thorough professional. Finally, after scores of auditions, the $180,000 needed to mount the show was squeezed out of seventy-two angels, but even then none of the blasé Broadway crowd took the project seriously.

Meeting for rehearsals in addition to Miss Morison, Miss Kirk and Alfred Drake were Harold Lang, choreographer Hanya Holm, musical director Pembroke Davenport and arranger Robert Russell Bennett. Ayers doubled by doing sets and costumes.

Among the performers, Cole took special interest in Lisa Kirk, a wildly exuberant personality whose vitality, voice and way with a lyric was a never-ending delight to him, especially when she sang "Always True to You in My Fashion." Although most of his associates had been convinced that a movie name such as Ann Miller was needed for the Lois Lane-Bianca role, Cole quietly went to bat for Lisa and got her the part. First, however, even though she had regularly been doing backers' auditions, she had to do a formal audition for the producers.

Early on in rehearsals, Harold Lang, who had been hired to play Bill Calhoun-Lucentio, became visibly perturbed over the fact that he had no solo. He was a well-established member of the American Ballet Theater and as rehearsals progressed he grew more and more unhappy.

Cole sympathized with him, but for the moment was without a workable idea. Then, one evening after rehearsal he invited Lisa Kirk to go back to the Waldorf-Towers for a drink. As they stepped into the elevator, Cole tentatively began to whistle a tune. He stopped, started again and pushed on to the finish just as the elevator door opened for the forty-first floor. As Miss Kirk stepped out, she remarked she had never heard that tune before and asked what it was.

"It's Harold's number," Cole replied. He eventually called it "Bianca." He had written it in the elevator between the first and forty-first floors.

Bella Spewack protested that Cole had promised to write no more songs, and thereafter he began to refer to her only as "Madame Spewack" and avoided accepting her telephone calls. Bella, naturally enough, felt that without her effort there would have been no show. She was hurt. A rift developed that was never entirely healed.

In addition to Lisa Kirk, Cole developed a great

admiration for Alfred Drake, who gave director John Wilson many inventive ideas in staging scenes. During the rehearsal period, Cole often invited Drake and Miss Kirk to the Waldorf for a drink. On some nights, the three of them would simply sit around and talk. On others, Cole would play and sing, maintaining all the while that he was good at neither.

The time came for a run-through at the New Amsterdam Roof. There amidst falling plaster and grimy walls, the pianist beat out the songs on an ancient piano. When the first act was finished, Saint Subber, whose mother ran a ticket agency, approached Bella Spewack and reported, "Mother says this is *schwatz* [weak]."

"Tell your mother to go home and sell tickets," Bella replied.

What Saint Subber did not tell her was that he also had Moss Hart hidden in the balcony and that Hart too had said, "Too bad; you haven't got it." He might easily have told Bella this because her confidence was such that, as she once said, by all the rules the house should have come down on her. "But I knew Cole had come through brilliantly. I knew what I had done and what Sam had done was right. We had nothing to change. I knew it so I didn't have to be superstitious. In the history of American musicals this is the only one where they didn't have to touch a scene or a song. In rehearsals, changes were made. I wrote three versions, but I knew eventually we'd go back to the first one—and we did. There were disagreements over 'Why Can't You Behave?' and over 'Bianca,' but the disagreements were all ironed out before we left town."

The last of November, six baggage cars and two parlor cars carried the scenery, costumes and acting company to Philadelphia for the December 2d premiere.

The Porters were to drive down, arriving in time for Cole to attend the final dress rehearsal. Paul had stocked their suites at the Hotel Barclay with all manner of special items, including a dozen boxes of Kleenex (which Cole preferred to the finest linen handkerchiefs), a piano and such favorite paintings as a Dali, a Grandma Moses and a

Picasso. Peppi and Berthe accompanied Cole, and Gracie was with Linda.

On the drive down in the Porters' Cadillac town car, they had a flat tire. Although it was changed quickly, Linda became chilled and developed pleurisy. Sick or not, she was determined to be on hand at the opening.

At the dress rehearsal, Cole and the Spewacks seemed confident. Others were convinced that this was another dud. The program concessionaire was so pessimistic that Dorothy Ross and her former husband George, who were the show's press agents, offered to buy the program man's share. He sold it to them, as well as the right to produce the programs. Later, Ross found others so skeptical about the show's chances that he hedged his bet by selling half the newly acquired share to stage manager Ben Francis.

None of this fazed the fearless Bella. At the end of the first half of the run-through, she got up and proclaimed, "It's great! It's wonderful!" Cole gave her a look that was enough to kill, she recalled. "And I turned to the men and said, 'Come on, boys. Tell him what you feel.' I didn't know what the orchestra felt, but they all came over and said it was wonderful. I was right."

John Wilson shared Bella's faith. On the afternoon of the Philadelphia opening, he sent a note to Linda, who was in bed with a fever. "Darling Linda: Who could have foreseen on the Lido in 1925 a Cole Porter *Kiss Me, Kate* staged by John C. Wilson!! Not Princess Jane, not even Elsa and certainly not John C. Wilson!! I am so proud and happy about it all and Cole aside from simply being a genius is the sweetest, kindest person in show business. Good luck tonight. And even if some of the lights don't work—they will by Saturday. All my love, Jack."

Although fighting for breath, Linda managed to take her place at the theater that night beside her husband. The audience was far from the brilliant ones that had so often assembled for his out-of-town openings. There was in fact only a token contingent from New York.

Even Selma Tamber had by now begun to wonder whether she could be wrong. But after the first act, she ran into comedian Milton Berle in the lobby. Berle was shouting that he had just telephoned New York that this was Cole's greatest hit, his greatest score, and that the Spewacks were at top form. "And all I could think," said Miss Tamber, "was how hard to put together it had been."

The final curtain fell at midnight, by which time it was apparent even to the doubters that this was the almost perfect musical show. Next day there was more than enough praise for everyone. After all the years in which out-of-town openings had been followed by desperate measures—writing new numbers, rewriting, tossing out the new numbers and adding others—the consensus was that no changes were necessary.

On December 8, Cole arrived in New York with the wonderful news about *Kate,* but was greeted with terrible news abut Linda, who had returned two days after the opening. Her lungs had become congested and she was seriously ill. During the previous night, she had nearly died. She was being kept alive by oxygen. Her condition was to change for the better and then for the worse for the next week. Alarmed, Cole reserved two private bedrooms, one for Linda and one for her nurse, on a through car to Phoenix, Arizona. They had decided that she should winter at the J6 Ranch near Benson, Arizona.

Unfortunately, an oversight occurred in regard to the trip. No one informed the Porters that there was a layover in Chicago at which time the cars were shunted to a siding and the heat turned off. When this happened, the nurse became panicky. She rushed out, located the Pullman porter and hysterically demanded to know whether he didn't realize that there was a dying woman in the unheated car. She so alarmed the porter that he arranged for an engine to be backed up to provide heat for Linda—but not before Linda once again had taken a turn for the worse. When Cole learned of the incident, he angrily threatened to file suit against the railroad, but when Linda's health improved in Arizona, his anger subsided.

On December 30, 1948, the evening of the New York premiere, Cole, as was his long-time custom, had bought

100 seats in the front rows of the orchestra and mezzanine for friends. He appeared outwardly calm, although he was fully aware of the truth in critic George Jean Nathan's observation: "The musical show, in a word, is like the other fellow's wife or sweetheart. For one man who shares his taste there are always those who wonder what he sees in her."

This had been the case with *Kate* during auditions, but by premiere night, the word of mouth had built high expectations. The show had received rave notices, sold out consistently in Philadelphia and come into town at a cost of $142,000. Cole's worry now, and it was a minor one, was that it had been oversold. The initial response opening night was clamorous, but watching the applause swell another person refused to express complete confidence until the end. It was Cole's mother, sitting in a fourth-row-center seat. After the first act, her escort, Dr. Moorhead, turned to her and said that it seemed as if Cole had another great hit, but the show-wise Katie looked at him quizzically and said: "We never know until after the second act, do we?"

Following the final curtain, Cole went to the Lytle Hulls for a drink and from there to the big opening-night party which Howard and Marguerite Cullman and Van and Sophie Schlee were tossing at 666 Park Avenue. As Cole arrived, Lisa Kirk recalled, Saint Subber, standing at the head of a long flight of stairs, shouted jubilantly that the *Times* notice was going to be a rave. Cole, she said, had been leaning heavily upon his cane; now he suddenly smiled, straightened up, tossed the walking stick aside and climbed the stair with a great show of verve.

During the evening, George and Dorothy Ross, Madi Blitzstein and Ingram Ash left the formal gathering to go to a penthouse in the Mayflower Hotel. There, they were to call in for the reviews. As one good notice followed another, a party spontaneously erupted. At first, a few chorus gypsies arrived, then some minor actors. Sandwiches and liquor were sent for. Then, quite unexpectedly, there was Cole, accompanied by several friends, all laden down with champagne. "May a poor little composer come in?" he asked.

To Dorothy Ross, who had always thought him self-absorbed and who could never bring herself to call him "Cole" despite the fact that he asked her to do so, it was a new view of the man. "He was at once shy, modest and triumphant. It was unforgettable," she said. "I'd written the notices out in long hand and here was this great man fondling them like a treasure."

Then Lem and Shirley Ayers, Saint Subber, the stars—everyone connected with the production arrived. After the notices were finally on the streets—much later than they are today—Ingram Ash went out to pick them up. "And I never saw anyone enjoy good notices as much as Mr. Porter," Dorothy recalled.

The daily reviewers hailed the show and welcomed Cole back to top form. The enthusiasm ranged from Robert Garland's benumbed "If this isn't the best musical comedy I ever saw, I don't remember what the best musical comedy I ever saw was called," through Richard Watts' "To Mr. Porter, the new musical comedy must be a particularly gratifying success, since there had been dark rumors abroad that the eminent composer had lost some of his old time power. There is no sign of any such decline in either the music or the lyrics of *Kiss Me, Kate*. There are some seventeen numbers, and all of them are worth listening to. There is no one song that struck me as standing out above the rest on first hearing and the lyrics are probably better than the tunes, but it all adds up to a vastly engaging score."

In *The New Yorker* Wolcott Gibbs noted that a man who would rhyme "Cressida" and "Ambassador" was capable of practically anything. Gibbs, whose admiration of Shakespeare was notably restrained, felt that this was, in every sense, a wonderful show and added that he couldn't think of a single sensible complaint to make about it.

For Cole, much as he enjoyed applause, universal praise would have been as uninteresting as a perfect Persian rug. Naturally, he clipped out and saved Harold Clurman's report in the *Saturday Review of Literature* saying that these were not his best songs "by a long shot."

Yet Cole, who equated success or failure with the enthusiasm his work generated, gloried in the acclaim he received from co-workers and friends. He even saved the letters of those who went out of their way to let him know they were delighted to have him back.

Alfred Drake wrote to thank Cole for the wonderful score and his many kindnesses. "I can think of no other production wherein I have been the recipient of so much consideration and thoughtfulness—so much of it from you. . . ."

Musical director Pembroke Davenport thanked Cole for his confidence and the freedom Cole had allowed him in his work. Not the least of his thoughtfulness, Davenport added, were flowers and gifts for Davenport's wife who was in the hospital and missing all the gala times.

Irving Berlin, who had also experienced the profound joy that accompanies a big-time comeback when he wrote *Annie Get Your Gun* (a job Cole had to turn down because he was busy with *Around the World*), wrote to congratulate him. Joshua Logan opened his note by admitting it was a fan letter. Helen Hayes regretted for the first time not owning the Koh-i-noor diamond so that she could tuck it in a nosegay as an appreciation for the joy he had given her with *Kiss Me, Kate*. She closed: "Bless you, you ever-bloomin' genius. Fondly, Helen."

On January 12, 1949, Cole received another note: "My dear Mr. Porter—I feel impelled to let you know how much I enjoyed *Kiss Me, Kate*. It has been many years that owing to increased deafness, I have not been in the theater, but your show is so well put on, acted, sung, so well written, one needed only one instead of all his senses to enjoy it. Sincerely, Bernard Baruch."

Variety put into print what all sentimental Broadway felt: that this was a thrilling story of show business, "the triumphant return of Cole Porter, the prodigal composer, to the ranks of the theatrical great."

Dr. Sirmay saluted *Kiss Me, Kate* as a masterwork in

light music. "In the artistic life of a composer—whether light or classical—he ordinarily creates only one perfect work. For Bizet, it was *Carmen*; for Mozart it was *Don Giovanni*; for Cole it was *Kiss Me, Kate*." Of its kind, each song is a gem—highly praised in 1948 and even more appreciated at the New York City Center of Drama and Music revival in 1965. Both in words and music, Cole succeeded in integrating the sounds of Shakespeare with those of the world of Broadway—all in a manner that is uniquely his own.

If, as Skitch Henderson remarked on the salute to Porter on NBC-TV's *Today* show, "The Bobolink Waltz" with its three variations might be passed off as a recently discovered Strauss waltz, it is one of the few songs by Cole that could be attributed to another composer—and it was written when Cole was eleven years old. Among composers, Cole is an original. Richard Rodgers and George Gershwin may be equally original, with Gershwin perhaps holding a slight edge, but Cole is a towering genius in words *and* music, while Gershwin needed a lyricist.

As a lyricist, Cole is rivaled only by Lorenz Hart. For those who would put forth Oscar Hammerstein, Hammerstein was a sentimentalist, who wrote excellent lyrics of a kind, but scarcely ever created a true comedy song. Hart and Ira Gershwin were funny, sarcastic and witty just as Cole was, but on occasion, too, Cole tapped emotional depths in his songs that have stood the test of constant repetition without loss of power.

It is in the creation of both words and music that Cole makes his strongest claims. The wedding of the two is so perfect that no two men could hope to achieve it. To do so, Cole generally first worked out the rhythmic impact of the song. Once this was clearly set, he created the lyric and then compsed the tune to the lyric. The result is a gaggle of singers' songs.

The songs, of course, reflect the man: witty, urbane and, although he strenuously rejected the designation, sophisticated. In *Kiss Me, Kate,* there is an effortless merger of high and low cultural references. Having had the advantage of a classical education with its emphasis on Latin and Greek—to say nothing of his later mastery of French, German, Italian and Spanish—Cole produced metaphors of a unique nature in popular music. Equally unexpected are the allusions to chemistry and biology which blend (seemingly with ease, but actually through hard work) with fashionable personalities, fads and foibles of modern society, in the larger sense. The humorless intellectual may detect more than a hint of *kitsch* in the juxtaposition of gangster slang and Shakespearean name-dropping found in "Brush Up Your Shakespeare" but even here the quality is high in terms of Broadway entertainment.

Kiss Me, Kate, after playing on and on at the Century Theater, moved to the Shubert where it eventually reached 1,077 performances. It was voted the Page One Award by the Newspaper Guild on March 29, 1949, and a month later, The Antoinette Perry Award. The national company, which opened in Los Angeles in July, 1949, continued its journeys for three years.

The British production which bowed at the Coliseum on March 8, 1951, with Patricia Morison, Bill Johnson, Julie Wilson and Walter Long in the leading roles, earned an ovation from first-nighters. The reviews were mixed. Dissenters called the script "mechanical, without heart" and the music "difficult." Yet the show ran for a total of 400 performances and in 1964 during the Shakespeare Tercentenary was revived for airing on BBC.

By 1965, the script had been translated into eighteen foreign languages. It was the first American musical to play Vienna, the home of European operetta, and was added to the repertory of the famed Volksoper Theater. It was also the first American musical ever to play in Germany, Iceland, Poland, Yugoslavia, Italy, Belgium, Hungary, Switzerland and Czechoslovakia. It has been done in Denmark, Sweden, Israel, Turkey, Spain, Brazil and Japan.

Was this the perfect musical success?

"Almost," Cole said. "Then, unfortunately along came a little thing called *South Pacific*."

Cole would have had to have been superhuman not to have regretted the temporary overshadowing of his work. And one evening shortly after *South Pacific* opened, he and a guest heard "Some Enchanted Evening" on the radio and the guest asked, "Cole, who wrote that song?"

"Rodgers and Hammerstein," he said. Then with a twinkle, "If you can imagine it taking *two* men to write one song."

CHAPTER XV

Ironically, the resounding popular acclaim accorded *Kiss Me, Kate* failed to buoy up Cole at the time of his greatest professional triumph. It was not that he no longer measured his own worth by the praise his work received, but that at this period of his life the strains that he had been undergoing for so many years seemed never to subside.

After remaining in New York for the recording of *Kiss Me, Kate* by Columbia Records, he departed for California where he wanted to supervise casting of the national company and to begin writing songs for a new show to be based on the Amphitryon legend. He had arranged, meanwhile, for Sturges to be at J6 Ranch in Benson, Arizona, to keep an eye on Linda, who was still bedridden as a result of the respiratory infection and complications brought on by the chill she suffered on the way West. Although Cole felt it necessary to stay in California, he rejoiced that he was within commuting distance of Linda. On February 5, he wrote her:

Dearest Linda,

I was very surprised, and so pleased to get your letter written on two postcards this morning. It also made me happy to read I should not worry about you, because until this note from you I did worry.

Please let me know, through Sturge, when you want me to come over. I am keeping from Friday to Monday free so that I can always fly over when you feel well enough for me to do so.

The ranch sounds like everything charming and it is a joy to know that you are there and not in that terrible New York.

I am talking to Sturge tonight. As a matter of fact, I think it's a good thing that you are *not* near the telephone.

All love,
Cole

P.S. I am sending you, under separate cover, a most beautiful present. My secretary, Mrs. Egan* gave it to me as she has never fallen out of love with Gracie [Linda's dog]."

Three weeks later, he flew to Arizona to stay four days with Linda and Sturges. Sturges was about to leave for Paris, so Cole arranged for Len Hanna and Winsor French to spend a week with Linda, to be followed by Constance Collier for a week, and finally for Celia Vom Rath to remain until the end of the month. He was also trying to persuade Linda to come to La Quinta, California, a resort near Palm Springs, during April. It would, he felt, be an ideal climate and would be within driving distance from his Brentwood place. Most importantly, it would keep her out of New York's April showers. She, on the other hand, was determined to open their Williamstown house by May 1. Cole felt this was sheer folly since the late Massachusetts spring might undo all the good that had been accomplished in Arizona.

He had another personal problem. For the past four years he had had his teeth checked every six months and

* Margaret (Tully) Egan, his West Coast secretary for many years.

his New York dentist had assured him that his mouth was in excellent shape. To his surprise when he consulted two California dentists both informed him that he had only four teeth in good condition, needed two bridges and was suffering from pyorrhea. One estimated the job at $9,500 and the other, whom Cole chose, at $8,000.

But mostly his mind was on Linda's health. On March 5, 1949, in his weekly letter to his mother, he gave her a rundown on his wife's condition.

> Dearest Ma,
>
> I went to Arizona last weekend and found Linda barely improved. The new drug [Aureomycin] which they had been giving her gave her such nausea that she had to give it up. The day before yesterday they began giving it to her again, with something to take to alleviate the nausea, so yesterday she was slightly improved, but the sleeplessness, the coughing and the struggle for breath all continue.
>
> I return there in two weeks and then the week following, I go again to start motoring with her, her nurse, her maid, her chauffeur and Paul to La Quinta, a resort on the desert only seven miles from Palm Springs, California. She will stay there at least a month.
>
> The great thing about her is that she is so philosophical. Her only remark during my last visit, showing that she was in the least discouraged was, "Oh, Cole, how I would love to bounce again!"

That spring Cole flew to Arizona every other week to visit Linda, who had decided to move from the J6 to the Hotel Conquistador in Tucson, where, he said, she found an "excellent bungalow for the usual modest price of $100 a day." There, too, she played guinea pig for a new drug, Chloromycetin, which Cole was hopeful would do the trick. He was pleased with the level walks which made it possible for her to take luncheon in the main dining room, after which she enjoyed a short drive, going to bed before dinner and remaining there for the evening. The tremor in her voice and her cough were still worrisome, but her sense of humor, he reported, was wonderful. "I suppose I shouldn't want to stop coughing, as I have coughed for so many years, if I stopped the shock might kill me," he reported her saying.

Finally on April 27, she insisted upon starting east on the train, going directly to her house in Williamstown. But in July, she experienced a seizure which made it necessary to rush her to an oxygen tent in a Bennington, Vermont, hospital.

Main Bocher, the couturier, who was a house guest every summer, notified Cole, who was in California, of the situation. Cole at once suggested that he fly to Albany, but Main talked it over with Linda's doctor, who said that since the attack was not terminal, he thought that Cole's unexpected arrival would alarm Linda, who knew he was busy working. Cole agreed, then later called again to say that he thought he really ought to fly to her side. Once more, Main repeated what the doctor had said.

Reluctantly, Cole gave up the idea of going to Bennington and instead wrote her a long, chatty letter, saying that he had been in despair when he first heard that she was in the hospital, "Then, my brain began to tick and I realized that this is a wonderful thing. I only hope that Dr. ———— will be more thorough so that you can have a complete recovery. It's been much too long and I can't tell you what great admiration I have for your patience. . . ."

Then he gave her gossip of the kind she doted on. He had heard, he said, that Irving Berlin-Moss Hart-Robert E. Sherwood *Miss Liberty* was a shambles. "This kind of news always terrifies me. To think that three such experts of the theater could go so wrong!" The evening before, he added, he had gone to a party at Katharine Hepburn's given for everyone connected with *Adam's Rib*. He had written "Farewell, Amanda" for the film, giving all profits to the Damon Runyon Cancer Fund.

She [Miss Hepburn] has a huge house overlooking Los Angeles. It has beautiful terraces and many acres. It used to belong to Charles Boyer and I can't understand why he ever built it, as the Boyers never entertained anyone except once when they invited Sturge to tea. We sat down in a dining room seating 300 people and the food was delicious. I think the nicest thing that has happened to me this summer has been getting to know Kate much better. She has great quality and I am devoted to her.

I think of you constantly, darling, and can't wait to see you. Jean [Linda's personal maid] writes that you already look like a different person due to the fact that you can breathe with ease.

All my love,
Cole

A few days later, he wrote once more, saying that his work went on daily and that by departure time on July 30, most of the refrains would be finished and many of the ensemble numbers for *Amphitryon*. After giving her a rundown on his social activities, he closed:

I have been in constant communication with Main and I was so delighted to hear last night that you were noticeably improved. It's all very well to ask me not to worry, but if you ever broke your fingernail I should worry. I have, however, used my head as much as possible and always insisted upon being optimistic. I know that you have this will power too and that this will, in a short time, make you fit again.

All my love, darling,
Cole

While Cole was worrying about Linda, he himself was down to 131 pounds and frequently unwell. "I think it must be in our blood to become thinner as we grow older," he wrote his mother. "As for myself I look practically like a withered grape." Yet that winter, spring and summer, he busied himself with auditions, work which he said he found depressing since all the young people tried so hard and spent so much money training their voices that he found it difficult to say no.

He worked hard on the musical version of *Amphitryon*, which he assured his mother in a letter was one of the funniest plots in the theater and not at all highbrow. She answered that it sounded like such a big show and she worried about its chances of success, but he insisted that it was no larger than *Kate* and added, "As for being afraid of it, you can't expect me to retire simply because I have a big hit on my hands. I doubt if I shall ever retire as I can't imagine living happily without my work."

As work continued *Amphitryon* became *Heaven on Earth* and then *Cloudburst* and Cole began to envision Carol Channing, David Wayne, Patricia Morison and Anne Jeffreys as the ideal cast.

Katie was still uneasy, so Cole invoked a little snobbism to allay her fears, assuring her that his collaborator Dwight Taylor was talented, experienced *and* the son of the late Laurette Taylor. These touches of snobbishness were always most blatant when he was playing the son intent upon impressing his mother.

He used it again that year when writing to warn her that he had endorsed Rheingold beer. After saying that he had done it to publicize *Kate*, he added that he had also received a nice check for his tax account and confided that the photographer Paul Hesse, who had taken the shots for the ad, was very well known and had taken some photos of him as a present.

On occasions when Cole was accused of snobbishness he always maintained that he was no snob, but just liked the best. Baron de Gunzberg, on the other hand, felt that all the expatriate Americans in the Porter set in the 1920's, with the exception of Sturges, were snobs. Whether Cole was or wasn't, he demanded the best in material comfort, amusement, service and companionship. But in regard to money, he exhibited a kind of reverse snobbism, assuring a friend who was planning to visit Palm Beach. "You'll be bored. They're *merely* rich."

Harry Krebs, a good friend in the 1940's, recalled that one particular acquaintance annoyed Cole by asking, "How's Vince?" Cole would ask, "Vince who?" "Vince Astor. Don't you see Vincent Astor." Although Cole might have had dinner with him the previous evening, he invariably said, "No. I seldom see Vincent Astor."

On July 11, the national company of *Kiss Me, Kate* was due to open. Shortly before, Selma Tamber, who was serving as general manager, was in the office of Western co-producer Edwin Lester, preparing for the opening-night party, when word was received that the scenery was on fire. Miss Tamber immediately rushed to the theater and was instrumental in saving most of the sets. One way or another word of her action reached Cole. When she returned to the hotel, she opened the door to her room—and became hysterical. In a very Porterian gesture, he had had the room filled with roses, roses and roses. Everywhere she looked there were vases of roses. And when she entered the bathroom even the bathtub and toilet bowl were jammed with roses.

Kate opened to excellent reviews and Cole now turned his full attention to the new show, auditioning half the score for Ayers and Saint Subber, who were pleased with it. Cole himself liked the romantic music and hoped that the remainder would turn out as well.

Before flying east, he turned down a Bing Crosby and a Betty Grable picture, decisions which were to give him much anxiety in the future.

Linda was on hand to greet Cole upon his arrival at Buxton Hill on August 1, but her condition was so shaky that he wrote to no one, not wanting to spread bad news. He at once bought an oxygen tent to be placed next to her bed for use in sudden crises. And he was shocked to see that she was compelled to use a wheelchair to get about and that her voice trembled when she talked. "It is pitiful," he confided to a friend. "She has, however, great courage and the will to survive which will help her greatly in the future. Sturge is here with all the gossip from the Continent, which she loves."

Quietly, Cole set about boosting Linda's morale. On September 18, he wrote a letter to Ethel Merman, which caused her to say he was "the most gracious, the kindest, the sweetest, and . . . there aren't enough adjectives to describe this great man, this great genius." The letter read:

> Dear Ethel: My Linda has been seriously ill for eight months. But if anything can make her well again, it is your broadcast every Sunday night at 9:30. I always listen too. You are wonderful and I sit beside her and watch her revel in your excellence. You probably know after a few years on the stage that no one can equal you. This is a love letter from Linda and me to you. My best to you all.
>
> From your devoted
> Cole
>
> P.S. If you have time, write Linda, tell her that you are so happy to hear from me that she is better (she is not) and that it gives you a great kick to know how she enjoys your program. This will do her great good, which she needs. The address is merely Williamstown, Massachusetts.

Miss Merman wrote Linda and then received this note from Cole:

> Dear Ethel: Your letter did the trick. You were a lamb to do this.
>
> Your devoted,
> Cole

That fall Cole received discouraging professional news. He had been hopeful that they could secure Carol Channing for the Juno part in the new show. In fact, he made a trip to New York to audition the score for her and her then husband, a professional football player and part-time detective. All evening, the husband had sat staring intently at him as he played and sang.

The next day Miss Channing called to thank Cole. "I really must apologize for my husband," she said. "When we got home, he said to me, 'That wasn't Cole Porter.' I asked whatever did he mean and he said, 'That wasn't Cole Porter. I saw *Night and Day*. And that's not Cole Porter.' "

The bad news was that Miss Channing had decided against his show in favor of *Gentlemen Prefer Blondes,* which was written by the Porters' long-time friend, Anita Loos.

By November the Porters had returned to the Waldorf-Astoria and Linda was no longer a great worry. "You ask for news of Linda," he wrote Sam Stark. "A month ago I felt she couldn't live more than half a year more. Today I believe that she may live and in comfort for quite a few years. This is all due to my having her apartment* air-conditioned. What I resent is that I thought of this and not her doctor. He should have thought of it years ago. What is more he has one of the phoniest smiles I have ever seen on any face. What's more he's a fashionable doctor. You call him and he's either gone to play golf or in the evening to some big ball, but she likes him."

Linda had, in fact, improved so remarkably that instead of spending the entire night in an oxygen tent, she would go into it only between 2:00 and 7:00 A.M. During the day, she was free to wander about in the dry air and could take a drive or a stroll in the park. Her condition was so much better that Cole even allowed himself to joke about it to Stark. "The only thing that worries me is that she is

* In 1936, the Porters had leased a huge apartment at the Waldorf-Towers at only $35 a day, because the management hoped their presence would help popularize the building. After Linda's health deteriorated, Cole's late-night piano playing disturbed her and they traded the large apartment for two smaller ones located directly across the hall from one another, making it possible for him to work at any hour.

scheming very soon to go to Mainbocher's to order a lot of new clothes," he wrote. "This will definitely kill her, but it is a beautiful way to die, I suppose. Old Mrs. Ogden Mills died fitting a dress at Callot's in Paris. And Mrs. Hamilton Rice, who was formerly married to George Widener, died fitting a hat at Reboux's. Perhaps Linda has become socially ambitious."

Cole's new show had now definitely been postponed. He had turned down the libretto submitted by Dwight Taylor, which he thought "underwritten, lacking love interest, and, above all, two great comedy scenes." It had been decided to hire Betty Comden and Adolph Green, who had written *On the Town*, *Billion Dollar Baby* and *The Barkleys of Broadway* (a film), to do a new script. "They are bright as buttons and write very fast and I believe they will deliver the goods in time so we can start rehearsals during the second week in January," Cole wrote Stark.

Dwight Taylor, meanwhile, was understandably upset by the turn of events and was demanding major upper-case billing (BOOK BY DWIGHT TAYLOR) while attempting to restrict the new writers to lower-case credit (Libretto by Comden and Green). Cole intended to point out, he said, that his songs could be used for other projects while Taylor stood to lose $1,500 a week if the show were not done.

The premise of Taylor's book lay in what happens when a god turns himself into a mortal. When Comden and Green turned in their version of the libretto, the premise of a god's night out had been turned into a baseball story. Cole and the producers agreed that the libretto, while funny, had little to do with the show they hoped to produce. Comden and Green were paid $10,000 and the search for a librettist continued.

What had been found by this time, after Judy Holliday rejected the role, was a leading lady: Charlotte Greenwood. Miss Greenwood had delighted New Yorkers in 1916 with her high-kicks and clowning in *So Long Letty* and, later, in other Letty shows. Miss Greenwood, who was rich, had last appeared on Broadway in 1926 in *Le Maire's Affairs*. In the meantime, she had turned down many scripts, but, as she told columnist Hedda Hopper, "When Cole Porter asks you that's a request from the top and I hope the combination of C and C (Charlotte and Cole) will be as bubbly as my favorite drink—ginger ale."

Once her role was filled, the rest of the casting was quickly completed with the signing of David Burns, William Redfield, Priscilla Gillette, Janet Collins, William Eythe, Barbara Ashley and George Jongeyans.

As it turned out, Selma Tamber found no difficulty in raising the financing for the show, which had now been renamed *Out of This World*. People whom she had had to beg to invest in *Kate* pressed money on her. Howard Cullman, for example, trebled the size of his investment; and Miss Tamber, who had had no share in the first show, bought into this one. Instead of the required $200,000 plus ten percent overcall, she could have collected $2,000,000. Broadway thought it recognized a sure-fire hit when it saw one.

Choreographer Agnes de Mille had been hired to direct the production. Hanya Holm, who had devised *Kate*'s dances, was to do these; Ayers was to design the sets and costumes again. Pembroke Davenport was once more to serve as conductor, and Robert Russell Bennett was to do the orchestrations.

Everything seemed to be meshing—except for one thing. They still had no acceptable script. While enthusiasm continued to be high everywhere else, Cole now began to have private doubts. He had admired Saint Subber and Lem Ayers for their willingness to give him the freedom to experiment when he was creating *Kate*. Now, when trouble developed, he missed a strong, sure hand. By this time, too, he had concluded that the comedy premise—a god gets tired of turning himself into bulls and swans and instead pretends to be an ordinary man in order to seduce the bride of an American tourist—seemed heavy and unworkable.

The hiring of Reginald Lawrence to doctor Dwight Taylor's book came too late. Cole had lost enthusiasm for the project and at that point refused to hold even one conference with his new collaborator. Thus, Lawrence has the distinction of having provided the book for a Cole Porter show without meeting the composer. Cole's score was simply superimposed on his book.

As rehearsals progressed, Cole almost totally detached himself from the proceedings. He sensed that a gigantic disaster was in the making, and after the great success of *Kate*, he regarded it as a personal humiliation.

The musical opened in Philadelphia early in November and played to sellout business. Yet the only elements of the production that showed off to advantage were the sets and costumes. Although Cole had written a score that has come to be considered one of his best by theater buffs, it was dismissed as very bad Porter since even those members of the cast who possessed good singing voices had already lost them from strain and worry by the time the show opened. Worse still, when it became apparent that the show was flopping, the relatively inexperienced producers took out one song after another until Cole forbade them to touch any others.

"I have never seen anyone suffer the way Cole did with that show. He was destroyed," Selma Tamber said fifteen years later. "I told him I was coming to New York to try to get George Abbott. I came in and called on Mr. Abbott. He consented to come down and see the show and we were all relieved."

When Abbott appeared, he agreed to take over on one condition—that Cole drop a number that Abbott felt was absolutely killing the show. Cole was so eager for help that he reluctantly agreed. The number was called "From This Moment On." It turned out to be the only song from the score that eventually became an established hit—after it was used in the film version of *Kiss Me, Kate*.

Abbott brought in F. Hugh Herbert, who was to rewrite the book, which might have been an advantage, save for one thing. Once Miss Greenwood learned her lines, she could not unlearn them. Nor would she talk to the two new men.

During the three weeks in Philadelphia, the show sold out and *Variety* tabbed it as superior to run-of-the-mill musicals, although inferior to *Kate.*

Its reception in Boston indicated that it was in serious trouble. Although Cole was reluctant to do any more work, he agreed to write a new song for Miss Greenwood. It was called "I Sleep Easier Now" and she found it "right in the middle of her vocal range."

In Philadelphia the show had been criticized because the chorus girls were overdressed and the boys scantily clad. In Boston, the second-string censor (a woman) objected to the scanty costumes worn by Venus (Gisella Svetlik) and Night (Janet Collins). Words in Cole's lyrics, the lady censor said, were not even suitable for "better-class gin mills." Nor, she said, did the ballet at the end of Act One leave anything to the imagination. Her pronunciamento naturally resulted in a box-office bonanza, and the producers alerted New York newspapers that the cuts would be restored for Broadway.

On December 21, 1950, the musical opened at the New Century, and Cole's behavior neatly summed up his style. He well knew what lay in store for him that evening, that the show was a horrendous flop, and there was no place he wanted less to be than in that theater. But as a gentleman and a professional, he felt compelled to attend.

To accompany him (because of the rumored trouble with the producers) he chose Mrs. Lemuel Ayers. They arrived at the head of the aisle just as the house lights were about to dim. Sensing his tension, Mrs. Ayers looked at Cole and smiled. He returned her smile, then announced determinedly, "I shall go slowly—and in my own way."

Next morning *The New York Times* and the *Herald Tribune* were negative. The *World-Telegram*, when it appeared, was mixed. The other five notices were enthusiastic, yet possibly the most devastating critique of the show lay in the fact that the high point of the evening was provided by Miss Greenwood's swinging her legs in the familiar cartwheel motion she had originated in 1916.

Soon after the opening, Ayers and Saint Subber left New York to supervise the London production of *Kiss Me, Kate.* Selma Tamber was put in charge of *Out of This*

World, which a number of theater parties, booked before the opening, kept running. Through these she managed to stave off collapse for 157 performances.

According to columnist Leonard Lyons, when Cole lamented the failure to George S. Kaufman, Kaufman alluded to the half-clothed men and the fully dressed women as the main reason for the show's lack of popularity. "After all," he told Cole, "nobody's ever heard of a butter and egg woman."

CHAPTER XVI

During the delay preceding the opening of *Out of This World*, friends noticed that Cole was behaving somewhat erratically. He had begun to experience severe depressions that would arise suddenly for no apparent reason. He lost interest in food and began suffering insomnia.

His fits of temper during the rehearsal period would hardly have been regarded as extraordinary when weighed against the outburst of a Jed Harris or a Tallulah Bankhead. Only because they were so alien to Cole's customary behavior did they cause some friends to fear that he might be losing control of himself.

What struck everyone as definitely odd was his great concern over his financial status. No reassurances were enough to still his fears. In May, he insisted upon calling a meeting with his advisers to determine exactly what he could and could not afford. Despite assurances to the contrary, he was fearful that he would be forced to give up the lease on his California house. In fantasy, Cole saw himself as relatively poor.

When the meeting took place, his advisers impressed upon him that it was not only possible but also desirable for him to spend at least six months of each year in California. There, he was entitled to write off sixty percent of his living expenses, although he could deduct only fifty percent at the Waldorf-Towers. ("I'm almost condemned to California," he chortled.) As for Williamstown, none of his expenses were deductible. ("It's my only extravagance," he sighed.)

On June 1, the Porters drove to Williamstown, expecting to spend a month, but left after two days of heat, rain and humidity. Then, accompanied by Howard Sturges, they fled to Mexico in mid-June. Cole found the weather in Guadalajara terrible and the life quiet, but he wrote friends that he and Linda were having enough fun to make up for the stifling heat.

On July 2, Linda returned east. Cole and Sturges went on to Los Angeles where Sturges was to stay for a couple of weeks before departing for Paris. They had hardly arrived in Brentwood when Cole fell into another of his severe depressions. What was alarming was that, although generally a perfect gentleman, he took to quarreling with close friends over trivial matters.

At a luncheon that summer, for instance, an incident occurred which friends found difficult to explain. Conversation had been good and the food was excellent. Cole had appeared untroubled and was the perfect host, keeping an alert eye for empty wine glasses, neglected guests and all the minor details. Like everyone else he seemed to be enjoying himself immensely until dessert was served. It turned out to be ice cream. Cole frowned and consulted the small handwritten menu that was always on the table.

"Wait," he cried. "We have fresh strawberries." He pressed the buzzer. When Max appeared, Cole asked him to bring in the strawberries.

Max hesitated.

Sturges spoke up to say that he guessed that he had eaten them for breakfast.

"All of them?" his host demanded angrily.

Sturges laughed and said he was afraid so. And all who were present were mystified by the uncustomary rage the response evoked.

There were other incidents, too, usually over something equally unimportant. And at other times, Cole would gloom around the house, calling Bob Raison, Sam Stark or some other friend and demanding to be cheered up.

Stark, who viewed Cole's behavior with some apprehension, attempted to banish his friend's unreasoning fears with logic. "What have you to be depressed about?" he'd ask. "You have great talent." This always elicited a groan. "You can go any place, have dinner any place, travel any place. Everyone welcomes you. You've met everyone you ever wanted to meet, except Churchill and Eisenhower. You can be a guest anywhere. What more can you want?"

"Cheer me up," Cole would reply. "I feel so low. So miserable. I'm depressed." He fretted that he would never again receive film offers and feared that if he did, he would be unable to make his old brain function any more.

In late summer, he returned east, going directly to Williamstown. Linda was startled by her husband's precipitous decline. "Cole is here and he looks so thin, poor darling. And he worries about everything—having no money, having no show, and so forth, all of which is perfectly absurd. And he can't be told. Sleeps badly and eats too little. It is a new Cole. I have never seen him in such a state. However . . . I can straighten him out and get rid of his nightmarish ideas for he really has nothing to worry about. . . ."

Once again, the question arises: why didn't Linda insist that her husband consult a psychiatrist?

The answer lies in the fact that both Porters had an unreasonable fear of and distaste for psychiatrists. In part, they felt a reluctance to reveal themselves to a stranger. It encroached on their natural reserve and offended their sense of propriety. Even in the professional situation, Cole regarded focusing on one's troubles as a lapse of good breeding.

Instead of consulting experts, Linda wrote friends asking them to Williamstown to cheer him up. On September 26, she saw her husband and Paul off to Paris via Pan Am.

Cole's emotional condition had been far more serious than she had at first estimated and she finally had persuaded him to have a checkup, which had revealed no real physical ailment other than an over-active thyroid. This, in part, accounted for his sleeplessness and loss of weight. "Pray God the change will put him on his feet. It is so distressing to see him in this state," she wrote Stark.

The projected six-weeks' holiday was terminated in less than a week, by which time Cole had fallen into a deep lethargy and intermittent delusions. Night after night, he lay sleepless in a darkened room, eyes wide open, staring at the ceiling. He had often said that he would never consider taking his own life unless he were involved in a scandal which disgraced his wife and his mother. Nevertheless, his depressions were sufficiently severe for Paul to maintain a careful watch over him.

From Paris, the two men flew directly to Boston where on October 3 and 4 Cole had another thorough medical examination. Then, on October 5, he returned to New York and secretly took Room 1039 at Doctors' Hospital. As usual, every precaution was taken to keep news of his illness out of the New York and Hollywood newspapers. If the story happened to leak out, all those immediately concerned agreed to say that he was there for thyroid treatments and a checkup.

Meanwhile, the severity of Cole's delusions had increased and doctors advised that he undergo shock treatment. After two treatments and two shots of curare for his legs, his improvement was so marked that Paul wrote Sam Stark:

> There is still much progress to be made, but there is great hope that in a week or two Mr. C.P. can be his old vivacious, charming, witty self again. There is nothing to worry about any more. I wire Mr. Sturges every night and talk to Mrs. C.P. every day, who is still in Williamstown until next Monday. She may be coming back to the Waldorf then. I assure you that everything is being done for Mr. C.P.'s health as well as comfort.

> I spend the days at Doctors' Hospital and sleep at the Waldorf in 41-C. Mr. C.P. is not allowed any visitors as yet. We are waiting till he asks for them when he is better.

Upon Linda's arrival in New York, she insisted that it was necessary for her husband to go to California regardless of his renewed fear of tax consequences. Meanwhile, at Doctors' Hospital, Dr. Moorhead, who himself was a patient, directed Cole's cure from a sickbed.

Beginning October 11, Cole had improved sufficiently so that for three successive nights he slept without drugs of any kind. By October 20, he had undergone five shock treatments and Dr. Moorhead, after discussing the patient's problems with the Porters, assured Linda that her husband would recover within a week or ten days.

Although the treatments diminished the intensity of Cole's depression, his anxieties still persisted. He felt that he had too many expenses. He fretted that he was being made poor by taxes. He lamented that he could not live as elaborately as he would have liked. He couldn't understand how he would ever be able to pay his hospital bills. In short, he felt that he was ruined financially.

In writing Sam Stark, Paul gave a graphic description of his employer's mental state:

> His thinking is along these lines. I am so depressed about giving up 416 and California altogether. The rent may be increased and I cannot afford living in California. What will I do with my beautiful things? Give them away? Store them? Ship them to New York? All my silver? Beautiful plates? What will I do with them? I love California so and because of my legs I cannot use a hotel swimming pool. I must tell the great team—Max and Helene—they'll have to go. All my friends are there, I'll miss them terribly. I always feel tops in the sunshine. . . . Right now a hurt on Mr. C.P.'s mind is the mistake he made about refusing the Crosby picture. But I always emphasize that the moguls

cannot indefinitely ignore his genius, being primarily good businessmen. For Mr. C.P. would be glad to accept any offer—or even one a year—even if this kind of book is not quite up to his talent. On that subject Mrs. C.P. rather favors the Broadway musicals and wants my boss to concentrate on them alone by living permanently in New York, by meeting the necessary important theater people and doing at least one show a year, which we have to admit she is quite right about. . . .

On November 1, Cole was out of the hospital but still recuperating. During his stay at Doctors' Hospital, his weight had fallen to 124 pounds. Upon his release, he was restless to be off for California, and even this anticipation indicated a recovery from the depths of his illness when time had been suspended.

Then Ed Sullivan proposed to devote two hours of his television programs to a Cole Porter Salute in late February. Cole called it "dull news," but readily agreed to postpone his California trip and even volunteered to appear on one program. The salute proved to be a turning point, giving Cole something to focus on besides his real physical woes and his imaginary problems.

By the time he arrived in Brentwood on February 28, he was basking not only in his much-loved sun but also in the warming glow of an offer from two new producers, who, from Cole's point of view at that particular time, had much to recommend them.

They were Cy Feuer and Ernest Martin, hard-headed businessmen who aggressively pursued success at any cost. Feuer, in addition, was an accomplished musician and theater man. Together, they had been responsible for *Where's Charley?* and *Guys and Dolls.* They now proposed to reunite Cole and the Spewacks for a new show.

Although Cole had become annoyed by what he considered Bella's excessive demands and she had been hurt by what she interpreted as lack of gratitude, he was eager to work with the Spewacks again and suggested that they come to California to collaborate. Unhappily, Sam was having a comedy tested in the English provinces and one delay followed another until it appeared that they would not arrive until the first of May.

Cole restlessly began to work on his own, but with little success. "I believe that it will take a little more application before I can get back in the groove, but once I do I shall be content again," he confided to his mother.

What he was not content with was his staff. Within ten days after arrival, he fired three cooks. The fourth was being retained only because Paul had been hospitalized. Consequently, Helene, an excellent cook, could not take over the kitchen because she was needed to assist Max, who had assumed Paul's valeting duties.

When Orry-Kelly, the costume designer, heard of Cole's problems, he suggested the late Fanny Brice's cook. Kelly hunted for her for two days and finally discovered that she had been working as a dietitian for the government since Miss Brice's death. The cook came to see Cole and he thought he had found a treasure. A week later, he reported to his mother: "Again I begin my letter with news about a cook. The cook from Fanny Brice, who was going to stay forever, stayed for five days."

His existence was also plagued by violent headaches. He had, he said, hired a trainer to direct his workouts and was swimming daily, hoping to improve his physical condition.

The following week, Cole had more show news. Feuer and Martin had warned that if the show were to be ready for the 1953 season work must begin with or without the Spewacks. They suggested instead Abe Burrows, who had successfully pulled together the book of *Guys and Dolls* after several other writers had failed to do so.

Cole, always eager to work with anyone who was highly successful, agreed. Once again he visualized Carol Channing in the leading role, and once again he was to be disappointed. Her advisers demanded that she have approval of all material written by Burrows or Cole. "This stipulation is not even made by top stars, such as Ethel Merman and Gertrude Lawrence, and these demands made it unreasonable to continue negotiations," he wrote Katie.

"Therefore, at the present moment we are hunting another star to write the show for. All of this means more and more delay."

The summer was marked by several small crises. Linda was undergoing a series of smothering spells, but her doctor thought that Cole's return east would alarm her and worsen her condition. Therefore, Cole again kept in touch by phone—and worried.

And then, Paul announced that his wife refused to return east and did not want him to go without her. "Losing Paul, for me, is like your losing Mamie [Katie's Indian maid]," Cole wrote Katie, "so you can imagine my worry. Until this new blow I always thought he would be with me for the rest of my life, and from his point of view I worry also that he makes this decision, as he never again can find a job where not only does he receive excellent wages, but has his room and board paid, plus all of his doctor bills that are not covered by insurance." When he told Linda about Paul, she advised him to say nothing until he was ready to leave California, for by that time Paul might have changed his mind.

Cole's headaches had increased in intensity so that it became difficult to work. In mid-May, he put himself in the hands of an expert and hoped for the best. He eventually learned that his headaches came from frontal sinusitis, a condition caused by chronic catarrh, which was not considered curable. "So I have resigned myself to it and behave as well as possible," he observed. Then, just when he thought he would never be better, the pain disappeared. After it had gone, he wrote Katie saying he would never know what drug had cured him since he had been taking so many. "At one time my sinus specialist felt so hopeless about curing me that he made me take an elaborate test with a brain specialist, to find out whether I had a tumor on the brain or not. This was a nerve-wracking experience as I had to wait for days before knowing the result. Luckily, the result turned out to be fine and my brain is in excellent condition, thank you."

Apparently, Katie had been hearing too much about his brain, for a week later, Cole responded to her latest letter:

Dearest Ma,

You write that at times you do not feel so well, but you never mention it to anyone as no one is interested in one's ailments. I am afraid I forgot that excellent axiom during the month of May when my head was driving me crazy. It was all such a mystery that I know now that I talked to my friends much too much about it. . . .

The work goes on slowly, as I still am waiting for my collaborator, Abe Burrows, to send me material. So far, I have only a very vague story outline and this limits me a great deal.

All my love to you, dearest Ma. Your letters are a joy, so please write and write.

Your devoted,
Cole

Early in July, Burrows turned in enough script so that Cole could begin to work seriously. The subject of the show touched deeply upon Cole's emotional investment in the past. It was set in Paris during the days of Toulouse-Lautrec and had suggested itself to Cy Feuer when he was looking at some Lautrec lithographs that he had brought home after being mustered out of the Army in Germany in 1945.

Cole, who had decorated his room with similar posters during his freshman year at Yale, had always retained an attachment for French culture. Now he was so caught up in the new project that he found it difficult at night to stop work and go to bed.

The collaborators met often during the evening to sit around and throw ideas at one another until they hit upon a theme that was potentially the basis for a song that fitted into the plot. Then they would part. Cole would go to work and later he would call Burrows and ask him to listen to the beat that he had worked out. "I understand from people who saw him when he called—I couldn't, I was on the other end of the phone—that he'd put down the phone and beat it out. Pah-pah-pa-pa-pah—and I'd begin to hum. 'Don't hum, don't hum!' he'd say. What he did was he got himself set with the beat—I never knew any other composer who does this—and that's how he got that unity. He'd do the beat, then match the lyrics to the beat, then write the tune to the lyrics."

Burrows found Cole amenable to endless working up of additional songs, but obdurate about changing any. "He wouldn't change a waltz into a beguine. He didn't like that. He'd look at you calmly and say, 'I'll give you another.' But he wouldn't change that one. He wouldn't bend a song. Songs get bent and changed and ruined."

Between the 8th and the 15th of July, Cole did not go out socially but worked continuously until he had caught up with Burrows. That same week, a great worry was removed from his mind. As the time approached for him to go east, he asked Paul whether he intended to remain in California. To Cole's joy, Paul said that he had talked the matter over with his wife and that she agreed that he should continue in his job for there was no place else where he could earn a comparable salary.

An unexpected complication arose when Katie Porter was stricken by a cerebral hemorrhage. By the time Cole arrived in Peru, his mother lay in her bedroom unconscious, while her Indian maids sat outside the door as if at the entrance of a church.

There was no hope, nothing to do except await the inevitable. Although he regretted not having been on hand when she was stricken, he bore up surprisingly well, turning to his best friend, work, to distract him.

In the later years of his own life, he often recalled how he had sat on the back porch at Westleigh Farms and out of necessity had beat out the raucous, orgiastic *Can-Can* finale as he waited his beloved mother's death. "It was," he said, "one of the strangest experiences of my life, but the number had to be done." It seemed to some as if in the telling he reassured himself that his actions would have met with the approval of the woman who more than anyone else was responsible for setting him on his life's course.

At 9:30 A.M. on August 3, the tenacious Katie died peacefully in her sleep. Her son, having accorded her respect, affection and all possible attention during her lifetime, was able to accept her death at ninety with outward equanimity. When Louise Bearss reported that Cole's mother had said, "Cole never gave me a moment's worry," he observed that mothers forget and forgive everything.

Linda, whose illness precluded her attending the funeral, more than ever seemed to be hanging on to life. The Porters customarily lunched together, but she was now unable to venture forth at night. Even so, she gallantly rose for a couple of hours each day, carefully made herself up and donned a tea gown to lie on the sofa in her drawing room.

Still struggling to retain her interest in life, that fall she ordered two new evening dresses from Mainbocher. Although far too ill to wear them, she had them hung in her closet so that she might look at them and maintain the fiction that one day soon she would be able to sally forth into the bright, chic world she adored.

"One got the feeling that beneath her optimism, she was simply clinging to life," Main said. "That is why I never could understand Lady Astor. Linda and Nancy were girlhood friends and once during Linda's illness, Lady Astor came to visit darling Linda. During the visit, she spied the dresses and said, 'Why don't you give me your Mainbochers? You'll never wear them.' With all her millions! The callousness of it."

That winter of 1952, in response to a friend's inquiry, Cole described his activities:

> You ask what I am doing. I continue to give small dinners in my little apartment here at the Waldorf. Last night [December 15], I had Charlie Chaplin and Harry Crocker (Oona was ill). The Bob Sherwoods and the Bill

Paleys. We had a wonderful time. Chaplin took the stage and went on and on. You would have liked it. Tonight Nicky de Gunzberg and I go to see the Balinese dancers, who opened last night. The papers are full of raves.

By the way, Noel Coward's play for the Lunts is one of the biggest hits of his life. We all believe it will continue for quite a few years. It opened last night in London to unanimous panning by the London critics. The play, however, is so strong and the Lunts such a delight that most people believe it can survive and do beautifully. I sent you Hedda Hopper's book. It is entertaining.

These two paragraphs in a way create a profile of Cole's enthusiasms in the later years of his life. Miss Hopper was a columnist on one of his favorite newspapers, the tabloid *Daily News.*

His enthusiasm for Noel Coward's *Quadrille* reflected his commitment to the comedy of manners, played by graceful players in eye-catching costumes against stunning settings. When a show of this type was not available, he also enjoyed vehicles such as *Edward, My Son* with Leueen McGrath and Robert Morley; *Twentieth Century* with Gloria Swanson and José Ferrer; *Affairs of State* with Celeste Holm; *Call Me Madam*; *Guys and Dolls* or any of Gian Carlo Menotti's works.

He did not enjoy *The Rose Tattoo,* although earlier he had admired *A Streetcar Named Desire.* But the slatternly characters in *The Rose Tattoo* offended his natural fastidiousness.

He continued to love the opera, and when a college professor wrote to learn what his favorite melodies were, Cole listed in order of preference: "Aria" from *Suite D* by Bach; "Isolde's Love Death" from *Tristan und Isolde* by Wagner; "Salce" from the last act of *Otello* by Verdi.

With Duke di Verdura, Cole spent hours discussing opera and another common interest, history. At Yale, he had made a poor showing in the subject, but as he grew older its fascination for him increased. During the 1950's, Cole had his secretary, Mrs. Smith, type out the line of succession of the various royal houses, which he Scotch-taped to the walls of his bathrooms in the Waldorf and in Williamstown.

Among actors, Alfred Lunt and Lynn Fontanne were favorites. (Miss Fontanne once confided to him that she maintained her youthful appearance by holding her head high so that the neck muscles had no chance to sag.) Ethel Barrymore, Ina Claire, Noel Coward and Carol Channing also appealed to him. On the other hand, no matter how superb the artistry of a Shirley Booth, a Maureen Stapleton or a Laurette Taylor, he was neither interested nor amused. Just as he preferred in life to associate with rich, celebrated, well-turned out people, so he preferred them in the theater.

Weekends during the fall and winter of 1952-53 Cole spent in Williamstown with Linda. The other four days he lived at the Waldorf, where he worked on *Can-Can*. By January, his time was taken up with auditions and finishing the score. During a telephone conversation with Cy Feuer, he once remarked that he was stuck for a rhyme to "the aurora borealis is. . . ." Later in the day, Feuer came up with "not as heated as a palace is. . . ." But Cole protested when Feuer called him, "That's the first one I threw away."

Cole's hopes for *Can-Can* were high, although a number of people had reservations about his score. For instance, Mitch Miller, who had not yet taken up a career as a community singmaster on television, was persuaded to attend an audition of the *Can-Can* score. Having unearthed such classics as Johnny Ray's "Cry," Frankie Laine's "Mule Train" and Rosemary Clooney's "Come On-a My House," Miller naturally was regarded as something of a modern Merlin. He listened to the songs, then rose and stalked across the room to the elevator without so much as a bob of the beard. Dr. Sirmay rushed after him to learn his opinion. In response to the doctor's question, Miller handed down his verdict. The music was bad and the songs had no future.

Cole, who had immersed himself in the music that had been popular in the French music halls circa 1890, was somewhat shaken by this response. He had attempted to produce modern equivalents of the various types of songs popular in Montmartre in that period. Miller's response made him wonder how well he had succeeded. What had complicated the task was that he had also made an effort to integrate the numbers with the book. In his enthusiasm he had written ten more songs than necessary. Nor was it like the old days when songs didn't have to make sense. Speaking to Seymour Peck of *The New York Times*, he recalled, "They [the songs] didn't come out of the book so much as now. Really, until Rodgers and Hammerstein, if you needed to change a scene, a girl could come out in front of the curtain and sing or dance or anything. But with *Can-Can*, I have worked since last June."

On February 16, 1953, the dancers went into rehearsal under the direction of choreographer Michael Kidd. A week later, the remainder of the company assembled. Abe Burrows was to direct the show, for which he had written the book. The story concerns a prudish French judge (Peter Cookson) who sets out to close down the raffish café run by La Mome Pistache (Lilo) because of the scandalous dances performed there by Claudine (Gwen Verdon) and other high-spirited young women.

Lilo had been imported from Paris to play the lead. Cookson, who had made a success as the fortune-hunting suitor in *The Heiress*, was making his musical-comedy debut as the judge. Yet the great find turned out to be Gwen Verdon, a tousled red-head who had appeared several times in films and on Broadway without making any lasting impression.

When the show opened at the Shubert Theater in Philadelphia on March 23, 1953, a strange phenomenon developed. There were no stars with a real box-office draw in the cast, the Porter score far from overwhelmed the critics, and audiences simply refused to accept a book that asked them to believe that some Frenchmen once possessed puritanical streaks. Yet even in the wake of the critical response, *Can-Can* drew a whopping—for those days—$50,250 in the second week of its tryout and by then had built up the largest advance in the history of that theater.

Feuer and Martin wasted no time in coming to a decision. They extended the engagement in order to give Abe Burrows, who had spent a year writing the libretto, three weeks to come up with a new one.

It was at this point that an incident occurred which caused Cole and me to become good friends. I had first encountered him in 1948 when I interviewed him about *Kiss Me, Kate* in his suite at the Barclay Hotel in Philadelphia. There he had been, amid his oil paintings, his recordings, his favorite crystal and other pet objects. He had seemed remote and somewhat bored. I had not liked him much and felt that he certainly lived up to Louis Sobol's description as the hardest man to interview since Calvin Coolidge. Although I had encountered him a couple of times in the next few years, he didn't remember me and my impression of him might have remained undisturbed had William Lowe, then the editor of *Look* magazine, not assigned me to interview him. We met at the Colony Restaurant in New York. On that night, two happenings made us friends.

About the first: When I opened the menu and discovered that it was in French, I wished that I were anywhere else in the world. Reluctant to admit to this renowned sophisticate that I couldn't read it, I listened carefully to Cole's conversation with the headwaiter. Catching the phrases "prosciutto and melon" and "an excellent seafood pancake," I promptly ordered them both.

"Two appetizers?" the waiter asked, somewhat incredulously.

"What a great idea!" Cole cried. "That's what we'll both have. With the seafood as the entrée."

The perceptiveness that impelled him to respond so swiftly and kindly to my predicament made it apparent that the legendary playboy was also a sympathetic human being. When I knew him a little better, I thanked him. "What a fool you were," he said. "Don't you realize that people *enjoy* teaching others? Besides, if you're not yourself, you're nothing."

Self-evident statements can sometimes strike home with great impact. His admonition turned out to be, for me, a valuable piece of advice.

The second incident meant little to me but a great deal to him. Not long before, he had been somewhat shaken by critical response to *Can-Can*'s score. That night at the Colony, I mentioned that Frith Banbury, an English director, had been greatly impressed, not because it was first-rate Cole Porter music but because it was Cole's impression of French music-hall songs of the 1890's in modern terms. Ever after, no matter how often I credited the remark to Frith, Cole insisted that I was the first person really to understand what he was trying to do in that particular score.

On the day of *Can-Can*'s opening, Burrows, Feuer and Martin sent Cole the traditional good-luck telegrams. "The Last of the Toffs," as Burrows dubbed Cole, sent Feuer a Grandma Moses, Martin a Utrillo, and Burrows received a Marcel Vertes painting of the first-act finale of *Can-Can*, which had been especially commissioned.

In assessing Cole's personality, Burrows once said that he had encountered many persons who through talent, beauty, luck, shrewdness or ruthlessness had managed to accumulate fortunes greater than Cole's, but not one of them knew as well how to enjoy the things money can buy.

On May 7, 1953, the show opened at the Shubert Theater in New York, receiving mixed notices with most of the huzzahs going to the dances created by Michael Kidd and to the piquant personality of Miss Verdon. Cole came in for much off-hand criticism for not having come up with another "Begin the Beguine," "Night and Day" or "Always True to You in My Fashion." In *The New York Times* Brooks Atkinson flatly declared that there was nothing original in the score and that the lyrics were unrelieved by humor. "And let's face it: both music and lyrics for 'Never, Never Be an Artist' would just about make the grade in a college show. . . . His [Porter's] score is not half as bright as the score Kay Swift wrote last season for Cornelia Otis Skinner's *Paris 90.*"

Cole took to his bed for several days after reading the reviews and remained depressed for weeks after. When reminded that in 1940 Atkinson had dismissed *Pal Joey* by announcing that it was impossible to take sweet water from a foul well, only to hail it in its 1954 revival, Cole refused to take comfort from critic-baiting.

Whatever Atkinson or Mitch Miller may have felt, the public decided that it wanted to see *Can-Can.* When the weekly reviews appeared, despite an acid verdict handed down by *Time,* Cole began to emerge in a noticeably improved position. The box-office line at the Shubert regularly spilled out into Shubert Alley. By May 9, when Cole left for California, the show was solidly sold out for six weeks ahead.

When Capitol's "original cast album" appeared, Dr. Sigmund Spaeth, the musicologist and tune detective, noted that "phonograph records have an embarrassing way of upsetting the dicta of drama and music critics. They often reveal qualities that easily escape first-night observers, and they have a permanence which permits a steady growth of appreciation through repeated hearings. Such hearings, after all, are the only fair test of music and perhaps also of theater in general." Dr. Spaeth found much to praise in the score of *Can-Can.*

The public agreed. By November 1953, columnist Ed Sullivan recalled the general disappointment expressed when the show opened in May. Now, he said, several numbers were taking over the jukeboxes. In December things looked even rosier. *Variety*'s listing of 1953's top popular hits—in a year when show tunes were not selling—included: "I Love Paris," "Allez-Vous-En, Go Away," "I Am in Love," "C'est Magnifique" and "It's All Right with Me"—five songs from the *Can-Can* score.

Cole's enthusiasm for the last song was tempered. During the Philadelphia tryout, he had wired Louis Shurr in Hollywood:

> I am sending today several copies of a song from show titled quote It's All Right with Me unquote which I wrote especially for you. Please scatter it among your dance orchestras but don't let them play it too fast as you should cry when you sing it.
>
> Love,
> Cole

Shurr scattered the copies, but very little happened until Lena Horne, a vocalist Cole admired, did an up-tempo version of the number. Suddenly it became a hit. The result: Cole hated it. In fact, several years later, when Geneviève, the French singer, recorded the *Can-Can* score and sent an album to him he praised her warmth, but added: "There are several songs in the score I'm not crazy about."

For him, the show remained something of a disappointment. Dr. Sirmay once said that the score was written with Cole's "heart's blood" in anticipation of an event which failed to come to pass. "He was a little sad and a little resentful that he received no recognition from the French government," Dr. Sirmay said. "I told him many times I would like to start a movement. No, he said, such a thing he didn't want. But this I know, he was expecting it. Not to get it hurt him deeply. After all, he wrote one of the greatest propaganda songs for Paris and France and it was a puzzle to me that people of secondary and third importance got honors from the government and he was not honored.

"He would not admit things hurt him, but they hurt him. Unfavorable words from the critics. The line, 'It is not from his top drawer.' After an opening, he would sigh and say, 'Once again it's not from my top drawer.' Again, they did not accept his work."

CHAPTER XVII

In 1953 Linda's illness, now definitely diagnosed as emphysema (a gradual loss of elasticity in the walls of the lungs), caused her to spend the greater part of her time in bed since most of her strength was expended fighting for breath. At times, too, her mind wandered, and then again she was bright and sharp, and the ghost of her celebrated vitality returned. Always then, she insisted that Cole pursue his career whether it entailed keeping an eye on the filming of *Kiss Me, Kate* or finding a new Broadway show.

He was in Hollywood on *Kate* business on May 16 when word came that Linda had taken a turn for the worse. This time the doctors offered no reassurances, nor did they advise Cole to remain in California in order not to alarm her. Instead he was urged to fly home at once. The strain which emphysema placed upon her heart and lungs had depleted her reserve strength, and the case was considered terminal.

Upon arrival, Cole found that her coughing attacks had greatly increased and that she was in continual pain. On one occasion, she coughed so violently that she fractured a rib. The face that had bespoken a special brand of beauty was now ravaged. Yet, briefly, she gathered her remaining strength and rallied. The self-control that she had exercised with magnificence over the years served as a support against the vagueness that age—she was sixty-eight—illness and extended medication had brought.

Slipping in and out of consciousness, she accepted her burden stoically. Just as she had embraced the various demands of life—making the transitions from the well-born but poor Kentucky beauty to that of the rich, vital young wife of an early 1900's playboy to that of the unbesmirched divorcee who was courted by top nobles of Spain and Italy to that of the devoted wife of the most sophisticated composer of light music in the United States—she now evidenced her willingness to face the demands made by death. She had possessed, as she would have readily admitted, at least the usual number of character faults, yet even these were displayed with grace.

As the days passed, at a time when she was suffering the agonies of slow suffocation, she clutched her husband's hand and, in a gesture that was designed to comfort him, whispered that death held no terror. "I want to die. I'm in so much pain," she said. Then, a longing both universal and futile emerged. "But I hate being forgotten and I'm not important enough. If only I were, so that a flower or something could be named for me."

Cole immediately vowed that there would be such a flower, a living memorial to her gallantry, her graciousness, her generosity and her beauty. That day he called his lawyer, John Wharton, who suggested contacting Marshall Field's gardener. The gardener set in motion a project that resulted in the announcement on August 28, 1954, that Cole had been granted a patent on the "Linda Porter rose." (The strain, originated by Pedro Dot of Barcelona, Spain, resulted from the crossing of two varieties of tea roses—the "Senator Potie" and the "Poinsettia." The blossom is pink, unusually fragrant and when fully opened measures between four and a half and six inches.)

Death came on May 20. After a service in New York on the 22nd, her body was taken to the Porter burial plot in Peru. Even though Linda had often expressed the desire to be buried on the hillside in Williamstown, Cole arranged that she be placed in the second space away from his mother, reserving the vacant one between them for himself.

When Cole left Peru for Hollywood after the funeral on May 23, he adopted the same posture as on his mother's death—of seldom referring to his grief and of immersing himself in work. Privately, he was shaken. There is a clue in the fact that he saved several of the condolences concerning Linda, whereas he had destroyed all the messages that came at the time of his mother's death.

Among those which he retained was a note written by Dr. John Moorhead, whom Linda had brought into Cole's life to see him through his catastrophic leg injuries. Dr. Moorhead wrote:

> Dear Cole:
>
> Telegram just received giving the sad news. Our sympathy goes out to you, and no one more than myself knows how hard the going will be for you. My memory takes me back to the long days of anxiety you gave her when you were hurt—how much she did to sustain you—and may I tell you again she was a pillar of strength to me also at times. Then it was your turn to understandingly and everlastingly bring strength and hope to her—and she knew, and how much she rejoiced in it! A rare person of infinite charm and understanding was Linda; and her belief and faith in you never failed even though fighting to get her breath.
>
> Let me be of any help if you need me.
>
> Very sincerely,
>
> M.

There were notes too from Anita Loos, Jean Howard and an especially touching one from Ellin Berlin:

> Dear Cole:
>
> I found the telegram waiting last night—and called Irving in California. We talked a long time about our lovely Linda. He asked me to write you for him as well

as me to say how sad we are—and how we remember and always will remember her beauty—not only her face and her voice, but everything that was Linda. And I speak of my abiding gratitude for her understanding and imaginative kindness to me when I was a not very happy child.

Devotedly,
Ellin

Because the Porters had so often been separated by illness and by his career, it was sometimes assumed that they were no longer close. While each enjoyed an unusual measure of freedom to lead a separate life, those who knew them best—Dr. Moorhead, Ethel Merman, Sam Stark, Louise Bearss—maintained that they remained devoted friends until Linda's death.

Schuyler Parsons, who knew Linda for fifty-two years and Cole for fifty, wrote me in 1965: "I think that Linda and Cole were far closer than most people think and that something went out of Cole when she died. She understood him perfectly and he was her care after his accident and filled her lack of not having children."

When her estate—$1,660,282—was settled Cole received a lifetime interest in it, with outright possession of the property in Williamstown and all of her personal possessions, including jewelry, silver, art books, art objects, etc., as well as income from various properties which were included in a trust fund, the principal of which reverted to her family upon his death. In a letter, she listed mementos which she wished him to distribute to friends but did not bind him to do so.*

Even though he made a great effort not to complain or depress his friends by indulging his grief, there was a

* Soon after he returned to New York, he carried out her wishes. Unable to bring himself to sell her jewels, he gave a favorite bracelet to Anita Loos; diamond and emerald clips to Jean Howard; and two diamond-emerald-ruby-sapphire bracelets and a clip to Natasha Wilson.

sadness about him. Once on a particularly gray afternoon while I was on a drive with him, he broke a lengthy silence to ask: "How can one help being depressed when all those you're closest to are dying?" After a pause, he said: "I asked Elsa, and she said, 'Rise above it! Rise above it!" He shook his head. "I'm afraid that she cares about no one but Elsa."

That was as close as he would allow himself to come to expressing grief. Fighting loneliness, he began to live his life even more by appointment, filling every moment with some kind of scheduled, organized activity.

In New York, he arranged for guests to be in the lobby of the Waldorf-Towers at 8:15, and he emerged from the elevator precisely on the dot, to be driven to Le Pavillon, arriving at 8:20, dining and leaving the restaurant at 9:40 for a 10:01 showing of a new film. On such evenings, the schedules were worked out with the precision of a military campaign.

This careful planning was carried out whether or not Cole was the host. In California, having heard that Mrs. Alex Steinert was an excellent cook, Cole wangled an invitation. Although the Steinerts had no servants, they were delighted. At 4:00 on the appointed day, Mrs. Steinert, who was in the kitchen preparing dinner, was startled to see Paul Sylvain drive up in a car, followed by Cole in a second car. The two cars paused for a moment, then moved on. That evening, at 7:59, Cole arrived, carrying flowers for Mrs. Steinert. After welcoming him, Steinert inquired whether he had driven by earlier. Cole nodded. He explained that he had wanted to time how long it took to get there and had wanted to set the route in his mind.

Precision was the key to his life. Letters were written at specific hours. Telephone calls were received at others. There was a time for dictation. His trainer, his barber, his doctors, his lawyers—all were expected to arrive either on the dot or a few minutes before a scheduled meeting. Even his pet dog, Peppi, saw him by appointment. When it was time for Peppi to be fed, Paul would bring him into the drawing room. There, Cole would be waiting to give him a dish of choice-grade steak. For several years this routine was followed. Then suddenly Peppi refused to eat. Cole sent him to the vet. There was nothing physically wrong with him. Still, he refused food. Finally, Paul said that he had an idea. The next evening when Cole gave Peppi his dinner, the dog gobbled it down greedily.

"Tell," Cole commanded. "How did you do it?"

Paul had simply replaced the steak with the cheapest-grade horsemeat.

Cole shrugged. "It's the old story," he said. "Too much caviar."

Even with all the organization and all the activity, he felt lost. What he needed now, he decided, was work, which Feuer and Martin provided—a musical version of *Ninotchka* (based on Michael Lengyl's screenplay). It was eventually to be called *Silk Stockings.*

Cole's relationship with Feuer and Martin had by this time shaken down so that he dealt chiefly with Cy Feuer, the creative half of the team. Originally he had entertained both the Feuers and the Martins, but gradually Ernie Martin, a shrewd dollars-and-cents businessman, began to feel that his concern with the commercial end of the theater bored Cole. So, with no ill-feeling on either side, they stopped seeing one another.

Privately, Cole held ambivalent feelings about them as producers. In many creative artists, there is both the extrovert who yearns for public acclaim and the introvert who wishes to please himself—the public be damned. Feuer and Martin served the extrovert brilliantly, but occasionally the introvert felt resentment.

For instance, Cole called me early one morning when I happened to be playing the *Out of This World* album. "What do you have on?" he asked.

I told him.

"I don't know why," he said.

"Because it's good," I answered.

The following weekend I was a guest at Buxton Hill. During one evening, Cole had the *Out of This World* album played. Afterward, he sighed and said, "You're right. The-quality is much higher than in *Can-Can.* Lem and Saint gave me wonderful freedom." He was silent, then added, "But when trouble started, they didn't know what to do."

In the new project, Cole was delighted to be working with librettists George Kaufman and Leueen McGrath because he admired Kaufman as a wit and Miss McGrath (Mrs. Kaufman) as an actress. In addition, from the moment the project was mentioned, a musical scheme for the show had popped into his mind. "The music," he said, "should be done in blacks and whites so that it will be perfectly obvious to everyone which are the Russians and which are the Americans."

When he completed the majority of the songs, he arranged for persons involved in the production to hear them. Ernest Martin was astonished to see that as the world-famed composer approached the piano, he was as timorous as an amateur. Martin had noticed this at the *Can-Can* audition, but had assumed that it was caused by the fact that Cole's previous show had been a disaster. Not so. "As he played the *Silk Stockings* songs," Martin said, "he was perspiring like a neophyte."

Cy Feuer was taken by Cole's great knowledge on a wide range of subjects, his exquisite taste, his enormous curiosity and his creative genius—all existing beside a wide streak of literalness. During conferences in which numbers were discussed, Feuer suggested a song for the three Soviet agents who were returning to Russia after having tasted the pleasures of Paris and having failed to lure the corrupted composer back home. Feuer thought there was a comedy number in their horror at being sent to "dreary Si-beer-ia."

Cole objected. "Oh, Cy, you're quite wrong about Siberia," he said. "When I spent a week at the Grand Duke's castle in Siberia it was truly beautiful."

Nevertheless, he wrote the number, although he complained to Feuer and George Kaufman that it was becoming increasingly difficult for him to think up new jokes, observing, "Oscar Hammerstein is never required to think up any jokes, but I'm always rebuked for not being up to my usual standard."

While working on the show in Williamstown, he would sit in his favorite red chair which stood beside the fireplace of his little cottage, ring for Paul and say, "My things."

Paul would set up a table on which he placed a container of pencils with sharp points. (When the lead wore off, the pencil was turned down as a signal that it needed sharpening.) In addition there were all the dictionaries, thesauruses and reference books, as well as a box of coughdrops, a box of Kleenex, enormous amounts of paper and a Cutty Sark and soda. When these were assembled, he would perch his shell-rimmed Benjamin Franklin specs on his nose and proceed to work.

On such weekends, Cole gave the outward appearance of having solved his grief. Yet, significantly, he avoided the big house and stayed in the small studio. Publicly, his excuse for not using it was that even when no one was in residence it required a staff of no less than six. However, Jean Wilson Gibb, the Scotswoman who had been Linda's personal maid and later became housekeeper for Cole at his cottage, noted that after Linda's death Cole never set foot in the big house. He would come as far as the front door, hand her a list of articles he wanted and wait outside while she gathered them up. On one occasion when it was raining, she urged him to step inside, but he refused.

While working on *Silk Stockings*, he decided to donate the property to Williams College, making the big house immediately available while retaining the use of the cottage. The weekend after this was put into effect, he, Baron de Gunzberg and Howard Sturges were constantly pestered by the stream of traffic going to and fro. Cole was annoyed. At one point the Baron asked him why he didn't have the big house blown up and move the cottage onto its foundation to take advantage of a view that included the formal garden and the purple-hued peaks of the Berkshires.

Cole enthusiastically put through a call to architect Jack Coble in New York. "I went right up the next weekend," Coble said. "And to my amazement the little house was built of solid brick and concrete. It weighed tons, but we found a man who said he could move it. It worked out and Cole was the best client I've ever had."

Once the decision was made to destroy the big house, Cole realized that he would need new accommodations in New York in order to have adequate space for the great treasures upon which Linda had expended so much energy and thought and care. After looking over apartments in various other hotels, he finally decided to remain at the Waldorf-Towers but to lease a larger apartment. The Towers might not be what it had been. "But then," he asked, "what is?"

On October 14, 1945, *Can-Can* opened to tepid reviews at the Coliseum in London and, despite the lack of enthusiasm for the tunes and lyrics and the outright dislike of the book, the production ran for 394 performances.

In New York, rehearsals for *Silk Stockings* were called on October 18. The Kaufman-McGrath script satirized Hollywood, Russia and various American and Russian attitudes. The story concerns the romantic involvement of an icy, defeminized Russian political agent (Hildegarde Neff) sent to Paris to watch over an impetuous musical composer, who is engaged in writing an "Ode to a Tractor" for a Hollywood-type musical. The agent herself becomes entangled romantically with a flashy Hollywood actor's agent (Don Ameche), who is there to look out for the interests of his heart-of-brass, movie-star client (Yvonne Adair).

Cole was pleased with the cast, but somewhat disappointed that Michael Kidd, who had done the *Can-Can* dances, refused to do this one because he felt relations between the two atomic powers were too strained to stand kidding.*

To Cole, Kidd's refusal typified the difficulty of doing a Broadway show. (The political situation simply did not concern Cole even if it meant life or death.) First choices were too often unavailable. Then, too, pressures were now much greater. Feuer and Martin were "afraid of no one in

* Eugene Loring finally was signed.

making their demands"—as he had good reason to know. Before he had finished his work, six numbers had been dropped and six new ones added. "If Ever We Get out of Jail," for instance, had been transformed into "As on Through the Seasons We Sail."

Snags continually developed. There was grumbling over George Kaufman's directorial methods. The plan to have Miss Neff talk-sing her songs in the Dietrich manner was not as effective as expected, especially for "Without Love," the number Cole considered the best in the show.

Yvonne Adair was plagued by illness. Suffering from shingles, she was hospitalized during rehearsals and there was concern that she would not be on hand for the Philadelphia opening. She wasn't. Her understudy, Sherry O'Neil, went on in her place. There were rumors that Yvonne would never return. To play safe, Ernie Martin wired Gretchen Wyler, a chorus girl who was trying to establish herself in films, offering her the chance to understudy the understudy. She took it.

The show opened to tumultuous praise. Philadelphia critics, one of whom attributed the lyrics to Kaufman and Miss McGrath, agreed that it was a "sure hit." Feuer and Martin, who had had four Broadway smashes and were determined to achieve another no matter what the cost, were not at all sanguine. Audience response varied, they felt, and since the show was doing sellout business, they extended the engagement for a week.

During the run, Cole suggested that I delay a story on the show that I was preparing for *Look* magazine. "We've found a wonderful new comedienne for the movie star," he said. "All she has to do is have her nose bobbed and her hair bleached platinum. You can scoop everyone."

Look had a six-week deadline so it was impossible to wait for the new girl. It was for the best. The comedienne with her new retroussé nose and platinum hair delivered her lines and sang her songs exactly as she had at her audition. With her new good looks, she couldn't raise a snicker. After two performances, Cole's great new discovery was finished.

Sherry O'Neil went on again, and then Yvonne Adair recovered sufficiently to return. Meanwhile, relations between the Kaufmans and the producers were deteriorating. Abe Burrows was brought in to make a few suggestions and, eventually, to rewrite the libretto. Kaufman relinquished his directorial reins to Cy Feuer and stopped speaking to the producers and to Cole, but not to Abe Burrows.

Instead of coming to New York, the production moved to Boston for four weeks. There it drew mixed notices and underwent further doctoring. The emphasis was changed from comedy-romance to laughs at any cost.

For reasons best known to themselves, Cole said, the producers decided to throw out every set, gown and prop that possessed any beauty.

Business continued at $49,000 and $50,000 a week. Still dissatisfied with the show, Feuer and Martin booked it into Detroit for three weeks. Cole's response was that if they kept it out of town much longer everyone would have forgotten what silk was and the title would have to be changed to *Nylon Stockings*.

Still more changes were made, but none of the actresses who had played the film star had got the expected laughs. "Josephine," intended as a raucous parody of the striptease, was turning out to be a protracted yawn. Nor were the other songs satisfactory.

Burrows changed the star from a dancer to a swimmer and gave her a piece of business—pounding the water out of her stopped-up ear—that countless television and nightclub comics have since appropriated.

At that point Cole asked me to gather swimming terms and books, hoping that there might be a song in them. There wasn't. After another false start, he decided that film techniques might serve as the basis for a low-comedy number. From various newspaper advertisements and trade papers, I culled color processes and screen techniques which seemed only slightly promising to me. Overnight, however, he turned out the ingenious "Stereophonic Sound." (For most of the other songs, the same research went on. Mrs. Smith supplied fabric names for "Satin and Silk." For "It's a Chemical Reaction, That's All," a researcher was sent to the Museum of Natural History.")

During this time, I had luncheon with Cole on three consecutive days. On the first we had macaroni and cheese. On the second, macaroni and cheese. And on the third—macaroni and cheese. As we were about to be served the third day, he said, "You must think I never have anything else. But it's so good for my digestion." There was no mention of tension or of pressures, but the menus were eloquent.

Privately he desperately missed Linda. Because she had stayed away from rehearsals and tryouts, people had erroneously assumed that she played a negligible role in his career. Yet he complained that he missed having her advice because it was she who always told him when to refuse to do more rewrites.

On February 3, Miss Adair's throat trouble forced her out of the show for the second act. This time, Gretchen Wyler, who had not yet shed her baby fat, stepped into the role. Then and there, the cliché that has served as the plot for thousands of Grade-B films and slick fiction stories was reenacted. The 156-pound, unprepossessing little chorus girl stepped into a featured role and stopped the show cold with a number that had been marked for oblivion. Lines that had never evoked a snicker brought roars. Miss Wyler not only made a name for herself, but literally saved the show.

Cole flew to Detroit to attend the Tuesday performance during the final week and returned to New York far from optimistic. He was off, he said, for Switzerland on the 19th, claiming that reservations had been made long ago and were too difficult to change, but it was evident that he had no heart for this opening night.

Realizing how much Cole missed Linda's guidance, some of their friends—Jean Howard, Natasha Wilson, Baron de Gunzberg, Duke di Verdura and Howard Sturges—had the traditional opening-night cigarette case made and presented it to him in memory of Linda. This one was gold and was adorned by a garnet and two Russian coins. It was the last of the collection.

On the 19th, he was off to Zurich in search of distraction in travel. Five days after he arrived, *Silk Stockings* opened at the Imperial Theater in New York where it became Cole's twentieth Broadway hit. For him, the show earned far better reviews than he had become accustomed to expect. "Paris Loves Lovers," "Without Love," "As on Through the Seasons We Sail," "Stereophonic Sound," "Silk Stockings" and "All of You" were singled out by more than one critic. Even Richard Watts was pleased. After years of lamenting that Cole was not up to his usual standard, Watts announced: "The music sounds fine right now, and Mr. Porter's work is famous and remarkable for improving with familiarity. . . ."

In Europe, during Cole's three-and-a-half-month sojourn, he lived on the scale he enjoyed most—luxuriously. From Zurich he wrote:

> Last night we were practically quoting Goethe in a little German restaurant here which nothing but the old aristocracy knows when in walked a sad-looking little man with bad teeth and so lonely. We had had several drinks and so we decided to take pity on him and asked him to join us.
>
> He turned out to be . . . (*over*)
> *DARRYL ZANUCK.*
>
> Best,
> Cole

Even when traveling, he took time to lavish attention on friends, laboriously composing the letters in his left-hand upside-down script and recopying them so that the surprising name came upon turning the page.

On March 15 from the Grand Hotel Continental in Milan, Cole wrote in great detail about the manner in which his party—Jean Howard, actor Robert Bray, Sturges—and he were traveling:

We're well organized for our trek to the west [Portugal]. For touring there is the 1955 red-leather-lined Cadillac. (I suddenly realized day before yesterday, that I had ordered it red-leather-lined because when Pep and Berthe make spots from their privates, it's so easy to wash leather. But Pep isn't here, nor is Berthe.) There is also a Pontiac station wagon. In this goes the luggage—so far 37 pieces—with Luigi and Paul on the front seat. On top of the Cadillac, there is a super-rack for extra luggage and it's held on by suction. This means that when one arrives somewhere and doesn't want to have a super-rack, one presses a button, there's no suction any more and everything is respectable again—no more rack—I don't understand this.

To continue, in the trunk of the Cadillac is my collapsible wheelchair. This means, what with the aid of Luigi, Paul and Bob, I can be carried up and down all the staircases and then wheeled around and around. The result is, as we have been sightseeing every day, that Luigi, Paul and Robert all come back to the hotel exhausted wrecks, and I'm still fresh and rarin' to go.

This Luigi is a great chauffeur from Rome and highly recommended but when I first saw him I was shocked by his clothes and also because he looked so much like Jackie Gleason. Sturge and I took him to a chauffeur's shop to get him the proper outfit to the last detail. He still looks like Jackie Gleason.

Today, we drove to Bergamo, the magic city on the hill, and tomorrow we lunch in Turin where I shall be carried upstairs and downstairs and wheeled around and around again to see beautiful treasures. I believe you would like seeing all these treasures. They're all so far from Fleur Cowles.

Best,
Cole

A few days later he dined with S.A. Le Prince de Polignac and S.A. La Princesse Charlotte de Monaco, the father and mother of Prince Rainier. Cole enjoyed seeing many other old friends and regretted only the attention he drew from the press. When he went to Paris again, he found it a "strange combination of joy and sadness." The sadness lay in friends who had grown old. "For instance, I lunched with Sir Charles Mendl today," he wrote Dr. Sirmay. "There were several young people there. And as he was helped in to lunch I realized that the guests were there because they were fond of him. He didn't know anyone was there except at rare intervals and I dread old age."

Although depressed by his aging friends and a city that no longer held quite the same charm for him, he was to take great satisfaction when the man from Chappell informed him that "C'est Magnifique" was at the moment the number-one song in France. "It is rather nice to find that when I tried to write a typical French popular song, that was dismissed by American critics, it has at last become a typical French song," he wrote Dr. Sirmay. He also asked him to congratulate Richard Adler and Jerry Ross for their work on *Damn Yankees*. He had read the numbers, he said, and found them delightful. "And, of course, 'Lola' is a masterpiece. Tell their publisher in their song 'Heart' on page five, stave one, measure two, the vocal note should be A not C. If Chappell did this to me, I'd raise hell."

From Paris he moved on to Rome and the rich rich, and then on to Athens. Finally on May 14, the party boarded Stavros Niarchos' beautiful ebony yacht, *Eros*, which Niarchos had kindly lent him for a two-week cruise among the Greek islands. Everything interested Cole, from the Argos theater to local characters. Of Mykonos, he noted in his trip diary: ". . . wandering through enchanting streets, 360 churches here, each offered by a sailor to his saint if he would return safe from the sea, the big shock, no noise because no cars, no telephones, the ladies all weave, the gentlemen all fish, a former top whore is now a top bootblack, bang-up lunch at a bang-up 'moderne' hotel, the local museum with our guide who suddenly made Greek vases interesting by explaining the process of their decoration, the village idiot on the quai, the boat that moved in and killed our view, the constant joy of this incredible gift from Stavros. . . ."

While Cole was abroad, work progressed on the remodeling and the decoration of 33-A (the new nine-room apartment at the Waldorf-Towers) and on the cottage in Williamstown. All spring Mrs. Smith had kept "the little boss" filled in on reports from the Waldorf: cartons of rare books, boxes of priceless art objects, the laying of the herringbone floor in the entrance hall (it came from a house in Versailles), the hanging of the thirteenth-century Chinese wallpaper. She was enthusiastic too about the black-gray-red color scheme for his bedroom.

Upon returning on June 7, Cole was pleased by all he saw, but particularly by the tortoise-shell leather walls and the brass-piping bookcases which decorator Billy Baldwin had devised for the library. He approved it at once and seldom thereafter made any changes in it.

Three nights after he arrived in New York, he went to see *Damn Yankees*, the Adler-Ross musical. Cole's generosity in regard to his colleagues—whether Berlin, Rodgers and Hart, Gershwin, Frank Loesser or, later, Lerner and Loewe—was widely recognized. Sammy Cahn, for instance, was overwhelmed when Cole agreed to allow him to make any changes he thought necessary in Porter lyrics for the second film version of *Anything Goes*. Afterward Cole wired Cahn, "Congratulations, you did a better job than I did," which moved Cahn to reply, "Thank you. You're more of a gentleman than a judge of lyrics." Nevertheless, Cole's enthusiasm was genuine. And for Adler and Ross he felt a particular enthusiasm. When in Europe, he had spread almost 100 copies of "Whatever Lola Wants" about England and the Continent.

Thus, on the morning of the 9th, Dick Adler was summoned from the barber chair to take a telephone call. The voice identified itself as Cole Porter. Adler countered that *he* was Irving Berlin, but eventually accepted the fact that Cole Porter—C-o-l-e P-o-r-t-e-r—was calling to invite him to drop by Michael's Pub for a drink after the show.

"That," Adler said later, "was the start of what developed into a wonderful relationship. Too short-lived because he was already quite an elderly man and I was just getting there. He taught me an awful lot. He was also the world's greatest song plugger for somebody else. Because when I went to Europe 'Lola' was being played all over—and it hadn't even been released. It was all due to Cole Porter."

What impressed Adler was that Cole evinced such curiosity about and interest in Ross' and his songwriting techniques. "He would always say: Now why did you do this? *He* was always curious. Here was a man in his sixties, the greatest songwriting genius of our time without any question—and if I'm offending some of my living friends I'm sorry—asking *me* why I'd done this or that. That shows the greatness of the man. He was curious about how my mind worked as a songwriter, not in telling me how his worked, although he did that too. He had an insatiable curiosity and that leads to greatness."

Because Cole was a skilled craftsman, Adler made it a point to draw him out on techniques and sent work for criticism. Then when Jerry Ross died in November, Cole sent Adler a two-page condolence telegram, urging him to drop by. Adler did. Cole spoke of Ross' tragedy and then urged Adler to avoid depression by getting back to writing at once. When Adler protested that he had no collaborator, Cole countered that since both he and his partner had written some of the music and some of the lyrics, Adler should write alone. Adler wondered whether he could do it. "Why not?" Cole asked. "*I* do."

During their friendship, Adler was always intrigued by the detailed analysis to which Cole would subject popular songs. About one such which had climbed to the top of the hit parade, Cole inquired in detail about the writer and why he had written this number. Then Cole took it apart, analyzed the words, the music and the relationship between these elements. "I kept asking myself, why? Why is the great master Cole Porter so interested in that mediocre song?" Adler said. "I finally decided that it was just his way of doing his ABC's for the day."

Cole once asked Adler how often he wrote a song, Adler said whenever he had an inspiration or a job. "Oh no," Cole cried. "You must write something every day—just to keep your tools sharp."

Several years later, Adler was to describe Cole as "the Adlai Stevenson of songwriters. . . . He was an aristocrat in everything he did and everything he wrote. Everything had class—even a little pop song like 'Don't Fence Me In.' There are no other writers like him. Larry Hart was a genius. He was brilliant and sophisticated, but he didn't have that kind of style nor did he write the music. Cole wrote exquisite melodies. And the openness and simplicity of them. I mean, when you go—you'd be so easy to love—with what we call footballs—whole notes—he knew how to write that open song that a singer can belt. He had that commercial instinct. He was also lucky to have lived and died at the right time, because he lived in an era of flourish. Before the mass media a man who had the sophisticated wit and style could express himself, be heard and appreciated. Today? With all his genius, who can say, but I'm afraid that at least a part of Cole Porter would be wasted."

Six days after his arrival in New York Cole went to Williamstown on June 13 to receive an honorary degree as Doctor of Music from Williams College. Two days later he and Sturges left for Brentwood where Cole pondered offers from three film companies and one from Feuer and Martin for Broadway show. This last was a proposal to convert the film version of *The Little Shop Around the Corner* into a musical comedy. Cole attended a screening and astounded the producers by turning the project down. "Until then," Ernie Martin said, "he had put complete trust in us."

In the latter part of July, Cole wrote that he had made a decision:

> . . . I am doing *The Philadelphia Story* at Metro-Goldwyn-Mayer. Of course, they have already changed

the locale to Newport, but that is to be expected. I like very much my producer, Sol Siegel, and John Patrick, with whom I am collaborating. It is also a rather easy job. I shall stay out here until November 1st on account of it and can finish whatever I have not done in New York. I resent missing October in New York, but I must count my blessings. . . .*

When Cole learned that Louis Armstrong was to appear in *High Society*, as they were calling the film, he decided that he would have to write a jazz number. As always, he approached the problem in a businesslike manner. He called Fred Astaire and suggested that they attend a "Jazz at the Philharmonic" concert. Later, he was introduced to jazz impresario Norman Granz on the telephone and Granz gave him a short introductory course in jazz terms. The eventual song was "Now You Has Jazz."

Besides Armstrong, the cast included Bing Crosby, Frank Sinatra, Grace Kelly and Celeste Holm.

Among the songs his favorite which he considered musically superior to the others, was "I Love You, Samantha." His hope was brightest commercially for "You're Sensational," which had lyrics peppered with slang. "True Love," eventually to emerge as the most-played song of the year, did not much interest him.

In October Cole sustained another emotional shock. His old and valued friend Howard Sturges suddenly died of a heart attack in Paris. Cole was shaken, probably more so than by the death of Linda or his mother, both of whom had been in ill health. Sturges had simply fallen dead without any warning signs to allow friends to adjust. In the wake of the shock, Cole began to feel more and more old.

Under the circumstances, it is not surprising that Cole's attention turned to his own health. Although he maintained

* Paramount Pictures, he later wrote, was remaking *Anything Goes* with a new story. The cast included Bing Crosby, Jeanmarie, Donald O'Connor and Mitzi Gaynor. Cole had nothing to do with it.

that it was probably an unnecessary precaution, he took to carrying a list of medication that he was currently receiving. Included were one Pyribenzamine, two Stewart's Formula and two Tocopherex High Potency pills taken with breakfast. In his pillbox, he carried two Bufferin and two Anacin tablets and two small pills for gout. The notation added that his gout seldom bothered him and he generally did not have to take them. Before retiring, he noted, he took, as he had for many years, four Carter's Little Liver Pills.

At the end of October, he left Hollywood via TWA, stopped over for three days in Peru and arrived in New York on November 1. For a month prior to his arrival architect Jack Coble had spent all his time getting the Williamstown cottage finished.

On that first weekend, Coble, Billy Baldwin and Baron de Gunzberg were on hand to witness Cole's reaction. "I was frightened out of my wits," Coble said later. "Well, the house was completely done. The lunch was on the table—everything. I didn't dare think what it meant if he didn't like it."

Cole did like it. His first reaction upon seeing the cottage on its new foundation was, "It looks as if it had been born there." Then he went inside, looked the place over and was delighted. Within fifteen minutes, everyone was relaxed and happy.

Thereafter, Cole began spending every weekend there if he was in the eastern part of the United States. Frequent weekenders included, among others, Louise Bearss, Jean Howard, Duke di Verdura, Baron de Gunzberg, Dr. Sirmay and Coble.

At this period, Cole and his longtime friend Elsa Maxwell had a mild disagreement. Like Cole, Elsa had borrowed Niarchos' yacht. Afterward Cole donated $10,000 in Niarchos' name to the Greek Archdiocese of North and South America. Then without warning, Elsa announced at a large dinner that she and Cole and a couple of other guests were going to give a party for Niarchos, to whom they were indebted. Because of the size of the gathering, the startled Cole foolishly said nothing.

Subsequently, he informed Elsa that he would not help underwrite the party because he had already arranged to give more than his share—$7,000—to a favorite charity of Niarchos'. Nevertheless, Elsa sailed ahead with the party and then told friends that Cole had welched on his obligation.

The next time they met, Cole confronted her and reminded her of their earlier conversation. She denied it had taken place and added, "Don't make excuses, Cole Porter. You're famous for being stingy. And when I leave, I won't kiss you goodnight."

Cole forgave her. The incident reminded him of an earlier one in which she had cabled him from France asking for $5000, saying that her mother was ill. Cole sent it promptly. Shortly after, Lady Mendl arrived in New York and announced that Elsa had asked *her* for $5000 for her sick mother. When Cole said he'd sent Elsa a like amount, Lady Mendl was outraged. Cole simply laughed.

That summer in Hollywood, he was approached by a guest at a party. The woman said that they had not met, but they belonged to the same club. Cole politely asked which one. "The Burying Elsa's Mother Club," the woman replied, adding, "Now don't be embarrassed. We're not alone. Several others here belong, too, but if you'll step to my car I'll take you to Elsa's mother—and it won't be in Forest Lawn, either."

When Cole returned to New York, he gave "a small dinner party for about forty guests"—one of whom was Elsa. At one point, he tapped his glass for silence and recounted the story. "No one laughed louder than Elsa," he told me later. "She said, 'Oh, Cole, you know I always do crazy things when I'm strapped.' Now how," he demanded, "can you resist anyone like that?" Cole and Elsa became friendly again and he even invited her to Williamstown for a weekend, although he later complained that she stayed in her room all day.

From the beginning of November until February 19, Cole enjoyed the country on weekends and the New York season during the week. Then in February, he flew to Switzerland, met other members of the party and traveled through Spain and Italy before flying on April 20 to Cairo where they stayed at the Mena House, a charming Edwardian-type hotel where Cole had arranged for their rooms to look out upon the changing light of the Sahara.

He was in his element here, having the opportunity to sample Arabian foods and to explore unfamiliar sights. One evening he and several others dined on the desert beneath a full moon and were entertained by an Arabian orchestra which accompanied two belly dancers, two Sudanese comedians and a beautiful white horse. In his journal Cole noted that the horse danced "in perfect rhythm and always on beat to the music even without his rider. In all my life I have never seen anything like this horse."

That night, the party stopped on the way home to view the Sphinx once again. As they sat there, an old Arab standing nearby suddenly cried, "Isn't it fantastic!" Cole tried to engage him in further conversation, but those were the only words the Arab knew, having heard thousands of American tourists utter them.

Among the stops were Beirut, Tripoli, Damascus, Jerusalem and Petra. On May 7, they toured the Holy Land, went on to Istanbul and then to the Greek islands for a second cruise on Niarchos' *Eros*.

June 5 saw Cole in New York for a few days, after which he dropped in on relatives in Peru before heading for Brentwood eager to get to work. At Metro, Arthur Freed was producing the film version of *Silk Stockings* with Fred Astaire and Cyd Charisse in the leads. For it, Cole was committed to write a rock-and-roll song. He confessed to Alex Steinert that he didn't know how, so Steinert brought him three or four examples. Cole listened to them, then added the Porter touch by writing the "Ritz Roll and Rock."

Cole's habits never ceased to fascinate Steinert, who was amused at the timetable precision: work fifty-five minutes, rest five. One day, Steinert arrived six minutes early. Cole greeted him, glanced at his watch and said, "We rest."

"One of the things that delighted me about Cole was that he knew what he wanted in the way of sound," Steinert once observed. "He knew good writing. He knew when to double a chord, he knew when not to double a chord. He was aware of voice leading, which is the secret of a great many of his things. And above all he had taste. One thing was very curious. Cole would take tremendous amounts of trouble in the first draft. He would take a great deal of time discussing whether to drop a note, whether to change a rhythm. He would find a section where the rhythm was static and something would have to be done about it to dress it up. Cole wanted the first draft as if it were orchestrated. He thought in terms of theater where you heard the melody—basically a more simple form of orchestration unlike band arrangements where everything is thrown in."

At one of these meetings, the two men discussed the moment, theatrical or musical or combined, that had made the greatest impression on each. After some consideration, Steinert found one definite choice. So did Cole. It turned out that both had chosen Nijinsky dancing *Petrouchka*, with Benois' settings and the original production. That combination of visual beauty, musical excellence, superb dancing and a good story, both agreed, was a perfect blending of the arts.

During the summer Cole also began to work on songs for MGM's *Les Girls*, which was to be directed by George Cukor. The producer, Sol Siegel, and screenwriter, John Patrick, were the team responsible for his previous assignment, *High Society*, which opened in August at the Music Hall in New York to mixed reviews and wide popular acceptance. Cole merely laughed at *Time*'s assessment of his songs—"fair to maudlin."

That September ASCAP gave him a citation and in October CBS-TV's *Ford Star Jubilee* was devoted to him. Both events celebrated his fortieth anniversary as a composer. At the time a newspaper reporter sought him out to talk about his music. Cole dismissed it. "There are practically no great songs. Grieg wrote one. Wagner wrote a few, and maybe there are two or three others. The standards in the classics are pretty high." His brainchildren, he maintained, were for the moment. "My songs last? I never gave it a thought. What's happened to Victor Herbert? Gilbert and Sullivan? It doesn't worry me a bit. My enjoyment was in writing them."

He remained consistent by leasing one of them as the basis for a television commercial, and during the preparation of the *Ford Star Jubilee*, he readily agreed to a network continuity-acceptance man's request for a new line in "Down in the Depths." "Even my janitor's wife/Has a perfectly good love life . . ." was changed because it reeked of class distinction. It became "Even my analyst's wife . . ." at Cole's suggestion.

At the end of the program, he made a two-minute appearance. "Then," he said, "I got out of town."

He arrived in New York on October 8. By this time "True Love" from *High Society* had become a major hit and MGM thought it stood a good chance of winning an Oscar. "I've sunk to new depths," Cole announced. "I've hired a press agent."

The "press agent" turned out to be an old friend, Stanley Musgrove, who had scored notable successes in publicizing other Award-nominated songs. Here, however, his hands were tied; Cole wanted no obvious promotion. So Musgrove was forced to concentrate on ingeniously disguised items for the trade papers. One suggestion he made was so outrageous that Cole immediately okayed it. Musgrove rented the marquee of a Sunset Boulevard theater in order to have a sign reading:

BING AND GRACE
SING "TRUE LOVE" IN HIGH SOCIETY

At Christmastime, Cole decided to return to Indiana to spend the holidays with relatives. A couple of days after Christmas Cole returned to New York to enter the hospital for observation. Tests revealed a large gastric ulcer, and on

January 8, 1957, he was operated on.

Shortly after release from the hospital, he decided to go to Montego Bay to recuperate. He took the house owned by the William Paleys for ten days and invited Baron de Gunzberg to go along. "I thought he'd love it," the Baron said. "But he was so nervous—and then we had an earthquake. Also, he'd just written a calypso number for *High Society* and he didn't want to hear calypso. We'd go into a bar and they'd start to play calypso. 'No, no, no, no!' he'd say, and give them a big tip not to play it. 'Don't these people realize I've written one myself?' he'd ask." After five days, Cole was so obviously not enjoying himself that they hopped a plane and returned to New York.

Although Musgrove had been successfully planting all kinds of stories about "True Love" in the entertainment pages of the Hollywood trade papers, he was unable to persuade Cole to attend the ceremonies.

On March 27, the night of the Academy Awards show, there was to be a screening of *Silk Stockings* for *Look* magazine (where I worked). I mentioned it, and Cole suggested that we dine together and then see the picture. After it was over, he asked me to go to the Waldorf-Towers to see the television show—the first mention of the Awards all evening.

The production numbers were terrible, and a filmed spot of Bing Crosby singing "True Love" was among the worst. However, the votes had all been counted long before, so no real harm was done. Finally, the winner was announced—"Que Sera, Sera."

The smile never left Cole's face as he picked up the telephone and asked for Western Union. To Musgrove, he sent the following message:

Whatever will be, will be, dear Stanley.

Cole

After the ulcer operation a tinge of melancholy settled over him. Possessions began to weigh upon him. He willed his clothing to the Salvation Army and changed his mind about giving friends the collection of cigarette cases. He felt that even women had given up carrying cases and decided to keep the collection intact by leaving it to a museum.

Williamstown with its beautiful foliage now became one of his chief joys. His only regret was that he could not move it to 42nd Street and Fifth Avenue since few guests were free to leave work Friday noon and stay away from the city until late Monday.

Once he spoke wistfully of ending his days in California where he would require a small house with lots of rooms—at least four for servants—and many acres.

Unwilling or unable to speak of real emotional problems, he fretted about money. "I worry about losing it," he said. "It's bad enough to be old without being poor." He worried, too, because he had disposed of 250 acres of the 750-acre farm which he had inherited. And he painted a gloomy picture of the Cole-Crane Trust running out and of the increase in taxes that would occur when it became a corporation.

Occasionally his problems appeared trivial even to him. Once he rode in silence for many miles, a frown clouding his face. When he spoke, he said he had an awful problem. "My mother's executor says I own three hundred houses in Omar, West Virginia. Now *what* am I going to do with them' Sometime later, when asked what he had done about them, he laughed and said, "I installed television sets in them, but it was a bad idea."

In April, 1957, he and Paul flew to Italy for a month, but Paul developed a back ailment and the trip was less successful than previous ones. Upon return, Cole urged his ailing valet to rest. So on May 27, Max Aydt arrived from California to replace Paul. Eighteen days later Cole, Max and another temporary valet set out for Brentwood.

In California, Cole's melancholy returned, increasing still further upon receipt of the news that Dr. Moorhead had died. Nor did the reviews of MGM's *Silk Stockings* lift his spirits. Not that they were bad, but they were a familiar story. In a letter to Dr. Sirmay, Cole observed, "Thank you very much indeed for sending me the notices of the film *Silk Stockings*. I was delighted to read in the [New York] *Post* that my music and lyrics are not my very best but at least are in my own style. I missed finding that I was not up to my usual standard." Melancholic or not, there were still flashes of wit.

He was at the time toying with the idea of doing a television musical with S. J. Perelman. On the one hand he suspected that this was a sure way to destroy "what little reputation I have left." Still, agent Irving Lazar, who "usually has excellent judgment," assured him that Perelman "could write the script without merely writing it for the mentality of a six-year-old!" What worried Cole was that the show, *Aladdin*, was rather like the *Cinderella* of Rodgers' and Hammerstein's television special. He worried, too, that the score of *Aladdin* would suffer the same fate as *Cinderella*.

He also complained to Dr. Sirmay that the score of *Les Girls* gave the impression of being negligible. Later, he admitted that he had done a bad job because he was suffering greatly from the ulcer while writing the score and should have given it up. He also concluded that an MGM staff tunesmith could have turned out a song for the vaudeville act, the only music actually needed.

At this time, Cole was working on the eight songs that were to make up the score of *Aladdin*. He proposed in the title song to rhyme Aladdin with gladden, sadden and madden. When he finished the song, he sang it to agent Bob Raison, who questioned the existence of such words. Upon being shown them in the dictionary, he mischievously revised his objection—the rhyming was not up to Cole's usual standard.

Cole thereupon called Richard Lewine, executive producer of the $500,000 CBS special, to ask whether the rhymes would do. "Mr. Porter, you may even rhyme it with Bernarr MacFadden—as long as we get the lyrics on time," was the reply.

Before returning to New York, Cole finished "Come to the Supermarket in Old Peking," "Make Way for the

Emperor," "No Wonder Taxes Are High" and "Aladdin."

In New York, he wrote a romantic waltz, experiencing some difficulty with it. When he played the song for Alex Steinert, Steinert greeted it with silence. Cole remarked that Steinert didn't seem to like his music.

Cornered, Steinert told him that it was bad Beethoven and not very good Porter. "There was a terrible silence," Steinert once recalled. "And he asked me what I meant by 'bad Porter.' I said it reminded me of other work of his. He was frigid for the rest of the time. When it got time to go, I said, 'Why don't you fire me?' He looked at me wryly and said, 'Because you are always right.'

"That was a Friday. By the following Monday, he had written a new waltz, adapting the lyrics from the first song. This turned out to be 'Trust Your Destiny to a Star.' I said, 'Ah, it's better than Beethoven.' And it went into the show."

The last song to be written for *Aladdin* was the one for the Emperor. And Cole complained that it was difficult because Chinese emperors seldom did anything except have their subjects beheaded. Research was to little avail. After great struggle, he came forth with "Wouldn't It Be Fun!"

Wouldn't it be fun not to be famous,
Wouldn't it be fun not to be rich!
Wouldn't it be pleasant
To be a simple peasant
And spend a happy day digging a ditch!
Wouldn't it be fun not to be known as an important VIP,
Wouldn't it be fun to be nearly anyone
Except me, mighty me!

It was the last song Cole ever wrote.

CHAPTER XVIII

On January 9, 1958, Mrs. Smith called my secretary at *Look* magazine and left a message that Cole was entering Harkness Pavilion on January 14 and would like me to dine with him on the evening of the 13th.

Since the 13th was a Monday and Le Pavillon was closed, he chose the Colony. Nothing was said about his impending hospitalization until I mentioned it while we were having coffee.

"It may be very serious and it may be nothing at all," he said, indicating that I understood the uncertainties of osteomyelitis, a disease he knew I'd had as a child.

Two days later, he called to report that his thirty-second leg operation had been minor, involving the removal of a small piece of bone. "When are you coming to dine?" he asked.

"At the hospital?"

"Why not? Paul brings the food from Le Pavillon or the Waldorf."

I laughed.

"*You*," Cole said, "are the only person in the world who would find that funny."

Although he gave up the idea of entertaining dinner

guests, he managed to turn night into day, having his cocktails when other patients were having dinner, delaying his dinner until 11:00 and sleeping throughout the next morning.

On February 14, he underwent his thirty-third operation, in which surgeons attempted to reconstruct the right leg following the January surgery. This leg never healed. Now, it failed to respond to antibiotics and became a serious threat to his life. For many years, Paul had dressed the legs twice weekly and the right heel twice a day, but it was becoming increasingly difficult for him to distinguish between the healthy and the unhealthy tissues.

Burdened with many troubles, Cole hardly noticed when *Aladdin*—with Anna Maria Alberghetti, Cyril Ritchard, Dennis King and Sal Mineo—was telecast on February 21, 1958. Since he always cut off all newspapers when he was ill, he was spared the curt dismissal it received from television critics.

He grew no better as time passed, and on April 2, Dr. Frank Stinchfield, Cole's surgeon, informed him that it was imperative that his right leg be amputated. He was allowed twenty-four hours to assent.

Upon hearing the news, Dr. Sirmay sought out Dr. Stinchfield and said that as a friend of long standing he wanted to know whether there was any alternative. There was not.

Cole faced this situation as he had faced many others—with Spartan calm. The night before the operation, he informed his valet, Paul, and his chauffeur, Andrew Bentley. "When Mr. Porter told me about the surgery, I just choked up," Bentley reported. "But he was the calmest man in the hospital."

Following the operation, Cole's system rebelled against the various shocks that had been visited upon it over the years. For five days, he hiccoughed continuously and had to be fed intravenously. Finally, on April 14—eleven days after the operation—he experienced a relatively good day and was able to eat a small amount of food.

The nurses now began getting him up and helping him

take a few steps each day in a walker. Since he was experiencing no pain for the first time in years, he found that he needed neither liquor nor pain killers.

He seemed to be facing the loss of his leg the same way he had accepted the accident—as a new challenge. In a cooperative mood, he agreed to put himself on hospital routine and to take his meals from the hospital's kitchen. He made plans to have his automobile converted so that he could drive when he was released. He said that he was anxious to work again. One visitor was invited each day to get him accustomed to the world of activity again. He looked forward to dismissal so that he could go to California where he was having a small elevator installed at 416 North Rockingham.

At Harkness Pavilion, he exercised in the gym daily, took sunlamp treatments and had Bentley bring Peppi to accompany him on his first drive.

But by the end of May he had begun to grow despondent about the possibility of ever acclimating to the artificial leg, which he complained weighed "eight tons." An expert had been flown in from Virginia to offer advice upon fitting it, but the leg, according to Cole, was "no good." No matter how great the pain, he said he would rather have kept his own leg.

On May 26, he was released from the hospital. To celebrate, he invited Mrs. John Wilson and Baron de Gunzberg to dine. Mrs. Wilson thoughtfully dressed to the teeth, wearing the jewels that had been Linda's.

The following evening, he began his custom of inviting one guest. The evening began as many such evenings had. Cole was full of wit, charm and enthusiasm, but after a single drink he lapsed more and more deeply into silence. When he spoke, it was to complain. He had begun to attend the Institute for Disabled Persons for "gait training" and he was discouraged at the difficulty he experienced in handling the leg, at the slow pace at which he moved and at the slow progress he was making. He was also beginning to complain that the stump of the leg was so sensitive that high-frequency treatment was needed to deaden the nerves. Although he looked fit, he maintained that the doctors didn't seem to think he was in good shape.

On June 9, 1958, Cole's sixty-seventh birthday, he was quoted in the Boston *Daily Globe* as saying, "I don't like to think about birthdays. I prefer to forget them." Robert Montgomery, an associate of John Wharton's, said that many legitimate-theater and motion-picture projects had been proposed but Cole was not yet ready to concentrate.

Six days later, in the company of Paul and Bentley, Cole left for Brentwood. There, he met daily with a trainer to continue his "gait training" and swam twenty minutes each day to get back into shape. He was thin, but physically in improved health. He could not, however, bring himself to accept dinner invitations. The last time he went out to dine was at the William Goetzes. In order to arouse no pity in the other guests, he arranged to have himself seated ahead of them. After attending that party, he confined his social activities to his own home.

By this time, phantom pains were causing him to feel itching and aching where his right leg had once been. Jean Howard gently urged him to consult a psychiatrist. Bob Raison suggested that he consider placing himself in the hands of a medical hypnotist. Cole indignantly rejected all suggestions. Although he had consulted medical doctors frequently throughout his lifetime, he now preferred to have no contact with them.

Then, in August, he suffered another psychological blow. Paul Sylvain entered the hospital for surgery. A malignant growth was removed. Cole was in despair as another of those closest to him was stricken. After several weeks, however, Paul returned to work. His doctors were hopeful about his prognosis. He was thin and pale, but remained an unwavering perfectionist. To lighten Paul's duties, Cole engaged a second man, who returned to New York with them on November 19.

This, too, proved unsettling. No sooner had they arrived than the new man charged several hundred dollars' worth of clothes (on the strength of his employment by Cole) and cashed bad checks at the Waldorf, disappearing just before his deeds were discovered.

In this atmosphere, Cole's depression became severe. Mrs. Smith lamented in a letter to Sam and Harriette Stark that "the little boss had not the strength that comes in a time of need, of a bolstering religion of even a Buddhist, a Seventh Day Adventist, a Jehovah's Witness—anything to take the place of just nothing. Without faith one is like a stained glass window in the dark. How to reach his particular darkness is an enigma."

Because he had no confidence in the artificial leg, Cole refused to go to public restaurants or to dine with friends in their homes. After he stopped going out, the legend grew that he had become a recluse. While it is true that there were seldom more than two or three guests at a time, there was at least one guest every night. Jean Howard, Ethel Merman, Louise Bearss, Mr. and Mrs. Arnold Whitridge, Mrs. Sumner Welles, Mrs. Lytle Hull, Colin Leslie Fox, Mr. and Mrs. Abe Burrows, Michael Pearman, Anita Loos, Mr. and Mrs. Cy Feuer, Garson Kanin and his wife, Ruth Gordon, Mrs. William Woodward, Saint Subber —these were only a few of the New Yorkers who were invited to dine on a more than occasional basis.

That winter, Paul went back to the hospital for a brief period, returned to his work at the Waldorf-Towers and then, in early May, entered the hospital as a terminal cancer patient. Cole, who had relied upon him for so much and who had come to consider Paul as much a friend as a servant, sadly observed again that "the gods seem to be punishing me for something."

He assumed the hospital bills and continued Paul's salary. When the sick man lingered past Cole's scheduled departure for California on June 15, Cole remained in New York. Finally, on June 26, at the urging of all concerned, Cole left for Brentwood. On July 21, Paul Sylvain died and it was upon his death that Cole at once set up a trust fund of $75,000 for Paul's two small daughters.

By August 6, Cole himself was back in the hospital, this

time with a kidney obstruction. Except for faithful old friends, he saw few people that summer. To those he did see, he apologized for being dull. Sometimes for several consecutive evenings, Bob Raison would be the only guest, struggling vainly to distract his host with anecdotes about the motion-picture business. Cole hardly seemed to hear.

When he returned to New York on October 27, his interest in food had all but disappeared. At lunchtime, he took to sitting with Mrs. Smith in her cheerful office in the corner of the apartment. When she found it difficult to keep conversation going, she suggested that perhaps he'd like her to read to him. He agreed. And one winter was spent on *Gone with the Wind*. Cole also enlisted her as a conspirator in disposing of the food for which he had no appetite.

She saw to it, too, that he was protected from everyone except those whom he wanted to see—sometimes, she realized, earning the enmity of people who felt she was failing to put their calls through.

Broadway projects were seldom considered, although she conscientiously attempted to bring each to his attention. For the most part, however, he impatiently waved them aside or referred them to his lawyers John Wharton and Robert Montgomery for assessment.

In January, the pendulum was on the upswing as Cole showed marked improvement in his walking. He now got about with two canes, instead of a cane and a valet. He began to read a bit of history once more and to enjoy listening to records.

Flashes of the famed Porter wit also returned. One time when Ethel Merman dined with him, she asked whether he had seen a mutual friend. He said he had; in fact, she had been there the previous evening. When Miss Merman inquired how she had looked, Cole replied, "She looked divine," paused and then threw away, "except her pearls were too long."

Encouraged by Cole's improvement, Dr. Sirmay offered him a choice of three musicals that spring. Cole turned them down. Dr. Sirmay also continued to urge him to play the piano once again and to think of writing. "I preached to him. I lectured him," Dr. Sirmay said. "In fact, I told Cole I would do anything in the world to make working easy for him. I pleaded with him to sit down and think, then to dictate a song." Dr. Sirmay refused to accept the supposition that Cole had lost his capacity to write. Cole was unable to cooperate.

One evening after dinner, Dr. Sirmay announced that it was time for Cole to return to the piano. They would, he said, play four-hands as they had done so often in years gone by. Cole meekly allowed himself to be led to the piano, and Dr. Sirmay chose an easy selection from Mozart.

Cole protested that he couldn't play it, but the doctor insisted that they try. After three or four bars, Cole gave up. He could no longer keep time.

"I can't. I can't. Leave me alone," he cried, with tears streaming down his cheeks. After that evening, the piano remained closed.

On his sixty-nineth birthday (June 9, 1960) representatives from Yale convened at Cole's apartment —he was too ill to go to New Haven—to confer an honor he had secretly coveted for many years. There, Secretary Holden presented Cole to Provost Steve Buck, who addressed him:

> Cole Porter:
>
> As an undergraduate, you first won acclaim for writing the words and music of two of Yale's perennial football songs. Since then you have achieved a reputation as a towering figure in the American musical theater. Master of the deft phrase, the delectable rhyme, the distinctive melody, you are, in your own words and in your own field, the top. Confident that your graceful, impudent, inimitable songs will be played and sung as long as footlights burn and curtains go up, your Alma Mater confers upon you the degree of Doctor of Humane Letters.

Promptly on June 15, Cole again set out for the West Coast. The unhappier he became, the stricter the schedule he maintained. Thus the June 15 arrival and the October 19 departure took on a kind of ritualistic importance.

In New York, too, the weekly schedule was unvarying—four days in the city, three in the country. Setting out for Williamstown, Cole descended to the lobby promptly at 12:15, greeted his guest (only one, since the other guest room was used by the valet, who was on twenty-four-hour call during weekends) and set off for Buxton Hill.

The menus in a way also reflected the ritualistic aspects of Cole's existence. Although he had by this time abandoned dressing for dinner, service was elaborate, with the inevitable small handwritten menu on the table. His gastronomic habits, however, reflected his own lack of interest in food. The week-end menu was always the same.

Lentil soup, a nut cup, broiled lobster, small potatoes in butter, string beans, green salad, lemon pie, Peru (Indiana) fudge and demitasse might make up the Friday dinner. For Saturday (or another day's) luncheon there would be cheese soufflé, green salad, a vegetable, fruit and demitasse. For dinner, there would be soup, a nut cup, barbecued chicken, rice, beans, mince pie and ice cream, Peru fudge and demitasse. For the next luncheon there would be liver and bacon, beet and watercress salad, floating island and demitasse. That evening, there would be vegetable soup, charbroiled steak, green salad, asparagus (from the garden if possible), potatoes, apple pie and cheese, Peru fudge and demitasse. In addition, there was both red and white wine at all meals.

Nor was the routine in the country surprising. It had for many years been his custom to take a drive through the Berkshires at 4:15 P.M. after having worked a bit. To the very end of his life, Cole maintained the schedule despite the pleas of Bentley and of his guests who pointed out how much more pleasant it would be to start earlier and to see the countryside's views. "I hate views," Cole responded.

Departure for New York on Monday morning occurred

at exactly 10:45. On several occasions, Cole, the guest and the staff were all ready to depart at 10:30. Once, a new valet asked, "Are you ready to leave, sir?"

"What time is it? " Cole asked.

"Ten-thirty, sir."

"Departure is set for ten-forty-five," Cole said, folding his hands and waiting for that moment to arrive.

From the summer of 1960 on, Cole was fortunate to have two Englishmen, Henry Burke and Eric Lindsay, as valets. Both were devoted to his well-being and did everything possible to make him comfortable. Eric was cheerful, introverted and infinitely kind. Henry was talkative, amusing and a great admirer of his employer's work. He was also an immediate link to the theater, seeing almost every play that opened on Broadway, whether a hit or a flop, and discussing it with his boss.

By November of that year, Cole was down to eighty pounds. Since he was also under sedation, it took only one Cutty Sark and soda for him to begin to feel the effects of the alcohol. As November wore on, he became increasingly weaker. Pressure was brought to bear for him to enter Harkness Pavilion for a checkup, which he did on November 26, 1960. The diagnosis revealed a general debility complicated by chronic pneumonia—"single pneumonia," as he always emphasized.

For the first few days, he was not allowed visitors; when Mrs. Smith let it be known that friends were calling about the possibility of coming up to see him, Cole sent word that he was not receiving anyone. In addition, he cut off all newspapers and correspondence, relying totally upon television, Henry and Eric for news of the outside world, "I always cut myself off when I'm ill," he said.

Then, on December 26, Bob Raison arrived in New York. When told that Cole was allowing no one in, Raison simply went to the hospital and appeared in Cole's room during visiting hours. After a few minutes of resentment, Cole decided to let him stay and had such a good time that he invited him back the next day.

Thereafter, a guest was scheduled for each afternoon in

the week. These were people with whom Cole could simply be himself, people who did not demand that he be the witty, word-weary, oh-so-clever Cole Porter. It was a time given over to reminiscences of his mother, his grandfather and life in Indiana. It was a return to the essential Indiana wit of J. O. Cole.

By January 9, 1961, Cole had gained sixteen pounds; he now weighed ninety-six. When his doctors tentatively suggested dismissal, he found that he had grown accustomed to hospital routine and was loath to face the outside world again. Finally, he was discharged after seven months and eight days.

Back at the Waldorf on July 4, he opened gifts that had arrived the preceding Christmas, spent a few days in the apartment and then, accompanied by Eric, Henry and Bentley, he was once again off for California.

He arrived thin and nervous, but after a couple of weeks of sunning, swimming and going to the UCLA clinic for walking exercises, he began to feel better, though not well enough to resume work. It was a quiet summer.

Upon return to New York in October, his life consisted of small dinners and quiet weekends in the country. The phantom pains still persisted, sometimes causing him to kick the artificial leg against the floor in frustration. On one such weekend when there was no guest, Ray Kelly drove over from Portland, Maine, to spend Sunday with him. That Sunday was an especially bad one for Cole, and Henry asked Kelly whether he would go into Cole's quarters and talk to him.

When Kelly walked in, Cole was sitting up in bed, beating it with his fists, saying, "If only I could die, if only I could die. . . ." Tears were streaming down his pain-wracked face. Suddenly he realized that someone was there.

"You could more or less see him pull himself together," Kelly said. "Then he looked up and smiled and said, 'I've been misbehaving, haven't I?' "

Some time later, Kelly made it a point to have a talk with Cole. "At one time, you could give him the devil and he'd fight back, but at the end there, he'd just agree with everything you had said. He'd just completely given up. It was a sad thing to see with a person of his ability and capabilities and one thing and another, but there was nothing anyone could do."

On March 30, 1963, Henry departed for a two-month vacation in England after having trained the temporary man in the requirements of the job. Since Cole enjoyed smoking before going to sleep, both Henry and Eric made it a practice to remain in the room until he had finished. The temporary man was given explicit instructions that he was not under any circumstances to leave his employer alone at night if he was smoking.

In a series of inexplicable mixups on Sunday evening, April 7, in Williamstown, not only did the temporary man leave Cole smoking in bed, but he also by mistake substituted Demarol for sleeping capsules.

No one knows exactly what happened, but by the time Cole realized something was wrong the bed was ablaze. He pushed the buzzer. The valet entered, saw the smoke, panicked and instead of beating out the fire ran to summon Bentley, who rushed over from his apartment above the garage and succeeded in smothering the flames, but not before Cole had been seriously burned.

Bentley called an ambulance, which rushed Cole from Williamstown to Harkenss Pavilion in New York where he was registered in Room 1036. There he remained for seventeen weeks, his misery so great that he scarcely responded when told that Peppi, who had been shipped ahead to California, had died on May 19.

Not until August was Cole released from the hospital, but by August 9, with the little finger of his right hand still bandaged, he left for Brentwood. During the siege in the hospital, the household had managed to keep the real story out of the papers, except for an inconspicuous item in *Variety*. Very few people were aware of this near tragedy or the suffering Cole went through from this new accident.

At this point Henry had been on the scene long enough

to become familiar with the effects produced by mixing little food with great quantities of medicine and Cutty Sark. He took it upon himself to tell his employer that the doctors had advised that he switch from Scotch to vodka. Surprisingly, Cole offered no opposition.

The ploy was a valuable one, for it made it possible for the drinks to be nine-tenths tonic and one-tenth vodka, since vodka has little taste. Then, as if he felt he had been too easy, Cole began to ask for Bloody Marys, a drink he had seldom requested previously. Because the tomato juice was considered harmful to his kidneys, the valets attempted to dissuade him, finally compromising on one Bloody Mary before dinner and vodka-and-tonics afterward.

With the diminishing of his alcoholic intake, Cole's outlook brightened. By the time he returned to New York in the fall of 1963, like the proverbial phoenix, he had renewed himself. He talked tentatively about attending the theater. He evidenced interest in reading the *Memoirs of Catherine the Great*, which he thought would make a good vehicle for Ethel Merman.

When I bought a paperback copy of the book, he took it and began to read with gusto. He continued reading it until Miss Merman announced her engagement to Ernest Borgnine and her decision to quit the stage. After that, according to Henry, Cole never read another page of the book.

There were, of course, many bad days, but there was no doubt that he was taking a renewed interest in life. Although he had for the most part given up seeing his socialite friends—with a few exceptions, such as Mrs. William Woodward, Mrs. Sumner Welles, Mr. and Mrs. Arnold Whitridge—he eagerly followed their activities, as well as those of the Jet Set.

Television, too, had become a focal point of his life and a target of his wit. One evening, when a weekend guest who was not favorably inclined toward panel shows asked Cole whether he wanted to watch "What's My Line?" since its lady villain, Dorothy Kilgallen, was absent, Cole nodded his assent. "I want to miss hating her," he explained.

Nor was this wit confined to television. When Colin Leslie Fox, the English boatsman and second Lord Hathaway, reported that he had just finished reading Somerset Maugham's *The Summing Up* and would like to meet the writer, Cole said, "Don't bother." Fox asked why; Cole merely repeated his original comment. Shortly after, the subject came up again, and Fox said that he had written Maugham about the book. "I hope," Cole piped up, "you said you knew me and I send my love."

On bad days, he simply sat. In an attempt to cheer him up, Mrs. Smith had recordings of various Broadway shows played during one luncheon. Upon hearing a score he'd written, he sat quietly until it finished, then shook his head in wonder and despair. "*How* did I ever do it?" he asked.

But for the most part throughout the winter of 1963 and the early months of 1964, he seemed to be experiencing a resurgence. In the spring, he began to seem slightly less alert, even though he was far from having relapsed into the state in which he languished for so long after the operation.

On June 9, 1964, Cole's seventy-third birthday, he invited me to dine, warning me that it wouldn't be exciting, as there would be no other guests. When I arrived at his apartment, not having seen him for eight days. I became alarmed. His hair, which was always neatly brushed, stood out on the left side of his head. His skin tone, usually aglow from recent sunlamp treatments, was a putty gray. The artificial leg had not been put on. And instead of his customary jaunty navy-blue suit with the untrimmed carnation in the lapel, he wore a dressing gown.

After wishing him happy birthday, I launched into a one-sided monologue of anecdote, opinion and aimless gossip, which I'd learned through experience generally evoked a response. This evening there was none. The curtain seemed to be down.

Initially I assumed he was suffering from birthday blues, but gradually I became aware that his body was periodically wracked by hiccoughs. Although he exhibited a contempt for middle-class conventions—rules against the use of toothpicks, excusing oneself for coughing, etc.—he apologetically told me that he had had the hiccoughs most of the day. When I suggested that perhaps he ought to call a doctor, he gave me an icy glare and changed the subject.

At 9:15, Eric announced that dinner was served. As usual I preceded my host into the dining area and walked to the window that overlooked the city, allowing Cole the opportunity to get to the table unobserved. Suddenly, an Oedipus-like cry of anguish sounded and was followed by the noise of wheels of the walker.

At the table, I noticed a scratch beside Cole's right eye. I also saw that his hands trembled greatly as he tried to light his cigarette. Apparently he realized I had heard the scream, because he explained that I would have to excuse him for not being good company. He had that morning slipped off the chair and fallen onto the stone floor in his bathroom, bruising the stump of his right leg. I again suggested calling a doctor, but Cole would not hear of it.

During dinner, he sampled the crabmeat cocktail, ate one olive, an inch-by-two-inch piece of steak and picked at a dab of ice cream. After coffee was served in the library, I suggested that I leave in order that he might get some rest.

"Stay," he said, adding that if he felt ready to retire he would let me know. Then he asked me to buzz Eric and ask for a codeine pill to stop his hiccoughing. Almost as soon as he had taken the pill, he fell asleep. I sat there for perhaps forty-five minutes; then he opened his eyes and, mistaking me for Eric, said, "I get up now."

I rang, and when Eric appeared I told him I was leaving and that I thought Cole wanted to go to bed. As I said goodnight, Cole reminded me that I was scheduled to go to Williamstown that weekend.

On Friday, June 12, Henry called to say that Mrs. Smith had been trying to reach me. The trip to the country was off. Instead, Cole was entering Harkness Pavilion. He had a fever and a high white-corpuscle count.

I was horrified when I heard that the doctor suspected that he had fractured his hip three days earlier in the bathroom fall. On his birthday, he must have been on the verge of shock. Yet there had been no one close enough to more than suggest that he see a doctor.

The fracture, luckily, turned out to be minor. But while Cole was in the hospital, the doctors took the opportunity to attempt to clear up a bladder infection which had been plaguing him and to build him up by intravenous feeding.

I went to visit him on the 14th and was heartened to find that he had improved to the extent that he was already resisting all the prescribed treatment of Dr. Dean and Dr. Atchley. He complained that lying on his side was uncomfortable; he groused at being forbidden alcoholic drinks; he demanded that he be allowed to smoke. In fact, he had abandoned all attempts to maintain a Spartan acceptance of his lot.

Whenever Henry and the nurse left the room, Cole demanded a cigarette. After the third one, I reminded him that he was to cut down. He responded with the familiar icy glare, then replied: "It's all I have left."

I gave him the cigarette.

The following Tuesday I went to see him again. After I had been there a little while, I left the room so that the nurse could attend him. When I returned twenty minutes later, Cole's face lighted up as he greeted me; then he called to Henry to ask when the other guests were arriving. Before anyone could answer, a look of despair crept over his face as he apologized, saying he was confused and had for the moment thought he was in California.

Dr. Dean and Dr. Atchley attributed these lapses to the drugs he was taking to clear up the bladder infection. They were, they said, pleased that his fever had subsided and his white-corpuscle count had dropped, but they predicted he would be hospitalized for at least a month.

Ten days later, he was released. On the 27th, he returned to his apartment where he remained until July 4, when he departed for what was to be his final visit to Brentwood.

After a shaky start, Cole once again seemed to be making a miraculous recovery. Bob Raison persuaded him that by having dinner served on trays and eliminating the trip to the dining room, he could see friends and yet remain immobile. Cole agreed.

That summer, for the first time in years, he began inviting new people, as well as the regulars. Actress Natalie Schafer was a frequent guest, as were actor John Cronin, screenwriter Frances Marion, film editor Peggy Gilbert, writer Hasse Nyborg, publicist Pat McDermott, Joan Blondell, Merle Oberon, along with many others.

Early in September, the phantom pains, which for a time had subsided, returned with increased intensity. Late that month, Bob Raison was spending a sunday at 416 North Rockingham when he realized that something was amiss. During the afternoon, he was out by the pool with Cole, reading the papers. Cole said that he was undergoing a new kind of pain and suggested that Raison go to the guest room. "I don't want you to see this," he said.

Raison, who had seen him through the depths following the amputation, said he'd stay. Cole spoke rather sharply to him, and Raison went to the guest room while Cole remained there, chain smoking—a new habit—and playing albums of his own songs. At dinner no mention was made of the incident.

Two days later, he phoned Raison to tell him that he was entering St. John's Hospital in Santa Monica and to ask him to reset all dinner engagements that had been made for the week. This request was complicated by the fact that he wanted no one to know he was hospitalized. Since the guests included Vivien Leigh, Merle Oberon, Julie Andrews and Tony Walton, Natalie Schafer, Peggy Elliot, Hasse Nyborg and George Cukor, the requested secrecy presented something of a problem in diplomacy; nevertheless Raison managed it.

As the only person who knew of Cole's hospitalization, Raison made it a practice to visit him daily. On the first day a nurse who was filling out the admittance form asked about religious affiliations.

"Put down none," Cole replied.

"Protestant?"

"Put down—none."

Raison spoke up to say that Cole had been a Baptist; why not put down Protestant?

Cole refused. Later, even when his condition had changed for the worse, he stood by his convictions.

Yet on the first day he was at St. John's, he seemed relaxed. He had a martini and, while Henry was out of the room, mischievously poured part of Raison's drink into his glass. (No mention was ever made of the cause of hospitalization—a bowel obstruction, which was not regarded as dangerous.)

The following day, Cole said that he could not drink because of X-ray tests he was about to undergo. Then in succeeding days, his condition began to deteriorate. He developed pneumonia. Since he had lost his appetite, intravenous feeding was begun. A flareup of the bladder infection developed. Simultaneously, Cole's frail body was seized by intense trembling.

When the shaking and the pneumonia began to disappear, Cole's delerium remained. The doctors in charge decided to call in Dr. Frederick Schlumberger for consultation. A new set of X-rays was taken, and it was discovered that a kidney stone had moved into and was wedged in a tube that connected the kidney and the bladder. This was causing the development of a toxic condition which would develop into uremic poisoning and would kill him if the stone was not removed. On the other hand, if the operation proved a success, he stood a good chance to recover.

Thus, on October 13, 1964, surgery was scheduled for 7:00 P.M. This late hour was chosen because the bladder infection from which he suffered is highly contagious and it was necessary to sterilize the operating room before using it again. The operation was a success and Cole withstood it well, although once again the trembling returned.

That final week, Stanley Musgrove and Bob Raison visited Cole daily, although he was unconscious and recognized no one. On October 15, Raison dropped by in the morning. That evening Musgrove arrived at the hospital. Cole was restless—turning, tossing and unconscious. The nurse was on duty. The valets were out to dinner. Musgrove stayed for a time, then left, drove back home and, on impulse, turned around and drove back to the hospital again. When he arrived, Cole was still restless.

A nurse came into the room and Musgrove stepped outside. At this point Henry and Eric returned from dinner. The nurse who was turning Cole on his side (because of the pneumonia) suddenly began to ring a bell. Three other nurses appeared and began flailing the patient's arms as if he were a drowning man. His heart had stopped beating. At 11:05, he was pronounced dead.

Next day, tributes appeared in the press all over the world. In New York, the *Herald Tribune* called Cole "The Gallant Singing Legend." The *Times* noted that the mere mention of all his songs caused one to be "flooded with the nostalgic glow of an entire era." *Variety* saluted his personal courage and described him as "one of the giant songwriters in the American musical theater." His fellow songwriters in the American Society of Composers, Authors and Publishers paid this tribute: "Cole Porter's talent in the creation of beautiful and witty songs was recognized as unique throughout the world. His brilliant contributions in the field of musical theater made him an international legend during his lifetime. . . ." And in the Columbia University *Spectator*, Stephen Handzo noted: "As Kern is the great romantic and Berlin is the great primitive, Porter remains the supreme sophisticate of American song." The *Daily News* summed up what many felt when it commented: "Porter's death marked the end of an era which beginning in the '20's and '30's revolutionized the Broadway musical—an entertainment many authorities consider the highest native American art form. There were three major composer lyricist teams: Richard Rodgers and Lorenz Hart, Jerome Kern and Oscar Hammerstein 2d, George and Ira Gershwin, and Cole Porter who worked superlatively alone."

As he worked, so he died.

When his body was taken to Peru, his valets accompanied it. In Peru, the instructions set forth in Cole's will were followed.

> I direct my Executors to arrange for no funeral or memorial service, but only for a private burial service to be conducted by the Pastor of the First Baptist Church in Peru, in the presence of my relatives and dear friends. At such service I request said Pastor to read the following quotation from the Bible:
>
> > *I am the resurrection and the life; he that believeth in me, though he were dead, yet shall he live; and whosoever liveth and believeth in me shall never die:*
>
> and to follow such quotation with the Lord's Prayer.
>
> I request that the foregoing be substantially the entire burial service, and that neither said Pastor nor anyone else deliver any memorial address whatsoever. I particularly direct that there be no service of any kind in New York City.

Thus, on a cold, rainy day in Peru, one part of the story ended. Cole's directions were carried out, and the man whom many consider the greatest composer of light music that America has produced was laid to rest between the two women who had played such important parts—one in preparing him and the other in everlastingly encouraging him to persevere so that he might fulfill the role he was destined to play in American music.

APPENDIX

NOTE: This is an attempt to assemble a list of Cole Porter's work. It is based on a variety of sources—theater programs, copyrights, ASCAP'S listing and Cole's own recollections. Records are sometimes contradictory. Nevertheless, I have attempted to check insofar as possible, and this is the result.

This appendix lists many songs which Mr. Porter composed for certain plays or pictures but were withdrawn by him. Therefore, the listing of these songs under the name of a play or picture does not necessarily mean that they were included in that play or picture.

1901:
The Song of the Birds

1902:
The Bobolink Waltz

1905-1909:

WORCESTER ACADEMY
Worcester, Massachusetts

Fi Fi Fifi
The Bearded Lady
The Tattooed Gentleman
Class Song—1909

1910:

Bingo Eli Yale — YALE
Bridget — New Haven, Connecticut

1911:

Bull Dog
Miss Chapel Street
(DKE smoker song, sometimes credited to 1910, sometimes to 1911.)

1912:

AND THE VILLAIN STILL PURSUED HER
Book: T. Gaillard Thomas 2d — Songs: Cole Porter

Songs:

We Are the Chorus of the Show
Strolling
The Lovely Heroine
I'm the Villain (introduced by E. Montillion "Monty" Woolley)
Twilight
Llewellyn
That Zip Cornwall Cooch
Charity
Queens of Terpsichore
Leaders of Society
Submarine
Barcelona Maid
Come to Bohemia
Dancing
Fare Thee Well
Silver Moon
Dear Doctor
Anytime

1912:

THE POT OF GOLD — December 4, 1912
Book: Almet F. Jenks — Songs: Cole Porter

Songs:

At the Rainbow
Bellboys
Longing for Dear Old Broadway
Melodrama
When I Used to Lead the Ballet
My Houseboat on the Thames
She Was a Fair Young Mermaid
Recitative
At the Rainbow
What a Charming Afternoon
Since We've Met
Exercise
We Are So Aesthetic
Scandal
I Wonder Where My Girl Is Now
My Salvation Army Queen
It's Awfully Hard When Mother's Not Along
I Want to Be Married
Ha, Ha, They Must Sail for Siberia
I Love You So
Loie and Chlodo
So Let Us Hail

1913:
THE KALEIDOSCOPE — April 30, 1913
No librettist credited — Songs: Cole Porter

Songs;

At the Dawn Tea
We Are Prom Girls
Chaperones
In the Land Where My Heart Was Born
Meet Me Beside the River
Beware of the Sophomore
Rick-Chick-a-Chick
Goodbye, My True Love
On My Yacht
We're a Group of Nonentities

Flower Maidens
Absinthe
The Absinthe Drip
As I Love You
Oh, What a Pretty Pair of Lovers
A Member of the Yale Elizabethan Club
Moon Man
My Georgia Girl

1914:
PARANOIA, or CHESTER OF THE Y.D.A.
By T. Lawrason Riggs and Cole Porter* April 24, 1914

Songs:

National Anthem
Entrance of Maidens
Oh, What a Lovely Princess
Won't You Come Crusading with Me
I Want to Row on the Crew
What Love Is
Down in the Dungeon Deep
Slow Sinks the Sun
The Prep School Widow
Idyll
I've a Shooting Box in Scotland (first version)
Down Lover's Lane
Flower Song
Dresden China Soldiers
Oh, What Terrible Suspense
Hail, Hail to Cyril

Miscellaneous Yale Songs:

Antoinette Birby
Moon, Moon
Washington Square

* Produced at Yale, although Riggs and Porter were doing post-graduate work at Harvard.

When We're Wed
When I Marry You
The Motor Car
I Want to Be a Yale Boy
A Football King
Morey's
Hail to Yale, Hail to Yale (music by Arthur Trootswyck, 1911)

1915:
Cincinnati — (Written by Porter for former Yale musical group's appearance before the Federation of Yale Clubs in that city.)

Esmeralda — (Lyrics and music: Cole Porter. Used in *Hands Up* on Broadway, August 23, 1915.)

Two Big Eyes — (Lyrics: John L Golden; music: Cole Porter. Used in *Miss Information* on Broadway, October 5, 1915.)

1916:
Cleveland — (Written by Porter for Federation of Yale Clubs gathering in Cleveland.)

1916:
SEE AMERICA FIRST — March 28, 1916
Book: T. Lawrason Riggs
Music: Cole Porter; lyrics: Riggs, Porter
Maxine Elliott Theater — 15 performances
Produced: Elizabeth Marbury — Staged: J. H. Benrimo

Cast: Clifton Webb, Red Eagle, Jeanne Cartier, Leo Gordon, Lloyd Carpenter, John H. Goldsworthy, Clara Palmer, Algernon Greig, Felix Adler, Roma June, Betty

Brewster, Gypsy O'Brien, Dorothie Bigelow, Sam Edwards, and others.

Songs:
I've a Shooting Box in Scotland (revised)
Oh Bright Fair Dream
Slow Sinks the Sun
Pity Me, Please
The Language of Flowers
Prithee, Come Crusading with Me
When I Used to Lead the Ballet (revised)
Something's Got to Be Done
Buy Her a Box at the Opera
Ever and Ever Yours
Lima
I've an Awful Lot to Learn
See America First

1918:

Alone with You	(Music: Melville Gideon; lyrics: Cole Porter. Thought to have been in an English production of *Very Good Eddie*.)
Altogether Too Fond of You	(Melvin Gideon, James Heard and Cole Porter. Credited to the English production of *Telling the Tale*.)

1919:
HITCHY-KOO of 1919 — October 6, 1919
Book: George V. Hobart
Music and lyrics: Cole Porter
Liberty Theater — 56 performances
Produced: Raymond Hitchcock — Staged: Julian Alfred

Cast: Raymond Hitchcock, Lillian Kemble Cooper, Sylvia Clark, Waneta Means, Charles Witzell, Mark Sullivan. James J. Doherty, Simone Cochet, Joseph Cook, Chief

Eagle Horse, Dan Brennan, Ursula O'Hare, Lucille Ager, Ruth Mitchell, Eleanor Sinclair, Billy Holbrook, Florence O'Denishawn, Josephine MacNicoll, Elaine Palmer, Princess White Deer and others.

Songs:

I Introduced
In Hitchy's Garden of Roses
When I Had a Uniform On
I've Got Somebody Waiting
Peter Piper
Bring Me Back My Butterfly
My Cozy Little Corner in the Ritz
An Old-Fashioned Garden
Another Sentimental Song
That Black and White Baby of Mine
The Sea Is Calling
I'm an Anesthetic Dancer

I Never Realized — (Music: Melville Gideon; lyrics: Cole Porter. Used in the English production of *The Eclipse* and in the 1919 edition of *Buddies* in New York for a time.)

1920:

Washington Square — (Lyrics: E. Ray Goetz and Cole Porter; music: Melville Gideon. Used in *As You Were*.)

Why Didn't We Meet Before?
Our Hotel
Look Around
— (Lyrics Clifford Grey; music: Cole Porter. These numbers were in the English production, *A Night Out*.)

1922:

MAYFAIR AND MONTMARTRE (revue, London only)
March 9, 1922

New Oxford Theater
Produced and staged: C.B. Cochran

Songs:

The Blue Boy Blues
Wand'ring Night and Day
Cocktail Time
Olga Come Back to the Volga
The Sponge

*Songs:**

PHI-PHI (London only) August 16, 1922
London Pavilion
Produced: C. B. Cochran

Song:

The Ragtime Pipes of Pan

HITCHY-KOO of 1922 (closed out of town)

Songs:

The American Punch
The Bandit Band
The Harbor Down Deep in My Heart
When My Caravan Comes Home
Love Letter Words

1923:

WITHIN THE QUOTA (ballet) October 25, 1923
Story: Gerald Murphy Music: Cole Porter
Produced: Ballet Suédois

* Most of Porter's work was cast aside and other songs were substituted.

1924:
GREENWICH VILLAGE FOLLIES (sixth edition)
September 16, 1924
Shubert Theater 127 performances
Produced: The Bohemians, Inc.
Staged: John Murray Anderson

Cast: Vincent Lopez and Orchestra, The Dolly Sisters, George Moran and Charles Mack, Dorothy Neville, Georgie Hale, Bobbe Arnst, George Rasley, Don Barclay, Julia Silvers, Billie de Rex, George Christie, Maisie Clifton, Roshanara, James Clemons, Ludmilla, James Naulty, John Sheehan, Robert Alton, America Chedister, Ethel Davies and others.

*Songs:**

Brittany
I'm in Love Again
Wait for the Moon
Syncopated Pipes of Pan
My Long Ago Girl
Make Ev'ry Day a Holiday
Long, Long Ago
Toy of Destiny
Bring Me a Radio
Broadcast Jazz

1925:
OUT O' LUCK December 17, 1925
Play C. S. "Tom" Cushing (Yale, '02) Songs: Cole Porter
Produced: Yale Dramatic Society Directed: Monty Woolley

* Most of Porter's work was cast aside and other songs were substituted.

Songs:

The Opera Song (introduced by John Hoysradt)
Butterflies
Madamezelle

Tour:

Bridgeport, Conn., December 17; New York, N.Y., December 18; Albany, N.Y., December 21; Rochester, N.Y., December 22; Buffalo, N.Y., December 23; Pittsburgh, Pa., December 24; Washington, D.C., December 26; Wilkes-Barre, Pa., December 28.

1926:
Hot House Rose
Weren't We Fools?*

1927:
The Laziest Gal in Town

1928:
IN THE OLD DAYS AND TODAY (nightclub revue)
May 12, 1928
Des Ambassadeurs Club, Paris

Cast: Frances Gershwin, Fred Waring, Buster West, Morton Downey, Evelyn Hoey, Clifton Webb, Dorothy Dickson and others.

Songs:

Keep Moving
The Lost-Liberty Blues
Gershwin Specialty
Omnibus
Pilot Me

* These songs were written for Fanny Brice but never used.

In a Moorish Garden
Almiro
You and Me
Fish
Military Maids
Blue Hours
Alpine Rose
Excelsior
Hans
Baby, Let's Dance
Old-Fashioned Girl
Old-Fashioned Boy
Fountain of Youth
Looking at You

1928:
PARIS October 8, 1928
Book: Martin Brown
Songs: Cole Porter, E. Ray Goetz, Walter Kollo
Music Box Theater 195 performances
Produced: Gilbert Miller in association with Goetz
Directed: W. H. Gilmore

Cast:

Andrew Sabot	Erik Kalkhurst
Harriet	Florence Edney
Valet	Reed Hamilton
Brenda Kaley	Elizabeth Chester
Cora Sabot	Louise Closser Hale
Guy Pennel	Arthur Margetson
Vivienne Rolland	Irene Bordoni
Marcel Prince	Theodore St. John

*Songs:**

Let's Do It
Don't Look at Me That Way
Two Little Babes in the Wood
Vivienne
I've Got Quelque Chose
Which
The Heaven Hop
Let's Misbehave
Dizzy Baby

1929:
THE BATTLE OF PARIS (film)
Paramount Pictures

Cast: Gertrude Lawrence, Charles Ruggles, Arthur Treacher

Songs:

Here Comes the Band Wagon
They All Fall in Love

WAKE UP AND DREAM (London) — March 27, 1929
Sketches: John Turner Hastings — Songs: Cole Porter
London Pavilion — 263 performances
Produced: C. B. Cochran — Staged: Frank Collins

Cast: Jessie Matthews, Sonnie Hale, George Metaxa, Tilly Losch, William Stephens, Elsie Carlisle, Douglas Byng, Fred Groves, Laurie Devine, Toni Birkmayer, Alanova, Tina Meller, the Berknoffs, Marge Finley, Chester Fredericks, Ann Codrington, Lance Lister,

* Songs listed for shows were often dropped, tried in another show and dropped again. "Let's Misbehave," for example, was dropped out of town in favor of "Let's Do It."

Moya Nugent, Emil Grimshaw Quartet, Antonio Rodriguez, June Roper, Jack Kinney.

Songs:

Wake Up and Dream
I'm a Gigolo
What Is This Thing Called Love?
Let's Do It
Looking at You
The Banjo, That Man Joe Plays
Agua Sincopada (tango, instrumental)
Tale of an Oyster (piano part, no lyrics)

1929:
FIFTY MILLION FRENCHMEN November 27, 1929
Book: Herbert Fields Songs: Cole Porter
Lyric Theater 254 performances
Produced: E. Ray Goetz Book staged: Monty Woolley

Cast:

Michael Cummins	Jack Thompson
Billy Baxter	Lester Crawford
Marcelle Fouchard	Dorothy Day
Louis	Ignatio Martinetti
Joyce Wheeler	Betty Compton
Emmitt Carroll	Thurston Hall
Gladys Carroll	Bernice Mershon
Peter Forbes	William Gaxton
Looloo Carroll	Genevieve Tobin
Sylvia	Fifi Laimbeer
May DeVere	Evelyn Hoey
Mrs. DeVere	Gertrude Mudge
Mr. Ira Rosen	Robert Leonard
Mrs. Rosen	Annette Hoffman
Junior	Larry Jason
Violet Hildegarde	Helen Broderick
Boule DeNeige	Billy Reed

Oscar	Lou Duthers
M. Pernasse	Mario Villani
Le Sahib Roussin	Jean Del Val
The Grand Duke Ivan	Mannart Kippen
Joe Zelli	Jean Del Val
Maître d'Hôtel	Oscar Magis

Songs:

A Toast to Volstead
You Do Something to Me
The American Express
You've Got That Thing
Find Me a Primitive Man
Where Would You Get Your Coat?
Do You Want to See Paris?
At Longchamps Today
The Happy Heaven of Harlem
Why Should I Have You?
It Isn't Done
I'm in Love
The Tale of an Oyster
Paree, What Did You Do to Me?
You Don't Know Paree
I'm Unlucky in Gambling
*Stepping Out
Why Don't We Try Staying Home?
That's Why I Love You
Watching the World Go By
Queen of Terre Haute
Please Don't Make Me Be Good
I Worship You

* Discarded from show.

1929:
WAKE UP AND DREAM (New York)
December 30, 1929
Selwyn Theater 136 performances
Produced: Arch Selwyn in association with C. B. Cochran
Staged: Frank Collins

Cast: Jessie Matthews, Jack Buchanan, William Stephens, Tilly Losch, Toni Birkmayer, Tina Meller, Dave Fitzgibbon, Jean Barry, Lance Lister, Marjorie Brooks, Claude Newman, Wyn Clare, Roy Mitchell, Frances Shelley, A. B. Imeson, Greta Wood, Douglas Phillips, Ann Barberova, Gomez Trio, Mary Tomlinson and others.

Songs:

Wake Up and Dream
I Loved Him But He Didn't Love Me
What Is This Thing Called Love?
Only a School Girl
Which Is the Right Life?
I'm a Gigolo
The Banjo, That Man Joe Plays
Looking at You
Agua Sincopada
I Want to Be Raided by You
I Dream of a Girl in a Shawl
If You Take One Pill
The Extra Man
The Lady I Love

1930:
THE NEW YORKERS December 8, 1930
Book: Herbert Fields Songs: Cole Porter, Jimmy Durante
Broadway Theater 168 performances
Produced: E. Ray Goetz Staged: Monty Woolley

Cast:

Nurse	Marjorie Arnold
Dr. Dortland Jenks	Paul Huber
Alice Wentworth	Hope Williams
Felix	Charles Angelo
Dr. Windham Wentworth	Richard Carle
Lola McGee	Ann Pennington
Gloria Wentworth	Marie Cahill
Alfredo Gomez	Maurice Lapue
James Livingston	Barrie Oliver
Mona Low	Frances Williams
Al Spanish	Charlie King
Jimmie Deegan	Jimmy Durante
Oscar Gregory	Lew Clayton
Grover McGeehan	Eddie Jackson
Butch McGeehan	Tammany Young
Burns	Ralph Glover
Dopey	Billy Culloo
May	Kathryn Crawford
Attendant at Sing Sing	Donald McGinnis
Plague	Stanley Harrison
Mildew	Oscar Ragland
	and Fred Waring and his Pennsylvanians

Songs:

Go Into Your Dance
Where Have You Been?
Say It with Gin
Venice
I'm Getting Myself Ready for You
Love for Sale
The Great Indoors
Sing Sing for Sing Sing
Take Me Back to Manhattan

Let's Fly Away
But He Never Says He Loves Me
Just One of Those Things (first song, not same as later one)
I Happen to Like New York
Let's Step Out

1931:
FIFTY MILLION FRENCHMEN (film) Warner Brothers

Cast: William Gaxton, Helen Broderick

1932:
GAY DIVORCE November 29, 1932
Book: Dwight Taylor, based on J. Hartley Manners' unproduced play; musical adaptation: Kenneth Webb and Samuel Hoffenstein Songs: Cole Porter
New York: Ethel Barrymore Theater 248 performances
Produced: Dwight Deere Wiman and Tom Weatherly
Staged: Howard Lindsay
London: Palace Theater, November 2, 1933
180 performances
Starred: Fred Astaire and Claire Luce

Cast:

Robert	Taylor Gordon
Guy	Fred Astaire
Teddy	G. P. Huntley, Jr.
Gladys	Jean Frontai
Doris	Mary Jo Mathews
Vivian	Helen Allen
Barbara	Betty Starbuck
Phyllis	Eleanor Etheridge
Joan	Joan Burgess
Joyce	Dorothy Waller
Waiter	Eric Blore
Ann	Billie Green
Hortense	Luella Gear

Mimi	Claire Luce
Porter	Martin Cravath
Tonetti	Erik Rhodes
Sonia	Sonia B. Fitch
Pat	Pat Palmer
Diana	Mitzi Garner
Claire	Edna Abbey
Elaine	Jacquie Simmons
Edith	Ethel Hampton
Evelyn	Grace Moore
Beatrice	Bobby Sheehan
Elizabeth	Hulda Hedvig
Mr. Pratt	Roland Bottomley

Songs:

After You, Who?
Why Marry Them?
Salt Air
I Still Love the Red, White and Blue
Night and Day
How's Your Romance?
What Will Become of Our England?
I've Got You on My Mind
Mister and Missus Fitch
You're in Love
It All Seems So Long Ago
Coffee
Fate
Gypsy Song
The Night of the Ball
Technique

1933:

NYMPH ERRANT (London)	October 6, 1933
Book: Romney Brent	Songs: Cole Porter
Adelphi Theater	154 performances
Produced: Charles B. Cochran	Staged: Romney Brent

Cast:

Winnie	Betty Hare
Edith Sandford	Winifred Oughton
Aunt Ermyntrude	Margaret Emden
Dr. Sandford	Ralph Roberts
Rev. Mr. Pither	Wilfred Caithness
Bertha	Hella Kurty
Joyce	Norah Howard
Henrietta	Doris Carson
Madeleine	Iris Ashley
Evangeline	Gertrude Lawrence
Miss Pratt	Moya Nugent
Andre de Croissant	Austin Trevor
Madame Celestine Arthur	May Agate
Hercule	Jean Davaut
Four Bored Visitors	Gerald Nodin, Annabel Gibson, Kenneth Ware, Betty Hare
Alexei	Alexander Ivo
Count Hohenadelborn-Mantalini	Morton Selton
Clarissa Parks	Queenie Leonard
Waiter	Kenneth Ware
A Frenchman	William Harn
Pierre Fort	Gerald Nodin
Pedro Bernanos	Taylor Reed
A Major Domo	Gerald Nodin
A Gondolier	Kenneth Ware
A Footman	David Shenstone
A Cook	Annabel Gibson
A Kitchen Maid	Betty Hare
Bessie	Sheila Marlyn
Mrs. Bamberg	Jessie Busley
Constantine	David Burns
Tourists	Gerald Nodin,

	Annabel Gibson, Kenneth Ware, Betty Hare
Demetrios Pappas	Arthur Grenville
A Greek Dancer	Eve
Other Greek Dancers (Mr. Cochran's Young Ladies)	Babs Blythe, Peggy de Beer, Margaret Braithwaite, Patricia Burke, Iris Houston, Barbara Glen, Sheila Marlyn, Bubbly Rogers, Pat Watson
Feliza	Winifred Oughton
Kassim	Ralph Roberts
The Dancer	Eve
Ali	Bruce Winston
An Attendant	William Harn
Haidee Robinson	Elizabeth Welch
Ben Winthrop	Walter Crisham
Wives	Marie Menckoff, Thea Camacho, Anita Leslie, Emma Trechman, Rosalie Corneille
1st Chorus Girl	Patricia Burke
2d Chorus Girl	Sheila Marlyn
An Electrician	Kenneth Ware
Stage Manager	Jean Davaut
Call Boy	Tommy Hayes
Persian Poitrine	Thea Camacho
Chinese Poitrine	Eileen Moore
Javanese Poitrine	Jackie Marcon
Hindu Poitrine	Nancy Millard
Two Girls from the Hostel	Marie Nenckoff, Rosalie Corneille
Les Deux Pious-Pious	David Shenstone, William Harn
Jo	Edward Underdown

Songs:

Experiment
It's Bad for Me
Neauville sur Mer
Beach Ball Dance
The Cocotte
How Could We Be Wrong?
They're Always Entertaining
Georgia Sand (instrumental)
Nymph Errant
Ruins
Carefree Carayatides
The Physician
Solomon
Back to Nature
Plumbing
If You Like les Belles Poitrines
When Tea Is Served
Entrance of Madeline
When Love Comes Your Way
You're Too Far Away
Count's Theme
Entrance of Greeks
Smirna
Harem Dance
Casanova
Sweet Nudity
My Louisa

1934:
WAKE UP AND DREAM (film) Universal

Cast: June Knight, Russ Colombo

THE GAY DIVORCEE (film) RKO Pictures

Cast: Ginger Rogers, Fred Astaire, Edward Everett Horton, Alice Brady, Erik Rhodes, Eric Blore

Note: Only "Night and Day" was used from the original score. Con Conrad's "The Continental," written for this picture, won an Oscar.

1934:

ANYTHING GOES — November 21, 1934

Book: P. G. Wodehouse and Guy Bolton; revised: Howard Lindsay and Russel Crouse

Songs: Cole Porter

Alvin Theater — 420 performances

Produced: Vinton Freedley — Staged: Howard Lindsay

London: Palace Theater — June 14, 1935

Produced: C. B. Cochran — 261 performances

Cast:

Bartender	George E. Mack
Elisha J. Whitney	Paul Everton
Billy Crocker	William Gaxton
Bellboy	Irvin Pincus
Reno Sweeney	Ethel Merman
Reporter	Edward Delbridge
First Cameraman	Chet Bree
Second Cameraman	Neal Evans
Sir Evelyn Oakleigh	Leslie Barrie
Hope Harcourt	Bettina Hall
Mrs. Wadsworth T. Harcourt	Helen Raymond
Bishop Dodson	Pacie Ripple
Ching	Richard Wang
Ling	Charlie Fang
Snooks	Drucilla Strain
Steward	William Stamm
Assistant Purser	Val Vestoff
First Federal Man	Harry Wilson
Second Federal Man	Arthur Imperato
Mrs. Wentworth	May Abbey

Mrs. Frick	Florence Earle
Reverend Dr. Moon	Victor Moore
Bonnie Letour	Vera Dunn
Chief Officer	Houston Richards
Ship's Drunk	William Barry
Mr. Swift	Maurice Elliott
Little Boy	Billy Curtis
Captain	John C. King
Babe	Vivian Vance

London Cast: Jack Whiting, Jeanne Aubert, Sydney Howard, Adele Dixon, Betty Kean, Peter Haddon

Songs:

I Get a Kick Out of You
Bon Voyage
All Through the Night
There'll Always Be a Lady Fair
Where Are the Men?
You're the Top
Anything Goes
Public Enemy Number One
Blow, Gabriel, Blow
Be Like a Blue Bird
The Gypsy in Me
What a Joy to Be Young
Kate, the Great
Pick Me Up and Lay Me Down
I Worship You
Blow, Gabriel, Blow (first version)
Mysteriously
Die Schoene Wirts-Tochter
Buddie Beware

Miscellaneous—1934:

Miss Otis Regrets She's Unable to Lunch Today
Thank You So Much, Missus Lowsborough—Goodby
You're Too Far Away

1935:
JUBILEE October 12, 1935
Book: Moss Hart Songs: Cole Porter
Imperial Theater 169 performances
Produced: Sam H. Harris and Max Gordon
Staged: Hassard Short

Cast:

The King	Melville Cooper
The Queen	Mary Boland
Prince James	Charles Walters
Princess Diana	Margaret Adams
Prince Peter	Montgomery Clift
Prince Rudolph	Jackie Kelk
Lord Wyndham	Richie Ling
Eric Dare	Derek Williams
Karen O'Kane	June Knight
Eva Standing	May Boley
Charles Rausmiller (Mowgli)	Mark Plant
Mrs. Watkins	Jane Evans
Laura Fitzgerald	Olive Reeves-Smith
A Sandwich Man	Charles Brokaw
Professor Rexford	Ralph Sumpter
The Beach Widow	Dorothy Fox
Cabinet Ministers	Leo Chalzell, Charles Brokaw
Lifeguard	Don Douglas
Announcer	Albert Amato
Master of Ceremonies	Harold Murray
The Drunk	Jack Edwards

The Usher	Ted Fetter
Keeper of the Zoo	Leo Chalzell

Songs

Begin the Beguine
We're Off to Feathermore
Why Shouldn't I?
Entrance of Eric
The Kling-Kling Bird in the Divi-Divi Tree
When Love Comes Your Way
What a Nice Municipal Park
When Me, Mowgli, Love
My Most Intimate Friend
A Picture of Me Without You
Ev'rybod-ee Who's Anybod-ee
The Judgment of Paris
Swing That Swing
Sunday Morning Breakfast Time
Mr. and Mrs. Smith
Gay Little Wives
Me and Marie
Just One of Those Things
Our Crown
Gather Ye Autographs
My Loulou
Waltz Down the Aisle
There's Nothing Like Swimming
Greek Scene: Wrestler's Music
Jubilee Presentation
Eric
Good Morning, Miss Standing
Sing Jubilee
Yours
To Get Away
Opening to Beach Scene

1935:
ADIOS ARGENTINA (unproduced film) Fox Pictures

Songs:

Don't Fence Me In
Chiripah
Sidecar

1936:
BORN TO DANCE (original film score)
Metro-Goldwyn-Mayer
Original story: Jack McGowan, Sid Silvers, B. G. De Sylva
Screenplay: McGowan and Silvers Songs: Cole Porter
Directed: Roy Del Ruth

Cast:

Nora Paige	Eleanor Powell
Ted Barker	James Stewart
Lucy James	Virginia Bruce
Jenny Saks	Una Merkel
Gunny Saks	Sid Silvers
Peppy Turner	Frances Langford
Captain Dingby	Raymond Walburn
McKay	Alan Dinehart
Mush McKay	Buddy Ebsen
Sally Saks	Juanita Quigley
Georges and Jalna	Themselves
Policeman	Reginald Gardiner
Floorwalker	Barrett Parker

Songs:

Rap Tap on Wood
Easy to Love
Hey, Babe, Hey!
I've Got You Under My Skin
Love Me, Love My Pekinese

Rollin' Home
Swingin' the Jinx Away
Who But You?
Entrance of Lucy James
Ours
It's De-Lovely
Goodbye, Little Dream, Goodbye

ANYTHING GOES* (film) Paramount Pictures

Cast: Ethel Merman, Bing Crosby, Ida Lupino, Charles Ruggles

1936:
RED, HOT AND BLUE! October 29, 1936
Book: Howard Lindsay and Russel Crouse
Songs: Cole Porter
Alvin Theater 183 performances
Produced: Vinton Freedley Staged: Howard Lindsay

Cast:

Reporters	Geoffrey Errett, Karl Kohrs, Bill Houston, Norman Lind, Vivian Vance, Betty Allen
Deputy Warden	Lew Parker
Warden of Larks Nest Prison	Forrest Orr
"Nails" O'Reilly Duquesne	Ethel Merman
"Policy" Pinkle	Jimmy Durante
Vivian	Vivian Vance
Anne Westcott	Dorothy Vernon
Grace	Grace Hartman
Lucille	Lucille Johnson
Cecile	Cecile Carey
Kay	Kay Picture

* Sold to television years later, its title was changed to *Tops Is the Limit.*

Irene	Ethelyne Holt
Betty	Betty Allen
"Fingers"	Paul Hartman
Bob Hale	Bob Hope
Sonny Hadley	Thurston Crane
Peaches La Fleur	Polly Walters
"Ratface" Dugan	Bill Benner
"Sure-Thing" Simpson	Prentiss Davis
"Flap-Ears" Metelli	Leo Schippers
"Louie the Louse"	Bernard Jannsen
Mrs. Peabody	May Abbey
Tiny	Anne Wolf
Louella	Jeanette Owens
Senator Musilovitch	Lew Parker
Senator Malvinsky	Robert Leonard
Senator O'Shaughnessy	Forrest Orr
Senator Del Grasso	Houston Richards
Sergeant-at-Arms	Norman Lind
First Expressman	Geoffrey Errett
Second Expressman	Karl Kohrs
Girl	Gloria Clare
First Marine	Frank Archer
Second Marine	Bruce Covert
Decorator	Houston Richards

Songs:

At Ye Olde Coffee Shoppe in Cheyenne
It's a Great Life
Perennial Debutantes
Ours
Down in the Depths on the 90th Floor
Carry On
You've Got Something
Goodbye, Little Dream, Goodbye
It's De-Lovely
A Little Skipper from Heaven Above
Five Hundred Million
Ridin' High

We're About to Start Rehearsin'
Hymn to Hymen
What a Great Pair We'll Be
You're a Bad Influence on Me
Red, Hot, and Blue
The Ozarks Are Callin' Me Home
Bertie and Gertie
Finaletto, Act II, Scene I
When Your Troubles Have Started
I Can Do Without Tea in My Teapot

1937:
ROSALIE (original film score) Metro-Goldwyn-Mayer
Screenplay: William Anthony McGuire; based on play by McGuire and Guy Bolton Songs: Cole Porter

Cast:

Rosalie	Eleanor Powell
Dick Thorpe	Nelson Eddy
King	Frank Morgan
Queen	Edna May Oliver
Bill Delroy	Ray Bolger
Brenda	Ilona Massey
Oloff	Billy Gilbert
Chanceloor	Reginald Owen
Prince Paul	Tom Rutherford
Mary Callahan	Virginia Gray

Songs:

Rosalie (five versions in addition to one used)
Who Knows?
In the Still of the Night
Why Should I Care?
I've a Strange New Rhythm in My Heart
Close
National Anthem (three versions)
It's All Over But the Shouting

Opening Romanza Sequence
I Know it's Not Meant for Me
Spring Love Is in the Air
To Love or Not to Love

Miscellaneous—1937:

A Fool There Was (Robbins music)

1938:
BREAK THE NEWS (film) Buchanan—G.F.D.

Cast: Maurice Chevalier

Song: It All Belongs to You

YOU NEVER KNOW September 21, 1938
Book: Robert Katscher, Siegfried Geyer and Karl Farkas; adapted: Rowland Leigh
Songs: Cole Porter, Leigh, Katscher, Dana Suesse, Edwin Gilbert, Alex Fogarty
Winter Garden Theater 78 performances
Produced: Messrs. Shubert in association with John Shubert
Staged: Rowland Leigh and George Abbott

Cast:

Gaston	Clifton Webb
Baron Ferdinand de Romer	Rex O'Malley
Chauffeur	Eddie Gale
Ida Courtney	Toby Wing
Maria	Lupe Velez
Henri Baltin	Charles Kemper
Mme. Baltin	Libby Holman
Louis	Wesley Bender
Headwaiter	Roger Stearns
Geoffrey	Dan Harden

General Carruthers	Truman Gaige
Comptroller	Ray Dennis

Songs:

I Am Gaston
Au Revoir, Cher Baron
Maria
You Never Know
What Is That Tune?
For No Rhyme or Reason
From Alpha to Omega
Don't Let It Get You Down
What Shall I Do? (lyric by Rowland Leigh)
Yes, Yes, Yes
Good Evening, Princess
Just One Step Ahead of Love
I'll Black His Eyes
I'm Yours
At Long Last Love

1938:
LEAVE IT TO ME — November 9, 1938
Book: Samuel and Bella Spewack — Songs: Cole Porter
Imperial Theater — 291 performances
Produced: Vinton Freedley — Staged: Samuel Spewack

Cast:

First Secretary	Ruth Bond
Second Secretary	Beverly Hosier
Buckley Joyce Thomas	William Gaxton
First Reporter	William Lilling
Second Reporter	Walter Monroe
Dolly Winslow	Mary Martin
J. R. Brody	Edward H. Robbins
Mrs. Goodhue	Sophie Tucker

Mrs. Goodhue's daughters	April, Mildred Chenaval, Ruth Daye, Audrey Palmer, Kay Picture
Reporter	Chet Bree
Photographer	George E. Mack
French Conductor	Walter Armin
Chauffeur	James W. Carr
Alonzo P. Goodhue	Victor Moore
Secretaries	Gene Kelly, Maurice Kelly, Roy Ross, Jack Seymour, Jack Stanton, Walter B. Long, Jr.
Prince Alexander Tomofsky	George Tobias
Jerry Granger	Dean Carlton
Colette	Tamara
Kostya	Joseph Kallini
Peasant	Peter Lopouhin
Sozanoff	Alexander Asro
Military Attaché	John Eliot
Naval Attaché	John Panter
Secretaries	Roy Ross, Jack Seymour, Michael Forbes, Thomas Jafollo
Waiter	Don Cortez
German Ambassador	Hans Hansen
French Ambassador	Walter Armin
Latvian Ambassador	Peter Lopouhin
British Ambassador	J. Colville Dunn
Italian Ambassador	Thomas Jafollo
Japanese Ambassador	George E. Mack
Mackenzie	Charles Campbell
Graustein	Eugene Sigaloff
Folkin	Ivan Izmailov
Secretary	Stanton Bier
Foreign Minister	Alexis Bolan
Stalin	Walter Armin

Songs:

How Do You Spell Ambassador?
We Drink to You, J. R. Brody
Vite, Vite, Vite
I'm Taking the Steps to Russia
Get Out of Town
When All's Said and Done
Most Gentlemen Don't Like Love
Comrade Alonzo
From Now On
I Want to Go Home
My Heart Belongs to Daddy
Tomorrow
Far, Far Away
To the USA from the USSR
Comrade Alonzo, We Love You
Just Another Page in Your Diary
Information Please
There's a Pan
When the Hen Stops Laying
Recall Goodhue (recitative)

1939:
THE SUN NEVER SETS (film) — Universal Pictures

Cast: Basil Rathbone, Douglas Fairbanks, Jr.

Song: River God

1939:
DUBARRY WAS A LADY — December 6, 1939
Book: Herbert Fields and B. G. De Sylva
Songs: Cole Porter
New York: 46th Street Theater — 408 performances
Produced: B. G. De Sylva — Staged: Edgar MacGregor
London: His Majesty's, October 22, 1942
178 performances

Cast

Jones	Hugh Cameron
Bill Kelly	Walter Armin
Harry Norton	Charles Walters
Alice Varton	Betty Grable
Florian	Harold Cromer
Louis Blore	Bert Lahr
Vi Hennessey	Jean Moorehead
May Daly	Ethel Merman
Alex Barton	Ronald Graham
Ann Barton	Kay Sutton
Manuel Gomez	Tito Renaldo
Charley	Benny Baker

At Versailles:

Le Duck de Choiseul	Hugh Cameron
Mme. LaDuchesse de Grammot	Kay Sutton
Mme. LaComtesse DuBarry	Ethel Merman
Mme. La Marquise Alisande de Vernay	Betty Grable
Captain of King's Guard	Charles Walters
Zamore	Harold Cromer
His Most Royal Majesty, the King of France	Bert Lahr
Mme. La Duchesse de Villardell	Jean Moorehead
Cosette	Audrey Palmer
René	Jack Stanton
Pierre	Roy Ross
Gateman	Carl Nicholas
Docteur Michel	Walter Armin
Henri	Johnny Barnes

Songs:

Ev'ry Day a Holiday
It Ain't Etiquette
When Love Beckoned
Come On In
Dream Song
Mesdames et Messieurs
Gavotte
But in the Morning, No!
Do I Love You, Do I?
Danse Victoire
Danse Erotique
DuBarry Was a Lady
Danse Tzigane
Give Him the Oo-La-La
Well, Did you Evah!
It Was Written in the Stars
L'Après Midi d'un Boeuf
Katie Went to Haiti
Friendship
What Have I?
Zombie Dance

Miscellaneous—1939:

At Last in Your Arms
I'm So in Love With You

1940:
BROADWAY MELODY OF 1940 (original film score)
Metro-Goldwyn-Mayer
Screenplay: Leo Gordon, George Oppenheimer; original story: Jack McGowan, Dore Schary
Directed: Norman Taurog Songs: Cole Porter

Cast:

Johnny Brett	Fred Astaire
Clara Brett	Eleanor Powell
King Shaw	George Murphy
Bob Casey	Frank Morgan
Bert C. Mathews	Ian Hunter
Amy Blake	Florence Rice
Emmy Lou Lee	Lynne Carver
Pearl	Ann Morriss
Juggler	Trixie Firschke
Masked Singer	Douglas McPhail

Songs:

I Concentrate on You
I've Got My Eyes on You
Please Don't Monkey with Broadway
Between You and Me
I Happen to Be in Love
Begin the Beguine (used from *Jubilee* score since that show was never filmed)

1940:
PANAMA HATTIE October 30, 1940
Book: Herbert Fields and B. G. De Sylva Songs: Cole Porter
New York: 46th Street Theater 501 performances
Produced: B. G. De Sylva Directed: Edgar MacGregor
London: Piccadilly Theater, November 4, 1943
308 performances

Cast:

Mrs. Gonzales	Conchita
Mac	Eppy Pearson
Skat Briggs	Pat Harrington
Windy Deegan	Frank Hyers
Woozy Hogan	Rags Ragland

Chiquita	Nadine Gae
Fruit Peddler	Linda Griffith
Tim	Roger Gerry
Tom	Raymond Blaine
Ted	Ted Daniels
Ty	Lipman Duckat
Hattie Maloney	Ethel Merman
Lelia Tree	Phyllis Brooks
Mildred Turner	Elaine Shepard
Kitty Belle Randolph	Ann Graham
Nick Bullett	James Dunn
Florrie	Betty Hutton
Geraldine Bullett	Joan Carroll
Vivian Budd	Arthur Treacher
Pete	Al Downing
First Stranger	Hal Conklin
Second Stranger	Frank De Ross
Mike	Jack Donahue
Whitney Randolph	James Kelso

Songs:

Join It Right Away
Visit Panama
American Family
My Mother Would Love You
I've Still Got My Health
Fresh As a Daisy
Welcome to Jerry
Let's Be Buddies
They Ain't Done Right by Our Nell
I'm Throwing a Ball Tonight
I Detest a Fiesta
Who Would Have Dreamed?
Make It Another Old Fashioned, Please
All I've Got to Get Now Is My Man
You Said It
God Bless the Women
Americans All Drink Coffee

1941:
YOU'LL NEVER GET RICH (original film score)
Columbia Pictures
Screenplay: Michael Fessier and Ernest Pagano
Songs: Cole Porter
Directed: Sidney Lanfield

Cast:

Robert Curtis	Fred Astaire
Sheila Winthrop	Rita Hayworth
Martin Cortland	Robert Benchley
Tom Barton	John Hubbard
Sonya	Osa Massen
Mrs. Cortland	Frieda Inescort
Kewpie Blain	Guinn Williams
Top Sergeant	Donald MacBride
Swivel Tongue	Cliff Nazarro
Aunt Louise	Marjorie Gateson
Mrs. Barton	Anne Shoemaker
Colonel Shiller	Boyd Davis

Songs:

Since I Kissed My Baby Goodbye
So Near and Yet So Far
The Wedding Cake-Walk
Dream Dancing
Shootin' the Works for Uncle Sam
Boogie Barcarolle
A-Stairable Rag

Miscellaneous—1941

My Barcelona Maid (written 1912; copyrighted 1941)

1941:

LET'S FACE IT — October 29, 1941

Book: Herbert and Dorothy Fields — Songs: Cole Porter

New York: Imperial Theater — 303 performances

Produced: Vinton Freedley — Staged: Edgar MacGregor

London: Hippodrome Theater, November 19, 1942

348 performances

Cast:

Polly Lee	Janice Joyce
Madge Hall	Marguerite Benton
Helen Marcy	Helene Bliss
Dorothy Crowthers	Helen Devlin
Anna	Kalita Humphreys
Winnie Potter	Mary Jane Walsh
Mrs. Fink	Lois Bolton
Mrs. Wigglesworth	Margie Evans
Another Maid	Sally Bond
Maggie Watson	Eve Arden
Julian Watson	Joseph Macaulay
Nancy Collister	Vivian Vance
George Collister	James Todd
Cornelia Abigail Pigeon	Edith Meiser
Judge Henry Clay Pigeon	Fred Irving Lewis
Molly Wincor	Marion Harvey
Margaret Howard	Beverly Whitney
Ann Todd	Jane Ball
Phillip	Henry Austin
Jules	Tony Caridi
Eddie Hilliard	Jack Williams
Frankie Burns	Benny Baker
Muriel McGillicuddy	Sunnie O'Dea
Jean Blanchard	Nanette Fabray
Lieutenant Wiggins	Houston Richards
Jerry Walker	Danny Kaye
Gloria Gunther	Betty Moran
Sigana Earle	Miriam Franklin
Master of Ceremonies	William Lilling

Private Walsh	Fred Nay
Dance Team	Mary Parker, Billy Daniel
Mrs. Wiggins	Kalita Humphreys

Songs:

Milk, Milk, Milk
A Lady Needs a Rest
Jerry, My Soldier Boy
Let's Face It
Farming
Ev'rything I Love
Ace in the Hole
You Irritate Me So
Baby Games
Rub Your Lamp
Cuttin' a Persian Rug
I've Got Some Unfinished Business with You
Let's Not Talk About Love
A Little Rumba Numba
I Hate You Darling
Get Yourself a Girl
Revenge
Aladdin's Dance
What Are Little Husbands Made Of?

1942:
SOMETHING TO SHOUT ABOUT (original film score)
Columbia Pictures
Screenplay: Lou Breslow and Edward Eliscu; adapted by George Own, from a story by Fred Schiller
Songs: Cole Porter
Directed: Gregory Ratoff

Cast:

Ken Douglas	Don Ameche
Jeanie Maxwell	Janet Blair
Larry Martin	Jack Oakie

Willard Samson	William Gaxton
Donna Davis	Cobina Wright, Jr.
Flo	Veda Ann Borg
Hazel Scott	Hazel Scott
Dan Howard	Jaye Martin

Songs:

Something to Shout About
You'd Be So Nice to Come Home To
I Always Knew
Hasta Luego
Lotus Bloom
It Might Have Been
Through Thick and Thin
I Can Do Without Tea in My Teapot

PANAMA HATTIE (film version) Metro-Goldwyn-Mayer

Cast: Red Skelton

1943:
SOMETHING FOR THE BOYS — January 7, 1943
Book: Herbert and Dorothy Fields — Songs: Cole Porter
Alvin Theater — 422 performances
Produced: Michael Todd — Staged: Hassard Short
Book directed: Herbert Fields

Cast:

Chiquita Hart	Paula Laurence
Roger Calhoun	Jed Prouty
Harry Hart	Allen Jenkins
Blossom Hart	Ethel Merman
Staff Sgt. Rocky Fulton	Bill Johnson
Sgt. Laddie Green	Stuart Langley
Mary-Francis	Betty Garrett
Betty-Jean	Betty Bruce
Micheala	Anita Alverez

Lois, Lucille	Barnes Twins
Lt. Col. S. D. Grubbs	Jack Hartley
Mr. Tobias Twitch	William Lynn
Corp. Burns	Bill Callahan
Sgt. Carter	Remi Martel
Melanie Walker	Frances Mercer
Burke	Walter Rinner
Mrs. Grubbs	Madeleine Clive

Songs:

See That You're Born in Texas
When My Baby Goes to Town
Something for the Boys
When We're Home on The Range
Could It Be You?
Hey, Good Lookin'
He's a Right Guy
The Leader of a Big Time Band
I'm in Love with a Soldier Boy
There's a Happy Land in the Sky
By the Mississinewah
Riddle-Diddle Me This

Miscellaneous—1943:

Glide, Glide, Glide — Army Air Force Aid Society
Sailors of the Sky

DUBARRY WAS A LADY (film) — Metro-Goldwyn-Mayer

Cast: Red Skelton, Lucille Ball, Gene Kelly, Tommy Dorsey

LET'S FACE IT (film) — Paramount Pictures

Cast: Betty Hutton, Bob Hope

1944:

HOLLYWOOD CANTEEN (film, all-star extravaganza)
Warner Brothers

Roy Rogers sang "Don't Fence Me In"

MISSISSIPPI BELLE (unproduced film) Warner Brothers

Songs:

Amos, Amas
My Broth of a Boy
School, School, Heaven-Blessed School
I'm Not Myself at All
In the Green Hills of County Mayo
Kathleen
Mamie Magdalin
When You and I Were strangers
So Long
Who'll Bid?
When a Woman's in Love
Loading Song
I Like This G.S.
Mississippi Belle
Hip, Hip, Hooray for Andy Jackson

MEXICAN HAYRIDE — January 28, 1944
Book: Herbert and Dorothy Fields — Songs: Cole Porter
Winter Garden Theater — 481 performances
Produced: Michael Todd — Staged: Hassard Short
Book directed: John Kennedy

Cast:

Lombo Campos	George Givot
Mrs. Augustus Adamson	Jean Cleveland
Eadie Johnson	Edith Meiser
Augustus Jr.	Eric Roberts
Mr. Augustus Adamson	William A. Lee

Joe Bascom (alias Humphrey Fish)	Bobby Clark
Montana	June Havoc
Picadors	Horton Henderson, Jerry Sylvon
Billy	Bill Callahan
Señor Martinez	David Leonard
Miguel Correres	Sergio DeKarlo
David Winthrop	Wilbur Evans
Henry A. Wallace	Byron Halstead
José	Paul Reyes
A. C. Blumenthal	Larry Martin
Tillie Leeds	Lois Bolton
Lydia Toddle	Virginia Edwards
Carol (Ex-King of Roumania	Arthur Gondra
Mme. Lupescu	Dorothy Durkee
Lolita Cantine	Corinna Mura
Dagmar Marshak	Luba Malina
Bolero	Alfonso Pedroza
Chief of Police	Richard Bengali
Lottery Boy	Hank Wolff
Mrs. Molly Wincor	Jeanne Shelby
1st Merchant	Paul Reyes
2nd Merchant	Horton Henderson
3rd Merchant	Ben Hernandez
4th Merchant	Jerry Sylvon
5th Merchant	Bobby Lane
Woman Vendor	Claire Anderson
Lottery Girl	Eva Reyes
Paul	Paul Haakon
Eleanor	Eleanor Tennis
Lillian	Marjory Leach

Songs:

Sing to Me, Guitar
The Good-Will Movement
I Love You

There Must Be Someone for Me
Carlotta
Girls
What a Crazy Way to Spend a Sunday
Abracadabra
Count Your Blessings
It Must Be Fun to Be You
Tequila

1944:
SEVEN LIVELY ARTS (revue) December 7, 1944
Sketches: Moss Hart, George S. Kaufman, Robert Pirosh, Joseph Schrank and Charles Sherman. Doc Rockwell's comments by Ben Hecht. Songs: Cole Porter. Ballet Music: Igor Stravinsky.
Ziegfeld Theater 179 performances
Produced: Billy Rose Staged: Hassard Short

Cast: Beatrice Lillie, Bert Lahr, Benny Goodman, Alicia Markova, Anton Dolin, Doc Rockwell, Nan Wynn, Jere McMahon, Paula Bane, Billie Worth, Bill Tabbert, Dolores Gray, Mary Roche, Albert Carroll, Michael Barrett, Dennie Moore, Thomas Kenny, Edward Hackett, King Ross, Teddy Wilson, Red Norvo, Morey Feld, Sid Weiss, Robert Austin

Porter Songs:

Frahngee-Pahnee
Big Town
Is It the Girl?
Ev'ry Time We Say Goodbye
Only Another Boy and Girl
Wow-oo-Wolf!
Drink
When I Was a Little Cuckoo
Dancin' to a Jungle Drum
Hence, It Don't Make Sense
The Band Started Swinging a Song

Pretty Little Missus Bell
I Wrote a Play
Where Do We Go From Here?
Dainty, Quainty Me
If I Hadn't a Husband

Miscellaneous—1944:

A Humble Hollywood Executive
Hereafter
Put a Sack Over Their Heads
It's a Big Night
It's Just Like the Good Old Days
Octette
A Sightseeing Tour
Here's a Cheer
It's Just Yours
That's What You Mean to Me

1945:
NIGHT AND DAY (biographical film) Warner Brothers
Screenplay: Charles Hoffman, Leo Townsend, William Bowers
Adaptation: Jack Moffitt
Produced: Arthur Schwartz Directed: Michael Curtiz

Cast:

Cole Porter	Cary Grant
Linda Lee Porter	Alexis Smith
Himself	Monty Woolley
Carole Hill	Ginny Simms
Gracie Harris	Jane Wyman
Gabriello	Eve Arden
Anatole Giron	Victor Francen
Leon Dowling	Alan Hale
Nancy	Dorothy Malone
Bernie	Tom D'Andrea
Kate Porter	Selena Royle

Ward Blackburn	Donald Woods
Omar Porter	Henry Stephenson
Bart McClelland	Paul Cavanagh
Wilowsky	Sig Ruman
Specialty Singer	Carlos Ramirez
Specialty Dancer	Milada Mladova
Specialty Dancer	George Zoritch
Specialty Team	Adam and Jayne Di Gatano
Caleb	Clarence Muse
Petsy	John Alvin
O'Hallaran	George Riley
Producer	Howard Freeman
Director	Bobby Watson
First Peaches	John Pearson
Second Peaches	Herman Bing
Herself	Mary Martin

Songs:

Night and Day
Let's Do It
What Is This Thing Called Love?
I've Got You Under My Skin
My Heart Belongs to Daddy (re-created by Mary Martin)
An Old-Fashioned Garden
In the Still of the Night
Just One of Those Things
You Do Something to Me
I Get a Kick Out of You
Begin the Beguine
Easy to Love
You're the Top
Miss Otis Regrets She's Unable to Lunch Today

1946:
AROUND THE WORLD IN EIGHTY DAYS

May 31, 1946

Book: Orson Welles — Songs: Cole Porter
Adelphi Theater — 74 performances
Produced: Orson Welles — Directed: Orson Welles

Cast:

A Bank Robber	Brainerd Duffield
A Police Inspector	Guy Spaull
Dick Fix	Orson Welles
London Bobbies	Nathan Baker, Jack Pitchon, Myron Speth, Gordon West
A Lady	Genevieve Sauris
Mr. Phileas Fogg	Arthur Margetson
Avery Jevity	Stefan Schnabel
Molly Miggins	Julie Warren
Passepartout	Larry Laurence
Mr. Benjamin Cruett-Spew	Brainerd Duffield
Mr. Ralph Runcible	Guy Spaull
Sir Charles Mandiboy	Bernard Savage
Lord Upditch	Billy Howell
A Serving Man	Bruce Cartwright
Another Serving Man	Gregory McDougall
A Station Attendant	Billy Howell
Meerahlah	Dorothy Bird
Two Dancing Fellas	Lucas Aco, Myron Speth
The British Consul	Bernard Savage
An Arab Spy	Stefan Schnabel
A Second Arab Spy	Brainerd Duffield
Snake Charmers	Eddy DiGenova, Victor Savidge, Stanley Turner
A Fakir	Lucas Aco
Maurice Goodpile	Guy Spaull
A Sikh	Spencer James
Mrs. Aouda	Mary Healy

A High Priest	Arthur Cohen
Various Sinister Chinese	Phil King, Billy Howell, Lucas Aco, Nathan Baker
Lee Toy	Jackie Cezanne
Two Daughters of Joy	Lee Morrison, Nancy Newton
Mr. Oka Saka	Brainerd Duffield
Circus Artists:	
The Foot Jugglers	The Three Kanasawa
The Rolling Globe Lady	Adelaide Corsi
The Contortionist	Miss Lu
The Hand Balancer	Ishikawa
The Aerialists	Mary Broussard, Lee Vincent, Patricia Leith, Virginia Morris
Assistants	Billy Howell, Lucas Aco, Gregory McDougall, Myron Speth
The Slide for Life	Ray Goody
Roustabouts	Jack Pitchon, Tony Montell
Clowns:	
Mother	Stefan Schnabel
Father	Nathan Baker
Child	Bernie Pisarski
Bride	Cliff Chapman
Groom	Larry Laurence
Minister	Arthur Cohen
Policeman	Jack Cassidy
Monkey Man	Eddy Di Genova
Kimona Man	Allan Lowell
Firemen	Bruce Cartwright, Gordon West
Dragon	Daniel DePaolo
An Attendant	Stanley Turner
A Bartender	Eddy Di Genova

Mexican Dancers	Dorothy Bird, Bruce Cartwright
Lola	Victoria Cordova
Sol	Brainerd Duffield
Sam	Billy Howell
Jim	James Aco
Jake	Spencer James
A Medicine Man	Stefan Schnabel
Other Medicine Men	George Spelvin, Billy Howell
Jail Guard	Allan Lowell

Songs:

Look What I Found
There He Goes, Mr. Phileas Fogg
Meerahlah
Suttee Procession
Sea Chanty
Should I Tell You I Love You?
Pipe Dreaming
If You Smile at Me
Wherever They Fly the Flag of Old England
Snagtooth Gertie
Indian Scene (vocal part)
Travel Valse
Melodrama
Suez (dance)
Missus Aouda
Storm at Sea

1948:
THE PIRATE (original film score) Metro-Goldwyn-Mayer
Screenplay: Albert and Frances Hackett. Based on play by S. N. Behrman
Songs: Cole Porter
Produced: Arthur Freed
Directed: Vincente Minnelli

Cast:

Manuela	Judy Garland
Serafin	Gene Kelly
Don Pedro Vargas	Walter Slezak
Aunt Inez	Gladys Cooper
The Advocate	Reginald Owen
The Viceroy	George Zucco
Gaudsmith Brothers	Nicholas Brothers
Uncle Capucho	Lester Allen
Isabella	Lola Deem
Mercedes	Ellen Ross
Lizarda	Mary Jo Ellis
Casilda	Jean Dean
Eloise	Marion Murray
Gumbo	Ben Lessy
Bolo	Jerry Bergen
Juggler	Val Setz
Trillo	Cully Richards

Songs:

Mack, the Black
You Can Do No Wrong
Nina
Love of My Life
Be a Clown
Voodoo

1948:
KISS ME, KATE — December 30, 1948
Book: Samuel and Bella Spewack
Music and lyrics: Cole Porter
New York: Century Theater — 1,077 performances
Produced: Lemuel Ayers and Arnold Saint Subber
Staged: John C. Wilson
London: Coliseum, March 8, 1951 — 400 performances

Cast:

Fred Graham	Alfred Drake
Harry Trevor	Thomas Hoier
Lois Lane	Lisa Kirk
Ralph	Don Mayo
Lilli Vanessi	Patricia Morison
Hattie	Annabelle Hill
Paul	Lorenzo Fuller
Bill Calhoun	Harold Lang
First Man	Harry Clark
Second Man	Jack Diamond
Stage Doorman	Bill Lilling
Harrison Howell	Dennis Green
Specialty Dancers	Fred Davis, Eddie Sledge

Taming of the Shrew players

Bianca	Lisa Kirk
Baptista	Thomas Hoier
Gremio	Edwin Clay
Hortensio	Charles Wood
Lucentio	Harold Lang
Katharine	Patricia Morison
Petruchio	Alfred Drake
Haberdasher	John Castello
Tailor	Marc Breaux

Songs:

Another Op'nin', Another Show
Why Can't You Behave?
Wunderbar
So in Love
We Open in Venice
Tom, Dick or Harry
I've Come to Wive It Wealthily in Padua
I Hate Men
Were Thine That Special Face

I Sing of Love
Kiss Me, Kate
Too Darn Hot
Where Is the Life That Late I Led?
Always True to You in My Fashion
Bianca
Brush Up Your Shakespeare
I Am Ashamed That Women Are So Simple
We Shall Never Be Younger
Bianca's Theme
If Ever Married I'm
It Was Great Fun the First Time
Petruchio's Theme
A Woman's Career
What Does Your Servant Dream About?
Tarantella/Pavane

1949:
ADAM'S RIB (film) Warner Brothers

Cast: Katharine Hepburn, Spencer Tracy, Judy Holliday, David Wayne.

Song: Farewell, Amanda*

Miscellaneous—1949

Hush, Hush, Hush
Tonight I Love You More Than Ever

1950:
OUT OF THIS WORLD December 21, 1950
Book: Dwight Taylor and Reginald Lawrence
Songs: Cole Porter
New Century Theater 157 performances
Produced: Lemuel Ayers and Arnold Saint Subber
Directed: Agnes de Mille

* Originally written as "Bye Bye, Samoa" during a cruise.

Cast:

Mercury	William Redfield
Jupiter	George Jongeyans
Helen	Priscilla Gillette
Waiter	Frank Milton
Art O'Malley	William Eythe
Night	Janet Collins
Vulcania	Peggy Rea
Juno	Charlotte Greenwood
Chloe	Barbara Ashley
Niki Skolianos	David Burns
Strephon	Ray Harrison
Venus	Gisella Svetlik

Songs:

I Jupiter, I Rex
Use Your Imagination
Hail, Hail, Hail
I Got Beauty
Where, Oh, Where?
I Am Loved
They Couldn't Compare to You
What Do You Think About Men?
I Sleep Easier Now
Climb Up the Mountain
No Lover for Me
Cherry Pies Ought to Be You
Hark to the Song of the Night
Nobody's Chasing Me
From This Moment On
You Don't Remind Me
Oh, It Must Be Fun
To Hell with Everything But Us
Hush, Hush, Hush
Midsummer Night
Why Do You Want to Hurt Me So?
Away from It All

Amphitryon
Tonight I Love You More
Entrance of Juno

1951:
I'm Dining with Elsa (mss.)

1953:
KISS ME KATE (film) Metro-Goldwyn-Mayer

Cast: Howard Keel, Kathryn Grayson, Ann Miller

Song: From This Moment On (added)

1953:
CAN-CAN May 7, 1953
Book: Abe Burrows Songs: Cole Porter
New York: Shubert Theater 892 performances
Produced: Cy Feuer and Ernest H. Martin
Staged: Abe Burrows
London: Coliseum Theater, October 14, 1954
394 performances

Cast:

Bailiff	David Collyer
Registrar	Michael Cavallaro
Policemen	Jo Cusanelli, Jon Silo, Arthur Rubin, Ralph Beaumont, Michael DeMarco, Socrates Birsky
Judge Paul Barriere	C. K. Alexander
Court President	David Thomas
Judge Aristide Forestier	Peter Cookson
Claudine	Gwen Verdon
Gabrielle	Mary Anne Cohan
Marie	Beverly Purvin
Celestine	Jean Kraemer

Hilaire Jussac	Erik Rhodes
Boris Adzinidzinadze	Hans Conried
Hercule	Robert Penn
Theophile	Phil Leeds
Etienne	Richard Purdy
Waiter	Clarence Hoffman
Le Mome Pistache	Lilo
Second Waiter	Ferdinand Hilt
Café Waiter	Jon Silo
Café Customer	Joe Cusanelli
Jailer	Deedee Wood
Model	Pat Turner
Mimi	Dania Krupska
Customers	Sheila Arnold, David Thomas, Ferdinand Hilt
Doctor	Michael Cavallaro
Second	Arthur Rubin
Prosecutor	Ferdinand Hilt

Songs:

Maidens Typical of France
Never Give Anything Away
Quadrille
C'est Magnifique
Come Along with Me
Live and Let Live
I Am in Love
If You Loved Me Truly
Montmart'
Allez-Vous-En, Go Away
Never, Never Be an Artist
It's All Right with Me
I Love Paris
Can-Can
Ev'ry Man Is a Stupid Man
Her Heart Was in Her Work
I Do

I Shall Positively Pay You Monday
The Law
Opening Act 1, Scene 1
Opening Laundry Scene
What a Fair Thing Is a Woman
Who Said Gay Paree?
To Think That This Could Happen to Me
If Only You Could Love Me
Nothing to Do But Work

Miscellaneous—1953:

The Crew Song
The Elizabethan Club (Yale Folio)

1955
SILK STOCKINGS — February 24, 1955
Book: George S. Kaufman, Leueen McGrath, Abe Burrows — Songs: Cole Porter
Imperial Theater — 478 performances
Produced: Feuer and Martin — Staged: Cy Feuer

Cast:

Peter Ilyitch Boroff	Philip Sterling
Hotel Doorman	Walter Kelvin
Hotel Manager	Stanley Simmonds
Flower Girl	Geraldine Delaney
Ivanov	Henry Lascoe
Brankov	Leon Belasco
Bibinski	David Opatoshu
Steve Canfield	Don Ameche
First Commissar	Edward Becker
Guards	Lee Barry, Dick Humphrey
Vera	Julie Newmar
Commissar Markovitch	George Tobias
Choreographer	Kenneth Chertok
Ninotchka	Hildegarde Neff
Reporters	

Reporters	Edward Becker, Tony Gardell, Arthur Rubin
Janice Dayton	Gretchen Wyler
Pierre Bouchard	Marcel Hillaire
Chief Commissar	Forrest Green
Minister	Tony Gardell
President of Politburo	Walter Kelvin
Saleslady	Ludi Claire
M. Fabour	Paul Best
Bookstall Man	Louis Polacek
French Comrades	Win Mayo, Arthur Ulisse
Movie Director	Paul Best
Assistant Director	Lee Barry
Sonia	Devra Kline
Grisha	Forrest Green
Anna	Alexandra Moss
Musicians	Maurice Kogan, Leon Merian, Mervin Gold
Guard	Edward Becker

Songs:

Too Bad
Paris Loves Lovers
Stereophonic Sound
It's a Chemical Reaction, That's All
All of You
Satin and Silk
Without Love
Hail, Bibinski
As On Through the Seasons We Sail
Josephine
Siberia
Silk Stockings
The Red Blues
If Ever We Get Out of Jail (became "As On Through the Seasons We Sail")
Why Shouldn't I Trust You?
What a Ball

Give Me Land
There's a Hollywood That's Good
Under the Dress
The Perfume of Love
Theme: Ode to a Tractor
Let's Make It a Night
Boroff's Ode
Art

1956
HIGH SOCIETY (original film score)
Metro-Goldwyn-Mayer
Screenplay: John Patrick. Based on Philip Barry's *Philadelphia Story*
Songs: Cole Porter
Produced: Sol Siegel
Directed: Charles Walters

Cast:

C. K. Dexter-Haven	Bing Crosby
Tracy Lord	Grace Kelly
Mike Connor	Frank Sinatra
Liz Imbrie	Celeste Holm
George Kittredge	John Lund
Uncle Willie	Louis Calhern
Seth Lord	Sidney Blackmer
Louis Armstrong	Himself
Mrs. Seth Lord	Margalo Gillmore
Caroline Lord	Lydia Reed
Butler	Gordon Richards
Lord's Butler	Richard Garrick

Songs:

True Love
Little One
Who Wants to Be a Millionaire?
You're Sensational
I Love You, Samantha

Now You Has Jazz
High Society Calypso
Well, Did You Evah! (revised)
Mind If I Make Love to You?
Let's Vocalize
High Flyin' Wings on My Shoes
A-Step Montage

ANYTHING GOES (remake, new story) Paramount Pictures

Cast : Jeanmarie, Donald O'Connor, Bing Crosby, Mitzi Gaynor

Porter songs plus new ones by Sammy Cahn and Jimmy Van Heusen

1957:
SILK STOCKINGS (film) Metro-Goldwyn-Mayer

Cast: Fred Astaire, Cyd Charisse

Songs (added):

Fated to Be Mated
Ritz Roll and Rock

1957:
LES GIRLS (original film score) Metro-Goldwyn-Mayer
Screenplay: John Patrick Songs: Cole Porter
Produced: Sol Siegel Associate Producer: Saul Chaplin
Directed: George Cukor

Cast:

Barry Nichols	Gene Kelly
Joy Henderson	Mitzi Gaynor
Lady Wren	Kay Kendall
Angele Ducros	Taina Elg

Pierre Ducros	Jacques Bergerac
Sir Gerald Wren	Leslie Phillips
Judge	Henry Daniell
Sir Percy	Patrick MacNee
Mr. Outward	Stephen Vercoe
Associate Judge	Philip Tonge

Songs:

Les Girls
You're Just Too, Too!
Ca, C'est l'Amour
Ladies in Waiting
Why Am I So Gone About That Gal?
Drinking Song

1958:
ALADDIN (original television score)

CBS-TV, February 21, 1958

Book: S. J. Perelman — Songs: Cole Porter
Produced: Richard Lewine — Directed: Ralph Nelson

Cast: Cyril Ritchard, Dennis King, Sal Mineo, Anna Maria Alberghetti, Basil Rathbone, Howard Morris, Una Merkel, Geoffrey Holder, Alexander Clarke, George Hall, John McCurry

Songs:

Trust Your Destiny to a Star
Opportunity Knocks
Aladdin
I Adore You
No Wonder Taxes Are High
Make Way for the Emperor
Come to the Supermarket in Old Peking
Wouldn't It Be Fun!

1960
CAN-CAN (film) 20th Century-Fox

Cast: Frank Sinatra, Shirley MacLaine, Maurice Chevalier

Songs (added, but written earlier):

The Inch Worm
Snake Dance

INDEX